# Gender, Violence, and Justice

# Gender, Violence, and Justice

—— *Collected Essays on Violence against Women* ——

Pamela Cooper-White

FOREWORD BY
Sally N. MacNichol

CASCADE *Books* · Eugene, Oregon

GENDER, VIOLENCE, AND JUSTICE
Collected Essays on Violence against Women

Copyright © 2019 Pamela Cooper-White. All rights reserved. Except for brief quotations in critical publications or reviews, no part of this book may be reproduced in any manner without prior written permission from the publisher. Write: Permissions, Wipf and Stock Publishers, 199 W. 8th Ave., Suite 3, Eugene, OR 97401.

Cascade Books
An Imprint of Wipf and Stock Publishers
199 W. 8th Ave., Suite 3
Eugene, OR 97401

www.wipfandstock.com

PAPERBACK ISBN: 978-1-5326-1229-9
HARDCOVER ISBN: 978-1-5326-1231-2
EBOOK ISBN: 978-1-5326-1230-5

*Cataloguing-in-Publication data:*

Names: Cooper-White, Pamela, 1955–, author. | MacNichol, Sally N., foreword.

Title: Gender, violence, and justice : collected essays on violence against women / Pamela Cooper-White ; foreword by Sally N. MacNichol.

Description: Eugene, OR; Cascade Books, 2019. | Includes bibliographical references and index.

Identifiers: ISBN 978-1-5326-1229-9 (paperback). | ISBN 978-1-5326-1231-2 (hardcover). | ISBN 978-1-5326-1230-5 (ebook).

Subjects: LCSH: Pastoral theology. | Theology, practical. | Interpersonal relations—Religious aspects—Christianity. | Women—Pastoral counseling of. | Abused women—United States.

Classification: BV4012 C651 2019 (print). | BV4012 (ebook).

Manufactured in the U.S.A.            03/12/19

# Contents

*Foreword* / Sally N. MacNichol | vii
*Acknowledgments* | xi
*Introduction* | xiii

1. Peer vs. Clinical Counseling: Is There a Place for Both in the Battered Women's Movement? (1990) | 1
2. Soul Stealing: Power Relations in Pastoral Sexual Abuse (1991) | 12
3. An Emperor without Clothes: The Church's Views about Domestic Violence (1996) | 20
4. Opening the Eyes: Understanding the Impact of Trauma on Development (2000) | 39
5. Functional Families for the New Millennium: Teaching Pastoral Care of Families with a Vision of Social Justice (2001) | 61
6. Keeping God's People Safe: Canons as Gift of Grace and Dance of Love (2002) | 76
7. Sexual Exploitation and Other Boundary Violations in Pastoral Ministries (2003) | 96
8. What Are We Teaching about Violence against Women? (2004) | 118
9. Feminism(s), Gender, and Power: Reflections from a Feminist Pastoral Theologian (2008) | 140
10. Forgiveness: Grace, not Work (2009) | 166
11. Intimate Violence against Women: Trajectories for Pastoral Care in a New Millennium (2011) | 177
12. Denial, Victims, and Survivors: Post-traumatic Identity Formation and Monuments in Heaven (2012) | 245
13. Sexual Violence and Justice (2015) | 262

# Foreword

Sally N. MacNichol[1]

FOR FORTY YEARS, REV. Dr. Pamela Cooper-White has maintained a strong and steady commitment to foregrounding the issue of violence against women in the field of pastoral theology, care, and counseling. As a New York City community-based domestic violence advocate and anti-violence activist who has spent many years working with victim/survivors of faith, the churches that blamed, or ignored, as well as the churches who have

---

1. Rev. Sally N. MacNichol PhD, is Co-Executive Director of CONNECT, a New York City non-profit organization dedicated to preventing interpersonal violence and promoting gender justice. She has been an antiviolence activist, advocate and educator for over three decades, counseling victims of domestic violence, designing and facilitating empowerment groups for survivors, working with men who batter and abuse, and training hundreds of staff from child welfare programs and community based organizations across New York City's five boroughs. Instrumental in developing CONNECT's wholistic prevention model, she has helped to cultivate and sustain hundreds of community partnerships in a wide variety of contexts, as well as serving on numerous committees working to reform NYC's domestic violence policies and practices.

Sally created and leads CONNECT Faith, a decade-long interfaith movement in New York City to build the capacity of religious leaders and communities of faith to work to end intimate partner abuse and co-occurring forms of family violence. CONNECT Faith currently partners with over 50 faith communities, offering customized training, support for education and awareness events, resource development, technical assistance for the creation of family violence ministries, consultation for safe practices and policies, and referrals for faith-based counseling.

Over the years, Sally has mentored many women (and some men) of faith as they developed their own ministries committed to addressing gender justice and preventing intimate violence, and has been a spiritual counselor to numerous survivors of abuse. Her interfaith theological roundtable has met faithfully every month for last ten years providing space for people of faith to deconstruct and transform the belief systems, theological norms, and faith community practices that support abuse. In 2012, Sally spearheaded the formation of the Ending Child Sexual Abuse (ECSA) Faith Collaborative, which developed and piloted the Safe Faith Community Project, a 9 month training program for churches working to address and prevent child sexual abuse.

tried to help, Dr. Cooper-White's work has been a valuable resource. I can't count the number of times I have taught and recommended her text *The Cry of Tamar: Violence against Women and the Church's Response* to clergy,[2] to members of a newly formed domestic violence ministries, to seminarians doing their field work in gender justice, to chaplains offering spiritual care to survivors, as well as to secular domestic violence advocates and social workers seeking to understand the role of faith in survivors' lives, and survivors themselves as they wrestle with the ways the theologies and practices of their faith community have helped or hindered their own paths to safety, justice, and healing.

How excellent then, that Dr. Cooper-White now offers us her collected essays on *Gender, Violence, and Justice*. Weaving theory, theology, and practice and entering the web of intimate violence at various points along the way, this volume, rooted in an uncompromising commitment to social justice, will help spiritual caregivers, faith leaders, and advocates address the suffering of survivors in more wise and compassionate ways.

One might think (hope) that essays written almost thirty, or even twenty years ago would have little relevance today. However, when it comes to gender, violence, and justice, the saying "the more things change, the more they stay the same" unfortunately applies. The pervasive and ongoing reality of violence against women and children and the urgent need for empowering practices and liberating theologies persist, despite a steady increase of awareness, advocacy, and services over the years. We are not exactly back where we started from. However, victim-blaming and pathologizing narratives and the terrible suffering they engender continue to prevail in both church and society at large.

There are, from my perspective, two important contemporary developments that make the essays in *Gender, Violence, and Justice* particularly

---

Sally serves on the board of Freedom House, one of the few domestic violence shelters in the country for people with disabilities, on the advisory board of House of Peace, a nonprofit organization working to address intimate violence in NYC's Muslim Communities, and on the steering committee of the New York City Elder Abuse Center of New York. She was honored ro be named a New York New Abolitionist and is the recipient of an *Agent of Change Award* from the New York City Coalition on Working With Abusive Partners (CoWAP), the *Seasoned with Hope* Award from New Hope for the World Ministries and the Unitas Distinguished Alumnae Award from Union Theological Seminary. Her published work includes "We Make the Road by Walking: Reflections on the Legacy of White Anti-Racist Activism," in *Disrupting White Supremacy from Within*, edited by Robin Gorsline, Jennifer Harvey, and Karin Case, and "Kin'dom Come: Houses of Worship and Gender Justice in the 21st Century," in *Learning to Lead: Lessons in Leadership for People of Faith*, edited by Rev. Willard Ashley. Sally earned her Masters of Divinity and Ph.D. in Systematic Theology from Union Theological Seminary in New York City.

2. Pamela Cooper-White, *The Cry of Tamar: Violence against Women and the Church's Response* (Minneapolis: Fortress, 1995; 2nd ed., 2012).

relevant. First, the anti-violence movement is presently engaged in a new and heightened round of scrutiny, questioning, and challenge. We are confronting the deleterious consequences of the "mainstreaming" of the movement—meaning the professionalization and de-politicization of the way the work is conceived of and done (as Dr. Cooper-White notes in her Introduction)—intensified by a more honest reckoning with who has been left out. Countless survivors, in particular survivors of color, immigrant survivors, LGBTQ survivors among them, have nowhere to turn for safety and justice. Fear of the police, lack of trust in the courts, and the threat of ICE (Immigration and Customs Enforcement—frequently present at court houses and emergency rooms) can make reaching out for help a more dangerous prospect than negotiating the violence of an intimate partner. A lack of support for grassroots efforts at prevention and culturally appropriate approaches to intervention and healing magnify the situation.

While there is no question that some survivors have been helped by mainstream remedies for domestic and sexual violence, there is also no question that many survivors who *have* sought help from mainstream systems and services have been re-victimized by "power-over" models of advocacy and counseling rife with the kinds of "clinical and pseudo-clinical pitfalls" Cooper-White illuminates and critiques in this volume. Linear concepts of healing, and monolithic and decontextualized understandings of human being that don't take into account the complex identities and social, political, economic realities of survivor's lives, endure. Grounded in a commitment to a praxis of humility, kindness and justice, the essays in *Gender, Violence, and Justice* can contribute to moving us—individual as practitioners, and collectively as a liberation movement—in another direction; towards an embrace of multiplicity (inner and outer[3]), relationality,[4] and respect for the resistance, resilience and creative possibilities of survivors.

A second and promising development is the upsurge in parishes and congregations that are a part of a wide variety of faith communities that *sincerely* want to address intimate violence in more than a perfunctory way. More sermons on domestic and sexual violence are being delivered. More women's ministries are addressing violence against women, and ministries specifically focused on offering safety, support, and healing for survivors of domestic and sexual violence are on the rise. Chaplains are recognizing that they need more training and skills to offer appropriate spiritual care to those who have suffered intimate abuse in their lifetime.

---

3. See Cooper-White, *Many Voices: Pastoral Psychotherapy in Relational and Theological Perspective* (Minneapolis: Fortress, 2007); and *Braided Selves: Collected Essays on Multiplicity, God, and Persons* (Eugene, OR: Cascade Books, 2011).

4. See Cooper-White, *Shared Wisdom: Use of the Self in Pastoral Care and Counseling* (Minneapolis: Fortress, 2004); and *Many Voices*, 2007.

In some ways, this development is connected to the first. The historical distrust, sometimes animosity, between the secular movement and religious leaders has been slowly fading over the last 20 years. Secular-religious partnerships are growing, particularly as secular advocates and activists realize that faith communities, particularly immigrant faith communities and communities of color, are, indeed, first responders and have a critical role to play in raising awareness, promoting safety, accountability and healing. This is heartening. However, if authentic and lasting transformation is to take place, a committed and rigorous exploration of the theological norms that deny or minimize the suffering of victim-survivors and/or collude with the strategies of power, control, and domination of both abuser and sometimes the church itself, is *essential*.

In my experience, it is here, at the crossroads of theology, spiritual care, and the church's response to intimate violence, that things often fall apart. When religious leaders are unwilling or unable to do the theological work required, even their most earnest efforts to offer safety and address the suffering caused by intimate violence fall short, and can even cause more harm. Take, for example, the issue of forgiveness, a central and searing concern for many Christian survivors, and a powerful tool in the hands of an oppressor. Having seen the anguish of victim/survivors pressured by pastors, spiritual caregivers, and whole congregations to forgive the people who have harmed them—and people who are still harming them—Pamela Cooper-White's incisive and extremely helpful theological analysis of forgiveness is an example of—and guide for—the kind pastoral and theological inquiry that must be engaged if churches (and the offices of pastoral counselors) are to become true sanctuaries of safety and healing.

An abiding faith in the God of justice, mercy and love, and compassion for the wounds of our humanity animate the prodigious clinical skills, theoretical insight, and theological acumen that show forth in these essays. They compel us to consider that, if we truly desire transformative change, it is possible—and indeed necessary—to embrace complexity and contradiction without sacrificing a strong ethical stance against intimate violence. Cooper-White's refusal to split the clinical and the social, the pastoral and the prophetic, spiritual care and justice-making make the collected essays in *Gender, Violence, and Justice* a valuable resource for the days ahead.

Sally N. MacNichol

August 2018

# Acknowledgments

IN NEARLY FORTY YEARS in movement to end violence against women, it is impossible for me to name everyone who has supported, taught, and challenged me in this work, but I am grateful to every one of my coworkers, clients, students, and teachers along the way, especially at Sojourn, Santa Monica, CA, and the YWCA Silicon Valley (formerly the Mid-Peninsula Support Network for Battered Women), Sunnyvale, CA—they continue to do the hard daily work of advocacy with individuals, families, and communities and I'm proud to have been involved directly in their work. I also want to highlight several grassroots organizations whose collegial consultations over many years have deepened my understanding and helped me to stay up to date on research, legislation, and activism: Help for Abused Women and Children (HAWC), Salem, MA; Futures without Violence (formerly the Family Violence Prevention Fund), San Francisco, CA; the Center for Domestic Peace/Marin Abused Women's Services, San Rafael, CA; the California Coalition against Domestic Violence (CCADV); the Women's Resource Center to End Domestic Violence, Decatur, GA; CONNECT: Safe Families, Peaceful Communities, New York City; and especially the FaithTrust Institute in Seattle, WA, for its education and advocacy work within religious communities. I also thank the Society for Pastoral Theology and the Psychology, Culture and Religion program unit of the American Academy of Religion for their support and encouragement over the years, and the editors of the *Journal of Pastoral Theology* and *Pastoral Psychology* (especially Lewis Rambo), for publishing many of the essays contained in this volume, as well as many other authors' essays on justice for women and persons of color—their commitment is evident in the contents of many issues over the past three decades. Finally, thanks as always go to my spouse, Michael, whose support for my work and whose advocacy for women, persons of color, and LGBTQ persons has been constant throughout his career, and to our daughter Macrina, whose editing help on this project was invaluable, and whose doctoral research on the neuroscience of open-mindedness is an inspiration!

# Introduction

THE SOUP WAS MADE and simmering on the old stove in the church kitchen. Cabbage soup and chicken broth with carrots and rice (oh, God, so much rice!), in a giant battered aluminum pot. There was bread. Coffee, tea, and water. I hope there were cookies, too. (I was a divinity and musicology grad student, vegetarian, and broke. It was my best effort at the time.) There were signs up all over the downtown area in my best poster handwriting: "Friday Night Suppers. Free! Join us from 5 to 7 p.m.!" The church council had reluctantly agreed to what they thought was a harebrained scheme. ("Homeless people, here in Salem, Massachusetts? I don't think so!") I'd preached my sermon about my love for Dorothy Day and the necessity of caring for the poor. The minister was encouraging, but at least in the beginning was leaving me to my own devices—communicating in not so many words, "Let's see how it goes." Were there any volunteers at the outset? I don't remember any. No guests came that first night.

The next week, I tried again. Where were the grizzled men I'd seen and spoken to on the benches in the courthouse square, with their bottles of booze not too carefully concealed in rumpled paper bags? Still, they didn't come. Until, a few weeks later, they did, and then, the Friday Night Suppers became a Thing. A good thing. A community. We ate, visited, cracked jokes, sang together. Sometimes they would ask what was a "nice suburban girl" like me doing with the likes of them, and sometimes the Big Questions of life and death—and poverty. They shared their life stories about the twists and turns that ended up with them sleeping down by the tracks. Some of the volunteers would say, with compassion, "There but for the grace of God go I." But I didn't buy that theology. For me, it was "Bad crap happens to people and God weeps—and gets back in there to make good happen, in spite of the obstacles we throw up in God's way."

When his leg got infected and he got a little paranoid, I took "Wes" to the ER and insisted that the doctors treat him. I helped a schizophrenic man come down from a terrifying hallucination about a murderous crow and got him to the ER, too. I followed "James" into an alley where he knew the stolen silver from the church (the church council's worst fantasy come true) had been stashed. I talked men into handing me their switchblades under less than favorable circumstances. When I look back now, I think I was stupidly fearless—but the men honored my innocence, and my unconditional love and trust in the goodness I saw in them. I was probably the safest young woman in Salem for a while. We later mourned James' death and celebrated his life after he was found dead by the railroad tracks. We added a clothes closet and optional worship. (I insisted on the "optional"—the material help we offered was to be free, with no conditions.) Volunteers came. I eventually moved on from that internship in a few years to take my first university teaching position, but the program grew to become a shelter, and numerous other churches joined in the work. Today, this fledgling enterprise is a thriving multi-service nonprofit organization, "Lifebridge North Shore."[1] Still, the first two weeks showed none of the promise the program was to become.

But around closing time on just the third night, still awaiting the first guest—and fearing that the church was going to shut me down—someone did come. A shy, thin white woman, "Sarah," with tired eyes and a haggard face tentatively entered the door with two children, a girl and a boy around ages 9 and 10. Over coffee, bread, and the meager soup, she haltingly told me her story. She had gone for help to the local grassroots agency for battered women, "HAWC" (Help for Abused Women and Children),"[2] which had its offices in the church's building next door. Her husband had been beating her, and had become increasingly violent over many years. She had reached a tipping point, and feared for her children's safety as much or more than her own. The kids were talkative, funny, and a little giddy that night. She had fled with them, and now was homeless. She was hoping eventually to move in with relatives in Brooklyn. In the meantime, the streets were safer than "home."

This was my first encounter with domestic violence, and I was floored.

Sarah and the kids kept coming to the Friday Night Suppers for several weeks after that, and then did find their way to Brooklyn, where I was able to visit them a few months later. They were doing OK. But I never forgot Sarah or the work of HAWC. And when I left Massachusetts for my first teaching job, I quickly got involved in the battered women's agency "Sojourn," in

---

1. Website at https://lifebridgenorthshore.org/.
2. Help for Abused Women and Children, Salem, MA—website https://hawcdv.org.

Santa Monica, California. Soon after, in my first ordained ministry position as director of the San Francisco Partnership Ministry, working with Southeast Asian refugees, I partnered with the Family Violence Project (now = Futures without Violence[3]) to provide advocacy and services for refugee battered women. From there, after a stint in the San Francisco Opera Chorus (unfinished vocational business), I went on to direct the Mid-Peninsula Support Network for Battered Women (now a program of the YWCA of Silicon Valley)[4]. A few years later, as director of the Center for Women and Religion at the Graduate Theological Union in Berkeley, I introduced courses on pastoral responses to violence against women, and on gender, power, and spirituality. During this transition back to academia—now in the field of pastoral theology, care, and counseling—I continued to write, teach, and advocate for an end to violence against women. I began support groups for women abused by their pastors and became involved in the movement to develop policies and strategies to end clergy sexual abuse of parishioners, both regionally and nationally. Growing out of these efforts, I wrote *The Cry of Tamar: Violence against Women and the Church's Response*, published in 1995 (with a second edition in 2012). For four decades, I have stayed involved in the movement in one way or another, these days mostly through teaching, preaching and public speaking.

After 40 years of engagement in this movement, some aspects of the dynamics of violence against women have become clearer to me, while in other ways, its continuing prevalence, and the cycles of resistance, advocacy, and backlash continue to baffle and dismay. When I was asked to provide a second edition of *The Cry of Tamar*, I was not surprised, but I was nevertheless saddened that it seemed necessary. On various online research sites, reader views keep increasing, and I have received requests for essays published on this topic in journals and anthologies over four decades—increasingly from international scholars and activists. The ongoing flow of requests was the catalyst for the present volume of collected essays. Colleagues encouraged me to gather these essays in one, easily accessible place for the sake of educating new generations of religious leaders and activists.

---

3. Website at https://www.futureswithoutviolence.org/. Note: all websites cited in this Introduction were active and accessed on Aug. 6, 2018.

4. Website at http://ywca-sv.org/our-services/support-services/domestic-violence-services.

## The View from Today

Some of the material in this volume—especially some of the earlier essays—may appear dated to those most familiar with the movement to end violence against women. Our insights and strategies have grown considerably since the first rape crisis centers and battered women's shelters opened in the late 1970s. Legislation is in place that had never existed before the 1980s, and public awareness has greatly increased. There is now a vigorous and growing international movement to end violence against women across the globe.[5] On the other hand, it is sometimes startling to see how much the knowledge we had at the beginning of the movement (speaking from the perspective of the U.S.)—and the commitment we had to articulating our resistance in connection with racism, classism, heterosexism and other forms of social oppression—has faded, been co-opted, and/or had to be re-invented in current times. Little specific attention has been paid to the sexual and domestic violence increasing the dangers faced by migrant women, both in the U.S. and globally.[6] Legislative gains have been eroded.[7] The Violence against Women Act ("VAWA"), drafted

---

5. Given momentum, at least in part, by the United Nation's *Decade for Women* begun in 1985 and its inaugural conference in Beijing, China. For documents on the conference, and information on past and future developments, see United Nations, "Gender Equality and Women's Empowerment Ten Years after Beijing—Where Do We Stand?" online at http://www.un.org/womenwatch/forums/review/; United Nations, *World Conference to Review and Appraise the Achievements of the United Nations Decade for Women, 1985: Nairobi, Kenya* (Pleasantville, NY: UNIFO Publishers, 1986), http://www.un.org/womenwatch/daw/beijing15/overview.html; see also http://beijing20.unwomen.org/en. Preparations are now underway for a 2020 "Beijing 25" conference, https://www.ngocsw.org/archive/ngo-csw-forum/preparing-for-2020. The World Council of Churches has also been active in global advocacy. See, e.g., Philippa Hitchen, "Thursdays in Black Campaign Relaunches Effort to End Rape and Violence," World Council of Churches June 19, 2018, https://www.oikoumene.org/en/press-centre/news/thursdays-in-black-campaign-relaunches-efforts-to-end-rape-and-violence; as well as the World YWCA "NoXcuses" and "Week without Violence" campaigns: #noXcuses@worldywca. For a brief discussion of intercultural complexities and recent history, see Pamela Cooper-White, "Global Efforts to Stop Violence against Women," in *The Cry of Tamar: Violence against Women and the Church's Response*, 2nd ed. (Minneapolis: Fortress, 2012) 9–13.

6. Summarized in Cooper-White, "Women Migrants, Gender-based Trauma, and Spiritual Care, in Isabelle Noth and Claudia Kohli-Reichenbach, eds., *Migration and Spiritual Care* (Göttingen, Germany: Vandenhoeck and Ruprecht, 2019) 17–45; see also Oliva Espín and Andrea L. Dottolo, ed., *Gendered Journeys: Women, Migration, and Feminist Psychology* (New York: St. Martin's/Palgrave MacMillan), esp. Part III "Violence, Resistance and Resilience," 145–226; and Smaïn Laacher, *De la violence à la persécution, femmes sur la route de l'exil* (Paris: La Dispute, 2010).

7. For more on legislative advocacy and challenges in the U.S., see Cooper-White,

by Sen. Joe Biden with Louise Slaughter of New York and first signed into law by President Bill Clinton in 1994, has made significant progress in reducing intimate partner violence and other crimes.[8] VAWA has been under continual threat at every funding renewal deadline, most recently in 2012–2013[9] due to objections by conservative lawmakers against protections in the law for same-sex couples and illegal immigrants.[10]

Corporate sponsorships and local, state, and national governmental and foundation grants have been a two-edged sword. They have "professionalized" our organizations—with the effects of both strengthening fiscal and structural viability, but also all too often making them into more mainstream non-profit agencies—concerned with excellent service provision to clients, but less able or committed to engage in social protest, especially around the larger issues of power and oppression.

## Forces of Backlash

At the time of this writing, we also live in a time of post-traumatic whiplash socially and politically in the U.S. After forty years of work, new understandings of gender and violence against women have emerged, and we have witnessed a perhaps unprecedented rise in women publicly calling men to account for sexual harassment and abuse—while at the same time we continue to elevate perpetrators to high office in both church and state. Many repeat offenders lie low for a while and then re-emerge to resume their careers with little public outcry, memory, or even awareness of their former malfeasance (by simply trading one arena of work for another and carrying on as usual). We (including 52% of white women[11]) elected Donald Trump, a racist perpetrator-in-chief whose abusive attitudes and treatment of women (public and, evidence would strongly suggest, private) are well known yet appear to be overlooked and, worse, tolerated by large

---

"Political Action and Gender Justice in the United States," in *The Cry of Tamar*, 3–9.

8. National Coalition against Domestic Violence (NCADV), online at https://ncadv.org/legislation.

9. [Currently, the VAWA is up for reauthorization again in 2018. —PCW, 2018]

10. "Renew the Violence against Women Act," *New York Times* editorial, Feb. 15, 2013. [Many of the same contested issues are expected in the next authorization debate; in the current political climate, the VAWA—and therefore the funding of state coalitions as well as many other protections, e.g., for immigrant women—are under threat. —Sally N. MacNichol, personal communication, Aug. 13, 2018.]

11. Exit polls, Election 2016, CNN, online at https://www.cnn.com/election/2016/results/exit-polls. Statistics for Black women and Latina women showed 4% and 25%, respectively, in the same poll; 41% of women overall; and 57% of all white voters.

swaths of the general population. Like most perpetrators, his violent words and behavior are minimized or denied (often with outright lies), both by himself and by those who choose to protect him. Abuse and exploitation of women follow him like Pigpen's cloud of dust in the comic strip "Peanuts," but he is hailed by many as the "leader of the free world." And his violent words gave tacit—and at times, more than tacit—permission for Americans who had learned to stifle their own hate speech in recent decades to emerge with a vengeance. The Southern Poverty Law Center (SPLC), which tracks extremist hate groups of all kinds, has documented two explicitly male supremacist groups in the U.S., which also incorporate homophobic and heterosexist hate speech on their web sites. SPLC views these sites as gateways to larger, racist "alt-right" groups, who also foster misogynistic and anti-LGBTQ hate-crime activity.[12]

Closely entwined with these social and political upheavals, and doubtless motivated by them, a fresh wave of outrage has erupted against this reality. The Women's March on Washington immediately following the Trump inauguration brought new urgency to progressive activism. The #metoo movement—already founded years before by Black activist Tarana Burke[13]—suddenly gained significant traction as women celebrities enlisted its name in exposing men's sexual harassment and abuse—first in Hollywood, and now increasingly in many other high-profile professional settings including journalism, finance, athletics, and the tech industry. Among the millennial generation, the word "feminist" has begun to emerge from the cloud of conservative scorn under which it had cowered for some years. The word "post-racial" (hopeful but overly optimistic and perhaps also propping up white denial and wishful thinking) has been retired from use following the end of the Obama presidency and in the wake of a rise in institutionalized and socially condoned violence against persons of color. The mask of white complacency is being ripped away by increasingly public revelations of racist violence that is, in fact, not new. Meanwhile, white supremacists are emboldened to increase this violence, supported by a current government that has sought to authorize such behaviors and attitudes, working to appoint and elect persons who

---

12. Southern Poverty Law Center, "Male Supremacy": https://www.splcenter.org/fighting-hate/extremist-files/ideology/male-supremacy.

13. For more info on Tarana Burke, see, e.g., Sandra E. Garcia, "The Woman Who Created #MeToo Long Before Hashtags," *New York Times*, Oct. 20, 2017: https://www.nytimes.com/2017/10/20/us/me-too-movement-tarana-burke.html. See also Burke's organization, Just Be, Inc., founded in 2006 in Philadelphia to empower young women of color: http://justbeinc.wixsite.com/justbeinc/home.

either tacitly or explicitly approve. White supremacist Conservative backlash is in the ascendancy at the current moment.

But it may also be well to remember that much of the abuse and exploitation of women committed by men in the so-called liberal era of the 60s and 70s was done explicitly in the name of sexual liberation and progressive social change, especially in more typically liberal contexts such as the arts and even among activist communities. And this strategy of psychological coercion was employed by clergy within religious institutions and communities just as much as in secular contexts. Christian churches have put policies in place in the 1980s and 90s to curb sexual misconduct by clergy and religious leaders, yet many still struggle to justly address the epidemic of child sexual abuse—especially in the Catholic Church—and still fail to fully enforce existing policies against adult-to-adult sexual harassment, abuse, and exploitation. Clergy are all too often still moved from parish to parish and district to district after cursory suspensions for supposed rehabilitation, and those who are permanently removed from ministry often find their way into allied professions such as counseling and social service work.

## Struggles in the Movement

It's a tricky time now *within* the movement to end violence against women as well. The #metoo movement has gained traction, but at what cost to its original intent? Beginning in grass-roots activism on behalf of struggling Black women, its public face is now mostly the face of white celebrities and women of considerable wealth.[14] It is as yet unclear how much the notoriety surrounding high profile executives and public figures who have been called out and punished for their abusive behavior will actually impact the misogyny and masculine privilege that pervades nearly all organizations, institutions, and communities. While I do not disagree that women in high-powered careers risk a great deal by coming forward with their allegations—and often do suffer harsh consequences, outside the glare of publicity—nevertheless, I think about how much *more* poor and middle-class women and women of color risk by doing so. As long as violence against women is normalized, privatized, and held in place by a continually pervasive social structure of patriarchy (yes, I still use that word!), how many women whose livelihoods are already fragile would be

---

14. This issue prompted a panel entitled "Me Too: Sexual Trauma and Sexual Shaming in the Era of #45," sponsored by the Psychology, Culture and Religion, and Womanist Approaches to Religion program units, at the American Academy of Religion, Denver, CO, Nov. 18, 2018, Stephanie Crumpton, presiding.

willing to risk everything for the sake of what will be viewed by many only as a private, personal vendetta, attention-seeking—or "making a mountain out of a molehill"?

The public whitening of the movement to end violence against women can also be seen in a related hot issue—especially in academia—that of "intersectionality."[15] What again began as a term to recognize the multiple oppressive structures and policies faced by Black battered women—first introduced by Columbia law professor and legal scholar Kimberlé Crenshaw[16]—quickly lost its roots in Black feminist activism, and became a generic term for the multiple demographic identifiers that most people of any race and any gender might be able to appropriate, shorn of any association with groups chronically targeted for oppression (e.g., an "white male, in my 40's, middle-class, college-educated, Christian, registered Independent, U.S. citizen born to U.S. citizens.") But "intersectionality" was not meant simply to denote *any* multiplicity of identities. It was born out of the necessity to recognize the pileup of obstacles that confront multiply oppressed persons, who simultaneously face discrimination and violence because they do not conform in one way or another to the white, middle-class, heterosexual, able-bodied male norm. This norm is so ingrained in U.S. society that it is cloaked in invisibility most of the time—affecting not only the ongoing prevalence of sexual violence, but impacting housing, medical care (too often normed on young male subjects), immigration and refugee relief, and access to all kinds of services because of political and funding barriers. A battered woman is oppressed, by definition. A Black battered woman, who may also be poor, or disabled, or lesbian, or transgender, faces multiple oppressions. This is the point that is too often lost in the public's appropriation of "intersectionality"—a concern within pastoral theology as well.[17]

Thus the complex issue of so-called "identity politics" (another term now deemed pejorative by the right) is valid and important, but it can also be twisted against progressive movements for justice, as the machinery of "divide and conquer" poisons the capacity of advocates to build alliances across oppressions. We are challenged to find common ground to build effective coalitions for change without appearing to make sexism, racism, heterosexism, and other forms of oppression equivalent, or to subsume one

---

15. For an excellent overview, see Patricia Hill Collins and Sirma Bilge, eds., *Intersectionality—Key Concepts* (Malden, MA: Polity, 2016).

16. Kimberlé Crenshaw, *On Intersectionality: Essential Writings* (New York: New Press, 2019).

17. E.g., Nancy Ramsay, "Analyzing and Engaging Asymmetries of Power: Intersectionality as a Resource for Practices of Care," in Ramsay ed., *Pastoral Theology and Care: Critical Trajectories in Theory and Practice* (Oxford: Wiley-Blackwell, 2018.)

within another, to essentialize, or to conflate them. We need to recover the intersections among sexism/misogyny (across all ethnicities) and racism (across all genders—more on gender below), which in my experience were much more prominent in the original movement to end violence against women—even integral to staff training—than they are today. Even the most radical white feminists today still struggle to recognize and combat our own racism. And churches—including the Black church—remain bastions of patriarchal privilege even while mobilizing for other forms of social justice and equality. To quote Crenshaw,

> Feminist efforts to politicize experiences of women and antiracist efforts to politicize experiences of people of color have frequently proceeded as though the issues and experiences they each detail occur on mutually exclusive terrains. Although racism and sexism readily intersect in the lives of real people, they seldom do in feminist and antiracist practices. And so, when the practices expound identity as "woman" or "person of color" as an either/or proposition, they relegate the identity of women of color to a location that resists telling . . . Because of their intersectional identity as both women and people of color within discourses that are shaped to respond to one or the other, the interests and experiences of women of color are frequently marginalized within both.[18]

## Building Alliances

In my teaching in the domain of pastoral and spiritual care, I have found it valuable, citing Emmanuel Lartey, to utilize the expression from anthropology:[19] "Human beings are like all others, like some others, and like no others." We all have common human needs, addressed in terms of basic survival needs and also political rights; we all belong to certain groups and group identities which are marked by distinct, local, and particular customs and traits (i.e., cultures and tribes); and we are all unique—including in our differences even from others who are in many ways "like

18. Crenshaw, "Mapping the Margins: Intersectionality, Identity Politics, and Violence against Women of Color." In Martha Albertson Fineman and Rixanne Mykitiuk, eds., *The Public Nature of Private Violence* (New York: Routledge, 1994) 93–118: https://www.racialequitytools.org/resourcefiles/mapping-margins.pdf.

19. Emmanuel Lartey, *In Living Color: An Intercultural Approach to Pastoral Care and Counseling*, 2nd ed. (London: Kingsley, 2003), 34, citing anthropologists Clyde Kluckholn and Henry Alexander Murray, *Personality in Nature, Society, and Culture* (New York: Knopf, 1948).

us." The challenge in providing spiritual care or psychotherapy with attention to the importance of the context in which people live their lives is to keep all three of these registers in awareness more or less continuously and simultaneously. It is also critical to recognize how power and privilege encircle—and circumscribe and invisibly define—these layers of cultural existence. I would suggest that the same is true for our advocacy work. We build bridges as allies around common human needs ("like all others"), we respect the distinctive values and experiences of different groups and the specific features of different forms of oppression ("like some others"), and we exercise care and empathy for the uniqueness of each individual person ("like no others") as we struggle together for the end of violence against women—and all people, creatures, and our planet.

This work of alliance-building may sound obvious, but in fact it is very, very difficult. These three layers of experience, values, and identity at times cause us to compete for token scraps from the institutional table rather than tolerate differences that are painful and nevertheless forge ahead with our urgent common work for meaningful, lasting change. Alliance-building calls for humility regarding those aspects of our lives in which we have unearned privilege; an openness to learning among all dialogue partners, with a "preferential option" for the voices of those who have historically been most silenced; and courage emerging from those aspects of ourselves that have experienced trauma and oppression. At the same time, as we embrace our passion for change, it is helpful to keep in mind that "speaking truth to power"—and to one another—"*in love*" can temper our own self-righteousness, stridency and judgmentalism, which too often can break down coalition building.

## The Impact of Trauma and Splitting

We are living, indeed, in a post-traumatic time and a post-traumatic culture, in which the increasing divide of wealth and power has not only built upon a legacy of past violence (including the original sins of chattel slavery, the genocide of Native American peoples, and the routine oppression of women across centuries)—traumas that urgently require healing of our North American culture[20]—but we are also living in a time of publicly tolerated violence that maintains an atmosphere of *ongoing* trauma. It is very difficult to heal from trauma when the trauma is still happening! It is all

---

20. These observations may well apply to other locations around the globe; I am speaking only for my own context here, and invite others to articulate helpful parallels to their own situations.

too easy in such a toxic environment to resort to psychological splitting into pure vs. evil, innocent vs. victimizer, and to fail to recognize one's own contributions to an ongoing spiral of violence, attack, and defense. As relational and feminist psychoanalyst Jessica Benjamin has often argued, when we fall into a "doer/done to" binary, creative thinking collapses.[21] This is *not* to say that violation of persons is categorically always "mutual"[22]—in fact, it very rarely is (see Ch. 11). There is almost always a power dynamic of domination that is chronic and one-way in intimate partner violence—with one identifiable victim and one batterer exercising control (see Chs. 3 and 11.) And sexual assault is an act of aggression, not just out-of-control sexuality (see Ch. 13).

There is also a popular myth that most victims are destined to become perpetrators in new relationships, or toward children in an intergenerational cycle. Although unhealed trauma *sometimes* begets unconsciously driven displacement of aggression onto new victims ("wounded people wound people"), this notion is vastly overstated. It comes from a common statistical category error: if a large majority of perpetrators were abused or witnessed violence as children (this is well established[23]), then it supposedly follows that abuse causes the abused to become abusers (not true). Researchers Stark and Flitcraft have found that 80–90% of men with a history of being abused do not become batterers.[24]

21. Jessica Benjamin, *Beyond Doer and Done to: Recognition Theory, Intersubjectivity and the Third* (New York: Routledge, 2017).

22. An often-critiqued term used by Murray A. Straus, Richard J. Gelles, and Suzanne K. Steinmetz in *Behind Closed Doors: Violence in the American Family* (New York: Anchor, 1981); cf. Michael S. Kimmel, "Gender Symmetry," *Domestic Violence: A Substantive and Methodological Research Review, Violence against Women* 8/11 (2002) 1332–63.

23. Numerous studies support this, e.g., National Institute of Justice, "Pathways Between Child Maltreatment and Adult Criminal Involvement" October 12, 2017. NIJ.gov: https://nij.gov/topics/crime/Pages/Pathways-between-child-maltreatment-and-adult-criminal-involvement.aspx.

24 Evan Stark and Anne Flitcraft, "Woman-battering, Child Abuse and Social Heredity: What Is the Relationship?" in Norman Johnson, ed., *Marital Violence* (London: Routledge & Kegan Paul, 1985) 147–71. (See also Ch. 3, this volume.) The direct effect of child abuse on later patterns of offending is still much debated in the literature. For example, one prospective study of children demonstrated that child victims of physical abuse do have a higher rate of "violent delinquency, aggression, and other socially relevant outcomes," as well as depression and anxiety (abating after age 21). The correlation with becoming "a perpetrator of romantic relationship violence" was statistically significant (to a lesser degree than some other problems in adulthood); there was no statistically significant correlation between abuse in childhood and becoming a victim of intimate partner violence in adulthood. —Jennifer Lansford, Shari Miller-Johnson, Lisa Berlin, Kenneth Dodge, John Bates, and Gregory Pettit, "Early Physical Abuse

The very terminology of "victim" can imply not only the legitimate horror of being victimized, but also a kind of assigned purity and innocence defined by helplessness, which erases the reality of survivors' agency. As pastoral theologian Jeanne Hoeft has eloquently described,[25] every choice made for the sake of survival in the midst of violation is in some sense a form of resistance.[26] Nevertheless, a climate of trauma, and its enablement by collective denial, is likely to persist until 1) victim-survivors are met with genuine justice and redress (no cheap grace or premature forgiveness); 2) there are safe contexts in which to heal (personally, inter-generationally, and historically), and 3) there is a genuine, enforced zero-tolerance for violence and abuse across the mainstream of institutions and social structures.

As with the term "victim," the language of "survivor" can trap a person in a moment in time, a moment of violation and response, narrowing her identity down to the effects of one dimension of her history. As I have written in *The Cry of Tamar*[27] and elsewhere (see Ch. 12), I believe we actually need "a category *beyond* 'survivor' that both retains the history of trauma and resistance, and the empowerment that the term survivor implies, but that also makes room for entirely new possibilities that neither deny nor focus exclusively upon past injuries in the formation of who she is today."[28] At the same time, I believe the therapeutic idea of "post-traumatic growth" all too often falls unintentionally into the pattern of "forgive and forget." I resist the notion that we should ever forget our histories, but rather incorporate them into the tapestry of all our experiences that have *both* injured

---

and Later Violent Delinquency: A Prospective Longitudinal Study," *Child Maltreatment* 12/3 (2007) 233–45, see Table 2. Online at https://www.ncbi.nlm.nih.gov/pmc/articles/PMC2771618/. Research methodologies and resulting statistical analyses vary widely among a plethora of studies on this topic. See also Daniel Goleman, "Sad Legacy of Abuse," New York Times, Jan. 4, 1989, who summarizes research that approx. 1/3 of childhood abuse victims abuse their own children—a significant number, but also denoting that 2/3 of childhood abuse victims do not perpetuate an intergenerational cycle of violence—online at https://www.nytimes.com/1989/01/24/science/sad-legacy-of-abuse-the-search-for-remedies.html.

25. Jeanne Hoeft, *Agency, Culture, and Personhood: Pastoral Care and Intimate Partner Violence* (Eugene, OR: Pickwick, 2009), also citing Sharon Lamb, *The Trouble with Blame: Victims, Perpetrators, and Responsibility*, rev. ed. (Cambridge: Harvard University Press, 1999).

26. See also Edward Gondolf and Ellen R. Fisher, *Battered Women as Survivors: An Alternative to Treating Learned Helplessness* (Lexington, MA: Lexington Press, 1998); Linda Gordon, *Heroes of Their Own Lives: The Politics and History of Family Violence* (1988; reprint, Urbana: University of Illinois Press, 2002).

27. Pamela Cooper-White, "Theorizing Trauma, Identities, and Victimization," in *The Cry of Tamar*, 2nd ed., Introduction, 13–21.

28. Ibid., 15.

us *and* helped us to grow—and I continue to maintain that even from a Christian vantage point, forgiveness is God's work, not a work of righteousness that we are required to accomplish.[29]

Consider also: perpetrators engender confusion in their victims; whereas victims and survivors habitually resort to self-blame (as an unconscious defense against complete loss of control). Just as interpersonal violence always includes, among other things, an element of mind-control and "gaslighting" to justify the abuse and cause uncertainty in the victim, the same dynamics of mind-control and spreading confusion are tactics of those who would grab institutional or societal power. The more totalitarian the authority in power, the more dishonesty and confusion will abound. In her classic book, *The Origins of Totalitarianism*, Hannah Arendt wrote, "The ideal subject of totalitarian rule is not the convinced Nazi or the convinced Communist, but people for whom the distinction between fact and fiction (i.e., the reality of experience) and the distinction between true and false (i.e., the standards of thought) no longer exist."[30] And the more dishonesty and confusion serve to cloak institutional violence, the more victims of oppression will be told they are to blame, in one way or another, for their subjugated circumstances. All of this is held in place—both in intimate and in public relations—by the silence and witting or unwitting complicity of the bystander. As Harvard trauma specialist Judith Herman has written,

> The knowledge of horrible events periodically intrudes into public awareness but is rarely retained for long. Denial, repression, and dissociation operate on a social as well as an individual level. The study of psychological trauma has an "underground" history. Like traumatized people, we have been cut off from the knowledge of our past. Like traumatized people, we need to understand the past in order to reclaim the present and the future.[31]

## The Role of the Bystander

Perhaps, as the rape crisis movement is now beginning to strategize, the most important target for education and prevention is not solely the perpetrator (who must be contained and stopped), nor solely the victim/survivor (who

---

29. Ibid., 251–261.

30. Hannah Arendt, *The Origins of Totalitarianism*, Part III "Totalitarianism" (New York: Harvest/Harcourt, 1973).

31. Judith Lewis Herman, *Trauma and Recovery: The Aftermath of Violence—from Domestic Abuse to Political Terror* (New York: Basic Books, 1997), 2.

deserves to be believed and justified, and offered support in healing), but the *bystander*. Bystander education has become a crucial tool in violence prevention, and one that appears to be having some positive effects on college campuses. Of course our efforts to effect social change must incorporate healing and empowerment for victim-survivors, and effective containment as well as treatment for offenders. But until we convince the bystanders (which means all of us, the whole society), we continue to apply bandages to wounds and not make significant inroads toward changing what is still, tragically in the U.S., a "rape culture"[32]—a culture of toxic masculine privilege and entitlement. To quote once more from *The Cry of Tamar*,

> In my view, both blaming the victim and idealizing victims as helpless innocent are two sides of the same coin, because both result in holding the victim responsible in different ways for the perpetrator's violence. We often still prefer to believe the excuses of perpetrators, consciously or unconsciously, and to empathize with their suffering, as a way of not having to do the hard work of holding them accountable and "rocking the boat" in our communities. But we are challenged to "do what love requires" (Mic. 6:4)—to hold in tension kindness, justice, and humility, not collapsing into just one or the other of these three prophetic mandates. Whether we identify ourselves as victims, survivors, perpetrators, bystanders, or all of these in varying proportions, we all share a communal responsibility to restore right relation. This will not be accomplished by giving in to minimization and denial, but by "speaking the truth [to power] in love."[33]

## Gender and New Challenges for the Future

Gender itself is emerging as an important challenge for the future of the movement to end violence against women. On the one hand, the male-female binary is being challenged and broken down by trans/non-binary gender activists who, in part inspired by the writings of Judith Butler[34] and Ann

---

32. Emilie Buchwald, Pamela R. Fletcher, and Martha Roth, *Transforming a Rape Culture*, 2nd ed. (Minneapolis: Milkweed, 2005).

33. Ibid., 21.

34. Most notably, Judith Butler, *Undoing Gender* (New York: Routledge, 2004), Judith Butler, *Gender Trouble: Feminism and the Subversion of Identity* (New York: Routledge, 2006).

Fausto-Sterling,[35] among others[36]—protest being boxed into stereotypical masculine vs. feminine identities, and seek to embody an identity that is free to incorporate or discard elements of each. This has "engendered" fierce debates in the LGBTQ community about the authenticity of identities—for example, (now traditional) "butch" Lesbian, transgender man, or queer/non-binary gender? Is "trans" a gender swap, or something less traditionally defined—an identity that transcends the binary and eschews all traditional gender norms—including the ways those norms are encoded in language, e.g., the use of masculine and feminine pronouns. Trans persons have been the targets of hate violence, equal to or even greater than violence toward gays and lesbians, and more than half have experienced intimate partner violence.[37] The rate of suicide, especially in adolescence and young adulthood, is 41 percent according to one very large-scale study—twice the rate of LGB adults, and almost 10 times the national average.[38] Pioneering organizations such as Community United against Violence (CUAV),[39] founded in 1979 in San Francisco and the Anti-Violence Project in New York[40] are important grassroots efforts to combat violence against all expressions of non-binary gender identity.

At the same time, self-identified or "cis" (non-trans) women continue to make up the vast majority of victims of gender-based and sexual violence. And nearly all trans murder victims are trans women of color.[41]

---

35. Ann Fausto-Sterling, *Sexing the Body: Gender Politics and the Construction of Sexuality* (New York: Basic Books, 2000, 2008).

36. Cf., in theology specifically, the challenge to heternormativity, including in our imaging of the divine, in Marcella Althaus-Reid, *The Queer God* (New York: Routledge, 2003). I thank PhD student Chanmi Byun for introducing me to this author in greater depth; see also Virginia Ramey Mollenkott, *Omni-gender: A Trans-religious Approach* (Cleveland: Pilgrim, 2001).

37. Violence against Trans and Non-binary People, 2015 survey, VAWNet, online at https://vawnet.org/sc/serving-trans-and-non-binary-survivors-domestic-and-sexual-violence/violence-against-trans-and. Human Rights Commission, "Violence against the Transgender Community in 2018, online at https://www.hrc.org/resources/violence-against-the-transgender-community-in-2018.

38. Ann P. Haas, Philip L. Rodgers, and Jody L. Herman, "Suicide Attempts among Transgender and Gender Non-conforming Adults: Findings of the National Transgender Discrimination Survey," American Foundation for Suicide Prevention/Williams Institute UCLA School of Law, Jan. 2014, online at https://williamsinstitute.law.ucla.edu/wp.../AFSP-Williams-Suicide-Report-Final.pdf.

39. See the website at www.cuav.org.

40. See the website at https://avp.org/. See also the National Coalition of Anti-Violence Programs, online at https://avp.org/ncavp/, which lists local organizations addressing violence against LGBTQ persons at https://avp.org/ncavp-members/.

41. Maggie Astor, "Violence against Transgender People Is on the Rise, Advocates

The work to end violence specifically against women—both cis and trans—is necessary. I see the issue of gender, as it has come under scrutiny particularly among millennials and academics versed in gender theory, as a thickly entwined reality of subjugation of both women and LGBTQ persons. In part, the term "intimate partner violence" or "IPV" has increasingly replaced the terms "domestic violence" and "woman battering," in recognition that violence occurs among multiple gender configurations (though still between 89–95% male-to-female), and couple arrangements (married, cohabiting, dating, etc.).

Without diminishing the particularities of violence targeting women and persons who do not conform in one way or another to stereotypical gender norms, I would argue that there is a common attack on the "non-masculine," and on anyone who embodies a challenge to the patriarchal structure of men—notably, in North America, white men—at the top of the power pyramid. The patriarchal preoccupation with being on top—in every way possible—assigns both women and non-gender-conforming persons to roles of subordination. Race and class privilege further complicate the debate, as race and class identities and issues can be misappropriated in fighting *against* gender reform.

At the same time, the meme of "toxic masculinity," originally born out of the (in many ways problematic) mythopoetic men's movement of the 1980s, has on the one hand promoted "healthy masculinity" as a way to mitigate the destructive impact of masculinity on men,[42] and has also created pockets of advocacy for non-stereotyping parenting and relationships among men that have a non-violent, pro-feminist, and anti-misogynist agenda. The Black feminist activist bel hooks has written a compelling argument for men becoming more relational as a way to combat both violence against women and harm toward other men and themselves.[43] But as Michael Kimmel argues,[44] turning around "aggrieved entitlement" will take more than persuasion that men feeling and expressing their feelings is a better way to live. The appeal to individual self-interest is not enough to overcome the gravity of the social construction of traditional gender

---

Say," *New York Times*, Nov. 9, 2017, online at https://www.nytimes.com/2017/11/09/us/transgender-women-killed.html.

42. For an analysis of this concept, see Michael Kimmel, *Angry White Men: American Masculinity at the End of an Era*, 2nd ed. (New York: Nation Books/Perseus, 2017), on his analysis of white masculine rage and "aggrieved entitlement." On the origins of "toxic masculinity," 104 et passim.

43. bell hooks, *The Will to Change: Men, Masculinity, and Love* (New York: Washington Square, 2004).

44. Kimmel, *Angry White Men*.

norms—and their attendant rationalizations for male privilege. The "men's rights" movement—a strong manifestation of masculinist backlash against feminist claims—feeds on cultural narratives of men's victimization and emasculation, and stokes the fires of violence against women.

It is important to note that not all men are themselves violent abusers of women—indeed, a majority are not. In another statistical category error, it has been assumed that if roughly 1/4 to 1/3 of all women are victims of domestic violence, the same proportion of men are perpetrators. With the reality of pattern offenders who continue to offend, leaving multiple victims in their wake, it can probably be said with some confidence that a smaller percentage of individual men is responsible for the large percentage of victims. This is a statistic we do not have. At the same time, the socialization of men to violence against both men and women is a dynamic in all relationships within a patriarchal society, and patriarchal patterns of dominance and submission require recognition and reform in all contexts and among all gender identities. Male socialization to "go along" and avoid confronting a peer around sexist—or racist—behavior is pervasive (which is why bystander education is so important). Men need to own up to ways in which masculinist socialization has been harmful to themselves and others, and to do the "men's work"[45] of confronting violence against women—especially among their peers in interpersonal situations.

A growing number of organizations work with perpetrators to stop patterns of abuse (including pioneering programs Emerge in Boston, Manalive in Marin County, California, the Duluth Domestic Abuse Intervention Project, and CONNECT in New York City).[46] Those utilizing best practices hold themselves accountable to the oversight of women's agencies with safety of victims as their first priority. CUAV and the Anti-Violence Project, noted above, also offer assistance to both batterers and victims with the LGBTQ community. All these organizations work collaboratively, not only providing direct services to clients, but also engaging in legislative advocacy and political activism.

---

45. Paul Kivel, *Men's Work: How to Stop the Violence that Tears Our Lives Apart* (Center City, MN: Hazelden, 2010).

46. For a complete list of batterers' intervention programs accountable to the battered women's movement, and a discussion of best practices, see David Adams, "Certified Batterer Intervention Programs: History, Philosophies, Techniques, Collaborations, Innovations and Challenges," *Clinics in Family Practice*, 5/1 (2003), online at https://www.futureswithoutviolence.org/userfiles/file/Children_and_Families/Certified%20Batterer%20Intervention%20Programs.pdf.

## Conviction with Complexity

It may be apparent in this Introduction, and increasingly throughout my writings on the issue of violence against women, that at times my initial deep grounding in the movement comes into tension with my training as a pastoral counselor and especially a psychoanalytically oriented therapist. I do struggle at times with the sharp edges of absolute right-and-wrong thinking in the movement, in light of the psychoanalytic awareness that everything is more complicated by unconscious motivations at individual, interpersonal, and societal levels of interaction. A rigorous, deeply held ethic is at times difficult to reconcile with the psychoanalytic embrace of ambiguity and complexity. Out of my feminist psychoanalytic perspective, I also continue to believe, as I wrote in *The Cry of Tamar*, that there are deep primal experiences in all of us regarding women as Other. Because we are all born from the body of a woman, and are completely at the mercy of our earliest caregivers during our infancy, we retain a mostly unconscious experience of Woman—as Other.[47] And while both girls and boys can grow up to be in awe—or fear—of this Other, women have the socially-encouraged chance to identify with and become Her, while boys are systematically pushed away and urged to suppress feelings of dependency. This differentiation is reinforced in families and on the playground and elsewhere by bullying and violence.[48] And differentiation + fear can all too easily become hatred. Sexism is not merely social and institutional male supremacy—it also is, or is fueled by, this fundamental fear-based misogyny. Like feminist writers Dorothy Dinnerstein and Nancy Chodorow,[49] who advocated as early as the 1970s for gender-non-stereotypical child-rearing to mitigate this primal internalization of woman as Other, I want to hold the complexity of this deeply rooted, collective unconscious dynamic in mind, and allow it to inform our non-sexist practices in family, church, and community, while recognizing that insight and the reform of relational practices are not

---

47. Articulated, e.g., through the lens of French psychoanalytic feminism in Luce Irigaray, *Speculum of the Other Woman*, trans. Gillian C. Gill (Ithaca, NY: Cornell University Press, 1985).

48. William Pollack, *Real Boys: Rescuing our Sons from the Myths of Boyhood* (New York: Random House, 1999).

49. E.g., Nancy Chodorow, *The Reproduction of Mothering: Psychoanalysis and the Sociology of Gender* (Berkeley: University of California Press, 1978); Dorothy Dinnerstein, *The Mermaid and the Minotaur* (New York: Harper & Row, 1976); Sherry Ortner, "Is Female to Male as Nature Is to Culture?" in *Woman, Culture, and Society*, ed. Michelle Zimbalist Rosaldo and Louise Lamphere (Stanford, CA: Stanford University Press, 1974); See also Cooper-White, *The Cry of Tamar*, 68–70.

enough in and of themselves to overturn centuries of patriarchal institutional privilege and discrimination.

It is my hope that in my writings in this volume and elsewhere, I have been able to assert an uncompromising stance for gender justice, while recognizing the complexities of human personalities and relationships, and the numerous socially constructed constraints that we internalize and that hold us bound. As a therapist, I want to explore the depths of individuals' complexity and multiplicity of self-states including self-blame, desire for revenge, claiming of agency and empowerment, healing, and growth through suffering without excusing violence or oppression or wishing them away. As a *feminist* therapist I also want to work toward empowerment of women and other persons targeted for oppression, keeping the larger societal issues of injustice always in view as a factor (both political and psychological) that we have all internalized both consciously and unconsciously, and which we need to remember and to contest. Clinical training and wisdom should not erase from therapists' and counselors' awareness that violence is wrong, period, regardless of anyone's internal motivations. No one deserves violence, no matter what. Neither relational conflict nor the dynamics of a perpetrator's unconscious personal history provide a valid excuse, or a "get out of jail free card" for terrorizing another human being. There are lines that simply must not be crossed. And from a theological point of view, the prophetic balancing act of the prophet Micah, holding kindness, justice and humility together must take precedence over any watered-down spirituality of self-absorbed niceness and cheap grace.

## Comments about This Volume

The chapters in this volume are organized chronologically, from the first essay I wrote on domestic violence in 1990, arguing that both advocacy and clinical counseling have a place in the battered women's movement, to a recent essay on violence and justice, exploring historic and theological foundations for an ethic and theology of sexual justice. In between, there are essays that are more theologically or theoretically focused, and others that are more practice-oriented. All were prompted initially by questions that were raised by colleagues, and later, by readers, extending and at times complicating assertions I had made previously—and always carrying the thread of my deep allegiance to the movement for social justice.

I have chosen not to update statistics in the body of these texts, for several reasons: 1) Official counts are always under-estimates, as it is well known by now that sexual and intimate partner violence—as well as sexual harassment and clergy sexual abuse—are routinely under-reported because victims fear disbelief or retaliation,[50] and childhood abuse is sometimes repressed until well after statutes of limitations for reporting have run out. The most recent National Crime Survey estimates that less than half of intimate partner/domestic assaults and only about 23% of sexual assaults are reported to police,[51] and only about ¼ of victims of intimate partner violence receive assistance from any victim service agency;[52] 2) Much social psychology research has tried to be gender-neutral in its data gathering, and therefore has been criticized methodologically by researchers identified with the battered women's movement;[53] 3) The more detailed the statistics being reported, the more variance there tends to be from agency to agency (including the Centers for Disease Control, the U.S. Census Bureau's National Crime Survey, and the U.S. Department of Justice/FBI), as well as independent academic researchers, although generalized prevalence statistics remain fairly consistent; and 4) Initially, it was important to publicize statistics in order to convince lawmakers, funders, and the general public that violence against women was a serious problem. But by now, haven't we done enough prevalence studies to know that this is an epidemic problem!?

It could be argued that after 40+ years of advocacy, education, prevention and intervention work, we would want to show evidence of improvement. The problem is that, in spite of reported declines in the official statistics (notably after the enactment of the VAWA legislation) for forcible rape (by about 9.5–10%),[54] and domestic violence (by 64–72%!),[55] in the

---

50. U.S. Bureau of Justice Statistics, Police Response to Domestic Violence, 5, online at https://www.bjs.gov/index.cfm?ty=dcdetail&iid=245.

51. U.S. Bureau of Justice Statistics, National Crime Survey 2016, p. 7. Link to full report online at https://www.bjs.gov/index.cfm?ty=pbdetail&iid=6166. Incidents involving serious injury were reported slightly more than half of incidents of intimate partner violence, with others reported less than half the time. Cf., BJS, "Police Response to Domestic Violence," which estimated that slightly more than half of all non-fatal incidents (56%) were reported in the years 2006–2015.

52. Ibid., 8.

53. Most criticism in this vein has been leveled at the National Family Violence Survey conducted by the Family Research Laboratory at the University of New Hampshire, e.g., Murray A. Straus and Richard J. Gelles, *Physical Violence in Families: Risk Factors and Adaptations to Violence in 8,145 Families* (New Brunswick, NJ: Transaction, 1989) and Straus, Gelles, and Steinmetz, *Behind Closed Doors*.

54. Between a peak of 109,062 in 1992 and 89,000 in 2008, with some fluctuation year to year, as reported by the U.S. Dept. of Justice/Federal Bureau of Investigation, Uniform Crime Reports, "2008 Crime in the United States," Table 1, http://www2.fbi.gov/ucr/cius2008/data/table_01.html.

55. Shannon Catalano, "Intimate Partner Violence Dropped 53 Percent from 1993 to 2010," online at https://www.bjs.gov/content/pub/press/ipv9310pr.cfm. In

most recent official report in 2016 by the U.S. Bureau of Justice Statistics (reflecting reports submitted by police departments), there were over 300,000 incidents of rape/sexual assault, and 1,109,610 incidents of domestic violence/intimate partner violence.[56] High levels of stalking, sex trafficking of (predominantly) women and girls, and sexual harassment (as evidenced by recent publicity) continue at astronomical levels. Clearly, violence against women and the non-masculine Other is still a massive social problem.[57]

## Hope for the Future

Although we have seen reports of improvements, especially since the enactment of the Violence against Women Act in 1994, we must still ask the question: Why is there still so *little* improvement after four decades!? Why is the work to end violence against women so hard to achieve?

One observation I have is that we have at times allowed the movement to end violence against women become mainstreamed, and we have lost the edge of our prophetic witness (see Ch. 11). This "mainstreaming" was often done with the best of intentions. We sought to increase the visibility of the problem, and to bring community resources to bear on solving it, and we built promising bridges with law enforcement and the judiciary through trainings and inter-agency coalition building.[58] But too much captivity to large institutions, corporations and governmental funders can blunt our voices of protest in favor of keeping our sponsors comfortable. In particular, we have tended to lose our philosophical grounding in a recognition of the ways in which violence against women intersects with other forms of violence and oppression. Have we "traded up," choosing corporate partnerships over our historical grassroots allies in anti-racism and community-based anti-violence work? We need to continue to keep alive strategies for

---

this official report, 85% of victims were female. NCADV attributes a decline of 72% in incidents of intimate partner violence to the Violence against Women Act of Congress (VAWA)—see https://ncadv.org/legislation. To see the TED talk on this hopeful progress by Esta Soler, founder of Futures against Violence on the history of the shelter movement and the impact of the VAWA act, online at https://www.futureswithoutviolence.org/our-mission.

56. BJS National Crime Survey 2016, 5. Population growth is also a factor.

57. See also a summary, periodically updated, by the National Coalition against Domestic Violence, online at https://ncadv.org/statistics; 11th annual National Domestic Violence Counts National Survey, Sept. 2016, online at https://nnedv.org/mdocs-posts/census_2016_handout_national-summary.

58. See online at https://ncadv.org/legislation; https://www.futureswithoutviolence.org/policy-advocacy/; https://www.futureswithoutviolence.org/aaron-polkey-2.

activism, coalition-building around the larger issues of institutionalized oppression and social—and political—change.

Where is hope? Are we simply to accept a theological view that sin abounds in this life? Is violence against women therefore with us until the apocalypse? And if so, should we simply pack away our picks and shovels and stop trying to erode the massif of violence against women? Is this some interim time that God has willed for a sinful humanity? I do not look for purity or perfection in life, which can again engender a kind of violent psychic splitting (see Ch. 12), but neither can I accept a theological fatalism about this world that urges us toward passive acceptance. I do not believe that violence is ever God's will, even temporarily, as a lesson or an interim necessity whose good outcome we cannot see. I reject "total human depravity," claiming the spark of original goodness that enables all of us to partner with God and God's intentions for the wellbeing of the creation.

As a therapist, I believe in the capacity for transformation, and as a feminist I believe in the possibility—at least in some times and places—of real social change. As a *pastoral* counselor and theologian, I also believe that resurrection and the eschaton are not a final, once-for-all cataclysmic overturning of the world's hierarchies, but rather a daily restoration of grace and renewal of life—God's abundant love overflowing into the world, against which we are as a species, finally, powerless to resist (although we often do our best and often appear to succeed in doing so). I stand with political theologians who speak of the power of hope,[59] and liberation theologians[60] who trust in God's solidarity and power to overcome oppression. I believe in our human capacity to join with God's desire for the flourishing of all life on

---

59. Classic texts include: Jürgen Moltmann, *Theology of Hope*, trans. James Leitch (Minneapolis: Fortress, 1993); Dorothee Soelle, *The Silent Cry: Mysticism and Resistance*, trans. Barbara and Martin Rumscheidt (Minneapolis: Fortress, 2001); Rebecca Chopp, *The Praxis of Suffering: An Interpretation of Liberation and Political Theologies* (1986; reprint, Eugene, OR: Wipf & Stock, 2007).

60. Some classic texts include: Gustavo Gutiérrez, *A Theology of Liberation: History, Politics, and Salvation*, trans. Sr. Caridad Inda and John Eagleson (1971; Maryknoll, NY: Orbis 2012); Ada María Isasi-Díaz, *En la Lucha/In the Struggle: Elaborating a Mujerista Theology* (Minneapolis: Fortress, 2004); Ivona Gebara, *Longing for Running Water: Ecofeminism and Liberation* (Minneapolis: Fortress, 1999); Delores Williams, *Sisters in the Wilderness: The Challenge of Womanist God-Talk* (Maryknoll, NY: Orbis, 1993; reissued, 2013). Specific to violence against women, see, e.g., Renita J. Weems, *I Asked for Intimacy: Stories of Blessings, Betrayals, and Birthings* (Philadelphia: Innisfree, 1993) and *Battered Love: Marriage, Sex, and Violence in the Hebrew Prophets* (Minneapolis: Fortress, 1995); Toinette Eugene and James Newton Poling, *Balm for Gilead: Pastoral Care for African American Families Experiencing Abuse* (Nashville: Abingdon, 1998); Traci West, *Wounds of the Spirit: Black Women, Violence, and Resistance Ethics* (New York: New York University Press, 1999); Stephanie Crumpton, *A Womanist Pastoral Theology against Intimate and Cultural Violence* (New York: Palgrave Macmillan, 2014).

the planet. As "Sarah" and her children so richly showed me, resurrection is possible—even one woman at a time. In these difficult times, it might be easy to believe that the light of truth and the power of love can be extinguished. I choose hope, and hope leads us to stay in the struggle.

# 1

## Peer vs. Clinical Counseling

*Is There a Place for Both in the Battered Women's Movement?*

1990[1]

AT THE PRESENT TIME, there is controversy among advocates within the battered women's movement, which is also relevant to other victim advocates, concerning the appropriateness of peer counseling or advocacy, vs. clinical counseling or psychotherapy. This controversy, which will be an important one for the 90s, lies within an even larger debate about whether social services or social action/community organizing, or some combination, is the more appropriate focus for agencies and programs that deal with domestic violence. For the purposes of this article, *peer counseling* is defined as counseling by non-licensed advocates who are roughly equal in age, status, and knowledge to those they are counseling.[2] In the battered women's movement, this may include both the volunteer paraprofessional (such as hotline volunteer) and paid shelter counselor/advocate, trained in the dynamics of domestic violence, crisis intervention, and problem solving techniques by senior shelter staff. Peer counseling emphasizes assisting women to identify various options and solutions for safety and empowering them to make their own choices. It avoids interpretation and diagnosis and stays out of the realm of the unconscious. In contrast to peer counseling, clinical counseling, or psychotherapy, refers to counseling by licensed, clinically trained professionals-psychiatrists, psychologists, licensed clinical so-

---

1. Based on papers presented to the Conference on Victim Services, Orange, California, May 1988; the 3rd National Nursing Conference on Violence against Women, Concord, California, May 1989; and the 5th National Conference of the National Coalition against Domestic Violence, Amherst, Massachusetts, August, 1990. This essay received the Annual *Response* Award for Practitioner Article, "Peer vs. Clinical Counseling," *Response to the Victimization of Women and Children* 14/1 (1991) 2–6.

2. Vincent D'Andrea and Peter Salovey, *Peer Counseling: Skills and Perspectives* (Palo Alto, CA: Science & Behavior Books, 1983).

cial workers, and licensed marriage, family and child counselors. While the techniques of licensed professionals vary widely, most operate within some model of mental illness, diagnosis, and treatment. Except for those who use cognitive-behavioral approaches, most work with unconscious material and interpretation as well as problem solving in the here-and-now. Clinical counseling and psychotherapy are nearly synonymous terms, although the latter implies greater emphasis on diagnosis and treatment of illness than the former. Clinical counseling and psychotherapy tend to be longer termed than peer counseling as the result of this depth perspective.

> Over the last 10 years, as domestic violence has become a more visible community issue, grassroots advocacy organizations have been joined by—or have themselves become—more mainstream social service agencies, addressing the multiple needs of battered women and their children. Organizational structures have often cited this trend, with larger, more hierarchical staff-patterns being seen as well as smaller, more consensus-based collectives: Many grassroots shelters have objected to the trend towards providing clinical counseling services. At the same time, many funders and more traditionally credentialed mental health and social service professionals have promoted it, even to the exclusion of the peer model.
>
> The objections of battered women's advocates include concerns that clinical approaches tend to discount the firsthand expertise of peer advocates in favor of academic credentials only. Many advocates are formerly battered women themselves, and/or have been working with domestic violence intervention long before it became generally recognized or addressed by clinicians. The grassroots women's movement also worries that by "professionalizing" work with battered women and their children, the social and political vision of the movement based on recognition of sexism, racism, and homophobia will be lost.[3]

The grassroots women's movement objects to victim-blaming models of psychotherapy, in which the battered woman is either someone to be healed or cured of her mental illness—hence, the terms "therapy," "treatment," and "patient" (e.g., psychodynamic/analytic approach)—or she is equally responsible for the violence in the family dynamic (e.g., family

3. For an interesting analysis of "power-over" dynamics and oppression, see Starhawk, *Truth or Dare* (San Francisco: Harper & Row, 1987). For the relationship between homophobia and domestic violence, see Suzanne Pharr, *The Connection between Homophobia and Violence against Women* (Little Rock, AR: The Woman's Project, 1986); and Kerry Lobel, ed., *Naming the Violence: Speaking Out about Lesbian Battering* (Seattle: Seal, 1986).

systems theory). Battered women have been mistakenly diagnosed on the basis of the *Diagnostic and Statistical Manual of Mental Disorders (3rd edition, revised)* ("DSM-III-R")[4] for behaving in ways that may have been their only alternatives for surviving life-threatening violence by their partners. The diagnoses in these instances include: masochistic, borderline personality, paranoid, or even schizophrenic behavior,[5] or (now in a provisional category) "self-defeating personality disorder."[6] Post-Traumatic Stress Disorder (PTSD), under which Lenore Walker assigns her "Battered Women's Syndrome,"[7] represents a more appropriate basis for diagnosing victim behavior. Walker's diagnosis has been recognized by some clinicians as more appropriate to victims of domestic violence. In this view battered women's symptoms are similar to survivors of war, out of whose experience after the Vietnam War PTSD was identified. (Even so, because the symptomatology is based on a male model of experience and reaction to stress and terror, it may not be entirely appropriate.)[8] Thus, until recently, it was easier for mental health practitioners to simply diagnose battered women as mentally ill than to consider the possibility of domestic violence—and in many cases this continues to be the prevailing practice (beginning with Freud's shift from believing his patients when they said that they were sexually abused by their fathers, the "seduction theory", to the position that such claims were usually fabricated—the oedipal theory[9]

---

4. American Psychiatric Association ("APA"), *DSM-III-R: Diagnostic and Statistical Manual of Mental Disorders, 3rd ed., revised* (Washington, DC: APA Press, 1987). [At the time of this *Collected Essays* volume, the DSM is in its 5th revision ("DSM-5," 2013). The personality disorders have been reorganized into clusters, with "Borderline Personality Disorder" listed, with no significant change in criteria, under Cluster B "dramatic, emotional, and erratic."—PCW, 2018]

5. Lynne B. Rosewater, "Schizophrenia, Borderline or Battered?" In Lynne B. Rosewater and Lenore Walker ed., *Handbook of Feminist Therapy* (New York: Springer, 1985) 215–25.

6. [This provisional diagnostic category was not incorporated in subsequent editions of the DSM. —PCW, 2018]

7. Lenore Walker, *The Battered Women's Syndrome* (New York: Springer, 1984).

8. [In response to this critique, the "A" criterion of exposure to "actual or threatened sexual violence" has been added in DSM-5 (2013). —PCW, 2018]

9. Janet Malcolm, *In the Freud Archives* (New York: Knopf, 1984); Jeffery Masson, *The Assault on Truth: Freud's Suppression of the Seduction Theory* (New York: Farrar, Straus & Giroux, 1984). [It should be noted that in recent decades, there has been some modulation of Masson's view that Freud entirely rejected the impact of trauma, although his focus did indeed shift from external to intrapsychic causes of neurosis. —PCW, 2018]

As an alternative to classical Freudian approaches,[10] family systems theory was actually a liberating approach when it was first put forward, because it presented the idea that the person identified by the family as being "sick" might actually be the family scapegoat. The theory acknowledged that a family member who shows symptoms—often the wife or the adolescent child—might be acting out or carrying issues for the rest of the family, and it held that all members have a responsibility for what happens within a family.[11] This view was liberating, in that it required the apparently more "normal"" or "healthy" family members to acknowledge their own roles in the family pathology and participate in making changes in order for the therapy to succeed. Battered women's advocates point out that this view can backfire miserably for a victim of abuse. They point out that, when it comes physical or sexual violence, the perpetrator alone must full responsibility for the abuse. It is a basic tenet of this view that no one, under any circumstance, deserves or provokes assault or violation.

Another popular trend in therapy, borrowed from chemical dependency treatment, examines relationship dynamics in tems of "co-dependency" or "women who love too much."[12] The battered women's movement objects that when this is applied to understanding victims of domestic or sexual violence, it tends to focus more on what the victim should or could do to change than on the perpetrator's responsibility. This is especially complicated when alcohol or drug abuse are actually present. It is considered to be a major pitfall of many social work and community mental health counseling approaches that they often blame the chemical or the addiction for the violence, whereas alcohol and drugs are usually the perpetrator's excuse for the violence, and not the cause.[13]

The dynamic of psychotherapy itself is held suspect by many battered women's advocates, since it calls for an expert or professional (often male) holding power over a client or patient. This is particularly true in more

10. [This comment refers to American "ego psychology," the postwar branch of psychoanalysis that dominated psychoanalysis through the postwar decades until the 1980s. Recent historical research has clarified that ego psychology became rigid and formulaic, and lost much of the social reform agenda of European analysis in the 1920s. See Russell Jacoby, *The Repression of Psychoanalysis: Otto Fenichel and the Political Freudians* (New York: Basic Books, 1983) 5–9. —PCW, 2018]

11. Murray Bowen, *Family Therapy in Clinical Practice* (New York: Aronson, 1978); Salvador Minuchin, *Families and Family therapy*. (Cambridge: Harvard University Press, 1974); Virginia Satir, *Conjoint Family Therapy*, 3rd ed. (Palo Alto, CA: Science-Behavior Books, 1988).

12. Robin Norwood, *Women Who Love Too Much*. (Los Angeles: Tarcher, 1985).

13. Family Violence Project, "Domestic Violence, Drugs and Alcohol: Proceedings of the Conference of the Family Violence Project, October, 1985," San Francisco, 1985.

psychodynamic models of therapy, where the phenomenon of transference (in which the client unconsciously relates to the therapist as primary parental figure) occurs or is deliberately elicited and strengthened by the therapist in order to work through early childhood traumas. At the extreme, the therapeutic "blank screen," by which a neutral non-responsive stance is maintained, is used by the therapist to refuse gratification of the client's infantile wishes for nurturing.[14] This eventually elicits an explosion of anger toward the therapist, patterned unconsciously after rage toward the early parent, and then this conflict can be worked through. Feminist criticism of this model is based on the alternative view that the client may, in fact, be angry at the therapist, and that some expectation of human warmth or empathy is not a sign of illness or unresolved conflict, but, rather a healthy understanding of what it means to be human.

Nevertheless, the power imbalance of expert-over-client must always exist to some extent in clinical counseling, and it is dangerous in any therapy to try to ignore it or wish it away. This power imbalance is the most important reason why any sexual contact between therapist and client is considered unlawful as well as unprofessional behavior, and is always the therapist's responsibility.

Finally, there is the criticism by the battered women's movement that the entire field of psychotherapy, dominated as it is by white, middle class, graduate-trained professionals, generally fails to take into consideration ethnic and cultural realities which further impact the struggles of battered women of color to survive. For many women of color, including both American-born and refugee and immigrant women, the whole notion of seeking "human services" from an unknown and impersonal institution or a white professional in private practice violates deeply held values around family, community, and cultural identity and solidarity.[15]

On the other side of the debate, mental health and social service professionals complain that, in its zeal for "political correctness," the peer counseling model discounts the skills and wisdom of clinical counseling and psychotherapy which have, in fact helped many battered women to free themselves and their children from a violent environment, and ignores the strides of feminist therapy in integrating the political and personal realms. Feminist therapy takes into account the harmful effects of sexism,

---

14. [A feature of ego psychology, described in note #10 above, and not commonly practiced today, including among most psychoanalysts. —PCW, 2018]

15. E.g., Evelyn C. White, *Chain, Chain, Change: For Black Women Dealing with Physical and Emotional Abuse* (Seattle: Seal, 1985); Myrna M. Zambrano, *Mejor Sola que Mal Acompañada: Para la Mujer Golpeada/For the Latina in an Abusive Relationship* (Seattle: Seal, 1985).

racism and homophobia in the society in which we live. It recognizes the presence of environmental stress, and seeks therapeutic change based on a model of empowerment in which clients recognize their own dissatisfactions, set their own goals, and make in formed choices and changes. This contrasts with the medical model that emphasizes diagnosis, prescription or therapy, and cure.[16]

In addition to this controversy, there is considerable debate on all sides of these questions about domestic violence research. At its 1988 national meeting,[17] NCADV formed an "Activist Research Task Force" to examine and critique current research on domestic violence, and to propose protocols for research methods appropriate for use in shelters. The position of this task force, as well as that of many researchers in the field, in light of this critique, was that some forms of research can be misleading and destructive. Also, the misapplication or misinterpretation of other research, which may, in its original context, be useful, can do further damage.

The article, "The Truth about Domestic Violence," by McNeely and Robinson-Simpson[18] provides an outstanding example of problematic research which has potentially destructive implications. Its controversial findings had potentially devastating implications for battered women's services and the training of clinicians. The article reported findings based on use of the Conflict Tactics Scale ("CTS"),[19] and studies by, among others, Susan Steinmetz.[20] The article stated that violence is equally or even more likely to be perpetrated by women partners as men. This finding was contrary to studies based on data from police, criminal justice agencies, divorce courts, and hospital emergency room records. Based on these data, 95–98

---

16. Detailed discussion of feminist therapy principles can be found in Lynne Rosewater and Lenore Walker, eds., *Handbook of Feminist Therapy* (New York: Springer, 1985), and specific guidelines for working with victims of domestic violence are contained in the National Coalition against Domestic Violence (NCADV)'s *Guidelines for mental Health Practitioners,* by Susan Schechter (Washington, DC: National Coalition Against Domestic Violence, 1987).

17. National Coalition against Domestic Violence, *Proceedings of the Fourth National Conference: "Bringing the Vision Home, 1978–1988"* (Seattle: NCADV, 1988).

18. Richard L. McNeely and Gloria Robinson-Simpson, "The Truth about Domestic Violence: A Falsely Framed Issue, *Social Work* 32/6 (1987) 485–90.

19. Murray A. Straus, *Conflict Tactics Scale Manual* (Durham, NH: University of New Hampshire Family Violence Research Laboratory, 1990).

20. Susan Steinmetz, *The Cycle of Violence: Assertive, Aggressive, and Abusive Family Interaction* (New York: Praeger, 1977); "The Battered Husband's Syndrome," *Victimology* 2/1 (1971) 499; and "Women and Violence: Victims and Perpetrators," *American Journal of Psychotherapy* 34 (1980) 339.

percent of victims of domestic battering historically have been women.[21] Estimates for the number of women expected to be battered in a given year have ranged from 25 percent[22] to 50 percent,[23] with 28 percent as the most common estimate.[24]

The findings of the McNeely and Robinson-Simpson article were vigorously rejected by five experienced battered women's advocates in a subsequent issue of the same journal.[25] There has been longstanding complaint that the CTS is an inadequate and misleading tool for gathering data. There are three main points in this criticism of special concern to feminists: first, the CTS asks respondents whether they ever hit, used a weapon, or otherwise did violence to their partner, and how many times, but it does not ask whether such acts were conducted in self-defense or whether injury resulted from them.[26] Secondly: it ignores the psycho-social context of male privilege and the dominant role socialization.[27] Third, although the test was principally designed to measure violence occurring in couples and families currently living together, there are no recommendations given to those administering the questionnaire that partners should not be interviewed together at the same time, or that any precautions for safety of victims should be taken in the interviewing process (Straus has acknowledged this as an omission and indicated that he would consider including such a section on safety for participants in a future edition of the

---

21. Federal Bureau of Investigation (FBI), *Uniform Crime Reports*. Washington, DC: U.S. Government Printing Office, 1982; Dobash, R. E., & Dobash, R. Lecture, University of Minnesota, Mar. 25, 1983 (cited in Joy Bussert, *Battered Women: From a Theology of Suffering to an Ethic of Empowerment*, New York: Lutheran Church in America, Division for Ministry in North America, 1986).

22. FBI, op. cit.

23. Lenore Walker, *The Battered Women's Syndrome* (New York: Springer, 1984).

24. Interview with Prof. Anna F. Kuhl, Dept. of Criminal Justice, San Jose State University, January, 1988.

25. Daniel Saunders, "Other 'Truths' about Domestic Violence: A Reply to McNeely and Robinson-Simpson," *Social Work* 33/2 (1988) 179–83; "Continued Debate: The Truth about Domestic Violence," Letters to the Editor by Terry L. Singer, Ann Darling, Jann Jackson, and Edward W. Gondolf, "Rejecting the Findings of the McNeely & Robinson article," *Social Work* 33/2 (1988) 189–91; See also McNeely and Robinson-Simpson's reply to Saunders, "The Truth about Domestic Violence Revisited," *Social Work* 33/2 (1988) 184–88.

26. Murray A. Straus, 1980; Straus and Richard J. Gelles, *Physical Violence in American Families: Risk Factors and Adaptation to Violence in 8,145 Families* (New Brunswick, NJ: Transaction, 1990).

27. Daniel Saunders, "Other 'Truths' about Domestic Violence."

*CTS Manual.*[28] As a result of these shortcomings, the validity of measures derived by using the CTS is compromised.

## Alternative Ways of Viewing the Problem

1. Perhaps it is a symptom of our socialization when problems are viewed in a linear way, in dichotomies such as either/or. It may be more useful to think of both peer and clinical counseling as a continuum in which a variety of helping methods can be used to varying degrees, depending on the needs and wishes of each battered woman.

2. Feminist therapy is a viable alternative to misleading and destructive models of psychotherapy that can lead to re-victimization. In feminist therapy the client's experience is validated, not merely diagnosed, and she is viewed as a *survivor* rather than a victim.[29] She is empowered to make change in a supportive environment, rather than treated, as in the medical model. *Many* specific therapeutic approaches can be helpful if applied within a feminist framework, including Rogerian/ humanistic therapy, Self Psychology,[30] Jungian/transpersonal approaches,[31] and techniques from family therapy.[32]

3. In keeping with the feminist approach, *NCADV* research protocols will propose topics generated from within the battered women's movement itself. Such research would focus on providing information to more effectively help survivors of domestic violence to become empowered. These protocols will also require a participatory research methodology, in which research is done in an empowering way with the full consent and understanding of the participants at every step. In this model, participants are seen as directly involved in learning from the research, rather than as subjects *upon* whom or *to* whom the research is being done, and who are expected to gain only indirectly from results.

28. Telephone interview with Murray Straus, Director of the University of New Hampshire Family Violence Research Laboratory, July, 1990.

29. Lenore Walker, "Feminist Therapy with Victims/Survivors of Interpersonal Violence," in Lynne B. Rosewater and Lenore Walker, eds., *Handbook of Feminist Therapy* (New York: Springer, 1985) 203–14.

30. Heinz Kohut, *How Does Analysis Cure?*, edited by A. Goldberg with P. Stepansky (Chicago: University of Chicago Press, 1984).

31. Barbara S. Sullivan, *Psychotherapy Grounded in the Feminine Principle* (Wilmette, IL: Chiron, 1989).

32. Harriet G. Lerner, *Women in Therapy* (Northvale, NJ: Aronson, 1988).

4. Some women who might never identify themselves as "battered," or come to a shelter for assistance, might seek professional therapy as a way out of their abuse. NCADV estimated in 1988 that only about 3 percent of battered women were being seen by shelters (due, in part, to the unavailability of facilities as well as the need for more culturally appropriate outreach and services for women in the Asian, Latina, Black, and other ethnic communities, and among lesbians and the disabled). It is the responsibility of advocates not to reject out of hand *any* of the options a battered woman may choose to free herself from a dangerous situation but instead to support those choices, even if they seem to lead away from the advocate's preferred methods of helping. While discussion of alternatives and challenging the victim to consider all available options may be fruitful, to impose a set of values on the victim simply replaces the dominance of the abuser and may lead to re-victimization. In order for a battered woman to become empowered, those who would help her must relinquish their desire to rescue her—especially in their way and on their terms—and to validate the victim's right to self-determination.

## Peer vs. Clinical Counseling

The concerns of the grassroots battered women's movement are valid ones. Much harm has been done to battered women, and many dangerously misleading ideas have been generated by professional mental health researchers and practitioners. Peer counselors/advocates ("advocates" refers to what many peer counselors in battered women's shelters are called) provide supportive presence and strategize options with a woman in crisis better than anyone else, regardless of credentials. It is important to recognize the wisdom and expertise of formerly battered women, and women trained by the battered women's movement, in the often subtle dimensions of socialization which underlie the violence.

Clinical psychotherapy or counseling should be seen as a complementary option to peer counseling under certain circumstances. Particular care should be taken in using clinical approaches.

1. It should consider the woman's safety *always*, without compromise, as the first priority;
2. It should be used to empower and not to control, supervise, treat, or cure the battered woman and her children, or to "save the relationship."

3. It should assist the woman to confront her own internalized sexism and assumptions of powerlessness, and be liberated from them;

4. It should be mutual, participatory and client-based, rather than exclusively therapist-controlled;

5. It should be undertaken with an understanding of related socio-political factors and not confine itself to scrutiny of purely individual client history and relationship dynamics;

6. It should take into account ethnic and cultural needs;

7. Under no circumstance should the therapist blame the victim.

## Integrating Peer and Clinical Counseling in Domestic Violence Programs

Both peer and clinical counseling have been found to be useful options by battered women. Some women may benefit from one approach but not the other. However, *both* approaches may be useful to the same battered woman at different stages of her efforts to break free and deal with the problem.

1. Peer counseling is probably the most effective in the initial crisis phase: (a) It provides validation, friendship, belief and support, and helps the client to explore strategic options, developing an action plan for getting free of the violence; (b) It assists her in the community, and provides advocacy with police, the courts, and social service, medical, and legal agencies; (c) It provides her with an analysis of the social and political reasons why battering happens, and helps her to realize that she is not alone, or powerless.

2. Clinical counseling may be most useful to the battered woman after the immediate crisis phase is past, and she is living free of violence. At this time, clinical counseling or psychotherapy may help her to address possible long-term effects such as depression or post-traumatic stress, to develop creative ways of channeling her anger, and to explore the basis for new relationships. The approach to this therapy should be grounded in a socio-political context that will foster her empowerment.

3. Personal involvement in feminist advocacy, education, and political activism in the community creates a stronger background for counseling than professional knowledge alone. For the clinical counselor, activism can be a nourishing ground for doing feminist therapy—a

balancing of the inner and outer perspectives. It further validates the steps the client herself is taking to advocate for herself with social institutions and in her relationships.

## Conclusion

By healing the rift between peer and clinical counseling in the battered women's movement, we continue to enact our belief that it is the victim's ultimate right to decide what is helpful to her and when, and we stand beside her as true advocates on her journey to greater freedom and wholeness.

# 2

## Soul Stealing

*Power Relations in Pastoral Sexual Abuse*

1991[1]

ONE OF THE MOST important tasks of the women's movement in the past two decades—if not the most important—has been to bring violence against women in all its forms out of the closet. Contrary to the opinion of a man who called in to a radio talk show to tell me that the work of battered women's shelters was "the promulgation of victimization," the often overwhelming task of bringing this information to light is one of empowerment. Understanding that knowledge is power, women have bravely spoken up about their experiences of abuse and formed supportive organizations that send a message to survivors of male violence: you are not alone. One out of three women in the U.S. is raped; one out of four (according to the FBI) or even one in every two (according to California's attorney general) is battered by an intimate partner; at least one out of four has been abused as a child; and at least one out of five is an incest survivor.

Despite an increased awareness of that violence, only a few works have addressed the issue of pastors' sexual abuse of parishioners. Most of these frame the problem as a psychosocial one rather than placing it squarely in the spectrum of power abuse. Important exceptions are Marie Fortune's *Is Nothing Sacred? When Sex Invades the Pastoral Relationship* (1989)[2] and Peter Rutter's *Sex in the Forbidden Zone: When Men in Power—Therapists, Doctors, Clergy, Teachers, and Others—Betray Women's Trust* (1990).[3]

---

1. Orig. publ. "Soul Stealing: Power Relations in Pastoral Sexual Abuse," *The Christian Century* (Feb. 20, 1991) 196–99; nominated by *The Christian Century* for the 1991 annual award for best full-length article, National Association of Church Publishers.

2. Marie Fortune, *Is Nothing Sacred? When Sex Invades the Pastoral Relationship* (San Francisco: Harper & Row, 1989).

3. Peter Rutter, *Sex in the Forbidden Zone: When Men in Power—Therapists, Doctors,*

My own observations are based on working more than ten years in the battered women's movement, in the church since 1984 as an ordained pastor, and since August 1989 as a consultant in a program for survivors of clergy exploitation. In convening a support group for such survivors, I have witnessed the lasting devastations that these women have experienced. The many parallels between male pastoral sexual abuse and wife- or partner battering have become increasingly clear, especially as the church is so often portrayed as family. (I agree with Fortune that we should be de-emphasizing the image of church as family in favor of images of *community* in which boundary expectations are more clearly defined.)

Pastoral abuse—pastors engaging in sexual or romantic relationships with their parishioners or counselees—is much more prevalent than is commonly supposed. Estimates exceed the 10 percent figure Rutter ascribes to male psychotherapists. The abuse often is seen by parishioners and denominational executives as something else—a problem with alcohol, for example, or an emotional or relationship problem of the pastor or the parishioner, or a parish conflict. A single pastor relating intimately with a single parishioner is typically seen as an acceptable and time-honored practice. I argue, however, that such intimate relating is *always* an unethical boundary violation and that it is *always* the pastor's responsibility to maintain the appropriate boundaries.

As with rape, a pastor's sexual or romantic involvement with a parishioner is not primarily a matter of sex or sexuality but of power and control. For this reason I call it *pastoral sexual abuse* rather than "pastor-parishioner relations" or, worse, a matter of private activity between consenting adults (which is almost always how the perpetrator will describe it). Even when adultery is involved, unfaithfulness is not the primary issue. I have found that ministers enter into romantic or sexual relationships with parishioners primarily because there is an imbalance of power between them at the outset and because they need to reinforce and heighten the intensity of that power dynamic. This need is driven by internal forces and is reinforced by societally conditioned expectations that women will function as a nurturing, sexual servant class.

Why should these relationships be considered abuse? If both the minister and the parishioner are single (usually not the case), what's wrong with their having a relationship?

As Fortune has outlined, there can be no authentic consent in a relationship involving unequal power. And no matter how egalitarian a pastor's style of ministry, he carries an authority that cannot be ignored.

---

*Clergy, Teachers, and Others—Betray Women's Trust* (Los Angeles: Tarcher, 1990).

I deliberately use the term "he" because, as in domestic violence, the vast preponderance of these cases involve male clergy. It is possible for a male parishioner, particularly one with special financial or organizational clout— a church council member, for instance—to harass a woman minister. It should also be noted that abuse also occurs between pastors and parishioners of the same sex. In such cases, the same power dynamics also pertain, further complicated by internalized homophobia and pressures and fears on the victim not to disclose or report.

The clergy role carries a great deal of power in and of itself, and one of the most insidious aspects of that power is the role of "man of God." In some sense the minister carries ultimate spiritual authority, particularly in the eyes of a trusting parishioner who looks to him for spiritual guidance and support. But the male minister also possesses other forms of power: as a man, he carries the power society confers upon men and socializes them to hold over women, often in the guise of being their protectors. He is often physically stronger and more imposing. He may be an employer. He may also assume a teaching or mentoring role which encourages women to listen to his advice and correction. Often he also functions as a counselor, with all the transference inherent in such a relationship.

Because of this power, ministers must not ever get involved with parishioners. (For a contrasting, less absolute viewpoint, see Karen Lebacqz and Ron Barton's article "Pastor-Parishioner Sexuality: An Ethical Analysis."[4] They argue that it may be legitimate for single pastors to fall in love with single parishioners. In this treatment of the theme, Lebacqz and Barton also caution that a complex power dynamic must be taken into consideration.)

In addition, the pastor must remain aware that dual relationships— where the pastor is also friend, spiritual adviser, pastoral counselor, administrator, CEO and even employer to his parishioners—can become exploitive or inappropriately intimate. While dual relationships are often difficult to avoid, pastors should be trained to be conscious of the potential for harm, and to understand that they hold the ethical responsibility as professionals for keeping the boundary intact.

The harm done to victims can best be understood in terms of the opportunities pastors have for ministry and how these opportunities are destroyed by violating sexual boundaries. In their counseling role, pastors have an opportunity to heal and strengthen fractured boundaries, and many parishioners suffering from childhood abuse have these fractures. Moreover, if a parishioner acts out sexually, the minister should recognize

---

4. Karen Lebacqz and Ron Barton, "Pastor-Parishioner Sexuality: An Ethical Analysis," *Explor* 3 (1988) 67–81.

it as a clear cry for help. The *last* thing he should do is read it as a valid invitation. It is even more reprehensible for him to initiate a sexual relationship and exploit this vulnerability. The pastoral relationship can and should be a sacred trust, a place where a parishioner can come with the deepest wounds and vulnerabilities—where she can even act out sexually. By modeling appropriate boundaries and healthy responses, the pastor can begin to empower her to heal those wounds. The harm done when this is exploited is no less than a violation of sacred space, which further ruptures and destroys the woman's boundaries, devastating her mental health and her sense of self. What every therapist knows (or ought to) about this should also be required training for every pastor.

Pastors have an opportunity to emphasize a power with rather than a power-over model in the parish. But sexual relationships with female parishioners reinforce a traditional male power dynamic and breed a closed, destructive parish model. In his pastoral role, the pastor has opportunities to validate the gifts and talents of his parishioners. When he focuses on a woman's sexuality, whether or not he denigrates her other abilities, those talents are discounted. Frequently the very talents that attracted him to her in the first place become discounted and devalued by him once the sexual relationship begins.

Finally, when a pastor violates a parishioner's boundaries he takes away the church's appropriate, powerful and sustaining spiritual guidance and support and, because of threats to her reputation, robs her of an important arena for her creativity and contributions. Many victimized women report that not only have they lost their parish community, but their trust has been so violated that they cannot go to any church.

Both pastor and victim lose. Their families lose. And the church loses. But the woman victim loses the most and, as things stand in most denominations, the pastor loses the least. Typically, when such a relationship or multiple relationships are uncovered, he gets a slap on the wrist, a lot of sympathy and is referred to a counselor. The parish is left to cope with feelings of betrayal and rage—most often directed at the woman as seductress. His family is angry at his betrayal (although they often minimize and deny it), and his wife is usually left feeling confused, abused and fearful. The family of the woman involved is generally broken up and the burden of blame placed on her. She loses her reputation, her parish, sometimes her job and even her whole life in the community. The best she can usually expect from denominational leaders is sympathy, not justice—that is, they take no action to prevent the pastor from doing it again, nor do they recognize the seriousness of his violation. At worst, she can expect to encounter disbelief or blame.

Like batterers, abusive pastors are frequently charming and charismatic in situations outside the abusive relationship. Because the real dynamic is power, not sex, they are often perceived as having strong leadership qualities and are often described as visionaries or political movers and shakers (or they believe that they are). They are often manipulative and foster a climate of secrets, gossip and an inner circle. As with batterers, there is no racial or class profile to this group.

In my experience, about half the time these men also abuse alcohol. But, as with domestic violence, drinking is not the cause of the abuse, although it is often used as the excuse. The common myth, probably held by his wife, the parish and the denomination, is that once he admits and deals with his alcohol problem, the sexual misconduct will stop. My experience is that sexual misconduct and exploitation does not stop until it is dealt with explicitly. A purely addiction-treatment model will not address a male power addiction, because the dependency model does not confront the root social forces sustaining and normalizing male power over women.

It is difficult to guess how consciously these pastors abuse women. They tend to see themselves, when questioned, as victims of female wiles. Sometimes—as when threatened with suspension by their denomination—they admit that they are in need of treatment to "build up their fortitude against being seduced." What they generally fail to see is their own responsibility.

The internal dynamics at work in these men may include: history of an abusive childhood; low self-esteem and a fear of failure; deeply held traditional values about male and female roles, however disguised in liberal rhetoric; poor impulse control; a sense of entitlement, of being "above the law," or other narcissistic traits; difficulty accepting responsibility for mistakes and difficulty establishing appropriate intimate relationships and friendships with male peers (he may have what Mary Pellauer calls a "Lone Ranger" style of ministry[5]).

No one type of woman is predisposed to victimization, however. In battered women's work, we know from experience that, contrary to prevailing myths and stereotypes, because of the way both women and men are socialized, any woman can be battered. There are some learned susceptibilities that incline women to overlook, forgive and tolerate a pastor's sexual exploitation: women's socialization to be polite, non-confrontational and accepting of men's behavior; their training and desire to heal men's wounds (these men often present themselves to women as needing their special love and healing); the sense of submissiveness as a Christian value,

---

5. Mary Pellauer, "Sex, Power, and the Family of God," *Christianity and Crisis* (Feb. 16, 1987) 47–50.

especially ingrained in churchwomen; and having one's identity defined by society as primarily sexual.

Particular situations add to a woman's vulnerability, and the typical clergy perpetrator has an uncanny knack—some women call it almost psychic in intensity—for zeroing in on women with these vulnerabilities (partly because the intimate details are being shared with them in counseling): divorce, marital conflict or abuse; a husband who shows indifference or is frequently absent; a time of career confusion (his encouragement can be very important); decade passages (a powerful man can validate her attractiveness); a child with special needs; particular dedication to the church—she may be a lay minister, a member of church committees, a church employee or a seminary intern (this makes for additional potential loss if she confronts him or says no); a personal history of family boundary violations—sexual, physical or psychological (this makes it harder for her to be clear about what is inappropriate on his part); power differentials such as a large age difference or his prominence in the community or denomination. Just about any life change that brings a woman in to talk with her pastor can be exploited as a gateway to satisfying his own power needs.

Many women neither stop nor report pastoral abuse, for several reasons. First, they usually feel responsible. But as Fortune has written, even if a woman initiated the sexual contact out of her own need or vulnerability, the pastor, like a therapist, has the responsibility to maintain the appropriate boundary. It was not her fault. Society blames women for attracting men—rape survivors usually feel that they are the ones on trial. "She must have done something to provoke it." This is further compounded by myths and stereotypes portraying male pastors as sitting ducks for the seductive maneuvers of female parishioners.

Victim-blaming, however, can also take the more sophisticated guise of clinical diagnosis of the women. Such "diagnoses" can range from masochism and personality disorder to "co-dependency" to woman-blaming-once-removed: blaming the perpetrator's mother for poor bonding and causing narcissistic wounds. Such strategies divert attention from the only appropriate focus: holding the abuser accountable for the abuse.

Second, the woman may fail initially to stop or report abuse because she feels validated by it on some level. It's flattering; it makes her feel special. At vulnerable times especially, this is compelling. Third, over time her self-esteem is seriously battered down by this relationship. Fourth, once the sexual relationship is begun, the man frequently engages in confusing behavior. Women have consistently reported extreme highs and lows in the relationship and an on-again, off-again quality. Promises of marriage are proffered and then withdrawn. Fifth, she may be sworn, with a religious intensity, to secrecy. "The parish would never understand our kind of love." In the worst cases this opens the door for multiple relationships with several parishioners at once.

The woman may not want to hurt his career. She may love him and believe he needs her. She may feel that the good times make the bad times worth it—or that the good times represent the "real him." She may be unwilling to hurt his wife and family or the church's reputation.

Once a certain determination to think about leaving has taken hold in her, however, fear keeps her stuck. She fears that no one will believe her when it's her word against his. She fears that she will be the one held responsible. She fears losing her church, community, her personal reputation and, if she is employed by the church, her professional reputation. She fears his retaliation sometimes within the sphere of personal and church life, but also sometimes in the form of physical violence, rape, or threats of violence.

Most chilling, she fears his retaliation on a spiritual level. This aspect became increasingly clear to me in work with the survivors' group. It is difficult for others to comprehend the sheer terror that accompanies this form of abuse. But often because of the image of charismatic spiritual power that these men have asserted and fostered, the women's terror is akin to actually being cursed or damned. Sometimes this kind of threat is made explicit by the abuser. Its power is clearly demonic in nature and intensity—victims fear that their very souls will be stolen.

Colleagues, counselors and denominational staff should be aware of several issues concerning treatment or intervention with abusive pastors. If the pastor has an alcohol problem, family disruptions, or a parish dynamic of secrecy and closed process, it is important to be alert to possible sexual abuse. Once sexual abuse has been identified, expect minimization and denial, expect to be diverted onto issues of alcohol abuse or extreme stress. Don't lose sight of the power pattern that is really operative and needs to remain the focus of treatment. To join in minimizing his responsibility is inadvertently to reinforce his behavior. Give an unequivocal message that all sexual or romantic relations with parishioners are wrong. Educate him on why they are wrong and how they have come to seem OK. All young men are socialized to some degree to see women as prey, seductresses who will say "No" and mean "Yes." Help him to see how this has harmed his ability to relate to women and thus harmed his ministry and his life.

The church needs a new ethical code that accurately names and recognizes the prevalence of the problem, offers justice rather than mere sympathy for victims—including clear policies and procedures for the support of victims and mechanisms for restitution—and that re-educates perpetrators rather than merely offering them sympathy. In conjunction with this treatment, local church and denominational offices have a responsibility to monitor and evaluate the counseling process. They need to outline clear consequences that include censure or suspension, with the goal of preventing harm to others.

Each judicatory body of each denomination needs a clear standard of behaviors and a clear disciplinary process that holds the pastor responsible for all sexual boundary violations. (In most states it will be essential that denominations take the initiative to adopt such policies, since attempts to legislate pastoral professional ethics, similar to laws regulating professional behavior of therapists and medical practitioners, have been blocked by church lobbies on the grounds of separation of church and state.) Each denomination also needs an established program of prevention and education about the root causes of male violence and power against women and a commitment to a vision of equality.

We need nothing less than a total paradigm shift: we need to stop treating the problem as only one of sexual morality, emotional instability or addiction, and address the power dynamics of these mostly hidden abuses. Only when this happens and the church stops engaging in denial and collusion can the church be a place of authentic power, healing and proclamation for both women and men.

# 3

## An Emperor without Clothes

*The Church's Views about Domestic Violence*

1996[1]

Once upon a time there was an emperor who was very vain about his elegant clothing. Two swindlers convinced him that they could make him the finest clothes he ever had, and set to work on an empty loom. Rumors of their fame began to spread, and even the emperor's high officials were convinced that the invisible garments were the finest they had ever seen. One minister even decided, "I know I'm not stupid, so it must be my fine position I'm not fit for. Some people might think that rather funny, but I must take good care they don't get to hear of it." And then he praised the material which he couldn't see and assured them of his delight in its charming shades and its beautiful design. The emperor finally went on parade with his new garments. Crowds gathered, and they all said how magnificently clad he was. No one dared admit they couldn't see the clothes, and many concluded there was simply something wrong with them that he appeared naked. Finally a little child said, "But he hasn't got anything on!" "Goodness gracious, do you hear what the little innocent says?" one whispered to another, until finally everyone shouted at last, "He hasn't got anything on!" The emperor was embarrassed, but he drew himself up and went on with the procession still more proudly, while his chamberlains walked after him carrying the train that wasn't there.[2]

---

    1. Orig. publ. as "An Emperor without Clothes: The Church's Views about Treatment of Domestic Violence," *Pastoral Psychology* 45/1 (1996) 3–20.

    2. Paraphrased from Hans Christian Andersen, "The Emperor's New Clothes," in *Eighty Fairy Tales*, trans. R. P. Keigwin (New York: Pantheon, 1976) 64–68.

THE CONSENSUS OF A group about what constitutes reality, even a small group, is extremely difficult to resist.[3] The consensus of an entire culture about reality is even more difficult to dispute or to contradict.

Battered women and their advocates have had to work very hard to get the church to acknowledge that domestic violence exists at all, except in rare instances. The myth of the happy family, and in particular, the happy Christian family, formed an imaginary cloak around an "emperor" who rules over his family with force, threats and terror. We have spent nearly two decades now debunking basic myths and stereotypes, educating the churches about the prevalence of woman-abuse, and the fact that it happens to white, educated, privileged women as well as poor women of color—and that it happens to women in our churches, at the hands of prominent, "upstanding, respectable," churchgoing men—including clergy. In many communities, this is still the struggle. In other communities; awareness has definitely increased, and with it, a commendable amount of concern and a desire to help. However, as people have acknowledged that domestic violence does, in fact, exist, new imaginary clothes have begun to replace the old. People continue to find ways to deny and minimize the terrifying extent of the problem of violence against women. The issue of domestic violence has passed in and out of the media spotlight, swinging between eroticized sensationalism on the one hand, and a dissociative effort to re-privatize, stigmatize, or ignore it on the other.[4]

This is understandable. Nearly everyone has some reason, conscious or unconscious, to want to hold this issue at arm's length. Women who have never experienced it do not want to believe that such horror could happen-and particularly, that it could happen to them. Women to whom it is now happening may be simultaneously relieved to know that they are not alone, but embedded in their own denial and minimization, which is one of the deadening effects of prolonged abuse. Women to whom it happened in the past often become staunch advocates for battered women, but without time and opportunity to work through their own experience, many former victims may instead repress and minimize their own history as a defense mechanism against despair and overwhelming rage. Men who do not batter may deny, either because they can't identify with it, or because they participate unconsciously at a level of secret collusion, a kind of male bonding around privilege,

---

3. Cf., Sigmund Freud, *Group Psychology and the Analysis of the Ego*, in J. Strachey, ed. and trans., *The Standard Edition of the Complete Psychological Works of Sigmund Freud*, vol. 18, 65–144 (London: Hogarth, 1955; orig. pub. 1921).

4. Wendy Kozol, "Fracturing Domesticity: Media, Nationalism, and the Question of Feminist Influence," *Signs* 20/3 (1995) 646–67.

shame, and even envy or vicarious gratification.[5] It is well known, of course, that batterers deny and minimize as part of their profile.

Everyone is in one of these categories. And every one of these categories is represented not only in congregations, but among seminary professors, seminarians, and the clergy. It takes a great deal of courage, or a great deal of personal or professional exposure to this violence—or both—to override these enormous pressures to deny, both internal and external. And many who do begin to turn against the tide feel waves of self-doubt about their perceptions, just like the emperor's officials.

As the 1990s have progressed, we have also found ourselves to be living in a political and economic climate which is less and less open to advances for women than during the heady decade of the 70s, when most battered women's shelters and coalitions were organized. In the social and political sphere, we have witnessed the rolling back of many advances previously gained. In many religious institutions, there is a false sense of complacency that "women's issues" have been largely resolved by allowing ordination and passing policies on inclusive language. In other institutions, there is a sense that feminism is passé, irrelevant, or a phase that we have outgrown. Those institutions and denominations which never acceded much to women's demands in the 70s and 80s—for example, over half of U.S. denominations still do not ordain women[6]—are now feeling less challenged than ever to change.[7]

The human tendency toward denial and minimization, then, can easily become a tool of larger social and political agendas to suppress the truth, part of a conservative backlash movement against hard-won rights for women. At the heart of the matter is the acceptance or denial of an analysis—basic to advocacy for battered women—that, like rape and sexual harassment, *battering is primarily a matter of power, control and domination*.[8] It is not

---

5. Peter Rutter, *Sex in the Forbidden Zone: When Men in Power Betray Women's Trust* (New York: Fawcett Crest, 1989) 70–74.

6. National Council of Churches, "1989 Yearbook Reports Increase in Number of Ordained Women" (NCC Office of Information, 475 Riverside Drive #1901, New York, NY 10115.) [In 1960, women were 2.3% of women clergy; in 2016 this rose only to 20.7%. —Eileen Campbell-Reed, "State of Clergywomen in America: A Statistical Update," Oct. 1, 2018, online at www.eileencampbellreed.org. —PCW 2019]

7. [According to the National Congregations Study (www.soc.duke.edu), 39.3% allowed women clergy in 2006–7, and 42.3% in 2012. However, female heads of churches in the same study were reported at 5.5% in 1998, 4.6% in 2006–7, and 6.2% in 2012. Cf., Carol Kuruvilla, "These Are the Religious Denominations that Ordain Women," Huffington Post Sept. 26, 2014, online at https://www.huffingtonpost.com/2014/09/26/religion-ordain-women_n_5826422.html. —PCW 2018]

8. Del Martin, *Battered Wives* (New York: Pocket Books, 1976); R. Emerson Dobash and Russell Dobash, *Violence against Wives: A Case against the Patriarchy* (New York: Free Press, 1979); Lenore E. Walker, *The Battered Woman* (New York: Harper

primarily a matter of the man simply "losing his cool," having "poor impulse control," or "deficits in communication skills." It is not primarily a matter of sexuality, capacity for intimacy, substance abuse, or personal pathology on the part of either the victim or the perpetrator. All of these factors may enter into the dynamic, but they are not the causes of the violence—although they are often the excuses. If intervention is to be successful, it cannot focus primarily on these excuses.

It seems that every few years a new explanation for battering crowds onto the therapeutic scene, based on phenomenological research. The more popular ones are gratefully adopted into pastoral counseling training in seminaries, by educators who are themselves concerned and eager to come to a better understanding of domestic violence-but often without being willing or able to face (at least fully) the single most important underlying factor, that of sexism and the power inequity between men and women, which is simply heightened to a more violent extreme in battering relationships.

In recent years, I have observed two main attempts to disarm the feminist analysis that battering is a matter of male power over women. First, there is a continuation of glossing over realities of the oppression of women in society, by adopting a variety of liberal, intellectual, and clinical or pseudo-clinical forms of (usually unconsciously) blaming the victim.[9] These ways of understanding domestic violence are attractive because they seem reasonable, even-handed, even gender-blind. The pastoral counseling profession has tended to adopt this attitude.

The second attempt to disarm feminist analysis is more straightforward: it recognizes the existence of voices for social and political reform regarding violence against women, but dismisses them as extremist, and scornfully labels them with the newly pejorative term "politically correct." I predict that this will become an increasingly powerful expression of conservative backlash in seminaries over the rest of this decade, even as it has established itself already on the agendas of college campuses and public school boards.

## Clinical Pitfalls

Examples of the first category tend toward clinical or pseudo-clinical explanations for battering. Four perspectives, very popular in pastoral counseling, come to mind. First comes the oldest and most traditional

---

Colophon, 1979).

9. Term borrowed from William Ryan, *Blaming the Victim*, rev. ed. (New York: Vintage, 1976).

pastoral/clinical viewpoint, drawn from [uncritical applications of] psychodynamic/psychoanalytic theory, that battered women are masochistic.[10] Using the American Psychiatric Association's *Diagnostic and Statistical Manual* (DSM),[11] battered women have also been frequently labeled with borderline personality disorder or even schizophrenia,[12] or (in a provisional category in DSM-III-R and thankfully eliminated from the DSM-IV) "self-defeating personality disorder,"[13] for behaving in ways which may have been their only adaptive choices for survival in the context of life-threatening violence by their partners.[14]

Many clinicians still have not recognized the more appropriate diagnosis, Post-Traumatic Stress Disorder, under which Lenore Walker assigns her "Battered Women's Syndrome,"[15] and the only formal diagnosis in the DSM that acknowledges past injury as the cause of distress.[16] Thus, until recently, it was easier for the mental health practitioner, including the psychoanalytically oriented pastoral therapist, to simply diagnose the battered woman than to assign responsibility to the batterer and confront the reality of her situation.

10. Robert D. Stolorow, "The Narcissistic Function of Masochism (and Sadism)," *International Journal of Psychoanalysis* 56/4 (1975) 441–48; Natalie Shainess, *Sweet Suffering: Woman as Victim* (Indianapolis: Bobbs-Merrill, 1984); contra Paula J. Caplan, *The Myth of Women's Masochism* (Toronto: Toronto University Press, 1985); Lenore E. Walker, "Inadequacies of the Masochistic Personality Diagnosis for Women," *Journal of Personality Disorders* 1/2 (1987) 183–89; R. Emerson Dobash and Russell Dobash, *Women, Violence and Social Change* (New York: Routledge, 1992).

11. American Psychiatric Association, *Diagnostic and Statistical Manual*, 4th ed. (DSM-IV) (Washington DC: APA Press, 1994).

12. Lynne B. Rosewater, "Schizophrenic, Borderline, or Battered?," in Lenore E. Walker and Lynne B. Rosewater, ed., *Handbook of Feminist Therapy* (New York: Springer, 1985) 215–25.

13. John Leo, "Battling over Masochism: Psychiatrists and Feminists Debate 'Self-defeating Behavior,'" *Time Magazine* (Dec. 2, 1985) 76; Walker, "Inadequacies of the Masochistic Personality Diagnosis for Women."

14. Cf., Jean Baker Miller, *Toward a New Psychology of Women*, 2nd ed. (Boston: Beacon, 1987); Miller, "Connections, Dis-connections and Violations," *Work in Progress* No. 33 (Wellesley, MA: Stone Center, Wellesley College, 1988); Janet L. Surrey, "The 'Self-in-Relation': A Theory of Women's Development," *Work in Progress* No. 13 (Wellesley, MA: Stone Center, Wellesley College, 1984); See also the Works in Progress Series, and many other papers available from the Stone Center, Wellesley College, Wellesley, MA (now online at https://www.wcwonline.org/JBMTI-Site/publications). [The Stone Center is now the Jean Baker Miller Training Institute, online at https://www.wcwonline.org/JBMTI-Site/introduction-to-jbmti. —PCW 2018] See also John Briere, *Therapy for Adults Molested as Children: Beyond Survival* (New York: Springer, 1989).

15. Lenore E. Walker, *The Battered Women's Syndrome* (New York: Springer, 1984).

16. [This also applies to the DSM-5 (2013). —PCW 2018]

A second, more recent clinical viewpoint is that of family systems theory. This seems increasingly influential in the pastoral psychology field, and is perhaps becoming the most standard clinical orientation in pastoral theological education. Family systems theory[17] was thought to be a liberating approach when it was conceived, because it put forth the idea that the person whom the family identified as the sick one, the "Identified Patient" (often the wife), might actually be carrying issues for the entire family. The seemingly more normal or healthy family members had to own their own roles in the family dysfunction and participate in treatment together for therapy to succeed. This approach can backfire miserably for a victim of abuse, however, because it all too often leads to blaming the victim for her victimization. Again, when it comes to crossing the line of physical or sexual violence, the perpetrator alone must take full responsibility for the abuse.[18] No one, under any circumstances, deserves or provokes assault or violation.

For example, Archie Smith, Jr., in his pastoral-clinical analysis of battering from a systems point of view,[19] acknowledges the feminist critique of family systems theory, especially as articulated by Michele Bograd.[20] But certain aspects of his approach, which overall carries a strong justice perspective, are still troubling: a largely uncritical mention of battered men, an uncritical acceptance of couples' counseling as a valid intervention without exploring the implications for the woman's safety, and an implication that the marriage itself as viewed through Ephesians 4, rather than the cessation of violence, is an appropriate focus of therapy.

Moreover, as pastoral therapist Christie Cozad Neuger has written in relation to working with depression in women, ". . . one significant difficulty with family systems theory is that systems therapists tend to see the family roles as equal in power and to ignore the fact that women have significantly less power in terms of cultural value, economic independence, vulnerability

---

17. E.g., Murray Bowen, *Family Therapy in Clinical Practice* (New York: Aronson, 1978); Salvador Minuchin, *Families and Family Therapy* (Cambridge: Harvard University Press; 1974); Virginia Satir, *Conjoint Family Therapy*, 3rd ed. (Palo Alto, CA: Science and Behavior Books, 1983); for a feminist synthesis of family systems and psychodynamic theory, see Harriet G. Lerner, *Women in Therapy* (New York: Aronson, 1988). [For an overview of feminist family therapy approaches and critiques, see also L. B. Silverstein and T. J. Goodrich, ed., *Feminist Family Therapy: Empowerment in Social Context* (Washington, DC: American Psychological Association, 2003). —PCW 2018]

18. Michele Bograd, "Family Systems Approaches to Wife Battering: A Feminist Critique," *American Journal of Orthopsychiatry* 54/4 (1984) 560.

19. Archie Smith, Jr., "The Significance of the Religion of Jesus to People Who Stand with their Backs against the Wall of Family Violence. A Vision for a New Humanity: Implications for the Pastoral Care of Souls," *Explor* (Winter, 1988) 26-53.

20. Bograd, op. cit.

to physical abuse, and so on."[21] She goes on to cite Rachel Hare-Mustin[22]: "by ignoring gender differences, the therapist supports them."[23]

A third approach uses an addictions paradigm. There has been a surge of interest in the use of the term "co-dependency," initially from the chemical dependency field, but now being applied almost universally—and especially to women. The concepts of "love addiction" and "women who love too much"[24] are now widely—but erroneously—applied to battered women.

The primary problem with this theory is that it again puts the focus on the *woman's* need to change, and erroneously assumes that certain neurotic personality traits pre-date her involvement in a battering relationship which predisposed her to becoming a victim. The difference, however, between the irrational compulsive behavior of a "relationship-addicted" woman (if one finds such a category useful at all) and a battered woman, is that the battered woman's seemingly irrational, compulsive behaviors, observable over time, are not pre-existing traits, but are the results of often futile attempts to cope and survive in an environment of terrorism.[25]

A particularly potent form of blaming the victim comes out of the addiction and recovery model, when it simplistically combines the concept of the "inner child" (often used in work with adult children of alcoholics and especially prevalent now in "recovery" programs for incest survivors) with Freud's concept of repetition compulsion. This produces the formula: The inner child seeks what is familiar, and is attracted to abusive partners in order to try to repeat and work out the pain of her past. For example, Robin Norwood, in *Letters from Women Who Love Too Much*,[26] the sequel to her best-selling book, wrote that women afflicted with this "disease" will "choose dangerous men and dangerous situations"[27] in order to produce an

---

21. Christie Cozad Neuger, "Women's Depression: Lives at Risk," in Maxine Glaz and Jeanne Stevenson-Moessner, ed., *Women in Travail and Transition: A New Pastoral Care* (Minneapolis: Fortress, 1991) 150.

22. Rachel Hare-Mustin, "The Problem of Gender in Family Therapy Theory," in Monica McGoldrick, Carol M. Anderson and Froma Walsh, ed., *Women in Families: A Framework for Family Therapy* (New York: Norton, 1989) 61–77.

23. Neuger, "Women's Depression," 150.

24. Robin Norwood, *Women Who Love too Much* (New York: Pocket Books, 1986).

25. Linda S. Brown, "What's Love Got to Do with It?: A Feminist Takes a Critical Look at the Women Who Love Too Much Movement," *Working Together* 7/2 (1986) 1; R. Moore and Valli K. Kanuha, "Co-dependency vs. Battered Woman Syndrome," special edition, *The Voice: National Coalition against Domestic Violence*, 1988; Dobash and Dobash, *Women, Violence and Social Change* (1992).

26. Robin Norwood, *Letters from Women Who Love too Much* (New York: Pocket Books, 1988).

27. Ibid., 92.

adrenaline rush, and that they will provoke violence by "clinging, placating, nagging and pleading."[28] The implication of this theory is that women actually seek out battering partners in order to somehow reenact and resolve past traumas. (If statistics that anywhere from 1/4 to 1/2 of all women are battered at some point hold true, then it seems apparent that batterers abound, and such women do not have very far to seek! More is at work here than the intrapsychic, unconscious compulsions of wounded women.)

Recognizing the limitations of this trend to see battered women in terms of "co-dependency" can be especially complicated when alcohol or other substance abuse or addiction are actually present. It is a common pitfall of many social work and community mental health programs that they often blame the chemical or the addiction for the violence, rather than recognizing it as the barterer's excuse, not the cause.[29]

Finally, neo-Jungian or transpersonal therapies are very attractive intellectually to pastors and pastoral counselors, because they explicitly strive to integrate the spiritual dimension with the psychological. This can be and has been very productively used by pastoral therapists in integrating dreamwork, active imagination, and archetypal symbology into Christian pastoral counseling.[30] Church programs on Jungian psychology and spirituality are very popular in some areas of the country. However, there are dangers associated with this orientation for battered women as well.

First; few if any contemporary approaches to Jungian analytical psychology to date have ever mentioned violence as a reality of women's experience. Moreover, there have been very few attempts to challenge its nineteenth century, Eurocentric and patriarchal bias, which underlay stereotypical definitions of masculine and feminine as archetypal.[31] Polly Young-Eisendrath and Frances Wiedemann have usefully reframed the notion of an archetype from an eternal, universal truth to a culturally-induced complex.[32] This helps to explain why masculine and feminine

---

28. Ibid., 267.

29. Family Violence Project [later renamed Futures without Violence], *Domestic Violence, Drugs and Alcohol: Conference Proceedings, October, 1985* (San Francisco: FVP, 1985).

30. E.g., John A. Sanford, *Dreams: God's Forgotten Language* (San Francisco: Harper & Row, 1989).

31. Naomi Goldenberg, "Jungian Psychology and Religion," in *The Changing of the Gods: Feminism and the End of Traditional Religions* (Boston: Beacon, 1979) 46–71; Goldenberg, *Returning Words to Flesh: Feminism, Psychoanalysis and the Resurrection of the Body* (Boston: Beacon, 1990); Demaris Weir, *Jung and Feminism: Liberating Archetypes* (Boston: Beacon, 1987).

32. Polly Young-Eisendrath and Florence L. Wiedemann, *Female Authority: Empowering Women through Psychotherapy* (New York: Guilford, 1987) 36–42.

archetypes such as the animus and anima seem to work for some people in analyzing their experience and dreams, but at the same time recognizes that these are not eternally ordained. An uncritical or simplistic acceptance of masculine and feminine archetypes will always be problematic to the extent that it selves to reinforce at a very deep, psychic level the idea that the "Feminine" is equated with weakness, passivity, receptivity and inaction. A battered woman could easily hear this as paralyzing rather than mobilizing her ability to be assertive, framing her anger and attempts to take action as unfeminine.

Further, within the transpersonal perspective, there sometimes emerges at the extreme an erroneous logic that people unconsciously call their affliction to themselves in order to "do their spiritual work." This is an example of the worst excesses of New Age spirituality, where a battered woman's "karma" simply replaces her "cross to bear." From this point of view, we all bring everything on ourselves, from abuse to cancer to natural disasters, simply by being out of harmony, or owing a debt of suffering from a former life. I have heard battered women struggle to understand what is happening to them by saying, "We must have known each other in a former life, because everything is so intense. This violence must be our way of working out unresolved issues in a past life." Again, for the battered woman, the focus of this approach becomes how the woman needs to change—in this case, to "evolve spiritually"—and the batterer's responsibility is largely ignored. This kind of fatalism inherent in New Age spirituality is more akin to rigid distortions of Calvin's theories of predestination than to anything new.[33]

What is seductive about all of these theories—except for, perhaps, the last—is that they all contain more than a grain of truth. They do seem to offer a fairly accurate phenomenological description of the dynamics of a battering relationship. They seem to go beyond the behavioral surface of a couple's interactions to the unconscious, intrapsychic forces at work in the relationship, and to the influential ghosts of each member's personal histories. They even seem offer a satisfying answer to the profound question "Why is this happening to me?" This is why psychoanalytic approaches are so genuinely helpful—and at times seductive. However, if the focus of treatment remains entirely upon the individual's personal past and an exploration of individual experiences of trauma, it often misses the social and political context which can lead not only to personal insight, but to empowerment. Judith Herman, in her recent book *Trauma and Recovery*,[34]

33. Cf., Pamela Cooper-White, Review of Barbara G. Walter, *The Book of Sacred Stones* (New York: Harper & Row, 1989), in *CTNS Bulletin* (Berkeley: Center for Theology and the Natural Sciences, Graduate Theological Union) 9/4 (1989) 12–14.

34. Judith Herman, *Trauma and Recovery* (New York: Basic Books, 1995).

eloquently sums up this perspective in relation to trauma survivors' cry for justice and society's dissociative inertia. Both personal and political healing and justice-making are needed.

Many women, particularly more affluent, white women, have utilized psychotherapy or clinically oriented pastoral counseling—because they can financially afford to do so—to recognize toxic relational patterns and to leave violent relationships and rebuild their lives. However, the pitfalls of these purely therapeutic approaches are serious. They focus on how the woman needs to change—behaviorally, internally, or both. In one way or another, subtly or forthrightly, they identify her problem as a pathology and give it a label: masochistic, self-defeating personality disorder, identified patient or "IP," co-dependent, love-addicted. They do not place responsibility for the violence squarely where it belongs: with the perpetrator. Very little attention, if any, is given to the man's responsibility for the violence. Clinical theories often unwittingly collude with batterers' prodigious capacity for self-justification. His abusiveness is generally attributed to childhood experiences of family violence—as witness and/or as direct victim. It may be true that a majority of batterers have such histories. But this does not adequately explain why most men with similar histories—80 to 90% according to a recent NIMH study[35]—do not batter, nor does it help a batterer to stop his violent behavior. More often, it simply gives him more sophisticated forms of rationalization and excuse. Finally, these theories focus first on the woman, and/or on the relationship, but fail to go beyond these intrapsychic and interpersonal dynamics to the wider social and political context that shapes and maintains violence against women in all its forms. No matter how far these psychological perspectives go into the unconscious, historical depths of individuals' and couples' psyches, they cannot fully explain—much less intervene and prevent—the violence because they entirely ignore the ground on which those individuals and couples stand. It is like digging a hole for planting without noticing whether one is digging in a fertile garden or a sandpit.

## Intellectual Backlash

What about the new attack on "political correctness"? This battle has largely been waged, thus far, on college campuses, in the debates of local school boards concerning curriculum, and in the popular media geared to ward

---

35. Evan Stark and Anne Flitcraft, "Woman-battering, Child Abuse and Social Heredity: What Is the Relationship?" in Norman Johnson, ed., *Marital Violence* (London: Routledge & Kegan Paul, 1985) 147-71.

affluent, educated and mostly liberal people in their 30s and 40s.[36] John Taylor wrote in *New York* magazine:

> [A] new sort of demagogic and fanatical fundamentalism has arisen . . . The new fundamentalists are an eclectic group; they include multiculturalists, feminists, radical homosexuals, Marxists, New Historicists. What unites them—as firmly as the Christian fundamentalists are united in the belief that the Bible is the revealed word of God—is their conviction that Western culture and American society are thoroughly and hopelessly racist, sexist, oppressive.[37]

And Philip Weiss, writing for *Harper's*,[38] has labeled male flashers as "performance art," and criticizes those who would call it sexual harassment. He disparages this "party of sensitivity" for what he sees as deliberately, and erroneously, inflating the prevalence and significance of this, date rape, and other male behaviors toward women.

The seductiveness of this critique is that it is tied to the issue of free speech. What was once a rallying cry for the "radical left" around issues of justice and exposing the intrigues and machinations of government and other colluding institutions—naming the emperor's nakedness—has been co-opted as rhetoric to justify bigotry, heterosexism, and hate-mongering.

The new "anti-PC" intelligentsia uses the liberal banner of free speech to champion the status quo of male privilege—put most bluntly, the "right" traditionally conferred upon men to leer at, comment upon, and touch women's bodies in whatever ways they, the men, so choose—in much the same way the anti-abortion movement has adopted 60s techniques of political activism and civil disobedience, and recent government administrations have reframed and attempted to subsidize traditional upper class privileges, such as private schools and regressive taxation,[39] under the banner of justice and constitutional rights.

What is at debate here is: at what point does a man's word to a woman cross the line from free speech to harassment, threat, or intimidation? "Free speech" advocates would say all speech is constitutionally protected, except for outright, provable threats of violent force or instigation of pandemonium

---

36. Helen Cordes, "Oh, No, I'm PC!" *Utne Reader* 46 (1991) 50–55.

37. John Taylor, "Political Correctness or Fundamentalism?" *New York*, Jan. 21, 1991, 32–40.

38. Philip Weiss, "The Second Revolution: Sexual Politics on Campus," *Harper's* (April 1991) 58–62, 64–72.

39. Ellen Teninty, "The Big Tax Turnaround," *Christianity and Crisis* 51/1 (1991) 12–14.

(like yelling "Fire!" in a crowded theater). But *who determines,* in daily life, or in the courts, what constitutes a reasonable threat? Women, who are burdened with a history thousands of years old, of socially condoned or ignored rape and assault, view the ugly surprise of a flasher, or the physical and psychological pressure of a date to have sex, in a very different light than the "reasonable *man*" of traditional English jurisprudence. It was this awareness that finally led to the establishment of the "reasonable woman standard" in the landmark sexual harassment case Ellison vs. Brady in 1991.[40] Women know in their bones, like species memory, that at any moment a situation of discomfort can explode into an episode of life-threatening violence—no matter whether they appear cool, frightened, disinterested, or angry. No matter how they respond to a potential threat, it may be the "wrong" choice and result in rape, injury, or death. This is no less true today than it was for Tamar (2 Sam. 13) or the Levite's concubine (Judges 19).

## Recommendations

The following are some recommendations for pastoral care and counseling with battered women:

First, the issue of domestic violence needs to be consistently, intentionally integrated in seminary education. To date, this is rare. Even though church communities and denominations are gradually growing in awareness of domestic violence, at least as an area of need for social services if not social activism, seminaries have been slow to respond. Adequate preparation for pastoral ministry must include providing a foundation in domestic violence, and more than just a passing mention in "Pastoral Counseling 101." It needs to be both a regular part of the academic curriculum (not just an occasional elective or summer offering), and an explicit item on the agenda for field education and internship experiences as well.

When pastors say "I've never had a battered woman come to me for help," it is often because battered women have very sensitive antennae for who can possibly hear their story without adding to their shame and fear. Pastors who do not give any signals that they are aware of the problem and equipped to be helpful may not be approached. This is not evidence that battered women do not exist among their flock. Time and time again, pastors have told me that after their first sermon on domestic violence,

---

40. Pamela Cooper-White, *The Cry of Tamar: Violence against Women and the Church's Response* (Minneapolis: Fortress, 1995; 2nd ed., 2012); Peter Rutter, *Sex, Power and Boundaries: Understanding and Preventing Sexual Harassment* (New York: Bantam, 1996).

suddenly several women quietly came forward with their stories. Seminarians need to be informed and sensitized, in order for battered women to feel safe coming to them.

None of this work is easy. It is also my impression from working and teaching in theological education that many seminarians bring their own personal histories of abuse, sometimes deeply repressed, to their seminary experience. Sadly, I believe there are many secret and unhealed stories of abuse among our clergy. Theological education must not only give students the tools to effectively recognize and help heal the violent wounds of battered women who come to them for support, but also tools for naming and grieving their own histories of abuse, working through them, keeping their own issues appropriately separate from those of the women who come for help, and knowing how to "re-charge their own batteries," to be effective "wounded healers," to borrow the language of Henri Nouwen.[41]

Pastoral counseling/psychotherapy with battered women needs to be highly self-monitoring to avoid victim-blaming. It must first be focused on the empowerment of the woman. This is done by helping her not only to explore her own internal dynamics, but by supplying her with information about the role and status of women in society, and the subtle ways in which both scripture and church tradition have been used to support the status quo rather than to give a message of empowerment and liberation. Counseling should be used to empower the battered woman, not to control, supervise, treat or cure her, or to "save the relationship." One of the best examples of scripturally based responses to questions asked by Christian battered women is found in a pocket-sized book, *Keeping the Faith*, by the Rev. Marie Fortune.[42]

At minimum, both pastor and pastoral psychotherapist should: (a) always, without compromise, *consider safety first*, and rely on the survivor's instincts to know what is safe for her; (b) believe her story; (c) talk about the violence straightforwardly and not be afraid to ask if she has been hit (recognizing the minimization and self-blame that is likely to be a part of her response); (d) encourage her to explore recourse to shelter/agency services, police, and legal help; (e) respect her right to self-determination; (f) be sensitive to ethnic and cultural factors affecting her decisions; and (g) assure her of God's love and help her to build a spiritual support community.[43]

41. Henri Nouwen, *The Wounded Healer* (Garden City, NY: Doubleday/Image, 1972).

42. Marie Fortune, *Keeping the Faith: Questions and Answers for the Abused Woman* (San Francisco: Harper & Row, 1988).

43. Caroline Fairless, "What Does Love Require?" unpublished M.Div. honors thesis, Church Divinity School of the Pacific, Berkeley, CA, 1988; Cooper-White, *The Cry*

In addition, certain common pitfalls of pastoral counseling with battered women should be avoided, whether the counseling is in a more therapeutic model or is part of a parish pastor's regular counseling work. There are the blatant pitfalls of sending her back home to pray, examining her own sinfulness and her own role—"What did you do to upset him so much?"—or trying to preserve the marriage at all costs because it is an unbreakable, sacramental union—no! The covenant of marriage has already been broken by the violence.[44] But there are also more subtle pitfalls: (a) being misled that everything is OK now because the couple is in the so-called "honeymoon" phase of the "Cycle of Violence" as outlined by Lenore Walker.[45] Be aware that this so-called "honeymoon" phase is no honeymoon for battered women.[46] Both partners may insist they are fine, but it is necessary to be aware of the escalating pattern of the Cycle, and also that true change on the part of the batterer cannot be measured by his words alone, but by long-term observable changes in *behavior;* (b) being misled that everything is OK now because of very persuasive minimization and denial on the part of the woman or the man, or both; (c) being misled because he is so nice and upstanding in every other context, possibly even in a highly regarded leadership role in the church; (d) using premature forgiveness as a Christian value, and bypassing the important stages of anger and grief that must be a part of a battered woman's recovery. Forgiveness is the very last stage of the healing process, and may take years, or may never be appropriate, particularly with a clearly unrepentant perpetrator.[47] It has been my contention, based on an examination of the biblical foundations of the concepts of forgiveness and reconciliation, that the frequent Christian emphasis on forgiveness between individuals needs to be replaced by a focus on reconciliation as the act of justice-making and restoration proper to the whole community of faith[48]; (e) using a couples' counseling format, with which the pastor may be very familiar, to work on "communication issues," etc., not

---

*of Tamar*, 2nd ed., 228–50.

44. Mitzi Eilts, "Saving the Family: When Is the Covenant Broken?" in Anne L. Horton and Judith A. Williamson, eds., *Abuse and Religion: When Praying Isn't Enough* (Lexington, MA: Lexington, 1988) 207–14; see also Fortune, *Keeping the Faith* (1988).

45. Walker, *The Battered Woman* (1979).

46. For a critique of this now popular terminology, see Dobash and Dobash, *Women, Violence and Social Change* (1992) 229.

47. Ellen E. Bass and Laura Davis, *The Courage to Heal: A Guide for Women Survivors of Child Sexual Abuse* (New York: Harper & Row, 1988) 150–51; Marie Fortune, *Sexual Violence* (New York: Pilgrim, 1983) 208–15.

48. Cooper-White, *The Cry of Tamar* (2nd ed.), "Reconciliation: Moving beyond Individual Forgiveness to Communal Justice," 251–61; see also chap. 10, this volume.

realizing that this can actually be dangerous for the woman. It is not a safe place for her to tell the truth of her experience. As part of the "honeymoon phase" and the couple's minimization and denial, they may both even ask for couples' counseling, but it is an unsafe intervention and should always be avoided;[49] (f) not thinking of domestic violence as a crime, neglecting to encourage her to seek help from police or legal recourse, because of seeing it as a purely private, emotional family matter; (g) wanting to be very active in the situation, to "rescue her."

*Pastors should not try to do the work that battered women's shelters and agencies are set up to do.* It is far better to refer, and then support the work done through that referral. Also, giving advice may merely substitute one dominant role (the pastor's) for another (the batterer's). Helping her identify her own options and respecting her self-determination are the most helpful ways to empower her. In the ideal, peer counselors in a local shelter or agency, clinical counselors or psychotherapists in the community, and pastoral counselors or parish pastors can work together cooperatively to assist in a woman's empowerment and healing.[50] These three forms of support may be especially useful at different stages, or to address different needs in the woman's life as she moves from the violent situation toward freedom.

*Peer advocacy,* that is, counseling by shelter workers, is probably most effective in the immediate crisis phase when a woman is realizing that she can no longer tolerate the abuse and needs to make a change in her life. This advocacy offers validation, friendship, belief, and support, and helps her to explore strategic options, developing an action plan for getting free of the violence (including as appropriate: restraining orders, legal advice, identifying relatives or friends who could help, getting medical assistance, transportation, and financial and job planning). The peer advocate is trained to "know the ropes" of the system, and can accompany her through the often overwhelming maze of bureaucratic procedures in court, and at social welfare agencies. The peer advocate is also trained to provide her with an analysis of the social and political reasons why battering happens, and to help her realize that she is not alone or powerless. Most shelters offer support

---

49. Susan Schechter, *Guidelines for Mental Health Practitioners* (Washington, DC: NCADV, 1987).

50. Pamela Cooper-White, "Peer vs. Clinical Counseling: Is There Room for Both in the Battered Women's Movement?" *Response to the Victimization of Women and Children: Journal of the Center for Women Policy Studies* 13/1 (1990) 2–6 (see Ch. 1 of this volume); Cooper-White, "The Respective Roles of Shelter Advocate, Pastoral Counselor and Psychotherapist in Working with Battered Women: A Cooperative Model," paper presented to the first Triennial Conference for Social Ministry Organizations, National Division for Social Ministry Organizations, Evangelical Lutheran Church in America (ELCA), Chicago, April 28, 1990.

groups for both residents and non-residents, which are an important first step toward validation and breaking isolation.

*Clinical counseling*, or psychotherapy, may be most useful after the immediate crisis phase is past, and the woman is living free of violence. At this time, if she chooses, a therapist may help the formerly battered woman to address possible long-term effects such as depression, post-traumatic stress, inability to trust, creative ways of channeling her anger, and establishing new relationships. Clinical counseling may also be valuable in the case of a woman who is determined not to leave the abusive relationship, and will not consult with peer advocates at a battered women's agency. In such a case, the woman may use therapy to gain the necessary support and understanding to allow her to seek appropriate crisis help from an agency or shelter when she is ready. In either case, clinical counseling or psychotherapy must be conducted from a feminist paradigm that does not pathologize women, and grounded in a socio-political context, which helps her to claim her power.

The parish pastor has a unique supportive role to play in empowering the religious battered woman. This may be concurrent with both the shelter crisis counseling and then the clinical counseling—neither as a substitute nor in competition, but to encourage and support changes as they may occur in her life, and to explore with her the spiritual and theological questions which will inevitably arise along the way. The pastor can have an invaluable role if (s)he is beginning to question long-held assumptions about biblical passages that may have reinforced her staying with the batterer. (S)he can then replace disempowering interpretations of scripture with healing, liberating ones. The effective pastor can support her in being wary of cheap promises and easy remorse without true, life-changing repentance on the part of the batterer, giving her permission to recognize such false promises for what they are. And the pastor can support her not only with kindness and empathy, but with a faith-grounded desire for justice, supporting her right to legal action and restitution. In other words, the pastor can, by her or his authority, begin to un-say all the negative messages absorbed from traditional church teachings that have reinforced her self-blame and low self-worth.

Parish-based pastors, as well as chaplains and pastoral counselors, have yet another special role. In addition to their individual pastoral role, it is their unique gift as representatives of their faith traditions to be able to help create communities of support for victims and survivors of domestic violence. Because of their grounding in the church, pastors, pastoral counselors and chaplains alike can help to educate a woman's own congregation, or if it is no longer safe for her to remain in that community, help her to identify a new church community where she can be embraced and understood. In this community of support, she should be able to feel free to disclose or not disclose as she chooses—never stuck in a closet of shame and fear of being disbelieved. By helping to create such a community, pastors, chaplains, and pastoral counselors can make a unique contribution in the life of a woman whose dominant feelings may have been reduced to loneliness, guilt, self-doubt, and terror.

Counseling with batterers requires highly specialized training and experience, and is not appropriate for pastors or pastoral counselors to undertake. The potential is great for being drawn quite unwittingly into the typical batterer's pattern of denial, manipulation, and self-justification. Unconscious collusion can, in turn, seriously compromise the woman's safety. The more a counselor thinks he or she can "handle the situation" (a common pitfall of pastors because of their frequent desire to rescue), the more dangerous this dynamic is likely to be. It is the pastor's responsibility to make a well-researched referral to a program which will effectively confront and change the man's behavior.

Battering men need to be referred to responsible batterers' programs which follow these minimum standards[51]: (a) clearly defines violence in intimate relationships as a crime; (b) defines violence as part of a pattern of coercive control that includes physical, emotional, sexual and economic abuse. Addressing this pattern of learned and socially sanctioned behaviors through peer resocialization is the foundation of program intervention[52]; (c) upholds the victim's safety as the first priority, especially given the potential for lethality and recidivism. Potentially dangerous interventions such as couples' and/or family counseling are excluded[53]; (d) holds the perpetrator accountable for the violence in the relationship—the perpetrator must accept personal responsibility and consequences for that behavior, and for changing it. (For example: a partner's behavior, or perceived provocation, or the perpetrator's own use of alcohol or drugs is not an acceptable excuse for the use of violence); (e) stopping the abuse is the priority and major focus, not other personal or relationship issues, e.g., focusing on keeping the couple together, or repairing couples' communication.

---

51. Barbara Hart, *Safety for Women: Monitoring Batterers' Programs* (Harrisburg, PA: Pennsylvania Coalition against Domestic Violence, 1988); J. Carter, Pamela Cooper-White, M. Cusick, Donna Garske, P. Kuta, J. Shattuck, and Hamish Sinclair, "Recommended Standards of Care in a Batterer's Intervention Program," Legislative Brief for the Criminal Justice Committee, California Alliance against Domestic Violence, 1989.

52. Edward W. Gondolf and David Russell, "The Case against Anger Control Treatment for Batterers," *Response* 9/3 (1986) 2–5; Richard M. Tolman and Daniel G. Saunders, "The Case for the Cautious Use of Anger Control with Men Who Batter," *Response* 11/2 (1988) 15–20.

53. Schechter, *Guidelines for Mental Health Practitioners*, 1987.

The responsibility of counselors finally extends to the wider community, and to culture. It is not purely a private matter of what goes on between the counselor and parishioner/client behind closed doors. What is spoken there, however confidential the particulars, will have a ripple effect on the growth—or continued unhealthy—of the whole society. If the counselor is also involved personally in advocacy, education and political activism in the community, that involvement creates a stronger background for effective counseling than when there is no involvement outside the counseling room. Activism can be a nourishing way of staying grounded, a balancing of "inner" and "outer" perspectives. It further validates the steps the battered parishioner/client takes to advocate for herself with social institutions and in her relationships, and models integrity and consistency.

The whole phenomenon of battering, and of violence against women in general, needs to be approached as much from the discipline of social and political ethics as from the field of pastoral psychology. It is not only useful but imperative to lay the social and political groundwork, and to provide the analysis that battering is a matter of power and control, not psychological pathology. In so doing, it is also imperative that all forms of oppression operative in our culture, including racism, heterosexism, and economic injustice, be understood as linked. In the context of theological education, it is especially important that we show how scripture and ecclesiastical polity and tradition not only have perpetuated, but at times have actively led the charge against women's equality.

## Claiming the Future

Where is hope? There are days, when I receive yet another phone call from a woman who has read something I wrote and wants to tell me her painful story (because she didn't know anyone else to safely tell), when I read one more news article about a woman raped in my community, when I listen quietly as a student or therapy client tearfully discloses her history of sexual abuse, that I want to lay down my head on my desk and weep—or sleep—for a year. Behind all theorizing and all theologizing are the lives of real women: aching, bleeding, burdened with terrifying secrets our society has labeled as shameful. I sometimes wonder if the most fundamental values of my Christian tradition—love, justice, peace, and compassion—really exist anywhere. Every theological supposition I know seems inseparable from a culture that denies what really happens to women (and to men), and, in fact, is constructed to perpetuate the lies.

And yet, we are here, we women are here, we are surviving in spite of everything, and we are speaking up. We are claiming the "authority of the future," as Letty Russell writes.[54] And we are claiming the authority of our lived experience, in counterpoint to all the abstract theory of male experts that has so often obscured the truth. As feminists, we are nothing if not eschatological, pointing prophetically toward our visions of "a mended creation."[55]

Under a miasma of denial and obfuscation, the emperor is naked. Ultimately, his many and various theories serve merely to explain away our pain and our oppression, and thus are bankrupt to heal and transform women's lives. We are called to "speak truth to power in love," naming the nakedness we see, even risking our respectability in society's eyes and becoming like the innocent little child of the fairy tale, and then—by going courageously through all the anguish that comes with really facing reality—finally, begin to mend the creation. We do this in partnership with a God who neither causes nor denies our suffering, but stands with us in it, and loves us into a future of wholeness and power.

---

54. Letty M. Russell, *Household of Freedom: Authority in Feminist Theology* (Philadelphia: Westminster, 1987) 18.

55. Ibid.

# 4

## Opening the Eyes

*Understanding the Impact of Trauma on Development*

2000[1]

"AND I SAY, HEY, what a wonderful kind of day, when we can learn to work and play, and get along with each other." Arthur, the latency-age aardvark who wears his baggy jeans and horn-rimmed glasses cavorts on his TV program early each morning. Along with his little sister, D.W., he learns not-too-terrible lessons about friendship, lying, recycling, chicken pox, homework, responsibility, and the death of hamsters. His TV audience of five- to nine-year-olds is brought along with him to learn these lessons gently and vicariously: The world is good. Responsibility is good. Lying is bad. Friends come in all shapes and sizes, but we can all get along. You'll get sick, but then you'll get to go to the fair anyway. Mothers are kind, grandmothers think the best of you, and fathers are honorable, if a little detached. This is the world of children as we adults want to believe it, sometimes remember it, and hope to help our own children experience it. It is also the world of child development as it has been largely taught and written about from Piaget to the present day.

Just as a child moves through the developmental eras of childhood from one evolutionary truce to another and literally cannot conceive of certain aspects of logic or reality that belong to a later phase of development, so our culture has only recently emerged (or, it can be argued, reemerged) from a long incapacity to recognize the reality of childhood sexual abuse and trauma. A quick review of the subject index in each of the developmental texts with which we have become familiar—Erik Erikson,[2] Robert Kegan,[3] and James

---

1. Orig. publ. in Jeanne Stevenson-Moessner, ed., *In Her Own Time: Women and Developmental Issues in Pastoral Care* (Minneapolis: Fortress, 2000) 87–102.
2. Erik Erikson, *Childhood and Society,* 2nd ed. (New York: Norton, 1963).
3. Robert Kegan, *The Evolving Self: Problem and Process in Human Development*

Fowler's now classic text on faith development[4]—reveals no mention of "trauma," "abuse," or "sexual abuse." These authors occasionally consider the idea of "crisis," but even this topic is generally framed as a naturally occurring disruption or loss that can eventually be accommodated, if not assimilated, as a growth-enhancing experience. Examples of crises include leaving home for the first time or losing a loved one. This exclusion of trauma and abuse is true even of Carol Gilligan's groundbreaking work *In a Different Voice*,[5] in which she presents the idea that women's and girls' development, particularly moral development, might not proceed along the same lines as those laid out by Kohlberg in his study of school-aged boys.

Sexual abuse and childhood trauma were just beginning to emerge into our public awareness in the late 1970s and early 1980s through the work of such authors as Florence Rush,[6] Judith Herman,[7] Roland Summit,[8] David Finkelhor,[9] and pioneering pediatricians Ruth and Henry Kempe.[10] The international journal *Child Abuse and Neglect* first appeared in 1976, and the U.S. Department of Health and Human Services conducted its first studies on child neglect and abuse reporting in 1978 and 1979. Two landmark empirical studies were published as recently as the mid-1980s, one a large-scale prevalence study of incest in the lives of girls and women by Diana Russell,[11] and another, the first study of sexual abuse of African American girls, by Gail Wyatt.[12]

---

(Cambridge: Harvard University Press, 1982). See also Robert Kegan, *In over Our Heads: The Mental Demands of Modern Life* (Cambridge: Harvard University Press, 1994).

4. James W. Fowler, *Stages of Faith: The Psychology of Human Development and the Quest for Meaning* (San Francisco: Harper & Row, 1981).

5. Carol Gilligan, *In a Different Voice: Psychological Theory and Women's Development* (Cambridge: Harvard University Press, 1982).

6. Florence Rush, *The Best Kept Secret* (Englewood Cliffs, NJ: Prentice Hall, 1980).

7. Judith Herman, *Father-Daughter Incest* (Cambridge: Harvard University Press, 1981).

8. Roland Summit, "The Child Abuse Accommodation Syndrome," *Child Abuse and Neglect: The International Journal* 7/2 (1983) 177–93.

9. David Finkelhor, *Sexually Victimized Children* (New York: Free Press, 1979); *Child Sexual Abuse: New Theory and Research* (New York: Free Press, 1984).

10. Ruth S. Kempe and C. Henry Kempe, *Child Abuse* (Cambridge: Harvard University Press, 1978).

11. Diana Russell, *The Secret Trauma: Incest in the Lives of Girls and Women* (New York: Basic Books, 1986).

12. Gail Wyatt, "The Sexual Abuse of Afro-American and White Women in Childhood," *Child Abuse and Neglect: The International Journal* 9 (1985) 507–19.

Two decades ago, the stark revelations of these authors about the nature and prevalence of child sexual abuse seemed at times shocking, subversive and radical. We now know, as we were just learning then, that from one in five to one in three girls, and one in sixteen to one in eleven boys are physically sexually abused by age eighteen.[13] The work of the Harvard Project on the Psychology of Women and the Development of Girls[14] and the Stone Center /Jean Baker Miller Training Institute of Wellesley College,[15] no doubt because of project members' commitment to the integration of feminist theory, have come the closest in recent years to incorporating an appreciation of trauma and sexual abuse into their theoretical and clinical writings on development. The Kempes' work was also significant, in that it was published in a series on child development

---

13. Diana Russell, Rachel A. Sherman, and Karen Trocki, "The Long-Term Effects of Incestuous Abuse: A Comparison of Afro-American and White American Victims," in Gail Wyatt, ed., *Lasting Effects of Child Sexual Abuse* (Beverly Hills, CA: Sage, 1988); Anthony Urquiza and Lisa Marie Keating, "The Prevalence of Sexual Victimization of Males," in Mic Hunter, ed., *The Sexually Abused Male* (New York: Lexington, 1990); David Finkelhor, "Risk Factors in the Sexual Victimization of Children," *Child Abuse and Neglect* 4 (1980) 265–73.

14. A number of writings have come from researchers connected with this project. See, e.g., Carol Gilligan, Janie Victoria Ward, and Jill McLean Taylor, eds., *Mapping the Moral Domain: A Contribution of Women's Thinking to Psychological Theory and Education* (Cambridge: Harvard University Press, 1988); Lyn Mikel Brown and Carol Gilligan, *Meeting at the Crossroads: Women's Psychology and Girls' Development* (New York: Ballantine, 1993); Jill McLean Taylor, Carol Gilligan, and Amy M. Sullivan, *Between Voice and Silence: Women and Girls, Race and Relationship* (Cambridge: Harvard/Belknap, 1996). Books on special topics by authors related to this group also include Dana Crowley Jack, *Silencing the Self: Women and Depression* (Cambridge: Harvard University Press, 1991); and Annie G. Rogers, *A Shining Affliction: A Story of Harm and Healing in Psychotherapy* (New York: Viking, 1995). A closely related, pioneering text is Mary Field Belenky, Blythe McVicker Clinchy, Nancy Rule Goldberger and Jill Mattuck Tarule, *Women's Ways of Knowing: The Development of Self, Voice, and Mind.* New York: Basic Books, 1986, 2nd ed. 2008; and Nancy Goldberger, Jill Tarule, Blythe Clynchy, and Mary Belenky, *Knowledge, Difference, and Power* (New York: Basic Books, 1998).

15. Jean Baker Miller, *Toward a New Psychology of Women* (Boston: Beacon, 1976, 1986); Judith V. Jordan, Alexandra G. Kaplan, Jean Baker Miller, Irene P. Stiver, and Janet L. Surrey, ed., *Women's Growth in Connection: Writings from the Stone Center* (New York: Guilford, 1991); Judith Jordan, ed. *Women's Growth in Diversity: More Writings from the Stone Center* (New York: Guilford, 1997); Jean Baker Miller and Irene P. Stiver, *The Healing Connection: How Women Form Relationships in Therapy and in Life* (Boston: Beacon, 1997). [See also the "Works in Progress" series and many other papers available from the Stone Center, Wellesley College, Wellesley, MA (online at https://www.wcwonline.org/JBMTI-Site/publications.) The Stone Center is now the Jean Baker Miller Training Institute, online at https://www.wcwonline.org/JBMTI-Site/introduction-to-jbmti. —PCW 2018]

and took a strong advocacy stance on behalf of the rights of children and the necessity of a community-wide response.

The split between the domains of developmental theory and the serious study of trauma is reflected in much of the literature up to the present. Both domains can be traced to Freud, but the split begins with Freud as well. Freud can be considered the first developmental theorist; he posited the three well-known stages of psychosexual development (oral, anal, and phallic/genital) in his *Three Essays on the Theory of Sexuality*.[16] But it is perhaps significant, as developmental theorists remain unaware of the impact of trauma in developmental theories to this day, that this developmental schema evolved as part of Freud's oedipal theory and represented a profound theoretical shift away from the so-called seduction theory of the previous decade, in which he attributed the symptoms of hysteria to sexual abuse by a father or father-figure. In this sense, the entire foundation of developmental theory, however accurate a depiction it may offer of certain psychic phenomena, is built on a "closing of the eyes," not against one's own oedipal wishes,[17] but against the horror of real abuse.

16. Sigmund Freud, *Three Essays on the Theory of Sexuality*, in J. Strachey, ed. and trans., *The Standard Edition of the Complete Psychological Works of Sigmund Freud* (London: Hogarth, 1962; orig. publ. 1905), Vol. 7, 145–248.

17. [In *The Interpretation of Dreams* (Standard Edition, Vols. 1–2 entire; orig. publ. 1900)—his first master work after the split with Wilhelm Fliess over Freud's rejection of the seduction (trauma) theory of hysteria—Freud himself referred to the metaphor of "closing the eyes" as one of denial (albeit of oedipal wishes). Following his father's death, Freud dreamed of a sign on which was printed "You are requested to close the eyes," (reported in a letter to Fliess, Nov. 2, 1896) or "You are requested to close an eye" (in *Interpretation of Dreams*). Freud interpreted this as a double meaning, referring to the duty of a (Jewish) son to close the eyes of his dead father, or—if winking (closing just one eye)—feeling guilt for having failed to take his duty seriously. This closing of the eyes has been interpreted by later analytic writers as Freud's obeying an inner wish/command to close his *own* eyes to his father's molestation of his siblings (noted by Freud to Fliess just three months later). Marianne Krüll, in *Freud and His Father* (New York: Norton, 1986), argues that Freud did indeed close his eyes at this time to his father's "perversion," and in so doing, turned away from the seduction theory (i.e., hysteria was caused by actual sexual abuse), reversing the logic in his oedipal theory so that it was now the child who desired his parent. Freud was long preoccupied with the symbolism of eyes. He associated eye symbolism with oedipal fantasies, and Oedipus' blindness as a symbol of castration (punishment for sex with his mother—in *Interpretation of Dreams*.) Freud may have closed his own eyes in denial, but the word "eyes" appears in *Interpretation of Dreams* at least 93 times! The theme of fear of losing one's eyes as a disguised fear of castration appears again in Freud's "The Uncanny" in 1919, in the grisly story of the Sand-Man from E.T.A. Hoffman's *Tales of Hoffmann*. For more on closing the eyes and denial, and more complete citations, see Cooper-White, *Old and Dirty Gods: Religion, Antisemitism, and the Origins of Psychoanalysis* (New York: Routledge, 2017) 245, 252n230. —PCW 2018]

Shift focus: A girl, let us say age eight, finishes watching Arthur and turns off the TV to get ready for her day at school. Last night Daddy came to her room again and did those things that belong to the awfulness of the night. She spent a long time floating somewhere along the ceiling while nightmare things were happening in the dark to her body far below. But that was night, and now it's day. She loads homework and lunch into a backpack and chooses her clothes—the flowered mini-dress and high platform sneakers. It's the outfit Daddy says he hates, because· it makes her look "trampy," and her mother defends: "Have *you* tried shopping for girls' clothes lately?" The young girl likes it because it makes her feel cool, a little more in control, and a little more like the other kids. It keeps her outsides feeling more okay and together when her insides seem to be falling apart in mysterious ways, more and more every day. She will try very hard today not to daydream, not to squirm where it hurts to sit, to pay attention so that she won't draw the teacher's attention to her again, to look and feel "normal," without monsters and terrors deep inside, the way she imagines it is for everyone but her.

It is the purpose of this chapter to return to developmental theories while opening the eyes, and to ask the question: How does the experience of early trauma, particularly sexual abuse, affect development? Does trauma derail or block development as it might be understood against the backdrop of normative developmental patterns? Or does it do something different altogether, creating a new, separate, or alternative pathway—or even multiple pathways proceeding at different rates? Many developmental theories and theorists could be engaged in such an inquiry. For the sake of brevity, I will focus on just three areas of developmental theory, but it is my hope that this examination will offer a method for further examining the impact of trauma and sexual abuse from many theoretical lenses. The areas I have chosen to explore are a number of theoretical perspectives grouped into three broad clusters of ideas. These three groups are: (1) developmental stage theories (including Freud, Erik Erikson, and the more recent author Robert Kegan); (2) relationally focused psychoanalytic theories, which have their own implicit or explicit developmental theory, including object relations, self psychology, and aspects of feminist relational theory; and (3) theories of faith development, beginning with the work of Fowler, which strive explicitly to incorporate a theological and spiritual dimension in development.

This chapter might strike some readers as heavily theoretical. It is my experience, however, that our practices of ministry, including parish ministry, chaplaincy, and pastoral psychotherapy, are subtly and even unknowingly formed by these theories as they trickle down into the culture from generations of psychological research, training and practice. It is important to know the origins of our assumptive practices in order to be better able to critique them and to choose whether and how to incorporate them into our own practices of ministry.[18]

This chapter is written primarily from the lens of pastoral psychotherapy. Theoretical constructs are ultimately only of use to the degree that they can be applied within the context of real relationships of trust and therapeutic safety. It is my intent, by bringing the all too often hidden realities of childhood trauma and especially sexual abuse into dialogue with developmental theories, to enhance the theoretically informed sensitivity of pastoral counselors and psychotherapists, so that previously unseen truths about trauma survivors' experience might be more readily perceived and empathically understood. It is my further hope that, although the long-term work of helping another to recover from sexual trauma belongs within the realm of a clinically trained therapist, the theoretical understandings offered here will also be of value to parish clergy, chaplains, and pastoral caregivers. Pastoral caregivers' sensitization to the inner dynamics of trauma plays a critical role, aiding in the deeply spiritual healing process of trauma survivors. The absence of such sensitization all too often unwittingly perpetuates cycles of self-blame, premature forgiveness, and re-traumatization.

## Stage Theories

In a film made late in his life, Erik Erikson talks about the popularity of his "eight stages of man."[19] In a touching personal moment, Erikson proudly shows the filmmaker a quilt or tapestry that someone had made for him in which these eight stages from infancy to old age were depicted artistically in sequential blocks of fabric. Those blocks are the way developmental stage theories are generally thought of and taught—as if they are a series of boxcars, one attached to the next as development proceeds. In such a "boxcar" conceptualization, events that are disruptive to development (whether conceived of as outer or inner events or conflicts) must be understood as impeding forward movement. Disruptive events, from minor challenges to crises requiring major life adjustments, are seen as either slowing development, stopping it at least for a time (as described in the

---

18. [See Cooper-White, "Thick Theory: Psychology, Theoretical Models, and the Formation of Pastoral Counselors," in Duane R. Bidwell and Joretta L. Marshall, ed. *The Formation of Pastoral Counselors: Challenges and Opportunities* (Binghamton, NY: Haworth, 2006) 47–67 and *American Journal of Pastoral Counseling* 8/3–4 (2006) 47–67; reprinted in Cooper-White, *Braided Selves: Collected Essays on Multiplicity, God, and Persons* (Eugene, OR: Cascade Books, 2011) 17–38. —PCW 2018]

19. Erik Erikson, "The Eight Stages of Man," in *Childhood and Society*, 2nd ed. (New York: Norton, 1963) 247–74.

language of "developmental blocks" or "fixation points"), or, in the worst case scenario, derailing it.

In such a conceptualization, the task of care and counseling is focused in linear fashion on getting development back on track. This healing is accomplished by addressing the crisis, perhaps helping the person to acquire new coping mechanisms to deal with what overwhelmed his or her existing capacities, or putting the person in touch with better external supports, so that when the crisis is resolved, development can once again move forward. This model has been taught extensively in counseling programs and has great practical utility, particularly when the disruptive event takes place within the framework of normal, though sometimes intensely painful life crises, such as illness, a difficult move, or the death of a close family member. Is this model adequate, however, when applied to the occurrence of severe trauma?

The term "trauma" is used in many ways. In its broadest sense, based on the original Greek meaning, it is simply any wound or injury. Under such an umbrella definition, *trauma* can mean any physical, psychic, or emotional insult. In this sense, a person might report to her partner at the end of a long day, "That meeting today was really traumatic!" For the purposes of this chapter, however, I use the term very specifically, following trauma specialists[20] to mean not simply any injury, but rather the deep injury that is accompanied by a feeling of helplessness powerlessness, an experience of pain combined with the terror of being overwhelmed, and in which normal coping mechanisms fail or are unavailable. This injury might occur as a single terrible event, or it might represent the cumulative effect of repetitive occurrences of abuse or neglect. Children's basic dependence on adults adds to the experience of helplessness and a perception that this abuse or neglect is just how life is.

The experience of acute or even chronic abuse certainly may be understood within the boxcar model as impeding or derailing development. If we take Erikson's model, it rivets our attention to consider the impact of severe neglect, or physical or sexual abuse on an infant whose earliest developmental issue is "basic trust vs. basic mistrust,"[21] corresponding with Freud's

---

20. For example, Lenore Terr, *Too Scared to Cry* (New York: Basic Books, 1990); Judith Herman, *Trauma and Recovery* (New York: Basic Books, 1992). This definition also conforms to the definition used for Post-Traumatic Stress Disorder in the *Diagnostic and Statistical Manual of Mental Disorders (DSM-IV)*, 4th ed. (Washington, DC: American Psychiatric Association, 1994) 424–28. [Note that the criterion of "sexual violation" was added in DSM-5 as a change from DSM-IV and previous versions. — PCW 2018]

21. Erikson, "Eight Stages of Man," 147.

oral stage. Erikson considered that "consistency, continuity, and sameness of experience provide a rudimentary sense of ego identity"[22] foundational to all further development and even to the possibility of religious faith in which "trust born of care is, in fact, the touchstone."[23] In the context of a traumatic early environment, the infant's fragile capacity for trust is shattered—if it is ever established at all—with devastating consequences for all subsequent development. The absence or destruction of a secure base of attachment[24] is considered by many traumatologists to be one of the deepest, most lasting forms of damage caused by abuse.[25]

It does not take too much imagination to consider the equally devastating consequences of trauma as it affects two subsequent stages in Erikson's theory (corresponding with Freud's anal and genital stages): "autonomy vs. shame and doubt," and "initiative vs. guilt." Abuse can also seriously interfere with developmental tasks at the later stages of "industry vs. inferiority"(roughly the school age or "latency" years), and "identity vs. role confusion" (adolescence). The impact of abuse can be seen through the lens of other developmental stage theories as well. For example, what damage does trauma inflict on a two- to four-year-old child at Robert Kegan's stage of the "impulsive" self,[26] in which the safety of the parental triangle is considered to be essential for the healthy exercise of fantasy, rivalry, and attachment, preparing her to meet the challenges around age five of relating to the wider world of reality and culture outside the family?

There is one serious conceptual problem with this boxcar formulation, however: biological maturation proceeds, even if development is damaged. In that process of maturation—simply "growing up"—physical, cognitive, and affective growth does continue, although it might be compromised in some areas, even very prominent areas. If we believe that trauma derails development, how do we explain the sexually abused child who nevertheless becomes an all-A student or star athlete, who perhaps takes refuge in her excellence, or the physically abused child of an alcoholic

22. Ibid.

23. Ibid., 250.

24. John Bowlby, *A Secure Base: Parent-Child Attachment and Healthy Development* (New York: Basic Books, 1988).

25. Bessel van der Kolk and Alexander McFarlane, "The Black Hole of Trauma," in van der Kolk, ed., *Psychological Trauma* (Washington, DC: American Psychiatric Press, 1987) 32; Jody Messler Davies and Mary Gail Frawley, *Treating the Adult Survivor of Childhood Sexual Abuse: A Psychoanalytic Perspective* (New York: Basic Books, 1994) 46.

26. Robert Kegan, *The Evolving Self: Problem and Process in Human Development* (Cambridge: Harvard University Press, 1982) 133–60.

or drug-addicted parent who nevertheless manages to function somewhat capably as the head of the household by the age of ten? Certainly, some sectors of the personality might be seen as stunted, missing, or suffering great pain, but nevertheless, other parts of the self continue to grow and even to exceed normal expectations.

Two other models might be helpful to place alongside the boxcar conceptualization. First, there is Anna Freud's concept of "developmental lines."[27] This concept is less widely known than Erikson's eight stages but arose from a similar motivation in the first generation after Freud to extend the application of psychoanalytic concepts beyond the clinical treatment of pathology to the consideration of normal development. Through her work with children at the Hampstead Clinic she founded in London, Anna Freud proposed the idea that there is not a single line of development but rather a number of lines running more or less parallel from infancy and on into adulthood. She identified five such lines, not as a definitive accounting but rather as examples: the line from "sucking to rational eating," from "wetting/soiling to control," from "irresponsibility to responsibility for one's own body," from "egocentricity to companionship," and most intriguingly, from "the body to the toy and from play to work."

Today, we might argue with specifics of Anna Freud's examples, which depended heavily upon oedipal theory and the notion of ego, id, and superego formation as central to development, and did not differentiate between boys' and girls' development. Later authors have expanded the concept to include many other proposed developmental lines. What might be most relevant for the study of trauma, however, is Anna Freud's further contention that normal development depends not only on the relatively untroubled progress of each of the lines, but also similar progress along all lines at once. Although she refrained from attributing pathology directly to a "disequilibrium" between developmental lines, she did identify this disequilibrium as a point of vulnerability, a "pathogenic agent."

How might severe trauma in childhood be understood in this conceptualization? Rather than impeding or derailing development altogether, if we think in terms of multiple developmental lines or "tracks," trauma might affect some but not all aspects of development, accounting for the appearance of competence and even precocity in many abused children. This also helps to explain why dissociation, however pathological it might seem later in life, functions to protect traumatized children. If certain experiences are too terrible to be assimilated, they may become encapsulated or frozen on

---

27. Anna Freud, "The Concept of Developmental Lines," *Psychoanalytic Study of the Child* 18 (1963) 245–65.

certain developmental lines, while other aspects of development are freed to proceed in relative coordination with maturation. This model might be helpful to pastoral caregivers and counselors by reminding us to consider multiple areas of growth within the same person and to hold in mind both the person's areas of strength or even overdeveloped capacities *and* underdeveloped areas of fragility, vulnerability, and fear.

A second model we might set alongside the boxcar model might be that of the concentric rings of a tree trunk. Using this image, we might imagine experiences during the earliest developmental eras in a child's life as encircled or nested within or beneath later ones. From this perspective, developmental achievements are layered together with the life experiences, joys, and crises of a particular period of time. New growth forms around the old, rather than replacing it. Nothing is left behind.[28]

Trauma in this model might then be seen as having a number of manifestations, from being encapsulated like a nodule that later layers of growth cover but leave intact, to spreading throughout a particular layer of the trunk, rendering the whole tree more vulnerable to the impact of disease, cold, and storms. Note that this model replaces the mechanistic image of a train with an organic one. Helping in this model would not be conceptualized so much as getting something back on track, as going deeper, toward the core of the organism to tend enclosed wounds in need of healing and regeneration. It then follows that the earlier the experience of trauma, the closer it is to the core of the person, which could be thought of as the soul itself. Deeper, longer-term work will likely be required for the healing process to take place.

## Relational Psychoanalytic Theories

We might gain a deeper appreciation of the impact of trauma on development, particularly very early development, by turning to a different set of theorists whose work, loosely bound together, represents a more relational conception of the development of the self. In this category I am including British and American objects relations, self psychology, the Sullivanian or interpersonal school and its evolution in the feminist work

---

28. This concept is somewhat like that of "domains" used by infant observation researcher Daniel N. Stern in his *Interpersonal World of the Infant: A View from Psychoanalysis and Developmental Psychology* (New York: Basic Books, 1985). Stern considers that a "phase" model of development in which phases are only revisited via regression is useful in understanding cognitive tasks but not an infant's sense of self. In Stern's conception, which is focused on the first eighteen months of life, "All domains of relatedness remain active during development" (p. 31).

of the Stone Center/Jean Baker Miller Training Institute, and the more recent relational and intersubjective schools of American psychoanalysis. It would be a vast oversimplification to imply that these schools are merely variations on a single theoretical conceptualization. Each represents a rich and complex system of thought that cannot be adequately represented in this chapter. Bearing this caution in mind, however, there are some common threads that are useful for our present purpose, which is to consider the impact of trauma on development and the implications of these theoretical understandings for healing.

All of these relational approaches share two important concepts: the centrality of human relations in development, and the intensely formative impact of the relations between caregivers and children going back to the earliest stages of infancy. First, let us consider the centrality of human relations in development. Beginning with Melanie Klein in the 1930s, the so-called object relations theorists began to detect the central significance of a drive or yearning for connection with an other (inelegantly termed "object seeking"[29]). In contrast with Freud's theories of drive satisfaction, the object relations theorists began to perceive that the other was not merely a target for instinctual satisfaction, but that connection with the other (both as fantasized and as experienced) was a strong motivating desire in its own right, even replacing sex and aggression as the central motivating factor in human behavior.

Through the work of W. R. D. Fairbairn and others, it increasingly came to be recognized that a variety of significant others, as experienced by the child, to varying degrees came to take up residence in the inner, psychic reality of the child from birth onward as "internal objects." Now not only or even primarily Freud's ego, id, and superego, but a host of satisfying, tantalizing, and tormenting figures or aspects of the self could direct behavior and color perceptions of the external world. These internal objects became the source for inner messages of self-worth, self-condemnation, inner conflict, and projection of old relational patterns onto real, external others. The point of intersection between the inner and outer realities, termed "potential space" by the British theorist D. W. Winnicott,[30] became a rich area for exploration, where fantasy and reality meet in a complex interplay of images and symbols, thoughts, feelings, and behaviors.

---

29. The notion of an "object" was derived from Freud but departed from Freud's theory that all motivation is grounded in biological instincts, the "drives" of sex and aggression, and that another person becomes the "object" or target for satisfaction of the drives.

30. D. W. Winnicott, *Playing and Reality* (New York: Basic Books, 1971).

Self psychologists, beginning with the work of Heinz Kohut in the 1960s and 70s,[31] although using different terminology, point also to the central significance of the child's lived experience of her caregivers, and particularly the role of an empathic environment early in life, to build the necessary inner psychic structures for self-soothing, self-regulation, and self-esteem. Interpersonal, relational, and intersubjective theorists also generally take the significance of real interpersonal relations as their starting point. Their differences lie mostly in implications for clinical treatment and the relative attention given to conscious vs. unconscious relationship between therapist and patient/client, but all would agree on the centrality of human connection as the starting point for development, clinical treatment, and living one's life in relation with others.

The second tenet of relational theories, particularly object relations and self psychology, is the central significance of the earliest period of development in infancy. Freud's own developmental stage theory spanned roughly the first five or six years of life, beginning with the oral stage at birth, through the anal stage of toilet training and socialization in toddlerhood, and culminating in the child's navigation of the oedipal stage. Developmental stage theories beginning with both Piaget and Erikson spanned even more of childhood, and Erikson set the precedent of examining ongoing development throughout the life span. This lens is an extremely valuable one from which to understand human development. Relational psychoanalytic theories, however, focus us more narrowly but in finer detail on the impact of caregivers at the earliest and arguably most formative periods of development: infancy and early toddlerhood. It might be useful to view Erikson and other stage theorists as providing us with a telescope for understanding the breadth of development over the course of a whole life, and relational psychoanalysts as providing us with a microscope to understand the nuances and complications of the period when the human person is most vulnerable, dependent, and in some senses—though by no means all—unformed and in a state of relative openness with the mother or other primary caretaker.[32]

---

31. E.g., Heinz Kohut, *The Restoration of the Self* (New York: International Universities Press, 1977). Thanks to June Fulton, Constance Goldberg, Chris Stephenson, and Cynthia Stone of the Institute for Clinical Social Work, Chicago, for their comments on this section of this chapter.

32. It should be noted that the idea that an infant comes into the world as a blank slate appears to be disproved by recent work in the field of infant observation, particularly Daniel Stern, *The Interpersonal World of the Infant*, and the temperament studies of Stella Chess and Alexander Thomas, *Temperament in Clinical Practice* (New York: Guilford, 1986); Thomas and Chess, *Temperament and Development* (New York: Brunner/Mazel, 1977); Thomas and Chess, *Dynamics of Psychological Development* (New

In this view, in infancy and early childhood, trauma can be extremely subtle because the infant is already in a state of helplessness and total or near-total dependency. Still using the definition of trauma as an overwhelming, terrifying experience, trauma in infancy can be a quite subtle pattern of unconscious inattention, neglect, or hidden hostility. Even a look or the absence of a look can combine with inner feelings and sensations to convey to the infant a message of malevolence, even hatred. In the earliest state of infant-parent merger, it has even been suggested that the infant is able to perceive the unconscious of the parent in a preverbal or pre-symbolic way.[33] Because trauma can be so subtle, emotional abuse or neglect is desolating, and actual physical or sexual abuse, devastating enough to an older child, can be experienced by a small child as psychically annihilating.

One tragic result of abuse in early childhood, in light of object relations theories, is the formation of inner objects that are neglectful, abandoning, and even persecutory. This is a process of mental and spiritual fragmentation. The smaller and more physically dependent the child is, the greater the need is in the child for some fragile faith in the goodness of the parent. The child, it is theorized, will therefore separate or "split" good and bad images of the parent in her own inner reality, some how segmenting off the experience of the terrifying parent from the needed good parent.[34] Often, the child will identify the bad with herself in order to keep the good and loving image of the external parent intact. In a mental process too early for actual words, a preverbal logic asserts itself: "If something is wrong here, it must be me, because the people I depend on must be good." The dynamic of secrecy that typically accompanies abuse, particularly sexual abuse, heightens a sense of shame and aloneness, and concretely results in isolation from others who could help. This negativity can haunt the child into adulthood with feelings of self-blame and an inner sense of damage or basic badness that was long ago separated from its actual origins in abuse. Particularly in cases of severe or repeated abuse, this inner, nonverbal, and potentially damaging logic begins to function as an organizer of experience, a limiting framework from which to understand and respond to subsequent life events.

---

York: Brunner/Mazel, 1980).

33. Malcolm J. Marks, "Conscious/Unconscious Selection of the Psychotherapist's Theoretical Orientation," *Psychotherapy: Theory, Research and Practice* 15/4 (1978) 354–58.

34. This process is eloquently described in Leonard Shengold, "Child Abuse and Deprivation: Soul Murder," *Journal of the American Psychoanalytic Association* 27 (1979) 539. See also Shengold, *Soul Murder: The Effects of Childhood Abuse and Deprivation* (New York: Fawcett/Ballantine, 1991).

This process is compounded by the nature of traumatic memory. Neuro psychological research on the effects of trauma is increasingly demonstrating that traumatic experience is not recorded as normal events are, in the form of narrative memory, but rather is encoded in other parts of the brain where the experience remains unsymbolized,[35] and therefore might initially be accessed only through bodily sensations and preverbal, body-based memories; unconsciously driven behaviors that might appear self-destructive; and physical illness. Furthermore, there is little or no differentiation in the early stages of development between the experiences of *body* and *self*. Violations of the body are violations of the whole self, often with disastrous consequences for the development of healthy boundaries and a sense of the integrity of the self.

The implications for healing from this theoretical perspective lie in bringing inner self-persecutory aspects of the self to light. This process is not one of exorcism, attempting to root out negative aspects of the self. As self-destructive as they might seem in the present, they once served a protective function, enabling the person to survive through some capacity for identification with the abuser on whom she depended, and perhaps in some cases later to fight back. Often, however, once the person grows up and begins to establish a life independent of her abusers, these negative functions have outlived their usefulness. Clergy and other helpers can support the person to build a conscious sense of self-worth and purpose, in tandem with more intensive psychotherapy designed to address the deeper, more unconscious aftereffects of trauma. The process of such psychotherapy with victims of sexual abuse and other trauma is one of identifying sensations and behavior that have never been verbalized or possibly even "digested" mentally in any symbolic form, and helping to move these from un-metabolized raw experiences through symbolization and verbalization to understanding.[36] No

35. Bruce D. Perry, Ronnie A. Pollard, Toi L. Blakley, William L. Baker and Domenico Vigilante, "Childhood Trauma: The Neurobiology of Adaptation and Use-Dependent Development of the Brain—How 'States' Become 'Traits,'" *Infant Mental Health Journal* 16/4 (1995) 271–91: http://www.trauma-pages.com/a/perry96.php; Bessel van der Kolk, *Psychological Trauma* (Washington, DC: American Psychiatric Press, 1987); van der Kolk, "The Body Keeps the Score: Memory and the Evolving Psychobiology of Post Traumatic Stress," www.trauma-pages.com/a/vanderk4.php; Allan Schore, *Affect Regulation and the Origin of Self* (New York: Erlbaum, 1994). [See also van der Kolk, *The Body Keeps the Score: Brain, Mind, and Body in the Healing of Trauma* (New York: Viking, 2014). For more sources, see David Baldwin's Trauma Information Pages: http://www.trauma-pages.com/. —PCW 2018]

36. This view is similar to that detailed by Davies and Frawley in *Treating the Adult Survivor of Childhood Sexual Abuse* (see above). It can also be understood from a Piagetian developmental perspective: the traumatic experience has remained at the sensorimotor level, and needs to be brought into representation through language for

single insight will be curative. Over time, however, as understanding grows, the experience of trauma can come to be incorporated as something that happened but that no longer has such controlling influence over the person's experience of herself and over her actions and choices.[37]

Feminist relational models speak similarly of the consequences of violence in terms of voice and the loss of voice. Mary Belenky and her colleagues, in their important study of "women's ways of knowing,"[38] interviewed women to investigate how women learn and organize their knowledge, including abstract critical thought and moral decision making but also their knowledge of self, others, relationships, and their whole world of experience. They identified "five different perspectives from which women view reality and draw conclusions about truth, knowledge, and authority."[39] They emphasize that these are not developmental stages per se, although their work does imply a hierarchy of complexity and maturity of thought. The first and most painful perspective they identify is that of "silence," in which women's experience of the absence of validation for their own self-expression, often combined with the presence of violence, created a disconnection between language and authoritative speech. Authority is viewed as external, unrelated, and uncaring. In this view, which complements the object relations perspective, helping must include a commitment to empowerment, of "hearing into speech"[40] by creating an environment of care that is empathic, connected, and deeply respectful.

Interpersonal, relational-cultural, relational psychoanalytic, and intersubjective theories all emphasize in various ways the two-person nature of the therapeutic relationship.[41] Rather than a classical stance in which the

---

growth and integration to occur.

37. Neuropsychological research appears to validate this process as even aiding in making positive changes in brain chemistry that help undo some of the early negative effects of trauma. See van der Kolk, "The Body Keeps the Score"; Perry, "Childhood Trauma"; [van der Kolk, *The Body Keeps the Score*. —PCW 2018]

38. Mary Belenky et al., *Women's Ways of Knowing*.

39. Ibid., 3.

40. Nelle Morton, *The Journey Is Home* (Boston: Beacon, 1985).

41. These theories differ in a number of respects. One important difference is the relative degree of attention paid to conscious vs. unconscious material in the therapeutic relationship. This difference is partly due to the intellectual and clinical heritage of each theory. Interpersonal and relational-cultural theorists trace their work back to Sullivan and Frieda Fromm-Reichman; relational theorists, to object relations; and intersubjective theorists, to self psychology. Interpersonal and relational-cultural theorists tend to work more in the sphere of conscious interactions between patient/client and therapist, and relational-psychoanalytic and intersubjective theorists are analysts, who tend to focus on apparent manifestations of unconscious dynamics in the transference-countertransference relationship between the therapist and patient.

therapist or counselor is the expert, and the patient or client is the object of treatment, these theories emphasize the mutual influence of therapist and patient. There is a recognition of a shared, co-constructed field of conscious and unconscious thoughts, images, feelings, and even bodily sensations that might arise between them as their exploration of the patient's suffering occurs in the context of deep connection. It is the therapist's responsibility to maintain good boundaries around the work in order to provide a safe container in which this deep work may occur. Within that safe container, a depth of shared experience can richly inform both partners in the therapeutic enterprise about the nature and origins of the patient's pain and the process needed for healing to occur.[42]

## Faith Development Theories

Let us return to the story of the eight-year-old girl. School has begun. The first class is on nutrition, and the teacher says, "Good eating is very important. Whatever goes into our bodies can make us healthy or unhealthy." She doesn't know why, but the pictures of fruits and vegetables the teacher shows suddenly make her want to throw up. Lately, she's been wanting to throw up a lot. Like when the Sunday school teacher started talking about good and evil. The teacher seems to think they should be able to understand this much more easily now, but for some reason it seems more complicated than ever. She can't figure out how Daddy, who is good, can make her feel so bad. So the badness must be in her. But God's a daddy, too, and he punishes badness.

Trauma is ultimately a spiritual assault. Because body and self are one in a child's experience, trauma strikes at the deepest essence or core of self and source of self-worth and integrity. Beginning as early as preschool age, children's experiences of Sunday school and formal church worship can compound the sense of powerless ness and alienate the abused child from a sense of God as a loving, protective resource. Religious images presenting God to children as all-powerful, all-knowing masculine Lord become easily equated in the child's mind with the abuser who exercises absolute power over them in terrifying ways. Especially when the abuser is the child's father or father-figure, church-authorized language and imagery presenting a powerful male

---

These differences are not absolute, however, and vary from one practitioner to another.

42. [On intersubjectivity, the use of the self, and mutual influence in the transference-countertransference continuum, see also Cooper-White, *Shared Wisdom: Use of the Self in Pastoral Care and Counseling* (Minneapolis: Fortress, 2004) and *Many Voices: Pastoral Psychotherapy in Relational and Theological Perspective* (Minneapolis: Fortress, 2011)—PCW 2018]

father-God combines with the lived experience of a powerful male father-abuser, and both images become mutually reinforcing.[43]

Theologian Jane Grovijahn has addressed the absence in existing theological frameworks of abuse survivors' experiences of God.[44] For Grovijahn, the body is unequivocally the site of religious truth.[45] She has offered us two new terms for better understanding survivors' embodied theological experiences: "Not-God" and "God-Gone-Wrong." These terms attempt more adequately to represent survivors' felt apprehension of God as "neglectful, abandoning, abusive, hostile or persecutory." As Ana-Maria Rizzuto powerfully demonstrated in a clinical study of psychotherapy patients' images of God, each individual's unique representation of God, or *God-imago*, depends heavily on internalized experiences of early caregivers and other significant others; experiences of oneself that might be invested with calm, conflict, or shame; and the way these experiences interact with the cultural surroundings and the belief system of the environment.[46] She emphasizes that "once formed, that complex representation cannot be made to disappear; it can only be repressed, transformed, or used."[47] Although Rizzuto does not directly address the impact of trauma on the inner evolution of the God imago, the implications are clear: abusive significant others will be internalized, not only as abandoning or persecutory inner "objects," but as the foundation for an abandoning or persecutory God.

James Fowler in his *Stages of Faith* introduced a now familiar and widely used framework for understanding individual differences in not only the content but also the formation of religious belief and meaning-making. Fowler's six stages of faith rely heavily on both Erikson's "stages of man" [sic], but also on the foundation of Piaget's stages of cognitive development, the premise being that the mode of thought possible for a child at various ages will strongly shape his or her developing faith conceptions. When we put this understanding of faith development together with the perspective of an abused child's inner experience of terror, abandonment, and violation, the overwhelming impact of trauma at the various stages becomes devastatingly clear.

43. For example, see interviews with incest survivors by Annie Imbens and Ineke Jonker, *Christianity and Incest*, trans. P. McVay (Minneapolis: Fortress, 1992).

44. Jane Grovijahn, "A Feminist Theology of Survival," PhD diss., Graduate Theological Union, Berkeley, California, 1997.

45. See also Elisabeth Moltmann-Wendel, *I Am My Body: A Theology of Embodiment* (New York: Continuum, 1995).

46. Ana-Maria Rizzuto, *The Birth of the Living God: A Psychoanalytic Study* (Chicago: University of Chicago Press, 1979).

47. Ibid., 90.

For example, in the first "pre-stage," termed "undifferentiated faith" by Fowler, the "seeds of trust, courage, hope, and love are fused in an undifferentiated way and contend with sensed threats of abandonment, inconsistencies and deprivations in a child's environment."[48] This is the normative definition of the first "pre-stage," however, in which an experience of basic care and protection (Winnicottt's "good enough" parental holding, both literally and symbolically[49]) is reliably present. This normative definition does not account for an environment in which abandonment, inconsistencies, and deprivations, as well as active violation of boundaries and overwhelming, frightening stimulation are the norm. Abuse and other forms of trauma at this earliest stage therefore undermine not only basic trust, as in Erikson's first developmental stage, but the whole foundation for trust in a caring, reliable, loving God. Because this stage of development is preverbal, traumatic experiences have even less likelihood of being recorded as any sort of symbolic or verbal memory and can lie dormant in inchoate, bodily form for years or even decades,

Trauma has a particular impact at each of the subsequent stages of faith. In Stage 1, "intuitive-projective faith," the child, roughly ages three to seven, is susceptible to be "powerfully and permanently influenced by examples, moods, actions and stories of the visible faith of primally related adults."[50] Because fantasy and external reality are fluidly related in this stage, real experiences of abuse and terror combine, sometimes catastrophically, with inner fantasies and nightmare images. God in this stage of imaginative and intuitive understanding of self and world can become a terrifying monster, or an absent, non-protecting parent who does not care. Perhaps in the best scenario, if there *is* some adequate caring or protection from an adult other than the abuser—a nurturing grandmother, a parent who learns of the abuse and takes a strong, protective stand—then there might also be some foundation in the child's inner life for imagining a rescuing God or avenging angel.

In Stage 2, "mythic-literal faith," located roughly during the school years, the child begins to appropriate the rules, norms, and stories of the wider community of institutions such as school and church. Here the impact of Sunday school lessons becomes formative. This fact points to the necessity for programs of Christian education and formation that reinforce not theologies of dominance and submission, but mutuality, care, hopefulness,

---

48. Fowler, *Stages of Faith*, 121.

49. D. W. Winnicott, *Maturational Processes and the Facilitating Environment* (London: Hogarth, 1965).

50. Fowler, *Stages of Faith*, 133.

and respect for the child's own thoughts, experiences, and perceptions about God, self, and others.

In Stage 3, "synthetic-conventional faith," usually corresponding with adolescence, the views and expectations of the wider world, and especially the judgments of peers, are ascendant. This is the stage of emerging ideological belief, but it is often embedded in what others think. The locus of authority is external. Fowler notes that a danger of this stage is that "interpersonal betrayals can give rise either to nihilistic despair about a personal principle of ultimate being or to a compensatory intimacy with God unrelated to mundane relations."[51] Abuse occurring or continuing during this stage is likely to trigger either outward conformity and compliance, coupled with an increasing inner sense of theft of identity and despair, or in other cases, intense rebellion, often in the form of self-destructive behaviors and peer alliances. God and religion might become an object of extreme scorn for the abused adolescent. Like the younger child, she will absorb the impact of abuse wordlessly in her body, but she now also has the intellectual capacity for both rationalization and cynicism. She might either rationalize the abuse, and identify with the needs of the perpetrator, or she might violently reject faith messages that seem fake, authoritarian, or smacking of collusion with her perpetrator. It should be noted that in Fowler's formulation, many people remain at this stage for life.[52] The remaining three stages occur past childhood and adolescence. Therefore, the occurrence of trauma during these stages falls outside the scope of this chapter. Nevertheless, a history of abuse might condition how these stages will be entered and lived, if at all. Also, the implied hierarchy of the further stages is challenged by the insights of Gilligan, and Belenky and her colleagues: women's and girls' development does not necessarily proceed directly from Stage 3 into a more rationally critical stage. The emphasis on critical analysis over emotional relatedness privileges the rational mind and does not give adequate attention to the emotions, bodily feelings, and wordless images as parallel, equally valid ways of knowing, growing, and relating both in connection with other people and with God. As this emphasis on critical analysis interacts with a history of abuse, it tends to privilege precisely the type of knowing that is least likely to provide access to knowledge of the abuse or its full impact. This lack of access in turn colludes with the messages of the perpetrator and the wider society to ignore, disbelieve, or forget that the abuse ever occurred.

---

51. Ibid., 173.
52. Ibid., 172.

Like the developmental stage theories discussed above, stages of faith must also be considered in light of the fragmentation and compartmentalization of survivors' experience into different sectors of the personality and memory. Again, there might be multiple developmental lines, and more than one faith stage might be operative in the person at different times and in different contexts of threat or safety. It seems to be the case that in many survivors' experiences, a part of the self containing the memory of trauma is walled off from other parts of the personality. Development may proceed extremely successfully by external appearances. Self-experiences of body and affect might be sacrificed to the task of successful daily living.[53]

Externally, such survivors might consciously give the appearance, both to themselves and others, of achieving an advanced stage of faith and intellectual theological integration based on Fowler's categories. Even a number of clergy and seminarians might fit this pattern. What is often missed, however, is the persistent inner sense of emptiness, fraud, self-doubt, shame, and incipient depression associated with earlier experiences of trauma. The depression of such individuals, sometimes masked by extreme industriousness, is a lid covering varying intensities of rage, pain, grief, and terror.

## Trauma and Women's Development

Why a chapter on trauma in a book devoted specifically to women's development? Developmental theories have cast male experience as the norm, as reflected in popular culture. Arthur the Aardvark is, after all, a boy, as was Charlie Brown before him, and as are a host of contemporary children's cartoon characters. Female characters have tended to be secondary, if not goofy, pesky, mean, bossy, or vapid, and there are few strong female figures even in educational television for children.[54] Allowing male development to set the authoritative standard has had the consequence of "normalizing" a lesser occurrence of abuse than is girls' reality. Girls are victims of sexual

---

53. There is some parallel here to D. W. Winnicott's notion of a "False Self" and a "True Self" (see "The Theory of the Parent-Infant Relationship" and "Ego Distortion in Terms of True and False Self" in *Maturational Processes and the Facilitating Environment*). The so-called False Self conforms to rigidly enforced expectations of caretakers, and the True spontaneous self is suppressed in the service of survival. I prefer the term *ambulatory self* or *coping self* to *False Self*, in recognition of the constructive and at times even heroic task of carrying on, coping, and succeeding that is performed by this aspect of the personality.

54. [There have been some positive changes in the past decade, including a number of Disney characters like the sisters in "Frozen," and more girls of color, e.g., "Dora the Explorer" and "Fa Mulan." —PCW 2018]

abuse about three times more often than boys, and the vast majority of abuse (81 to 95 percent) is committed by men against girls.[55] These statistics in no way excuse or minimize the devastating impact of sexual abuse of boys[56] but are reflective of the whole continuum of violence against women and girls that continues to be a characteristic feature of our society.[57] The very nature of many developmental theories might be seen, in contrast to women's ways of knowing, as showing traces of masculine thought process, to the extent that they organize the messiness of human growth into rational, linear taxonomies.

Further, the focus of traditional developmental psychology on *individuals'* development is challenged by feminist models of care that call for attention to the "living human web."[58] Healing of abuse requires not only a sensitized response to individual victims and survivors, but a contextualized awareness and response. In the words of a recent book, we all live in a "rape culture"[59] in which women's and girls' experience is surrounded every day by media messages that female bodies are meant to be used as commodities, and that violations of female body-selves will be ignored, tacitly condoned, or blamed on them. In the privileging of the rational, the sources of women's knowledge of abuse in body, image, and emotion will be discounted, and truth-telling can become a Cassandra-like exercise in futility and ostracism.

The "closing of the eyes" is not only an individual but a systemic and societal response. It is natural to recoil at the prevalence and the horror of the sexual abuse of children. The widespread existence of sexual abuse defies our beliefs about ourselves as a democratic society that is both rational and decent. This unwillingness to see is further compounded in the church, where we want to believe that Christians are loving and nice. Ultimately, our

---

55. Studies by Finkelhor and J. Landis, summarized in Herman, *Father-Daughter Incest*, 13; also extrapolated from statistics for female perpetrators in Russell, *The Secret Trauma*, 218, also citing Finkelhor, *Sexually Victimized Children* (New York: Free Press, 1979). For further discussion of prevalence of abuse and the myth of the rarity of abuse, see Pamela Cooper-White, *The Cry of Tamar* (Minneapolis: Fortress, 1995) 152ff. (2nd ed., 2012, 175–76).

56. Two excellent resources for male survivors are Mike Lew, *Victims No Longer: Men Recovering from Incest and Other Sexual Child Abuse* (New York: Harper & Row, 1990); and *The Sexually Abused Male*, ed. Mic Hunter.

57. Cooper-White, *The Cry of Tamar* (2nd ed.).

58. Bonnie Miller McLemore, "The Living Human Web: Pastoral Theology at the Turn of the Century," in Jeanne Stevenson Moessner, ed., *Through the Eyes of Women: Insights for Pastoral Care* (Minneapolis: Fortress, 1996) 9–26. See also Pamela Couture, "Weaving the Web: Pastoral Care in an Individualistic Society," in *Through the Eyes of Women*, 94–106.

59. Emilie Buchwald, Pamela R. Fletcher, and Martha Roth, eds., *Transforming a Rape Culture* (Minneapolis: Milkweed, 1983; 2nd ed., 2005).

pastoral response must be one not only of care and compassion, and belief toward individual victims and survivors—although this is the very least we must offer. We must also make sexual abuse and trauma visible. This step is the first toward changing the social, political, and ecclesiastical contexts that sponsor abuse through denial and inertia. Only in this way will we fully validate the authority of women's and girls' experience and vision. By so doing, we open our eyes, and thus open the way to God's own healing and justice-making to move among us and transform our world.

# 5

## Functional Families for the New Millennium

*Teaching Pastoral Care of Families with a Vision of Social Justice*

2001[1]

IN A *NEW YORKER* cartoon from long ago, there is a picture of a large auditorium with three lone audience members scattered among rows of empty seats. A banner hangs across the stage announcing the purpose of the gathering: "Annual Convention of Adult Children of Functional Families." The cartoon represents a viewpoint that is common in our heavily psychologized society—almost nobody is free of "dysfunction," or "normal" (and perhaps we wouldn't want to be anyway)! At the same time, however, the cartoon also speaks to a bias in terms of what we tend to focus on, as a culture, when we consider family life. Due in no small part to the primacy of the a psychiatric model, in which all problems that in another era might have been understood as the domain of the "cure of souls" are now diagnosed, prescribed and treated, we tend to view families through the lens of pathology. If an individual family or a societal family issue comes into view, it is most often because there is a problem or social ill to be diagnosed and remedied. In the teaching of pastoral care with families, this has tended to have two results, both absorbed from secular psychological models, especially family systems theory: first, the focus on pathology has tended, however subtly, to dominate the subject matter taught. Second, as a result, the internal workings of an individual family have tended to be the focus of investigation, rather than the impact of the outer world (including the relative social reali-

---

1. Orig. publ. as "Functional Families for the New Millennium: Teaching Pastoral Care of Families with a Vision of Social Justice," *Seminary Ridge Review* 4/4 (2001) 36–49.

ties of privilege and prestige, poverty, discrimination, and injustice), or the potential impact for good by the family upon that world.

This preoccupation with pathology and the internal life of families has begun to be challenged in recent decades, both in secular family systems theory, and in the discipline of pastoral theology. In particular, in the last decade, pastoral theologians have increasingly been writing on issues of concern to women, African American couples and families, and the intersection of individual persons and families with issues of racial and economic justice and social change. The purpose of this article, then, is to ask: how in our teaching of pastoral ministry with families can we challenge ourselves to shift our inherited focus away from models overemphasizing pathology and the privatization of family life? Or, to frame this positively: how can we model in our teaching a more balanced view of families, noticing strengths and potential for joy as well as illness and sorrow, and in every case in some way capable of becoming (to quote Herbert Anderson and Susan Johnson) a "just community" that in turn becomes a "crucible of justice" for the wider world?[2]

There are at least four elements which I have found helpful to hold in balance in the teaching of pastoral care of families: 1) first, celebrating the *strengths* of families—holding a balanced view of families' capacities, resources, and joys, as well as problems and dysfunctionality. Such a view calls for a redefinition of the very notion of "family" itself, beyond Victorian and 20th century white middle class norms.

2) Closely related to this, is the element of remembering the *contexts* in which families live. Families do not form their patterns of functioning and relating in isolation from the rest of society. Just as a traumatized individual may learn to survive by adopting patterns of relating that do not always conform to "normal" behavior, families also survive in hostile or oppressive conditions by adopting patterns that may deviate from dominant cultural norms. Some of these patterns may, in fact, become harmful to members of the family over time, but they must first be understood in terms of how they evolved, and how their first purpose was adaptive and oriented toward survival. And some of these patterns may be healthy.

3) Families, like individuals, have a spiritual life that needs to be attended and nurtured. We can look for the *"thin places,"* to borrow a phrase from Celtic spirituality, those places where the veil (or illusion) separating the sacred from the secular, or the spiritual from the everyday, is most transparent. We can help families to identify moments and occasions in

---

2. Herbert Anderson and Susan B.W. Johnson, *Regarding Children: A New Respect for Childhood and Families* (Louisville: Westminster John Knox, 1994).

which the sacred is most apparent in the things of their everyday life, and glimpses of the spiritual aspect of our lives are most apt to break through into ordinary awareness. These three dimensions are all important, and already reframe family care beyond the diagnosis of pathology toward the identification of strength.

4) Attention to these three domains of family life already refocuses the pastoral care of families away from pathology and toward a more balanced view of families' strengths and capacity for spiritual growth. But attention to these three domains is still incomplete without asking the question: spiritual growth *for what?* Finally, families are not strong and joyful only to produce internal harmony among family members, or a privatized form of satisfaction, safety, and happiness. As with the individual spiritual journey, families are places where people are joined together by blood kinship or by choice, to support one another not only in attaining personal happiness, but also in engaging with the wider world in ways that ideally will make a positive difference. To put it more theologically, families are ideally places where family members, both individually and collectively, are supported in living out their call by God, to live more and more fully into God's own Realm of peace and justice here on the earth. For Christian families, this is specifically the *living out of their baptismal call*, their call to ministry.

## What Is a Healthy Family? Celebrating Families' Strengths

In another recent cartoon, a young boy with punk hairstyle and an earring sits at dinner with his mother, father, and sister, and declares, "This family is *way* too functional!" The cartoon focuses on the boy's adolescent rebellion, and the humor hangs on the irony of the boy's already having appropriated the psychological lingo of the very culture he purports to be rejecting. But the image of the family itself remains unchallenged at a more tacit level. The family is white. The father, presumably just back from work, wears glasses and a white shirt and tie. It is ambiguous whether the mother has been working outside the home or in the home. She also has glasses, and wears a neat sweater and skirt, as does the daughter. In addition to his hair and earring, the boy's T-shirt is black, signifying his status as rebel, but also as "other." They sit in a dining room, with a separate kitchen partially visible through a doorway. The table is set with a tablecloth and laden with full plates of food, and a shiny sideboard contains an additional bowl of fruit. The image emphasizes comfort and wealth, presumably as a product of cleanliness, hard work, and the presumption of knowing what is "appropriate" behavior.

At the turn of the 21st century, this image of the nuclear family, including its one rather well socialized rebel, is a cultural icon of the American middle class. Many families do, in fact, resemble this model, or hold a belief that they do. But many do not. It is crucial in teaching pastoral ministry with families that we not, however inadvertently, elevate the icon of the white nuclear family above other models that may be equally or even more healthy for the contexts in which they live. In many cultures, more than two generations, and often more than two marital partners and their children, live together under the same roof. And although the Victorian family norm specifies that the races of the marital partners must be the same, while the genders must be "opposite," both of these factors are clearly changing in modern families, and such differences should not be pathologized.

Of course, the relative health or "functionality" of a family has never been assessed simply by a narrowly defined standard of the generations, racial composition, biological relatedness, and genders of its members—although deviations from the norm have tended to predispose traditionally trained clinicians to expect pathology. But the health of family ultimately depends not on its external demographic characteristics, but on its quality of communication, support of its members, and even capacity for joy and generosity.

What, then, are the signs of health and functionality in a family, and how can we identify and encourage these in the families who come to us for pastoral care and counsel? There are clearly many ways to theorize about what makes a healthy family.[3] A consensus view of family systems experts would likely include at least three elements: boundaries, rules, and roles. A fourth element, borrowing from object relations and psychoanalytic group relations theory, would be the capacity to hold opposite feelings together in tension rather than splitting into factions or dyads holding polarized beliefs. All four of these elements contribute to an overall sense of truth and transparency in communication, mutual support, and room to grow that in turn potentiates more joyful and generous living.

We can celebrate the strengths of families by noticing where boundaries seem to be both consistently present, and at the same time flexible and porous, giving family members "room to breathe." Boundaries are both internal

---

3. Maria Krysan, Kristin Moore, and Nicholas Zill studied 15 research models of successful families, and identified nine separate constructs common to most research: communication, encouragement of individuals, commitment to family, religious orientation, social connectedness, ability to adapt, expressing appreciation, clear roles, and time together, in "Identifying Successful Families: An Overview of Constructs and Selected Measures," project funded by the U.S. Dept. of Health and Human Services (Washington, DC: Child Trends, Inc., 1990).

and external, defining the spaces between individual family members, and also between the whole family and the outside world. Where boundaries are too rigid, there is isolationism. Where boundaries are not present enough, there can be experiences of invasion, intrusion, or merger. The woes of such boundary problems are well known, and do involve serious harm to family members, up to and including severe trauma and abuse. But often there may be some healthy boundary keeping to be found even in a family with longstanding boundary pathology. Perhaps it will be found first in the behavior of the "identified patient," a family member whom the family identifies as problematic or deviant, but who in effect is demonstrating to both the family and the world that there is another way to be. The marriage partner who begins to assert the need for greater inter-dependence and less dependence; the adolescent who breaks a rule in order to assert a need to break out of a stifling set of role expectations; the child who breaks the boundary of secrets between the family and the outside world by whispering to a trusted Sunday school teacher, "my uncle touched me"—all these family members are showing signs of health and new growth that can be nurtured and attended for what they signify about what needs to change.

Similar to boundaries, rules in families can also be rigid or flexible. In healthy families, there is a reasonable degree of structure in the form of rules, spoken and unspoken. Rules are simply the expectations that family members come to have of one another, and generally live by. In nurturing families, rules are at the same time clear, and flexible. There are few "should's," and the important ones involve health, growth, and safety (not how family members "should" feel or think). Expectations are stated out loud, are consistent, and make sense. Few challenges to a family's regular expectations are answered by "because we've always done it that way" or "because I said so!" Often such challenges are responded to with concise explanations, such as "because if you don't get enough sleep you won't be able to feel energetic and do well tomorrow" or "because if you don't let me know where you are I won't be able to reach you in an emergency."

Occasionally, also, challenges to expectations may cause a re-evaluation of what may have become habitual and outlived its usefulness. A child may reasonably challenge a parent by saying, "I know you have said that I have to have all my homework done before I go out to the movies on Saturday. But I'm older now, and you know that I'm pretty good at organizing my work. I would like you to trust me to have everything done by Monday, even if it's not done by Saturday night." A parent might well then respond, "OK, let's try it the next couple of weeks, but if it turns out that you end up in a big time crunch on Sunday night, then we will go back to the old rule. Deal?" "Deal." In this example, a rule is clear and consistent, but negotiable within reasonable limits. Decisions are not based on reflex responses, but on a balance of trust and common sense.

Again, in teaching pastoral ministry with families, we can emphasize looking for places in the family where rules and expectations are working well. Teach our students to ask, "What are the expectations that your family has come to live by that you think work well for all of you?" rather than probing for places where rules are either too rigid, too loose, or too inconsistent. How can the family's own strengths be developed and transferred to other situations where the family needs help?

A third element in family life is the roles people play. The idea of roles has been a mainstay of family systems theory.[4] For example, one member of the family might be the Caretaker, another the Star, another the Troublemaker or the Screw-Up, and another the Clown. There is often confusion about this category. Students new to family theory often believe that the presence of roles in a family is automatically a sign of pathology. But this is not necessarily the case. We can look, rather, to see whether roles, like boundaries and rules above, are flexible. Also, we can look to see whether they are ego-syntonic, that is, does the role fit the innate temperament, personality, and goals of the person, and, importantly, his or her ideal sense of self, or is the role s/he plays thrust upon him or her? Do the roles in a family shift or even trade back and forth over time, or as circumstances within the family or external pressures shift and change? Rather than looking askance upon all roles in family life, we might again want to ask, "Do you feel you play a particular role in your family? How does this work for you, and for the others? Do you like this role and does it feel like the 'real you'"?

We can also foster increasing amounts of role fluidity within families, while at the same time supporting roles that enhance the division of labor and sense of authentic self of each family member. In particular, we need to encourage the role of "caretaker" to be shared, so that no member cares for all the others all the time in a rigidly identified way, especially if this comes to be at the expense of *his* (stereotypically as highly pressured breadwinner) or *her* (stereotypically as emotional nurturer and family nurse) own growth and development. Adults should, on the other hand, be the ones to do more of the caretaking than the children (especially young children). As pastors, we can

---

4. Murray Bowen, *Family Therapy in Clinical Practice* (Northvale, NJ: Aronson, 1995); for an application to congregations see also Edwin Friedman, *Generation to Generation: Family Process in Church and Synagogue* (New York: Guilford, 1985) and Peter Steinke, *How Your Church Family Works: Understanding Congregations as Emotional Systems* (Bethesda, MD: Alban Institute, 1993). Transactional Analysis, popular especially in the 1970s and 80s, similarly emphasized the "scripts" people play habitually in their lives, e.g., Claude Steiner, *Scripts People Live: Transactional Analsyis of Life Scripts* (New York: Bantam, 1974).

support parents to find ways to cope with the stresses and demands of life, so that they may be in a position to take joy in this responsibility, and children can take joy in being children, not "parentified" mini-adults.

Finally, maturity in families, as in individuals, consists in the capacity to hold opposites together, in tension. A key sign of health in a family—or any group, such as a church council or committee—is the ability to say "I can see some truth in another point of view." This can play out in families in a variety of ways. In small children, this might mean being able to realize "Mom is angry at me for running and breaking the lamp, but I know she still loves me"—or, even "I'm angry at Mom, but I also love her." In adults, it might mean, "I'm upset with my partner for forgetting that important commitment, but I know s/he also is thoughtful about a lot of things," or even, "I'm furious at my spouse, but I still love him/her." It might mean, "I feel like hitting my child for breaking that expensive lamp, but I can also recognize how little s/he is and not act on that impulse, take a deep breath, and talk to him/her instead."

Wherever we see family members struggling to hold together good experiences and bad, neither idealizing the family or individuals within it as "all wonderful," nor devaluing them as "all bad," we can affirm that life in families and in the world is deeply complex, at times confusing, but always rich with possibility. Where complexity is allowed, and negative feelings such as anger, fear, disappointment, shame, grief, and sadness can be expressed openly, people will feel more loved, because they will feel known and accepted for who they really are. This, in turn, generates energy, and a sense of inner security and strength to face whatever external pressures face the family, individually and as a group. Complexity makes room for more painful feelings to be expressed, but it also, finally, makes room for joy, and in turn, greater generosity and finally, altruism toward others beyond family.

## Remembering the Contexts in Which Families Live

It is important in assessing the strengths of families that we also consider these in relation to the contexts in which they live. Family theorists Betty Carter and Monica McGoldrick have, in particular, brought greater awareness to the reality that families not only deal with internal stresses from events generated from within individuals, the immediate and extended family, but also many external stressors as well.[5] They describe a confluence of

---

5. Betty A. Carter and Monica McGoldrick, eds., *The Expanded Family Life Cycle: Individual, Family, and Social Perspectives*, 3rd ed. (Needham Heights, MA: Allyn & Bacon, 1999). See also 5th ed. by Monica McGoldrick, Nydia A. Garcia, and Betty A.

"*horizontal stressors*," which are generated by developmental and historical changes that impact the family across time, and "*vertical stressors*"—more chronic or enduring sociocultural, political and economic forces that result in disappearance of community, more work and less leisure, less time to nurture friendships, and, at the most overarching societal level, racism, sexism, classism, ageism, heterosexism, consumerism, and poverty.[6] These vertical stressors have the effect of grinding down individuals and families, creating stress-related "symptoms" that are better understood as socio-cultural in origin rather than primarily intrapsychic or intrafamilial.

Carroll Watkins Ali has described a pastoral counseling client, "Lemonine," who suffered from what might have been classically diagnosed as anxiety with acute psycho-somatization.[7] An examination of Lemonine's economic circumstances showed that her "symptoms" were in fact natural responses to an unbearable degree of economic and social oppression. In Watkins Ali's words, "Truly, life was Lemonine's presenting problem. There are no other diagnoses in the traditional sense."

It is crucial in our teaching of pastoral care to hold together individual and family health and "functionality" with the wider social, political, racial, and economic situation in which the family lives. What might be unhealthy for one family might be an adaptive arrangement that enhances another family's ability to survive and thrive in spite of external hostility. For example, it was long thought in family theory that two (heterosexual) adult partners were needed for healthy child rearing, and that "cross-generational alliances," that is, strong decision-making and emotional bonds across the generations, were pathological. This, of course, could still be the case, if, in an intact marriage or committed partnership, one partner is displaced in authority and emotional closeness by an unhealthy, enmeshed bond maintained by the other partner with a grandparent, or with one of the children. However, in many families, the model of two adults + child(ren) does not pertain. The healthy support of a single parent may indeed come from a grandparent, aunt or uncle, or close church or community member who serves as a surrogate parent and role model. Extended family may also play a much larger, much healthier role than has been normed according to twentieth century white, middle class values.

As pastors, and as students of pastoral care, we need to remember to ask the questions: how is what this family is telling me and showing me an

---

Carter (New York: Pearson, 2015).

6. Ibid., 6.

7. Carroll Watkins Ali, *Survival and Liberation: Pastoral Theology in African American Context* (St. Louis: Chalice, 1999) 4–5.

indication of the pressures they are under, not only from within, but from the community and from larger social, political, and economic realities? How are the things they are doing ways of adapting and coping with these pressures? We must also look to our own countertransference, or our own blind spots, to remind ourselves that the pressures—and privileges!—we may experience are not the same as those of the families we serve, and that we should not assume that they are coping with the same issues, nor should we judge their adaptations by our own. Often, when we discipline ourselves to pay attention to the wider contexts affecting families, we may realize that many modes of care in which we have been traditionally trained are insufficient. Again, to quote Watkins Ali, "a communal strategy of a network of care and resources was required to meet Lemonine's needs." Feminist, Womanist, and liberationist models of care have increasingly insisted that the role of pastor itself must expand beyond individualistic notions of one-to-one pastoral care, to become a "facilitator of networks of care."[8] The traditional functions of pastoral care as "healing, sustaining, guiding, and reconciling"[9] must be extended to include "nurturing, empowering, and liberating"[10] with an awareness of context always held in mind.

## Looking for the "Thin Places"

Families, like individuals, also have spiritual lives that needs specific, intentional focus and nurture. As Lauren Artress, Canon for Special Ministries at Grace Episcopal Cathedral in San Francisco, is fond of reminding us, "We are not human beings on a spiritual journey; we are spiritual beings on a human journey." The spiritual life of families does not occur in isolation from its other activities, relationships, and routines. Nor is the spiritual life of a family defined exclusively by its church attendance (or lack thereof!). In teaching pastoral care, we can lift up the role of pastor as nurturer of spiritual formation of families, and the individuals within them. If we view Christian education as a lifelong *habitus* of ongoing discernment of God's will for each of us, and not simply a Sunday morning curriculum for people under age 18, we can open up a realm of possibilities for the fostering of

---

8. Bonnie Miller-McLemore, "The Living Human Web: Pastoral Theology at the Turn of the Century," in Jeanne Stevenson Moessner, ed., *Through the Eyes of Women* (Minneapolis: Fortress, 1996) 9-26; see also Pamela Cooper-White, "The Living Human Web: Emerging Paradigms in Pastoral Care," *Parish Practice Notebook* (Lutheran Theological Seminary at Philadelphia) 63 (Spring, 2001) 1-6.

9. William Clebsch and Charles Jaekle, *Pastoral Care in Historical Perspective* (Northvale, NJ: Aronson, 1995).

10. Watkins Ali, *Survival and Liberation*, 9.

spiritual growth in families. Christian education and spiritual formation are a crucial aspect of pastoral care. Multi-generational Sunday schools, adult education,[11] small group ministries and Bible studies[12], developmentally appropriate curricula for children that foster questions and exploration[13], and the growing adult catechumenal movement[14] all provide arenas in which people of all ages can explore the meaning of their own baptismal call. For this reason alone, they deserve to be elevated as one of the central sacramentally-based ministries of the church.

Beyond curricula and programs, we can also in our pastoral care help families to become attentive to the "thin places"—those times and places in which we are more likely to catch glimpses of a deeper wisdom, a sense of calling, or a spiritual insight in the everyday. The ancient Celts identified such places in the actual geography or landscape of their world. Some families may appreciate being encouraged to seek out actual places to plan a spiritual pilgrimage or family retreat. Such places might be long revered historical pilgrimage sites such as Jerusalem, Wittenburg, Canterbury, the Isle of Iona, Chartres Cathedral, or the Metropolitan Cathedral of San Salvador (which houses the tomb of Archbishop Oscar Arnulfo Romero). Other sites might be as privately meaningful to a family as a favorite campsite in the woods, or a tiny church where great grandparents were baptized, married, and buried. Pilgrimage destinations may also represent crucial moments when the family's history intersected with larger world events, such as a house that served as a hiding place on the underground railroad, the Gettysburg battlefield, the Registration Hall on Ellis Island, the Holocaust Museum, or the Vietnam Memorial.

---

11. For a discussion of the unique challenges of religious education with the adult learner, see Margaret Krych, "Lifelong Learning: Called to Learn and Teach," *Parish Practice Notebook* 62 (Winter 2001) 6–9.

12. E.g., the Augsburg Fortress "Intersections Small Group Ministry Series." For an overview of this series, see *Starting Small Groups—and Keeping Them Going* (Minneapolis: Augsburg Fortress, 1995).

13. E.g., Christian Montessori models such as the "Cathechesis of the Good Shepherd," Sofia Cavaletti, Ed., *The Good Shepherd and the Child: A Joyful Journey* (Chicago: Liturgy Training Publications, 1996), and Gianna Gobbi, *Listening to God with Children: The Montessori Method Applied to the Catechesis of Children*, transl. R. Rojcewicz (Loveland, OH: Treehaus, 1998); Jerome Berryman's *Godly Play: An Imaginative Approach to Religious Education* (Minneapolis: Augsburg Fortress, 1995); and the *Journey to Adulthood* curriculum for youth (Leeds, MA: Leader Resources, 1998).

14. E.g., *The Catechumenal Process* (New York: Church Publishing, 1988); Michael Merriman, ed., *The Baptismal Mystery and the Catechumenate* (New York: Church Publishing, 1990); Gordon Lathrop, "Catechumenate for Adults: Being Formed in the Faith," *Parish Practice Notebook* 62 (Winter 2001) 1–5.

But being attentive to the "thin places" does not require us to leave our homes and go anywhere. The family itself has been referred to as a "forming center,"[15] in which the faith of each of its members will be shaped by the quality of its spiritual life—and this will be true whether the spiritual life of the family is explicitly grounded in a faith tradition, or implicitly formed by the idolatries of secular work, television, addictions and consumerism. The family can function, in fact, as the "domestic church,"[16] a phrase that has been reclaimed in recent decades, hearkening back to ancient times in which the hearth was the center of human spiritual gathering. We can encourage families to observe the liturgical seasons at home as well as in church, and feel the rhythms of the church's life and story change with the shifting patterns of nature, light, and weather. We can encourage families to ponder how their story and the story of the faith coincide and interweave.

These observances can happen not only at Christmas and Easter, when rituals often come as part of the family's inherited traditions, but especially at other times when the family may be less constrained by long-standing customs and expectations. Families can reclaim ancient religious rituals and seasonal observances that promote spiritual awareness, family togetherness, and fun,[17] for example, making an Advent wreath to have on a dining table, or in Lent, making pretzels (recalling their origins in an ancient prayer posture of crossed arms) or hot cross buns. They can observe saints' feasts and festivals at home by reading stories of the saints, and what their lives might mean today.[18]

15. Marjorie Thompson, *Family the Forming Center: A Vision of the Role of Family in Spiritual Formation* (Nashville: Upper Room Books, 1996).

16. Cited by Pope Paul VI, "Dogmatic Constitution on the Church," *The Documents of Vatican II*, Ed. W. Abbot (Baltimore: America Press, 1966) 29; Thompson, *Family the Forming Center*, 25–30; and see especially Edward Hays, *Prayers for the Domestic Church: A Handbook for Worship in the Home* (Leavenworth, KS: Forest of Peace Publishing, 1989).

17. Two excellent resources include Joanna Bogle, *A Book of Feasts and Saints*, 3rd ed. (Leominster, UK: Gracewing, distrib. Harrisburg, PA: Morehouse, 1992), and Gertrud Mueller Nelson, *To Dance with God: Family Ritual and Community Celebration* (New York: Paulist, 1986).

18. A number of standard resources are arranged in order of the liturgical year so that families may readily find the saints and festivals appointed for each week, e.g., in the Lutheran tradition, see Philip Pfatteicher, *Festivals and Commemorations: Handbook to the Calendar in Lutheran Book of Worship* (Minneapolis: Fortress, 1982); in the Episcopal tradition, see *Lesser Feasts and Fasts 1997* (New York: Church Publishing, 1997\*), and Sam Portaro, *Brightest and Best: A Companion to the Lesser Feasts and Fasts* (Cambridge, MA: Cowley, 1997); in the Roman Catholic tradition, see Leonard Foley, O.F.M., *Saint of the Day: A Life and Lesson for Each of the 173 Saints in the New Missal* (Cincinnati: St. Anthony Messenger Press, 1997), and John Delaney, *Saints for All Seasons* (New York: Doubleday, 1979). [Cf., *Holy Women, Holy Men* (New York: Church Publishing,

Perhaps one of the easiest ways for families to be intentional about their spiritual life as a family is the table grace. This, in turn, requires some intentionality about gathering around a common table on some regular basis. As the family gathers at the end of the day to share what each member has experienced, learned and felt during the day, graces can provide a moment for regathering in love and focusing on God's presence. Families may recite old, familiar graces, but also may find spiritual nourishment in a number of new anthologies of graces drawn from a variety of centuries and cultures[19]. They may also be encouraged to try their hand in creating new graces that incorporate the particular concerns or celebrations of their day or week.

Finally, we can simply encourage families to keep their eyes and ears open for the stirrings of the spirit in any moment, and every moment. We can teach that prayer need not only be a verbal communication to God, nor must it involve a specific time, place, or wording. Every act, however simple, can itself become a form of prayer if it is infused with an intention to make it an offering to God. This is not unlike the practice of "mindfulness" described by the Buddhist priest and Nobel laureate Thich Nhat Hanh. He wrote, "Wash every dish as if it were a baby Buddha."[20] The spiritual life is not apart from daily life, on some higher plane, but "the word is very near to you; it is in your mouth and in your heart, so that you can do it." (Deut. 30:14) Simply by keeping this in mind, families will find that their whole way of being can be subtly but deeply transformed over time. Priorities will shift, and everyday actions and words will take on new meanings in the light of consciously practicing one's faith.

This brings us back to the centrality of each family member's baptismal call. For what is discernment and a practice of mindfulness, if it is not to grow more deeply into the knowledge of what God is calling each member of the family to do and to be? Edward Wimberly, in his *Counseling African American Couples and Families*, has written:

> Family members and marital partners are to live in their relationships in such a way that all family members are free to grow into their full possibilities as full participants in God's unfolding drama of salvation and as members of the eschatological community

---

2010). Resources in this section emphasize Christian sources; readers are encouraged to supply relevant examples and materials from other traditions. —PCW 2018]

19. E.g., June Cotner, ed., *Graces: Prayers and Poems for Everyday Meals and Special Occasions* (San Francisco: HarperSan Francisco, 1994); Marcia and Jack Kelly, eds., *100 Graces: Mealtime Blessings* (New York: Random House, 1997); and M.J. Ryan, ed., *A Grateful Heart: Daily Blessings for the Evening Meal from Buddha to the Beatles* (Berkeley: Conari, 1994).

20. Thich Nhat Hanh, *Being Peace* (Albany, CA: Parallax, 1988).

... [T]he ultimate end of growth facilitation is participation in the unfolding drama of God's salvation. The purpose of the eschatological community is to make people ready to assume their roles and vocations in God's salvation endeavor. Consequently, marital and family relationships serve a greater end.[21]

The family as a whole, and also each individual within it, has a vocation, a calling. One sign of health in a family is that *every* member's vocation is sought and honored—there is no one vocation that is supported at the expense of others. All vocations, at least by turns, are fostered and cultivated intentionally by the whole family as a group and by each member within it.

The spiritual life of families, then, is finally always a living into the eschatological hope of God's Realm of peace and justice that is paradoxically both not-yet and also here-now as we live more and more into its reality. It is at this point that the family's spiritual life, if lived with intentionality, leads the family to transcend itself, and to reach out to the world beyond its walls, not only to make contact, but to make a difference.

## Helping Families to Live Out Their Baptismal Call

Robert Bellah and other social scientists have called for a radical revisioning of the individualism that is rampant in contemporary American culture.[22] In the book *Habits of the Heart*, Bellah and his colleagues have written of the dangers of viewing the family as a private cocoon or haven from the rest of society:

> The family is the core of the private sphere, whose aim is not to link individuals to the public world but to avoid it as far as possible. In our commercial culture, consumerism, with its temptations, and television, with its examples, augment that tendency. Americans are seldom as selfish as the therapeutic culture urges them to be. But often the limit of their serious altruism is the family circle. Thus the tendency of our individualism to dispose "each citizen to isolate himself from the mass of his fellows and withdraw into the circle of family and friends" that so worried Tocqueville, indeed seems to be coming true. "Taking care of one's own" is an admirable motive. But when it combines with

---

21. Edward Wimberly, *Counseling African American Marriages and Families* (Louisville: Westminster John Knox, 1997) 5, 7.

22. Robert Bellah, ed., with Richard Madsen, William Sullivan and Steven Tipton, *Habits of the Heart: Individualism and Commitment in American Life* (Berkeley: University of California Press, 1985).

suspicion of, and withdrawal from, the public world, it is one of the conditions of despotism Tocqueville feared.[23]

The word *apathy* itself (*a*-pathy) means lack of suffering. The desire to avoid suffering, upon which most family isolation is based, can put blinders on a family's vision, leading to a seemingly *in-nocent* (not-knowing) disregard for the common good. In its extreme, this can result in complete isolationism. Theologian Dorothee Soelle has defined apathy as "a social condition in which people are so dominated by the goal of avoiding suffering that it becomes a goal to avoid human relationships and contacts altogether."[24]

In their book *Regarding Children*, Herbert Anderson and Susan Johnson have identified four themes from the Christian tradition that move family theory beyond an internally focused, privatized concept of family health toward a larger, more theologically grounded vision of family living: hospitality, compassion, justice, and reconciliation.[25] While secular family systems theorists rarely use the term "community" in relation to the family itself, Anderson and Johnson draw on the Judeo-Christian insistence on hospitality as a central aspect of morality, to reframe the family as a community that is hospitable, compassionate—able to respond "with tenderness to the least fortunate or most vulnerable in its membership without blaming them, humiliating them, or diminishing their identity,"[26] and moreover, a community that is *just*. They assert that "the family is a just community when it acts as a moral agent."[27] This challenges privatized notions of family, and presses toward a vision of families who collectively participate in the wider process of social change. As Anderson and Johnson point out, it not only "takes a village to raise a child," but it also takes individual children and adults, families and groups to raise a village.[28] The family, thus, in Anderson's and Johnson's view, must become a "crucible" of social responsibility, in which "the needs of the individual and the needs of the community are negotiated and balanced."[29]

Teaching pastoral care, then, requires moving beyond the teaching of care as nurture of individuals' and families' growth, toward the fostering of those strengths and attributes in families that are most likely to lead toward a capacity for a commitment to constructive change in the world. What

23. Ibid., 112.
24. Dorothee Soelle, *Suffering*, trans. E. Kalin (Philadelphia: Fortress, 1975) 36.
25. Anderson and Johnson, op. cit., p. 71 *et passim*.
26. Ibid., 78.
27. Ibid., 82.
28. Ibid., 104.
29. Ibid., 107.

conditions in a family make it more likely that family members will grow up with a passion for engaging in action for social change? In order to inquire about what constitutes such commitment, social researchers Daloz, Keen, Keen and Parks interviewed 145 individuals whom they identified as having a commitment to the common good. This commitment was evidenced in their ability to articulate how their life work served the well-being of society as a whole, as well as qualities of perseverance, resilience, and ethical congruence between everyday life and work. Through these interviews, the authors identified several key factors that appeared to be significant in the development of these "lives of commitment." Not surprisingly, family of origin figured centrally in their participants' responses. The key factors included a loving home environment in childhood, the example of at least one parent who worked actively for the public good, opportunities and challenges to be of service to others during adolescence, exposure to cross-cultural experiences, and a good mentoring experience in young adulthood.[30] The more such experiences were present, the greater the likelihood was that individuals would grow into a mature adult life of commitment to the common good—and, we might infer, cultivate a family life that would carry on this commitment into the next generation.

## Concluding Thoughts

In conclusion, the teaching of pastoral care encompasses far more than the transmission of skills for the traditional functions of "healing, sustaining, guiding, and reconciling," although these remain as important aspects of care. Pastoral care for the new millennium requires further skills: a diagnostic openness to look for strengths as well as weaknesses or symptoms of pathology and a widening of the very definition of family itself; cross-cultural and cross-class competencies, sensitivity, and appreciation; attention to the contexts in which families live; and attention to spiritual formation that will, in turn, foster the conditions for families and the individuals within them to live out their unique baptismal callings toward the incarnation of God's realm of peace and justice for all. And then comes the most personal challenge of all on this threshold of the new millennium: how will we ourselves nurture one another and our own families, so that we may faithfully discern and live out our own baptismal callings? Especially for those of us who teach pastoral care: how shall *we* practice what we preach?

---

30. Laurent Daloz, Cheryl Keen, James Keen, and Sharon Parks, *Common Fire: Leading Lives of Commitment in a Complex World* (Boston: Beacon, 1997) 17.

# 6

## Keeping God's People Safe

*Canons as Gift of Grace and Dance of Love*

2002[1]

THIS PAPER WAS WRITTEN at the request of the Episcopal Church's national Task Force on Title IV Canon (church law and polity) Revisions during the fall of 2002. Its purpose is to serve as a catalyst for further discussion of the theological grounds and rationale for understanding the underlying purposes of disciplinary canons, and in particular, addressing continuing concerns about sexual abuse in the church and "keeping God's people safe."[2] The intent here is not to present *the* single, definitive theological statement on this subject, but rather, to offer some constructive theological and ethical "food for thought" as our church, among many, moves toward deeper formulations of our the theological foundations and rationale for canon revision.

What is the ultimate purpose of disciplinary canons?

In my view, the canons of the church represent "law" in its highest sense—as a God given expression of care for the ordering of the church that is grounded not merely in restraint of evil (as often is the case in secular

---

1. Printed in the *Report to the 74th General Convention* (New York: Church Publishing, 2003) 357–68 as "Some Thoughts toward Canon Revision: Canons as Gift of Grace and Dance of Love," https://www.episcopalarchives.org/e-archives/gc_reports/reports/2003/bb_2003-R040.pdf/. I am grateful for feedback in 2002 from members of this Task Force: Les Alvis and Margo Maris, and especially Timothy Sedgwick for his careful reading of an earlier draft; and to Guy Lytle and Timothy Sedgwick for encouraging wider theological discussions about canon law in the Episcopal Church. [For more on the recent history of Title IV revisions, see https://www.episcopalnewsservice.org/2012/08/14/title-iv-continues-to-attract-debate/; Cooper-White, videotaped interview on Title IV training, General Convention, July 2018. —PCW 2018]

2. Episcopal Diocese of Chicago, *Keeping God's People Safe: Sexual Misconduct: Policies, Procedures, Prevention*, August 1, 1994.

law),[3] but focused on creating a community in which every member is supported in living a life grounded in desire for God, and the joy of being in harmony with the original goodness of God's creation.

This is the church's earthly vocation, and the vocation of its ministers—who ultimately include *all* the baptized, "lay persons, bishops, priests and deacons" (*Book of Common Prayer*, 855—hereafter *BCP*[4]).

There is, as well, a distinctive vocation to serve within this community, among those who hold ordained and other professional leadership roles within the church's earthly organization: to "equip the saints for the work of ministry" (Eph 4:12), assisting each and every child of God to discern more and more fully his or her own unique vocation from God toward the living of God's own Realm of peace, justice and freedom, encapsulated in Jesus' summary of the law: "You shall love the Lord your God with all your heart, and with all your soul, and with all your mind.' This is the greatest and first commandment. And a second is like it: You shall love your neighbor as yourself.' On these two commandments hang all the law and the prophets" (Matt 22:37–40; also in Mark 12:28–34; Luke 10:25–28).

Perhaps in an ideal world, there would be no need for canons at all. Yet the church, like all earthly human institutions, participates in the paradox of God's Realm: the mystery of the already-not yet character of God's final redemption of the world.

Jesus came to proclaim that God's Realm of peace and justice is already here, now, and it is up to us to live daily into that already given reality, which exists now in *kairos* time, God's time-in-eternity; yet the fallenness of creation persists in the daily tick tock *chronos* time of our creaturely existence. Thus the church both participates in the Church Eternal in which all human

---

3. I was delighted to discover a parallel formulation of this distinction between secular law and canon law as grounded first in theology, in Jesuit theologian Ladislas Orsy, *Theology and Canon Law: New Horizons for Legislation and Interpretation* (Collegeville, MN: Liturgical, 1992). While Orsy's project focuses on the interpretation, implementation and reception of Roman Catholic canonical revisions since Vatican II (especially the latest revision of law in the Code of 1983), and therefore must contend with arguments concerning magisterial authority that do not apply in the Anglican context, his fundamental thesis of grounding canon first in theology is relevant to this committee's project: "Since the church is . . . the continuation of the incarnation, we may say that it exists for the sake of redeeming human persons. To understand canon law as having a function in our redemption is to distinguish it sharply from civil law, and to collocate it in a spiritual order which is never purely juridical" (29).

4. The Episcopal Church, *The Book of Common Prayer and Administration of the Sacraments and Other Rites and Ceremonies of the Church: Together with the Psalter or Psalms of David—According to the Use of The Episcopal Church* (New York: Church Hymnal Corp., 1979).

community is perfected and made at one with one another and with God; and at the same time is an earthly creature.

This duality mirrors the mystery of Christ's own incarnation, at once divine and human. The church, as the Body of Christ in the world, is at once divinely ordained, and bound by earthly limitations. The canons, and in particular those canons that govern the relations among persons in community including matters of *professional* conduct and accountability, at their best serve as a bridge between these two dialectical poles of the church's earthly existence. Canons are thus both an expression of God's gracious gift of law to aid human persons in governance that is loving, merciful and just: "Oh, how I love your law! It is my meditation all day long" (Ps 119:97)—and also an expression of the just and peaceful vision of the Church Eternal, toward which the church on earth aspires, and awaits in the final day of God's coming.[5]

As this gift of God, the canons participate in a vision of just and peaceful relationality that dwells at the heart of the church's Trinitarian faith. In the words of the "Virginia Report" of 1997 by the Inter-Anglican Theological

---

5. The Rev. Dr. Francis Bridger of Trinity College, Bristol (also citing Roman Catholic moral theologian Richard Gula), has argued convincingly for the re-appropriation of the term "professional," not in the sense of secular occupation, but as "standing for *(professio)* a set of transcendent values and principles which derive from a theology of vocation," being called as Christians to be "signs and agents of God's love." Francis Bridger, "A Theological Reflection," in *Guidelines for the Professional Conduct of the Clergy,* The Convocations of Canterbury and York, February, 2002, 1–8. Analogies to this eschatological approach can be found in both Catholic and Lutheran understandings. Orsy, op. cit., writes: "On the level of ideals the next revision of canon law should begin by examining all our institutions, one by one, in order to determine the theological values which the law must uphold and serve. Then it should assess how far the existing norms measure up to the theological demands. If they do not, they should be duly amended. Obviously a dream; although this was the historical process by which our laws were conceived and established in the first place. On the level of our fallen world (by which I mean a world affected by original sin and its consequences) we can take many small steps toward the ideal. By upholding the organic relationship between theological concepts and practical norms, we can in our daily work defend and promote the integrity of the church. By integrity I mean an internal harmony and unity, where all norms of action flow from a vision. In this, obviously, we shall never achieve perfection; it ought to be an on-going process" (117–18). In Lutheran theology, this mirrors Luther's emphasis on the distinction between law and Gospel, and the later doctrine, derived from Melanchthon, known as the "two kingdoms doctrine," in which there is a recognition that in the kingdom on earth, governed by law, human agents are divinely ordained to approximate divine justice, but the fullness of salvation and grace is only reached in the heavenly kingdom, when in the fullness of time God redeems all creation through the lovingkindness of God's grace.

and Doctrinal Commission in response to a call from the Lambeth Conference of 1988:[6]

> The unity of the Anglican Communion derives from the unity given in the triune God, whose inner personal and relational nature is communion. This is our center. This mystery of God's life calls us to communion in visible form. This is why the Church is called again and again to review and reform the structures of its life together so that they nurture and enable the life of communion in God and serve God's mission in the world.

In practice, this means that the canons must be congruent with the church's moral theology.[7] As Episcopalians and members of the Anglican communion, the church's moral consensus is not derived only from magisterial authority, and is not implemented through a top-down hierarchy. We draw, rather, on the oft cited "tricycle" of scripture, tradition, and reason/experience, which had its classical sixteenth-century articulation at the time of the Elizabethan Settlement in the writings of Richard Hooker, and has been a continuing theme in the works of other Anglican divines throughout the centuries.[8]

*Scripture* (the large wheel of the tricycle), as in all Protestant traditions, is primary. Rich in general guidelines for Christian community and the moral life of the baptized, Scripture grounds the community of faith both in Christ's teachings, rooted in turn in the Jewish commandment of love of God and neighbor, and in the example of Christ's own *kenosis*, his freely self-giving love (Phil 2:6–7). Scripture provides general rubrics for the conduct of Christian community as well, especially in the Epistles, e.g., to seek the fruits of the Spirit: love, joy, peace, patience, kindness, goodness, faithfulness, gentleness, and self-control (Gal 5:22–23).

Scripture is often mute or contradictory, however, when it comes to the specific ways in which particular communities bound by their own chronological, cultural, racial, ethnic, and other aspects of social location, work out the time and context bound problems and conflicts that arise in the course of living out their particular vocations.

Canons, therefore, must also draw on both *tradition* and *God-given reason and experience* to interpret Scripture contextually for the sake of the church's sense of vocation in its own unique time and social location.

---

6. Robert Eames, "The Report of the Inter-Anglican Theological and Doctrinal Commission," Anglican Consultative Council, 1997, 1.11.

7. Orsy, op. cit., 119ff.

8. Richard Hooker, *The Lawes of Ecclesiastical Polity* (Cambridge: Harvard University Press, 1977–1981).

Tradition is embodied in the history of the church catholic, and the deposit of canon and interpretation that has come down to us through time. The explicit recognition of the importance of culture and context as a dimension of both tradition and reason has emerged in the discourse of Anglican churches worldwide especially in recent decades: "Anglicanism sees reason in the sense of the 'mind' of the culture in which the Church lives and the Gospel is proclaimed, as a legitimate and necessary instrument for the interpretation of God's message in the Scriptures."[9]

Reason, valued in Anglicanism following the long tradition of natural law back to Aristotle and through the Thomist Catholic tradition, is the God-given human ability to interpret and make moral decisions—not only based on rational thought, but also sense, feeling, and experience. In Hooker's words:

> Whatsoever either men on earth, or the Angels of heaven do know, it is as a drop of that unemptiable fountaine of wisdom, which wisdom hath diversely imparted her treasures unto the world. As her waies are of sundry, so her maner of teaching is not merely one and the same. Some things she openeth by the sacred books of Scripture; some things by the glorious works of nature; with some things she inspireth them from above by spiritual influence, in some thinges she leadeth and trayneth them onely by worldly experience and practice. We may not so in any one special kind admire her that we disgrace her in any other, but let all her wayes be according unto their place and degree adored.[10]

Reason and experience also need not be narrowly defined as drawing only on theological discourse narrowly defined as such, but may draw equally and be informed in a mutual dialogical relationship with the secular disciplines of sociology, psychology, law, medicine, and others, in a relationship of "critical correlation."[11] In fact, following Hooker, Anglicans in our incarnational approach find that the Holy Spirit can speak to us freely through the signs and practices of our embodied contemporary world, and

---

9. Eames, op. cit., 3.10.

10. Hooker, *Lawes*, II.1.4. "Hooker based his insistence on the role of reason in church polity on the idea of reasonable law, which he took to be manifest in the workings of God and the various orders of creation." A.S. McGrade, "Reason," in Stephen Sykes and John Booty, eds. *The Study of Anglicanism* (Minneapolis: Fortress, 1998) 108.

11. This concept of correlation is found first in the work of Paul Tillich, *Systematic Theology*, I (Chicago: University of Chicago Press, 1951) 18–28, and elaborated as a discipline of mutual dialogue in David Tracy, *Blessed Rage for Order: The New Pluralism in Theology* (New York: Seabury, 1975) esp. 45ff.

the best recorded wisdom of thoughtful people from a variety of traditions, cultures, and disciplines. "The Word of God is addressed to the Church as it is part of the world."[12]

The following therefore assumes that canon law is not a static body of legislation and ecclesiastical jurisprudence which is changed in order to "perfect" it, but, rather, a living, breathing, dynamic document that represents the best wisdom of God's people in a particular time and place, *"leges ecclesiae semper reformandae,"*[13] even as the church on earth is *semper reformanda*. As Hooker asserted, Christ has not forbidden change: "Christ hath not deprived his church so far of all liberty in making orders and laws for itself."[14]

To summarize, then, if the canons are to be understood as an incarnational, dynamic gift of God, they may even further be understood sacramentally, as a means of grace by which the visible church is given the power to order its common life for holy purpose—to promote human communion that reflects as closely as is humanly possible the unity and relationality of God.

What form of governance, and in particular, ecclesiastical discipline, then, does our present time and context call forth from us, as the Protestant Episcopal Church in America in the first decade of the twenty-first century? Different eras in church history have focused on different aspects of ecclesiology and clerical conduct. Most recently, much of the focus has been on uncovering formerly hidden practices surrounding clergy sexual misconduct, on disputes over human sexuality more generally, and concerns about the boundaries of intra-Anglican church collegiality and intrusions between ecclesiastical jurisdictions. In addition, financial misconduct, other forms of abuse of authority, and refusals of local Episcopal oversight have harmed the church's trust and unity.[15]

In particular, our North American experience in just the last decade has included a growing, painful awareness of sexual abuse and exploitation

12. Eames, op. cit., 3.10.
13. Orsy, p. 18.
14. Hooker, *Lawes*, III.11.13.

15. More subtle forms of unethical practices by clergy that often do not rise to the level of ecclesiastical discipline have also caused harm to the church's trust and unity. These involve breaches in such areas as truth-telling, use of discretionary funds, confidentiality, plagiarism, authority in teaching and preaching, representation of credentials, role in society, representation of personal piety, ignoring the power inherent in the clergy role and the related requirement of non-maleficence, the need to be liked, and ministering only to certain groups or persons, outlined by Phillip Cato in "Beyond Sex: A Broader Look at Clergy Ethics," *Leaven: A Journal of the National Network of Episcopal Clergy Association*, Oct. Nov. 2002, 1ff.

in the home, in public institutions, and in the church. Sexual misconduct, including sexual harassment, abuse, and exploitation, have been identified in recent years as constituting a serious problem affecting the integrity of the ministry, and the capacity of the church to be a safe and just place for all people. Research studies have estimated that up to 20% or more of clergy have violated sexual boundaries with parishioners (a higher percentage than any other professional group).[16] This problem, once cloaked in secrecy, is now being addressed in healthy ways by our church denominations and by individuals and groups within the church who are committed to promoting positive professional sexual ethics and models of self-care, boundaries and wellness among church workers. However, while important strides have been made to address this issue, serious problems persist, as demonstrated by the recent vividly painful disclosures of the Roman Catholic Church, and continuing devastating cases of misconduct in our own communion.

The ultimate goal of the canons in such a context, it seems to me, must be directed toward the *restoration of right relation in community*, through truth telling, healing of the wounds in this part of the Body of Christ, and reconciliation—not in the sense of cheap or premature forgiveness, but in the sense of the whole community, the whole church.[17] It is important to note that such reconciliation is not an end-in-itself. The goal of reconciliation is not solipsistic, but missional. As I have written in *The Cry of Tamar*, to "reconcile" translates the Greek words *apokatallatto, katallasso/katallage*, and *diallattomai*, all of which mean a thorough change:

---

16. A range of 12–20.7% can be extrapolated from a *Christianity Today* survey, reported in "How Common is Pastoral Indiscretion?" *Leadership* (Winter 1988) 1. [Online at https://www.christianitytoday.com/pastors/1988/winter/88l1012.html.] A doctoral study at Fuller Seminary shows fully 38.6% of respondents having had sexual contact with a parishioner. Richard Allen Blackmon, "The Hazards of the Ministry" (unpublished Ph.D. dissertation, Fuller Seminary, 1984). In my own most recent research among pastoral counselors and clinical social workers, respondents estimated a mean prevalence of sexual misconduct of 14.5% among pastoral counselors; and 82% had heard a client report of a clergyperson crossing a sexual boundary with him or her, with a mean of over four incidents told to each therapist. Cooper-White, "The Use of the Self in Psychotherapy: A Comparative Study of Pastoral Counselors and Clinical Social Workers," *American Journal of Pastoral Counseling* 4/4 (2001) 14.

17. I have written more extensively about this distinction between individual forgiveness and reconciliation as a communal activity in the Conclusion to *The Cry of Tamar: Violence against Women and the Church's Response* (Minneapolis: Fortress, 2nd ed. 2012) 251–61 (see esp., 260–61). The theological method of *The Cry of Tamar* is one of critical correlation, in which social and psychological knowledge and in particular the insights of traumatology are brought into fruitful engagement with constructive ethical and theological reflection.

> To be reconciled is to be changed through and through. This is the precise meaning of the passage in Paul's second letter to the church in Corinth, entreating Christians to be ambassadors for Christ's reconciling love for the world, and themselves to be reconciled to God. (2 Cor. 5:18–19). It is in this sense of thoroughgoing change that Paul promises unity and peace between Jew and Greek (Eph. 2:14–16), humanity and God (Rom. 5:10; Col. 1:19–23). We are called by the gospel to *restore right relation*,[18] not just between individual men and women, and not in the sense of premature or cheap forgiveness, but in the sense of the whole community, the whole church. We are called by baptism to be *re-concilers*, that is, restorers of the *concilium*—the whole community of God, called and blessed as God's children, and equally precious in God's sight.[19]

This, then, empowers the church in turn for its mission-to proclaim and live out the Good News of justice, peace, and reconciliation in the wider world.

How do we do this? I would propose that, if the canons are to provide us with a bridge between the needs of the earthly church for healing and justice, and the vision of the Church Eternal to live into the re-establishment of right relation that is finally the Realm of God, they must then address at least four areas of both moral theology (vision) and ecclesiastical polity *(praxis)*: 1) safety; 2) truth-telling; 3) healing; and 4) reconciliation.

## Safety

In all areas of discipline, the most fundamental ethical/theological principle is one of safety. In secular ethics, particularly the ethics of allied helping and healing professions, this is made plain in the classical dictum: *Primum non nocere*—first do no harm. But in the church, again, we are guided not only by the negative avoidance of evil, but the positive vocation to love and justice. In our Baptismal Covenant, we are called to "seek and serve Christ in all persons, loving our neighbor as ourselves," and to "strive for justice and peace among all people, and respect the dignity and freedom of every human being." (*BCP*, p. 305). Safety within the church, paradoxically, is the necessary pre-condition for the missional goal of taking risks for the

---

18. Carter Heyward has written extensively about the call to right relation, with perhaps the most systematic elaboration in her first book, *The Redemption of God: A Theology of Mutual Relation* (Lanham, MD: University Press of America, 1982).

19. Cooper-White, *The Cry of Tamar*, 2nd ed., 261–62.

Gospel. Risks taken for the sake of the Gospel are never imposed or coerced. Safety within the Body of Christ is what nurtures and empowers Christians to take up the cross, not submitting passively to involuntary suffering, but having the courage to confront evil and injustice as they encounter it in both the church and the wider world.[20]

Sanctuary is at the heart of Christian ecclesiological tradition:

> Throughout history, the Church has been understood to be a 'sanctuary,' a place of safety for all who enter. This has been profoundly demonstrated in times of strife, war, plague, tragedy, oppression, and chaos. The Church with all its ministers is both sign and symbol of the Divine Reality of Christ's compassion and justice.[21]

This raises an important definitional question: *Who constitute the ministers of the church, who, for the purpose of canon law are accountable to canonical discipline?* As stated above, our catechism makes explicit that the ministers of the church are comprised of *all* the baptized, "lay persons, bishops, priests and deacons," with the laity in first place (*BCP*, p. 855). While Paul makes it clear that there is a variety of gifts and forms of service which are all interdependent in the Body of Christ (Rom 12:3-8; 1 Cor 12:4-11, 27-31), there is an over-arching call to right relation that is incumbent upon all baptized Christians as the "priesthood of all believers." The canons should offer a process that recognizes the responsibilities and accountability of the ministry of the baptized in our relations with one another at all levels of the church's earthly organization (in practical terms, encompassing both "paid" and "volunteer" workers). This means guidelines not only for ethical, non-exploitative behavior by all Christians toward those whom we serve in our

---

20. Feminist theologians have rightly challenged a reading of the cross as a justification for involuntary suffering by the oppressed and a glorification of suffering as "divine child abuse." E.g., Joanne Carlson Brown and Rebecca Parker, "For God So Loved the World?" in Joanne Carlson Brown and Carole Bohn, eds., *Christianity, Patriarchy and Abuse* (New York: Pilgrim, 1989) 26; and Rita Nakashima Brock, "And a Little Child Will Lead Us: Christology and Child Abuse," in *Christianity, Patriarchy and Abuse*, 42–61. In my view, Christ's surrender to the cross is not redemptive because of his suffering, which is never redemptive in itself, but rather because of his choice to remain faithful even in the face of death, against the oppressive powers and principalities of his day. (*The Cry of Tamar*, 2nd ed., 53) God does not cause suffering, but rather, as Latin American Liberation theologians have powerfully asserted, God stands in solidarity with those who suffer. E.g., Jon Sobrino, *Christology at the Crossroads* (Maryknoll, NY: Orbis, 1978); and Jon Sobrino and Juan Hernandez Pico, *Theology of Christian Solidarity*, trans. P. Berryman (Maryknoll, NY: Orbis, 1985). See also Sally B. Purvis, *The Power of the Cross: Foundations for a Christian Feminist Ethic of Community* (Nashville: Abingdon, 1993).

21. Episcopal Diocese of Chicago, *Keeping God's People Safe*, 5.

communities (again, the negative imperative), but for the faithful living out of our baptismal call to love and justice, and means to call one another to account when we fall short. In the words of the Diocese of Virginia,

> Christians have a high calling. Christ invites and empowers us to live out our lives in the love he shows us. Our identity as Christians is both gift and demand. Promised fullness of life, we are called to the self-giving of the cross, to faithfulness, compassion and justice. Our faith is framed between acknowledgement of our arrogance, sinfulness and brokenness, and commitment to the renewal of human life through dying to self. That renewal encompasses "the healing, wholeness and liberation promised by God's grace to every facet of human life" which is the task of ministry.[22]

While ordained clergy are not to be understood, then, as having a "higher" calling, they have historically been understood as "set apart" for specialized service to the church and the world. This is true across a spectrum of understandings of ordination within the Anglican tradition, from the more Catholic or sacramental understanding of ordination as an "indelible mark" (Hooker's view)[23] or ontological status, to the more Protestant or functional understanding of ordination as a vocation or profession with a unique authority and status within the church.[24] This is equally true across the spectrum of ordained ministries of deacons, priests, and bishops, and therefore the canons should reflect a parallelism in disciplinary processes among all three Holy Orders.

Ordained clergy in all three Holy Orders are called to particular forms of equipping ministry, whether service (*diakonia*), sacramental leadership (*presbyteros*), or oversight (*episkope*). Such ministry is set apart always for the sake of others, by preaching the Word, administering the Sacraments "to equip the saints for the work of ministry, for building up the body of Christ." (Eph 4:12) This vowed responsibility creates an asymmetry of power and authority that is at once both spiritual and temporal in the involvement of clergy with the lives of those whom they serve (both in the church and the

---

22. Diocese of Virginia, "Theological Basis: For All Christians," in *Policy and Procedures on Sexual Misconduct in Pastoral Care*, November, 1998, p. I: http://www.thediocese.net/Diocese/cpsm/policies.htm, or from The Mayo Memorial Church House of the Diocese of Virginia, 110 W. Franklin St., Richmond, VA 23220-5095.

23. Hooker, *Lawes*, V.1.

24. For a discussion of this question, see Owen Thomas, "Ministry: Is There a Theological Difference between a Lay Person and an Ordained Person?" in *Theological Questions: Analysis and Argument* (Wilton, CT: Morehouse-Barlow, 1983) 119–23. See also Timothy Sedgwick, *The Making of Ministry* (Cambridge, MA: Cowley, 1993).

wider community).²⁵ In both biblical and traditional sources, this asymmetry has been recognized in the form of a particular responsibility, as stated in the ordinal of the 1979 *BCP*, "to do your best to pattern your life in accordance with the teachings of Christ, so that you may be a wholesome example to your people" (*BCP*, 532), and that candidates for both the diaconate and the priesthood must be certified before ordination as having a "manner of life . . . suitable to the exercise of this ministry." (*BCP*, 526, 538).²⁶ In the words of the pastoral epistles: "Train yourself in godliness, for while physical training is of some value, godliness is valuable in every way" (2 Tim 3:7b–8a).

## (1) Truth-telling

*"For nothing is hidden that will not be disclosed, nor is anything secret that will not become known and come to light. Then pay attention to how you listen."* (Luke 8:17–18a). The canons should offer an ecclesiastical process that creates a safe space for disclosure of the truth, and strives to eliminate a climate of toxic secrecy and shame, for victims in cases of personal harm, and for those accused of offending, alike. Such processes should not threaten victims with re-traumatization by forcing disclosures for which they are not sufficiently healed or encounters with (alleged or admitted) offenders.

25. Roman Paur, OSB, Executive Director of the Interfaith Sexual Trauma Institute, has written: "Clergy and religious frequently, if not typically, are quite unaware of their relational 'power,' and often do not appreciate how they are perceived by the faithful within their congregations or, for that matter, by people at large. They can express genuine surprise and consider themselves even powerless and ineffective toward achieving their pastoral goals. Such lack of awareness can jeopardize relational integrity by minimizing appropriate differences in wanting to be perceived as just another guy or crossing lines of professional propriety with indifference or distortions of transference and countertransference. Power is more a matter of how clergy are perceived by others than how they perceive themselves. In any case it is imperative that clergy be clear about who they are in their various roles and the relational requirements those roles impose on them. Power derived from the authority of pastoral appointment is rooted in the co-unity of the faithful and in the service of their safety, freedom, and growth." In "Recommendations of the Executive Director: The Humanity of Belief Systems, Twelve Critical Issues," Interfaith Sexual Trauma Institute website: http://www.csbsju.edu/isti/reco=endations/english/dir rec.htm/.

26. Cranmer's words from the ordinal in the first *Book of Common Prayer* carried even more solemn warning: "Have always printed in your remembrance, how great a treasure is committed to your charge. For they are the sheep of Christ, which he bought with his death, and for whom he shed his blood. The Church and Congregation whom you must serve, is his Spouse, and his body. And if it shall chance the same Church, or any Member thereof to take any hurt or hindrance by reason of your negligence, ye know the greatness of the fault, and also the horrible punishment which will ensue."

Similarly, processes should not confuse assignment of responsibility with shaming offenders. In the words of one policy from another communion, "A church that balances the needs of individuals with the comfort and admonition of a caring community will be in a better position to exercise discipline without harshness or resentment. The sharing of burdens and failures can be such a regular part of church life that correction and comfort from others will be expected. The speaking of truth in a spirit of love and self-control helps build a climate that counters the worldly practice of concealment and defense. If a congregation (church body/structure) is accustomed to confrontation alongside forgiveness and acceptance, the secular practices of concealment and contempt will be given up."[27]

Another perhaps more distinctly Anglican way of thinking about this truth telling might be to connect it sacramentally to the Eucharist, as *anamnesis*. The central feature of the Eucharist itself is the *anamnesis*, the recalling of God's saving acts in history and in the lives of believer. In the words of liturgy scholar Marion Hatchett, "Anamnesis is the antithesis of amnesia. A person with amnesia has lost identity and purpose. To know who you are, to whom you belong, and where you are headed, you must remember."[28] Especially in situations of trauma, the importance of remembering and telling are crucial for healing of both individuals and communities. The participation of the community as witnesses to the truth is a crucial element in healing and justice. As Elie Wiesel has written, "Let us remember: What hurts the victim most is not the cruelty of the oppressor, but the silence of the bystander."[29] Those not directly involved in the traumatic events have an equally important role to play in the work of truth-telling and remembering

---

27. New York Conference, United Church of Christ, Syracuse, NY, 1990, "Guidelines for Responding to Allegations of Professional Misconduct by Authorized Ministers..." also citing H. Newton Malony, Thomas L. Needham and Samuel Southard (Eds)., *Clergy Malpractice* (Philadelphia: Westminster, 1986) 86–87, reprinted in M. Fortune et al., eds., *Clergy Misconduct: Sexual Abuse in the Ministerial Relationship: Workshop Manual*, 1992 (Seattle: Center for the Prevention of Sexual and Domestic Violence, 1914 N. 34lli St. Ste. 105, Seattle, WA 98103), Appendix I, p. 11.

28. Marion J. Hatchett, *Commentary on the American Prayer Book* (New York: Seabury, 1981) 366. For a discussion of *anamnesis* in the context of Anglican views on healing and suffering, see also David H. Smith, *Health and Medicine in the Anglican Tradition* (New York: Crossroad, 1986) 21ff. Smith is an Episcopal medical ethicist, Professor of Religious Studies at Indiana University, Bloomington, and Director of the Poynter Center for the Study of Ethics and American Institutions.

29. Themes of remembering, knowing vs. not-knowing, and breaking silence are pervasive in the writings of Holocaust survivor Elie Wiesel, e.g., "We Must Remember," in Irving Abrahamson, ed., *Against Silence: The Voice and Vision of Elie Wiesel* (New York: Holocaust Library, 1985) 3:192–3; and "The Call to Remember," in Abrahamson, *Against Silence*, 1:112–14.

The Greek word for witness is *martys* (martyr). The work of faithful listening and witnessing is, indeed, wrenching and sacrificial. The canons must continue to offer a process to support the community's willingness to know painful truths in the face of prevailing cultural denial.[30]

Given the continued prevailing disbelief about abuse (which has not suddenly gone away in the wake of two decades of disclosures) and the natural tendency toward minimization and denial,[31] the church must not retrench on mechanisms designed to maximize and protect a fair hearing of the most vulnerable, i.e., as in the "reasonable woman standard" established in secular law,[32] those alleging abuse, and more generally, the laity, women, persons of color, and children, and other groups who have experienced systematic and institutional oppression both in the secular society and in the church.[33] Grounded in Christ's own teachings that the last shall be first, the canons need to reflect a "preferential option" for the vulnerable, in order to apply the necessary counter-cultural strength needed to resist the prevailing preferential option in society for those traditionally endowed with institutional power and cultural privilege. This does not mean denial of due process, but does call for preserving canonical safeguards and protections that take into consideration the courage required for victims to come forward with complaints, their fear of disbelief, ostracism, retaliation, even spiritual harm[34] and the prevailing societal tendency toward denial.

Processes should also be refined in order to

---

30. For more on the importance of a community of witnesses and a social context that values justice, see Judith Herman, *Trauma and Recovery* (New York: Basic Books, 1992) 8–9.

31. For more on the psychological mechanism of denial as a group phenomenon in the face of humancaused trauma, see Judith Herman, *Trauma and Recovery*, 8–9; Cooper-White, *The Cry of Tamar*, 2nd ed., viii–ix.

32. In the landmark case Ellison v. Brady (U.S. Court of Appeals, 9th Circuit, No. 89-15248, 1991, 878ff), two nominally conservative, male federal appellate court judges established the "reasonable woman" standard, with the following historic statement: "We believe that in evaluating the severity and pervasiveness of sexual harassment we should focus on the perspective of the victim. If we only examined whether a reasonable *person* would engage in allegedly harassing conduct, we would run the risk of reinforcing the prevailing level of discrimination. Harassers could continue to harass merely because a particular discriminatory practice was common, and victims of harassment would have no remedy." A more lengthy excerpt and discussion is given in Cooper-White, *The Cry of Tamar*, 93.

33. For a list of basic principles necessary to safeguard victims and prevent further harm, see Cooper-White, *The Cry of Tamar*, 2nd ed., 143–48.

34. For survivor testimonies and a discussion of the spiritual damage of clergy sexual misconduct, see Cooper-White, "Soul Stealing: Power Relations in Pastoral Sexual Abuse," *The Christian Century*, February 20, 1991, 196–99; and Cooper-White, *The Cry of Tamar*, 2nd ed., 149–50.

a. assist those who (in a very small minority of painful cases)[35] are falsely accused in being restored to their community without stigma, and

b. assist those against whom complaints are founded to own their responsibility for the impact of their behaviors and to take appropriate steps toward both healing and restitution. Canons should offer mechanisms by which the church can rightfully enforce appropriate consequences aimed toward the protection of potential future victims and the safety of the community, without shaming the offender or implying a level of personal or spiritual condemnation that is not within the purview of humanity to impose.

Existing canons have too often focused only on individual clergy and complainants, however. Canons should further offer a process by which the *full community* also takes responsibility for systemic sources of abuse, and in specific instances, for corporate responsibility via silence, or even unwitting collusion, with abusive dynamics, patterns, and behaviors on the part of clergy and other church leaders. While confidentiality and safety must take first precedence, the effort of any ecclesiastical process should always be to help safely move all affected parties- not only victims and offenders, but secondary victims such as family members, friends, and ultimately the whole congregation and wider community—toward greater transparency, honesty, and as appropriate, ownership of responsibility for the next steps toward healing and restoration of trust, justice and safety.

This greater accountability of the wider community may further be understood as a call to every ecclesiastical level, from national church, to province, to diocese, to local parish and mission. In the words of Roman Paur, churches must confront an underlying "ecclesial culture of abuse: The fundamental challenge of religious leaders across faith systems is to examine how abuse of power through the sexual misconduct of clerics is reinforced by their interpretive documents and traditions. Such an examination is formidable because it goes to the core of structural and institutional identity as evolved over time, claims on originating sources, understanding of ordained and lay leadership, and mandates of mission and purpose."[36]

---

35. See "The Clergy Nightmare: False Allegations," in Cooper-White, *The Cry of Tamar*, 2nd ed., 162–63.

36. Paur, "Recommendations of the Executive Director," 1.

## (2) Healing

The word healing corresponds with the Teutonic root word *haelen/helen*, linking it with "health" and "wholeness." The Latin parallel is *salvare*, from which we get both "salve" and "salvation." Thus, healing and salvation belong together.[37] For most Anglicans, salvation is ultimately understood as the reconciliation between humanity and God, a healing or re-whole-ing of humanity's original turning away from the inherent desire for God. Sin is therefore understood most deeply as a condition of alienation,[38] of separation, or isolation, both from God and from others in creation. For Hooker, *participation* was a central theological theme.[39] Baptism is the sacrament of incorporation into the Body of Christ, the initiation into full participation which is then renewed in the sacrament of Holy Communion. The "Real Presence" of Christ in the Eucharist was not for Hooker a technical change in the elements of bread and wine themselves, but rather, the transforming presence of Christ in the hearts of the believers who receive them, through "our participation of his body and blood"[40]—echoing Cranmer's eucharistic prayer, "that we may be made one body with him, that he may dwell in us, and we in him" (*BCP*, 336).[41]

While only God can bring about the ultimate salvation of reconciliation between humanity and God's own self, the church through its long tradition of "cure of souls" has worked in more humble ways toward healing and wholeness for individuals within their particular communities. The traditional functions of pastoral care have always involved healing, sustaining, guiding, and reconciling,[42] and more recently have also been understood to include nurturing, empowering, and liberating.[43] If sin is the ultimate condition of alienation, then human illness, injury and hunger may also be understood not merely as wounds to be physically treated, or problems

---

37. For a more detailed discussion of pastoral understandings of healing, see Larry Kent Graham, "Healing," in Rodney J. Hunter, ed., *Dictionary of Pastoral Care and Counseling* (Nashville: Abingdon, 1990) 497–501.

38. John Macquarrie, *Principles of Christian Theology*, 2nd ed. (New York: Scribner's, 1977) 71–72.

39. Hooker, *Lawes*, V.57.

40. Hooker, *Lawes*, V.67.5.

41. Cf., Hooker's statement, "that mutual inward hold which Christ hath of us and we of him, in such sort that each possesses the other by way of special interest, property or inherent copulation" (*Lawes*, V.56.1).

42. William Clebsch and Charles Jaekle, *Pastoral Care in Historical Perspective* (Englewood Cliffs, NJ: Prentice Hall, 1964).

43. Carroll Watkins Ali, *Survival and Liberation: Pastoral Theology in African American Context* (St. Louis: Chalice, 1999) 9.

to be fixed, but rather as manifestations of alienation and isolation to be healed, i.e., "re-wholed." Examples in the Gospels of Jesus' own healing ministry frequently addressed not only an individual's need for physical healing, but restored that person to community.

The healing that is facilitated through canonical processes will not, and possibly should not, take away the realities of pain and injury. But the memory and experience of that injury can be transformed, by God's grace, through processes that both honor the truth, and restore wounded individuals to community. Episcopal ethicist David H. Smith has written, "The salvation that is made possible by the incarnation does not fundamentally consist of bringing suffering to an end. Rather, salvation involves God's participation in suffering, to establish community between suffering humankind and himself. Salvation does not mean an end to suffering; it means an end to *isolated* suffering."[44] Perhaps paradoxically, experience has shown that those ecclesiastical processes that do not rush to cover over truth or prematurely seek an end to pain, usually result—over time—in more lasting and profound healing from pain and suffering for all involved. The truth-telling involved is also, in and of itself, one crucial dimension of justice. Truth-telling, healing and reconciliation are all intimately intertwined with justice.

Some might want to argue for a separate category at this point, entitled "Justice." While I agree with others who have written extensively on the healing of the trauma of exploitation and misconduct by church leaders, that there can be no complete healing without justice,[45] I have also come to believe that there is a false dichotomy between the two. This begins with the error of separating God's own love from God's judgment.

God's judgment is a loving word. As Phillip Bennett has written, "How can we reconcile God's love with God's judgment? The most satisfying answer I have found is that God's judgment is God's love, in its penetrating, unremitting power. God's judgment is never divorced from God's love; it is not some angry part of God which is split off from God's mercy and gentleness. Instead, God's judgment is the way we experience pure and constant love which sees and knows us to our core . . . our layers of self-deception and avoidance of intimacy must be unwound until love can touch us to our core."[46]

---

44. Smith, *Health and Medicine in the Anglican Tradition*, 8.

45. For a thoughtful discussion of the relationship between justice and mercy and the importance of remediating injustice as part of the healing process, see Marie Fortune, *Is Nothing Sacred?: When Sex Invades the Pastoral Relationship* (San Francisco: Harper & Row, 1989) 108–29.

46. Phillip Bennett, *Let Yourself Be Loved*, (New York: Paulist, 1997) 25. Bennett is an Episcopal priest in the Diocese of Pennsylvania, spiritual director and psychoanalyst.

While all judgment ultimately belongs to God, the church's discipline should be a mirror of that all-knowing, all-compassionate loving judgment of God. The healing functions of pastoral care have often been considered incompatible with justice. However, we are enjoined to do both together: "What does the Lord require of you but to do justice, and to love kindness, and to walk humbly with your God?" (Mic 6:8). The canons offer an opportunity to effect both in a process that integrates healing mercy with appropriate discipline. The canons should facilitate a process in which the very process of truth telling itself, this anamnesis, is so safely and compassionately facilitated that it has the potential to bring all parties alike to their knees, not in shame, but in awe of the mystery of being so truly and deeply known. In such a process, consequences and responsibility may come to be experienced by offenders not as punishment, but as part of the healing process itself, a means by which those who have caused injury can begin a process of repentance in its true sense, re-turning to align oneself again with God's will. Note that this is not the same as relieving offenders of consequences for past behavior, nor does it assume reinstatement to the office and practice of ordained ministry, because the safety of the whole community must take priority over the privilege of clergy. But this orientation to discipline as healing recognizes the intrinsic human worth and dignity of all participants in any ecclesiastical process, including those who have caused great harm.

Much has already been written and need not be duplicated here about the specific ways in which healing can best be effected for victims, offenders, family members, and congregations, particularly in cases of sexual and/or financial misconduct where clergy misconduct has caused personal injury.[47]

---

[See also 2nd rev. ed., 2015—PCW 2018]

47. For example, for resources on healing for victims, see, e.g., Cooper-White, *The Cry of Tamar*, 163–65 and 228–50. Re: healing for offenders, see Cooper-White, *The Cry of Tamar*, 2nd ed., 158–65, ; Gary Schoener et al., "The Betrayal of the Pastoral Relationship," "Sexual Exploitation by Clergy," and "Intervention," Ch's. 9, 20 and 32 in *Psychotherapists' Sexual Involvement with Clients: Intervention and Prevention*, 1990 (Walk-In Counseling Center, 2421 Chicago Ave. So., Minneapolis, MN 55404); some useful considerations of treatment and institutional responses are also found in Glen O. Gabbard, "Sexual misconduct," *Annual Review of Psychiatry*, 1994, 433–56; and Gabbard and Eva P. Lester, *Boundaries and Boundary Violations in Psychoanalysis*, (Washington, DC: American Psychiatric Press, 1995) 87–121 and 175–196. For resources for congregational healing, see Larry Kent Graham, "Healing the Congregation," *MCS Conciliation Quarterly* (Spring, 1991) 2–4, 15; Chilton Knudsen, "Trauma Debriefing: A Congregational Model," *MCS Conciliation Quarterly* (Spring, 1991) 12–13; Nancy Myer Hopkins, "Symbolic Church Fights: The Hidden Agenda When Clerical Trust Has Been Betrayed," *Congregations: The Alban Journal* (May/June, 1993) 15–18; and Hopkins and Mark Laaser, eds., *Restoring the Soul of a Church: Healing Congregations*

The canons should continue to make these distinctions. In brief: victims require intensive healing in the realm of treatment for post-traumatic stress. Offenders require long-term healing to address issues of narcissistic wounding, together with appropriate containment. Family members of both victims and offenders often require assistance in the form of family therapy. The community also requires healing in the form of traumatic debriefing and the normalization of a wide variety of reactions and feelings.

Further, it is absolutely necessary for discipline to be seen as a part of pastoral care. Discipline and consolation, reformation and reconciliation, fellowship and guidance are all part of the practice of discipline. It is difficult to bring all these elements to bear in each and every case of misconduct, but it is also clear that we have a greater problem when any of these elements are missing."[48]

## (3) Reconciliation

The final purpose of the canons is to establish processes by which conditions are created in which God can bring about reconciliation in the wounded community, so that the church is freed and strengthened for mission in the world. I am defining "reconciliation" in the biblical sense of thoroughgoing change or transformation described above. The marks of such reconciliation would include a felt sense of restoration of safety, trust, and justice—all precursors to a communal praxis of *agapic* love that is "unstuck," spontaneous, free and fruitful. Reconciliation is, ultimately, the work of the Holy Spirit, not the earthly church or its agents. However, in the sense described above in which canons offer a bridge between the earthly church and the Church Eternal, the canons can help facilitate the conditions in which this work of the Spirit can occur.

Furthermore, reconciliation must be understood a *process*, not an event. The canons can offer a spacious process in which the ongoing support for both healing and ownership of responsibility can be given the time they need, with enough flexibility to recognize that timelines for healing will vary from individual to individual, parish to parish, and diocese to diocese.

---

*Wounded by Clergy Sexual Misconduct* (Collegeville, MN: Alban Institute and Interfaith Sexual Trauma Institute, 1995). For an overview from a systems perspective, see also Candace Benyei, *Understanding Clergy Misconduct in Religious Systems* (New York: Haworth Pastoral Press, 1998).

48. New York Conference, United Church of Christ, Syracuse, NY, 1990, "Guidelines," 14.

The ultimate goal of reconciliation and restoration of the community is not an end in itself, and does not stop at the goal of attempting to satisfy immediately affected individuals or groups, but is finally always directed toward the restoration of mission.

Mission is disabled by fractures in trust and safety. Reconciliation is not only meant to reinstate good feeling among believers, although this is a welcome outcome. In its fullest sense, reconciliation, transformation, enables the community to move again from a preoccupation with internal concerns to an outward focus, even evangelism, bringing once again the good news *(evangelio)* of God's undying compassion, passionate mercy, love and justice to the rest of the world.

## Conclusion

Finally, all canons must be grounded in an *imago Dei*.[49] The canons of the church help us in our earthly pilgrimage to create right relation. Right relation depends not solely upon rules for behavior, or categories of virtues that can enhance civility (as in secular ethics), but more fundamentally upon an understanding of our identity as children of God—to know who we are, as human beings created in the image and likeness of God. I believe a Trinitarian understanding of God is most helpful in underpinning all our relational practices,[50] including those guided by canonical process, because in the Trinity, we comprehend God as Being-in-Relation in God's own essence. Taking the Rublev icon of the Trinity as her exemplar, Elizabeth Johnson has written about a trinitarian image of God as fluid, multiple, and profoundly relational. Johnson finds support for this idea in Aquinas: "relation really existing in God is really the same as His essence, and only differs in intelligibility. In God relation and essence do not differ from each other but are one in the same."[51]

Quoting Catherine LaCugna, "To be God is to-be-relationally."[52] Johnson concludes with the following Johannine-inspired statement, which perhaps offers us a summary of the theology that should undergird all efforts at canonical revision:

49. Orsy, 29–30. While Orsy makes this assertion, he does not go further in proposing a specific *imago Dei*.

50. Cooper-White, "Higher Powers and Infernal Regions," *Pastoral Psychology* 50/5 (2002) 319–43. [See more recently Cooper-White, "A Relational Understanding of God," Ch. 2 in *Many Voices: Pastoral Psychotherapy in Relational and Theological Perspective* (Minneapolis: Fortress, 2009) 67–94.]

51. Elizabeth Johnson, *She Who Is* (New York: Crossroad, 1994) 227–28.

52. Cited in Johnson, *She Who Is*, 228.

At its most basic the symbol of the Trinity evokes a livingness in God, a dynamic coming and going with the world that points to an inner divine circling around in unimaginable relation. God's relatedness to the world in creating, redeeming, and renewing activity suggests to the Christian mind that God's own being is somehow similarly differentiated. Not an isolated, static, ruling monarch but a relational, dynamic, tripersonal mystery of love—who would not opt for the latter?[53]

Canons, like all human products, are not infallible. I have hoped to show in this paper that they are, nevertheless, gifts of grace from God, and though we have them "in earthen vessels," we are called to continue to discern how God would ask us to shape them anew for our own time and context. If we are faithful in our discernment, our canon revisions may indeed help us to approximate more closely in our church on earth that Realm of human community which is God's *perichoresis*, the divine relational dance of peace and justice, safety and freedom for all people, now, and until the Time to come.

---

53. Johnson, *She Who Is*, 192.

# 7

## Sexual Exploitation and Other Boundary Violations in Pastoral Ministries

2003[1]

THE INCLUSION OF THIS chapter in the third volume of the *Clinical Handbook of Pastoral Counseling* signals an important and healthy shift in awareness in religious institutions surrounding clergy professional sexual ethics and the problem of sexual misconduct. A great leap in awareness has occurred over the course of the last decade, in part prompted by religious institutions' growing commitment to address other forms of domestic and sexual abuse. Clergy violations of sexual boundaries with members of their congregations, once almost universally cloaked in secrecy, denial, or patterns of blaming the victim, are now much more visible as religious institutions have begun to make serious efforts toward policy making, preventative education, screening of candidates for ministry, intervention in reported cases of misconduct, and healing for individuals, families and congregations in the aftermath of abuse. The codes of ethics of the American Association of Pastoral Counselors and the Association for Clinical Pastoral Education both formally prohibit sexual behavior with clients, patients, and students/supervisees.[2] AAPC further prohibits sexual behavior with research sub-

---

1. First published as Chapter 16 in Robert J. Wicks, Richard D. Parsons and Donald Capps, eds., *Clinical Handbook of Pastoral Counseling*, Vol. 3, (Mahwah, NJ: Paulist, 2003) 342–65.

2. AAPC Code of Ethics, 1994, principles IIIG and VC); www.acpe.org. [AAPC is less specific since its reorganization as a non-certifying body. Its Ethics statement now reads, "Establish and maintain appropriate professional relationship boundaries. We will make every effort to be transparent with congregations and other public constituencies about the boundaries we hold." ACPE Standard 101.3 (2016), online at https://www.manula.com/manuals/acpe/acpe-manuals/2016/en/topic/standard-101. —PCW 2018]

jects, and employees other than spouses/domestic partners.[3] Nevertheless, continued attention to the issue of sexual boundary violations by clergy is necessary, in order to build on the pioneering work done in the last decade, and to more fully institutionalize a commitment to making all pastoral ministries and all places of worship harbors of safety for all people.

The high prevalence of clergy sexual misconduct is increasingly being verified by research.[4] Surveys of female ministers, rabbis, church workers, and women congregants have shown rates of experiencing sexual harassment in the religious context ranging from 21 to 77%. Surveys of ministers in a variety of denominations show self-reported percentages of sexual contact ranging from 5.8 to 38.6%. In other studies, 70% of clergy report knowledge of other ministers who have had sexual contact with congregation members. Preliminary results from my own research suggests that as many as 85–90% of pastoral counselors have treated clients bringing reports of sexual exploitation by their clergy.[5] Although sexual boundaries can be violated by both male and female clergy, in both heterosexual and same-sex relationships, experts continue to estimate that the vast preponderance of sexual misconduct (90–95%) is between male clergy and female congregants. As with all child sexual abuse, sexual abuse of children in religious settings is also committed largely by male clergy or congregational leaders.

Pastoral counselors may be called upon to assist in situations of sexual misconduct in several ways: 1) counseling victims of clergy sexual misconduct; 2) counseling clergy who have crossed sexual boundaries with congregation members; 3) couples' and/or family counseling with the families of victims or offenders to deal with the secondary traumatization of family members and the disruptions of family relationships in the aftermath of the misconduct; 4) consulting to congregations in need of healing during and after the disclosure of sexual boundary violations, and to interim clergy and "after-pastors" who are ministering to congregations in the aftermath of misconduct. This chapter is intended to provide a grounding in basic

---

3. ACPE, op. cit., 2016, Standards 101.6, 104.1.

4. Marie Fortune, *Clergy Misconduct: Sexual Abuse in the Ministerial Relationship Workshop Manual*, rev. ed. (Seattle: Center for the Prevention of Sexual and Domestic Violence, 1997). For other resources including DVDs, see online: http://www.faithtrustinstitute.org/resources and https://store.faithtrustinstitute.org/.

5. Pamela Cooper-White, "The Therapist's Use of Self: Countertransference in Pastoral Counseling and Clinical Social Work," unpubl. PhD dissertation, Institute for Clinical Social Work, Chicago, 2001 (ProQuest #3023407); key findings reported in Cooper-White, "The Use of the Self in Psychotherapy: A Comparative Study of Pastoral Counselors and Clinical Social Workers," *American Journal of Pastoral Counseling* 4/4 (2001) 5–35; and summarized in Cooper-White, *Shared Wisdom: Use of the Self in Pastoral Care and Counseling* (Minneapolis: Fortress, 2004) 155–80.

definitional, ethical, and psychological understandings of the dynamics of clergy sexual misconduct with congregation members, and to offer some basic guidelines for counseling in these several situations. Of course, no one pastoral counselor can or should serve all the many persons affected in any given case of misconduct. A collaborative team approach is recommended, in which pastoral counselors, consultants, and judicatory staff may work together as appropriate, respecting the roles, boundaries, and primary accountabilities of each. In every aspect of this work, the safety of past, present and future potential victims, the cessation of harmful behaviors, and the re-establishment of safety and justice must be the first priority. Counselors who plan to specialize in this area, or who find themselves called upon to do this work because of a specific request for help or a referral, can avail themselves of the growing body of literature available on this subject, but they should also seek specialized training and clinical supervision before declaring this as a specific area of competency.

Clergy sexual misconduct has been analyzed from two different but complementary perspectives: 1) ethical analyses, aimed primarily at prevention, appropriate intervention, and justice-making; and 2) psychological or psychodynamic analyses, which provide a deeper understanding of why sexual misconduct occurs, how it typically is enacted, and what prevention and intervention measures are needed to address the deeper impact of misconduct on individuals, families and congregations, and to promote safety in our houses of worship. Both approaches are helpful to pastoral counselors in understanding the complexities of individual cases.

First, some definitions are needed to clarify the various types of clergy sexual misconduct. It should be noted that in actual situations of sexual misconduct, many of these categories overlap or co-exist.

## Definitions

*Sexual harassment* refers to inappropriate sexual language or behavior within the context of an employment, teaching, mentor, or colleague relationships between the persons involved. Sexual harassment, as legally defined by Title VII (Section 703) of the 1964 federal Civil Rights Act, was declared by the Equal Employment Opportunity Commission (EEOC) in 1980 to be a form of sex discrimination that is an unlawful employment practice.[6] As defined by the EEOC, sexual harassment includes "unwelcome sexual advances, re-

---

6. U.S. Equal Employment Opportunity Commission, "Enforcement Guidance," No. N-915–050, online at https://www.eeoc.gov/eeoc/publications/upload/currentissues.pdf/.

quests for sexual favors, and other verbal or physical conduct of a sexual nature when 1) submission to such conduct is made either explicitly or implicitly a term or condition of an individual's employment, 2) submission to or rejection of such conduct by an individual is used as the basis for employment decisions affecting such individual; or 3) such conduct has the purpose or effect of unreasonably interfering with an individual's work performance or creating an intimidating, hostile, or offensive working environment."[7] Case law has further applied these EEOC definitions to educational settings under Title IX of the Education Amendments of 1972.[8]

The first two criteria in the law constitute what is understood as *quid pro quo harassment* (from Latin, meaning "this for that"), in which the employee or student is expected to submit to sexualized behavior in exchange for fair supervision, i.e., continuation of employment, promotion, fair evaluation, grades, or recommendations. The third criterion, which is sometimes more difficult for victims to prove, is called *hostile environment* or *condition of work harassment*, in which a sexualized atmosphere is created that a victim finds difficult to tolerate. Hostile environment harassment is the more common form of harassment because it is more subtle. But it is equally damaging, since it often has the effect of driving a victim away from an economic, educational, or vocational opportunity, and also frequently results in stress-related health problems. If a victim does manage to tolerate the hostile atmosphere, in the interests of keeping her job or educational situation, this often is taken (erroneously) as proof of her consent. *Gender harassment* is also a form of hostile environment harassment, in which the atmosphere is not necessarily sexualized, but the victim's gender itself is a target of hate speech and often accompanied by discriminatory practices. Racial and gender harassment are frequently combined to target women of color. Gender harassment is also frequently targeted at LGBTQ persons.

*Sexual abuse* technically refers to sexual contact with a minor, or with an adult person who is legally incompetent to consent. Any physical contact with a person under the age of 16 to 18[9] constitutes felony abuse, regardless of consent or even invitation by the minor. Even apparently consensual sexual activity with a minor constitutes statutory rape in all fifty states in the U.S.

---

7. Code of Federal Regulations, Title 29—Labor, Part 1604 "Guidelines on Discrimination Because of Sex," Section 1604.11 "Sexual harassment . . . Harassment on the basis of sex is a violation of section 703 of title VII. 1," online at https://www.gpo.gov/fdsys/pkg/CFR-2016-title29-vol4/xml/CFR-2016-title29-vol4-part1604.xml.

8. Title IX provisions online at https://www2.ed.gov/about/offices/list/ocr/docs/shguide.pdf.

9. [The "age of consent" varies by state, along with prohibited age differences. https://www.legalmatch.com/law-library/article/age-of-consent-by-state.html. —PCW 2018]

Medical professionals, social workers and counselors are mandated to report child abuse to the proper child protective agencies in all fifty states. Sexual abuse of adults who are deemed unable to consent has also been recognized in most states, and most states now have adult protective services agencies. An "incompetent" or "endangered" adult is defined as any individual aged 18 years or older who is, using an example from Indiana state law, "incapable by reason of mental infirmity or other incapacity of either caring for themselves or managing their property, and is harmed or threatened with harm as a result of neglect, battery or exploitation."

The term sexual abuse is also frequently used more generally to refer to any sexual language or behavior which exploits the vulnerability of another person, including vulnerability due to a power differential in roles, for one's own sexual gratification. Sexual contact by clergy with congregants or parishioners of any age is now a crime in thirteen states, mostly in the context of providing pastoral or mental health counseling; Minnesota, Utah, and Wisconsin specifically include clergy as counseling professionals by definition; Arkansas, Texas, New Mexico, Alaska, California, Connecticut and Kansas broadly recognize a perpetrator as one who has a "position of authority" over the victim.[10]

*Sexual exploitation* is a betrayal of trust in a pastoral relationship by the development or the attempted development of a sexual or romantic relationship. Sexual exploitation occurs when any ordained priest, minister, pastor, rabbi, professional pastoral counselor, chaplain or lay staff member in a defined ministry role (e.g., Stephen Minister, Lay Eucharistic Minister, Minister of Music, Youth Minister, etc.), participates in sexual behavior with any person served in that worker's ministry. Because of the unequal power inherent in all pastoral relationships, this holds true even when the person served initiates or apparently consents to the sexual behavior. Exploitative behavior can range from sexualized verbal comments, overt and covert seductive speech, gestures, and requests for sexual favors, to erotic kissing or touching, to sexual intercourse. In sexual exploitation, both the person who is the recipient of the sexual behavior, and the office of ministry itself are being exploited for the sexual gratification of the religious leader who engages in the sexualized behavior.

---

10. [Updated from Bradley J. B. Toben and Kris Helge, "Sexual Misconduct of Clergypersons with Congregants or Parishioners—Civil and Criminal Liabilities and Responsibilities," https://www.baylor.edu/content/services/document.php/96096.pdf; see also "The Silent Majority: Adult Victims of Sexual Exploitation by Clergy—State Laws": http://www.adultsabusedbyclergy.org/statelaws.html. It should be noted that state laws change frequently, and should be consulted directly for current information. —PCW 2018]

Sexual misconduct is a violation of professional sexual ethics by clergy, counselors, chaplains, and other helping and teaching professionals, and may encompass any or all of the above categories of behavior.[11]

## Ethical Analysis

Until recently, clergy sexual misconduct was generally understood under the rubric of personal morality of the clergyperson. Sexual contact with a member of the congregation was, and still frequently is, regarded as an "affair," identifying the wrong done by clergy as adultery, or in the case of single clergy, violating religious norms prohibiting sexual activity outside the marital bond. This view is severely limited, however, by failing to recognize the professional ethical dimensions of sexualized language and behavior by clergy with members of their congregations. Recent ethical analyses have recognized that there is not only a personal moral dimension to sexual misconduct, but also a professional duty or fiduciary trust, to care for congregants.

As the Rev. Marie Fortune has so clearly outlined in her pioneering book *Is Nothing Sacred?*,[12] the primary issue is that in any professional helping relationship, there is an imbalance of power that eliminates the possibility of authentic consent on the part of a congregant. In Fortune's words, "Consent to sexual activity, in order to be authentic, must take place in a context of mutuality, choice, full knowledge, and equal power, and in the absence of coercion or fear. When there is an imbalance of power in a relationship, these necessary factors will not be present."[13] Sexual relating with persons in one's professional care is wrong for four interlocking ethical reasons: violation of professional role, misuse of authority and power, taking advantage of vulnerability, and absence of meaningful consent.[14] The

---

11. See, e.g., Marie Fortune, *Is Nothing sacred? When Sex Invades the Pastor-Parishioner Relationship* (San Francisco: Harper & Row, 1989); Pamela Cooper-White, "Soul Stealing: Power Relations in Pastoral Sexual Abuse, *The Christian Century* (February 20, 1991) 196-99. [See Ch. 2, this volume.]; Cooper-White, *The Cry of Tamar: Violence against Women and the Church's Response* (Minneapolis: Fortress, 1995; 2nd ed., 2012);William E. Hulme, "Sexual Boundary Violations of Clergy," in Glen O. Gabbard, ed., *Sexual Exploitation in Professional Relationships* (Washington, DC: American Psychiatric Press, 1995) 177-92; Stanley J. Grenz and Roy D. Bell, *Betrayal of Trust: Sexual Misconduct in the Pastorate* (Downers Grove, IL: InterVarsity, 1995); Jan Erickson-Pearson, *Safe Connections: What Parishioners Can Do to Understand and Prevent Clergy Sexual Abuse* (Chicago, IL: Evangelical Lutheran Church in America, 1996).

12. Marie Fortune, *Is Nothing Sacred?*

13. Ibid., 38.

14. Marie Fortune, *Clergy Misconduct . . . Workshop Manual*.

authority of the pastoral office, however much the offending clergyperson may wish to downplay it, precludes a peer relationship in which the term "consenting adults" could be meaningful.

The clergy role carries a great deal of power in and of itself, especially for male ministers, infused with popular ideals about being a "man of God." Clergy may have multiple levels of spiritual and institutional authority in relation to congregants, not only in the general sense as a visible leader or "CEO" of the congregation and many of its committees and sub-groupings, but also with varying degrees of formal institutional authority as an employer, administrator, teacher, supervisor, mentor, and spiritual guide. Clergy frequently also act (with or without formal clinical training) as pastoral or spiritual counselors to congregants and their family members, sometimes briefly, but sometimes over long periods of time, with all the transference inherent in all counseling relationships. Home visitation and pastoral care in hospitals and nursing homes gives clergy and chaplains intimate access to congregation members in their most private settings and at their most vulnerable times.

Because of the unequal power and authority inherent in the pastoral relationship, it is always the responsibility of the clergyperson, as professional, to maintain appropriate boundaries. Although the majority of cases of clergy sexual exploitation occur at the clergyperson's initiative, sometimes members of the congregation attempt to initiate a sexual or romantic relationship. Sometimes vulnerable congregants are attracted by the power of the clergy role itself, and the healing it seems to offer. In such cases it is unequivocally the clergyperson's responsibility to recognize the underlying need represented by the congregant's overtures, and to say "no" compassionately but clearly. This both protects the safety and dignity of the congregation member, and preserves the integrity and the genuine healing potential of the pastoral relationship.

Clergy sexual misconduct causes harm to both primary victims, those who have been directly harassed, abused or exploited, and many secondary victims—the families of both victim and offender, members of the congregation, the denomination, and even the surrounding community. Because of the universal imbalance of power between clergy and members of their congregations, and the potential for widespread harm, denominations have increasingly developed policies over the last decade that strictly prohibit sexual contact with congregants, and also limit the pastoral counseling role of clergy serving in congregations. In some policies, single clergy dating of single members of the congregation is permitted, but is strictly circumscribed by admonitions to openness with congregational leaders and denominational authorities, adequate supervision, and provision of alternate pastoral care of these congregation members. While professional opinions vary on this somewhat,[15] the practice of single clergy dating single congregation members, even with appropriate disclosure to congregational and denominational leadership, presents a high risk for harm, not only to the member, but also in the potential for divisiveness in the whole congregation, and should be avoided.

Finally, a theological understanding of clergy sexual ethics makes clear that the exploitation of congregation members violates fundamental biblical tenets of care for the vulnerable. Clergy sexual misconduct is not only a wrong because it stands outside accepted personal moral standards for both clergy and laity, but because it is a violation of justice. Persons join congregations in good faith, expecting their religious institutions to be places of safety and inspiration. Clergy sexual misconduct violates this trust. Because clergy and religious institutions come to represent the divine in many people's imaginations, sexual violations may even have profound repercussions upon congregation members' ability to trust God.

## Psychodynamic Analysis

The issue of keeping good boundaries, while first and foremost an ethical duty, is not *only* an ethical matter, but also a profoundly psychological one. Ethical analyses are crucial in educating clergy about the importance of prevention of harm, and in educating religious institutions more generally about the need for policies with clear-cut reporting procedures, fair processing of complaints, and clear-cut consequences for misconduct that prevent harm to future potential victims. Yet policies and prohibitions, however clear, have never altogether stopped an offender caught in the grip of a powerful unconscious impulse. Because being "above the law" is a common psychological defense in the profile of clergy sexual offenders, ethical education and policies may be regarded as applying to everyone else, but not to him. Some understanding of the unconscious dynamics of sexual misconduct is helpful, both in screening candidates for ministry, and in recognizing and intervening in cases of abuse.

The unconscious dynamics of clergy sexual misconduct can be understood in two ways, first, through the transference-countertransference relationship, and second, through an understanding of the psychological profile of clergy who cross sexual boundaries with those in their care.

15. Karen Lebacqz and Ronald G. Barton, *Sex in the Parish* (Louisville: Westminster John Knox, 1991); Peter Rutter, *Sex in the Forbidden Zone: When Men in Power Abuse Women's Trust* (Los Angeles: Tarcher, 1989).

As in all helping relationships, there is a transference-countertransference dynamic operating in and between both the clergyperson and the congregant or student or counselee. *Transference* refers to the expectations, fears and wishes that a congregation member unconsciously projects or *transfers* onto the clergyperson from early childhood experiences with caregivers and other powerful figures during his or her formative years. *Countertransference* refers to the parallel childhood-based projections transferred by the clergyperson onto the congregant or counselee, as well as a wide range of feelings, thoughts and fantasies that may be evoked by the transference of the counselee. Transference and countertransference are universal phenomena in helping relationships, *whether or not the helping professional is aware of the dynamic.*

The less trained or aware the professional is the dynamic of transference and countertransference, the more likely he is to fail to recognize the pulls and impulses arising from the dynamic, and to behave reactively rather than therapeutically. In particular, most psychotherapists are trained to recognize the specific phenomenon of *erotic transference*, involving an intense feeling of love and desire on the part of a counselee. They know not to react sexually but to use this phenomenon as information to guide them in appropriate care for the client. However, many clergy who have had little or no formal clinical background may not recognize the transferential dynamic for what it is, and find themselves feeling flattered and enthralled in a countertransference reaction of grandiosity and sexual arousal.

The element of grandiosity aroused in the countertransference points to the other important aspect of psychodynamics in clergy sexual misconduct, namely, the inner psychological structure of clergy who cross sexual boundaries. Various typologies of offenders have been proposed, including a two-fold typology of "wanderer" vs. "predator,"[16] a four-fold typology including psychotic/bipolar, predatory, lovesick, and masochistic,[17] and a six-fold typology ranging from uninformed/naïve, healthy or mildly neurotic, severely neurotic and/or socially isolated, impulsive character disorders, sociopathic or narcissistic character disorder.[18] These typologies are useful

---

16. Fortune, *Is Nothing Sacred?*

17. Glen O. Gabbard, *Boundaries and Boundary Violations in Psychoanalysis* (New York: Basic Books, 1995).

18. Gary R. Schoener and John C. Gonsiorek, "Assessment and development of rehabilitation plans for the therapist," in Gary R. Schoener et al., *Psychotherapists' Sexual Involvement with Clients: Intervention and Prevention* (Minneapolis: Walk-In Counseling Center, 1989) 401–20; cf., J. Reid Meloy, "Narcissistic Psychopathology and the Clergy," *Pastoral Psychology* 35/1 (1986) 50–55; Conrad Weiser, *Healers—Harmed and Harmful* (Minneapolis: Fortress, 1994).

when studied by trained mental health professionals for the purposes of diagnosis, prognosis, and, when deemed possible, appropriate methods and length of time for rehabilitation.[19] One pitfall of these typologies, however, is the misuse of such typologies by judicatory executives and by the offender himself. Because of a widespread culture of optimism within religious institutions, offenders may be rushed through inappropriate, brief pseudo-rehabilitation and reinstatement, because judicatory staff, clergy colleagues, and others involved in the situation may have a strong wish to see the offender incorrectly as a "wanderer" or a "neurotic." Experts at rehabilitation of clergy offenders estimate that at least half of all offenders, and generally all repeat offenders, actually fall on the side of the spectrum of more serious woundedness and poor prognosis for rehabilitation.[20]

Another way of understanding boundary violations from the inner dynamics of the offenders is that there is a strong unifying thread of narcissistic wounding running through the entire range of clergy offenders. Narcissism, because it has its origin in the first years of life, is very difficult to heal. It impairs a minister's professional judgment in a way that puts him particularly at risk for crossing boundaries, because it damages his capacity for empathy and causes him to seek gratification of his own needs first, regardless of the cost to others. Even a "wanderer" or "neurotic" clergyperson may show narcissistic wounding through manipulative behaviors, externalization of blame, and a tendency to use others, especially to meet personal needs in times of stress. Through the lens of self psychology, it has been proposed that the sexualization of usually non-sexual activities and relationships can be seen as an effort to enliven a sense of deadness inside, or to soothe a sense of inner fragmentation or emptiness, and is, in fact, a hallmark of narcissistic character structure.[21] Rutter has also suggested from a Jungian perspective that male offenders may project longed-for aspects of their own inner life onto the woman who

---

19. See also Barbara Sanderson, ed., *It's Never OK: A Handbook for Victims and Victim Advocates on Sexual Exploitation by Counselors and Therapists* (Minneapolis: Task Force on Sexual Exploitation by Counselors and Therapists, Minnesota Department of Corrections, 1989); Glen O. Gabbard, *Sexual Exploitation in Professional Relationships* (Washington, DC: American Psychiatric Press, 1989); Glen O. Gabbard, "Psychodynamics of Sexual Boundary Violations," *Psychiatric Annals* 21 (1991) 651–55; Glen O. Gabbard, "Psychotherapists Who Transgress Sexual Boundaries with Patients," *Bulletin of the Menninger Clinic* 58 (1994) 124–35.

20. Gabbard, *Boundaries and Boundary Violations in Psychoanalysis*, x, 135–41, et passim; Schoener and Gonsiorek, "Assessment and development of rehabilitation plans for the therapist."

21. Arnold Goldberg, *The Problem of Perversion: The View from Self Psychology* (New Haven: Yale University Press, 1995).

has come for help.[22] She may then be used unconsciously by the offender as an *anima*-figure or muse, artificially creating a sense of wholeness that can only really be achieved through an internal process of integration, not through enactment of projection-laden fantasies.

Narcissism begins with early childhood wounding, or deprivation—sometimes quite subtle—in which the normal grandiosity of the very small child is not mirrored, or is even crushed, leaving a great psychic hole to be filled. Unconscious defenses are erected, concealing the core wound, but empathy is seriously impaired, resulting in behavior that may in turn victimize others. The narcissistically wounded professional tends to conceal his insecurities and cravings for attention under a behavioral style of specialness—a style often condoned or even reinforced by the ministry setting. A primary sign of narcissistic wounding is a tendency toward entitlement. Wants are equated with needs. Because manipulation and the projection of a star image are common to narcissistically wounded people, empathy and conscience are often convincingly feigned. But at the core of the person's soul is overwhelming despair, emptiness, and fear. For this reason, there is often difficulty establishing appropriate intimate relationships and peer friendships, often resulting in a "Lone Ranger" style of ministry.[23] Other people are used compulsively and heedlessly in an attempt to keep the demons of worthlessness at bay. This is why it is also advisable when sexual boundary crossings are uncovered to look for other violations of fiduciary trust as well, such as financial misconduct. Boundary violations that may stop short of sexual involvement but may lead to what some researchers have called the "slippery slope phenomenon"[24] include giving of personal gifts, establishing an inappropriately intimate friendship and relying on the congregation member or counselee to set limits, or privately attending concerts or movies together. By showing the congregant or counselee his "private side" by swearing or engaging in activities that others would probably regard as unusual for a clergyperson, or even illicit, such as smoking marijuana together, or engaging her in other behaviors that would normally be considered private, a clergy person creates an aura of specialness around the relationship. Undue special treatment of a congregant or counselee, attempts to isolate her from family and friends, isolating oneself from one's family, friends and colleagues, seeking repeated reassurance from consultants, can also be signs of gradual

---

22. Rutter, *Sex in the Forbidden Zone*, 45.

23. Mary Pellauer, "Sex, Power, and the Family of God," *Christianity and Crisis*, (Feb. 16, 1987) 47–50.

24. Gabbard, *Boundaries and Boundary Violations in Psychoanalysis*, 25 et passim.

sexualization of the relationship.[25] Imposing secrecy on the congregant or counselee about the relationship or any aspect of it is a serious warning sign of the development of an inappropriate relationship. All these behaviors serve to enhance the professional's sense of importance, and the resulting excitement or risk is used unconsciously to inflate an underlying sense of flatness and malaise caused by the original narcissistic wound.

It is perhaps important also to note that there is no single profile for victims of clergy sexual offenders. While offenders often seem to have an uncanny ability to ferret out vulnerabilities and exploit them, no member of a congregation is immune to exploitation because of the transferential dynamic and the power imbalance in the pastoral relationship. Everyone brings certain vulnerabilities and lifelong desires for growth, inspiration, and wholeness to their church or temple, and legitimately so, because the quest for wholeness is at least one central dimension of all religious life. It is precisely the exploitation of these vulnerabilities and desires for wholeness that constitutes such a profound betrayal of trust, and causes such psychological and spiritual harm to victims.

## Counseling for Victims

By the time a victim seeks counseling, she has probably already gone through a significant process of struggle and discernment. She is likely to be aware of a variety of painful and confusing feelings around attempting to end an exploitative relationship, or in its aftermath. She may have read something about clergy sexual misconduct that struck a responsive cord. She may have been suffering in isolation for a very long time, not even knowing how to name her suffering as abuse, or having any idea that there might be somewhere she could turn for healing and justice. She may also be struggling with feelings of guilt for disclosing the nature of the relationship to anyone, even a therapist, because perpetrators often swear victims to secrecy, sometimes with the implication of a holy vow.

Post-traumatic symptoms are common, including nightmares, intrusive thoughts and memories, disturbances in relating with others, and self-destructive behaviors. Depressive symptoms are also common, sometimes to the level of a major depressive episode, including depressed mood, excessive guilt and feelings of worthlessness, sleep disturbances, and changes in appetite.

25. Kenneth S. Pope, Janet L. Sonne, and Jean Holroyd, *Sexual Feelings in Psychotherapy: Explorations for Therapists and Therapists-in-training* (Washington, DC: American Psychological Association, 1993).

Most victims initially blame themselves, and threads of this self-doubt may persist for a very long time. In the aftermath of sexual exploitation by a clergyperson, victims often feel confused, hurt, angry or shaken up, or may be wondering why it seems unusually difficult to heal from the ending of the relationship. However, they may have little understanding that they have been wronged in an institutional, ethical sense. As in other forms of sexual and physical abuse, there is a dynamic of victim-perpetrator splitting, in which the perpetrator generally presents himself as the victim, and the victim as the "true" perpetrator. Within the relationship, victims are often told explicitly or implicitly, "You make me do this, I can't help myself even if I know better." This kind of thinking serves to relieve the perpetrator from feeling responsible, and causes the victim to feel at fault from the very first moment the clergyperson began to fantasize about her. Prevailing myths about the seductiveness of female congregants and the supposed naivete and innocence of clergy reinforce this dynamic. Some Christian professional journals for clergy continue to emphasize the pastor's struggle to resist temptation, and continue to portray clergy as innocent sitting ducks for the seductive wiles of female parishioners.[26]

Because of these dynamics, there are seven principles that govern the therapeutic process with victims of clergy sexual misconduct:

1. *Convey your belief in the client's experience.* Because clients are so prone to doubting themselves, and because prevailing social and institutional views still tend to place blame upon victims, this is healing in and of itself. It may be necessary to reinforce many times over that both therapist and client can trust her inner process to know what is true and how to proceed.

2. *Convey to the client that the abuse was not her fault.* Some educational work is often appropriate, explaining that it is always the responsibility of the clergyperson to maintain appropriate sexual boundaries. It may also be helpful to refer clients to appropriate literature about sexual boundary violations and to current professional ethics standards for clergy, and to provide some direct analysis of the abuse of power inherent in sexually exploitative relationships. Such educative efforts may help to validate the client's trust in her own perceptions of her experience, and to reduce self-blame and shame.

3. To the extent that it is appropriate, *offer some form of institutional acknowledgement and apology.* As a religious professional, you may at least in the broadest sense represent institutional religion in the client's

---

26. e.g., Louis McBurney, "Seduced," *Leadership* (Fall, 1998) 101–106.

eyes. It is appropriate to say "As a minister/rabbi/imam/priest, I am deeply saddened by what you are telling me. The events you describe should never happen to anyone, and I am very sorry for what you have experienced and the pain you are in now."

4. *Respect client self-determination concerning any decision to report or take action.* As in all good counseling, the principle "follow the client's lead" becomes even more important when working with victims of clergy sexual misconduct. Counselors frequently may feel outrage on the client's behalf, and feel an impulse to push the client toward reporting or taking some other form of action. Counselors may even wish to disclose the abuse or take action directly with judicatory bodies. Concern about potential future victims and a desire to bring the offending clergy to justice may fuel these impulses. It is important to remember that the client can only feel empowered by allowing her to reach decisions about action in her own time and her own way. Further, acting or pressing the client to act before she is ready may jeopardize her safety.

5. *The victim's safety is always the first priority.* Any decision to report or act belongs to the victim. Reporting may carry serious risks of re-traumatization, both because the relevant institutional body may not be prepared to make a safe and just response, and because the perpetrator may retaliate. Offending clergy often have a wide sphere of influence in which they can inflict harm to the reporting victim's personal reputation, professional status and goals. Clergy fearing report or institutional discipline sometimes even threaten physical harm. Therefore, client self-determination must be respected.

6. *State your commitment to confidentiality.* While keeping confidentiality is ethically mandated in all counseling, it is especially crucial to state this clearly and directly to the client in cases of sexual abuse, because the client's trust has already been ruptured by the abuser, and may be particularly vulnerable to re-injury. This commitment may need to be re-stated at various times, as the client remembers and re-experiences fears and doubts in the area of trust. The usual exceptions to confidentiality, as in cases of abuse of a minor, or where the client has threatened harm to herself or another, must be carefully explained, and whenever possible, handled as collaboratively with the client as possible in order to minimize her further sense of disempowerment and rupture of trust.

7. Finally, *be active in promoting justice.* While it may not be possible to intervene directly in a particular case, due to considerations for the

client's own self-determination and safety, it is possible to advocate for changes that will advance safety and justice in your own institutional settings and communities. Therapeutic work to empower individual clients is a trust that is strengthened at its foundations by one's own commitment to systemic change.

## Counseling for Offending Clergy

Given the psychological profile of offenders offered above, and in particular the prevalence of narcissistic wounding, the question of rehabilitation and reinstatement becomes a matter of more subtlety and discernment than simply designating a specific period of time for therapy and re-education. The kind of therapeutic process necessary to address such deep-seated characterological patterns at minimum takes years, not months. Even then, evidence of true "amendment of life" for a clergyperson who has crossed sexual boundaries with a person or persons in his care would, at the very least, have to include questions such as: Does the clergyperson genuinely and spontaneously take full responsibility for his past behaviors, without excuse or qualification, or does he still at least partially frame his own experience of the misconduct as one of having been victimized himself (whether by the victim, by the congregation, by his family, or by the judicatory body or "the system")? Is he able to talk about the past, focusing genuinely and spontaneously on the pain that was caused to others, or is this still an area he seems to avoid, minimize, or neglect to bring up until someone else raises it? Does his request for reinstatement to the roster seem motivated by a genuine desire to serve others, or does it still seem driven by his own interests and desire for status?

It is unfortunately very easy for counselors working with offenders to be pulled into an empathic dynamic that joins with the offender's own minimization or denial, or to be distracted by the presentation of other issues. Once uncovered, clergy sexual misconduct is often misattributed, even by mental health professionals, to alcohol abuse, mismanagement of personal stress, or "sex addiction." Treatments designed around these framings of the problem will not bring about genuine rehabilitation, because they miss the underlying dynamic of abuse of power, and fail to address the underlying dynamic of narcissistic entitlement.

Counselors working with offenders need to maintain an unequivocal stance that all sexual or romantic relating with congregation members or others in their care is wrong, period. Empathic joining may be possible around a shared desire for rehabilitation, but the goal of therapy is *not* reinstatement per se, but to help the offending clergy to take responsibility for his actions. This may or may not lead to reinstatement. Treatment will require a long period of exploration of the deep origins of the clergyperson's sense of entitlement and use of others in attempts to shore up a fragile sense of self. The counselor's empathy should be mobilized away from collusion with the offending clergy's sense of entitlement, and toward uncovering the offending clergy's patterns of disavowal of destructive sexualized behaviors and impulses.

Because of the dangers of manipulation and co-optation, pastoral counselors interested in working with offenders should avail themselves of specialized education and clinically supervised training hours. Some resources for training are listed at the end of this chapter.

## Counseling Family Members

Family members of both victims and offending clergy are often the secondary victims who are forgotten in institutional processes of discipline and healing. There is still little written on this particular aspect of clergy sexual misconduct.

Family members of victims may go through a range of feelings upon learning of the sexual abuse. Shock, betrayal, anger toward the victim, anger toward the offending clergyperson, and anger toward the congregation and the religious institution are common. Family members often blame the victim, asking questions like "Why didn't you just say no?" and "Why couldn't you see through him?" Feelings of shame, embarrassment, and humiliation can affect family members as well as victims, and these are often displaced onto the victim herself.[27]

Family members often feel tremendously out of control in the aftermath of disclosure of abuse, and may attempt to regain control through conscious or unconscious efforts to control the victim. They may begin to "carry" feelings for the victim herself, such as anger or hurt, making it difficult for the victim to identify her own feelings, and they may co-opt her own process for healing by attempting to direct her responses. They may also displace this need for control onto the religious institution, and its representatives. Family members may press religious institutions for a speedy response, and become enraged on behalf of the victim when justice is slow, partial, or not forthcoming.

---

27. Ann-Janine Morey, "Blaming the Woman for the Abusive Male Pastor," *The Christian Century*, (October 5, 1988) 866–69.

Family members need support in coming to terms with their own grief and anger, and differentiating these from the reactions of the victim. The usual goal of conjoint therapy of enhancing individual members' capacity for self-differentiation while remaining connected becomes paramount in work with families of survivors of sexual abuse. Family members often need help in withdrawing their own projections about what happened, and processing their feelings and responses as their own. Like the victim herself, family members almost always suffer a sense of betrayal of their own trust, and if they are also members or clients of the congregation or agency in which the abuse occurred, a sense of loss of their own religious community or support system.

Family members of victims can also be helped in strengthening communication skills, in particular learning to listen more empathically to the victim regarding her feelings, and what kinds of support she does and does not need.

Family members of offenders are also secondary victims of the sexual misconduct. The marital betrayal of the spouse may be doubly harmful, because it carries not only the pain of infidelity to the marriage, but also the pain of infidelity to the office of ministry, about which the spouse may care deeply and may be deeply invested. The spouse of the offending clergy may wish to deny that the abuse occurred, and so unconsciously collude with the clergyperson's own patterns of minimization and self-justification. She may feel rage toward the "other woman," and a wish to blame the victim for having seduced the spouse. Spouses of offending clergy not infrequently also report dynamics of power, control, and/or abuse within their own marital relationship. The disclosure of abuse of a member of the congregation may cause the spouse to recognize more fully the abusive dynamics of the marriage.

Often, the families of offenders not only lose their religious community, but a special status or role within it, and experience feelings of shame, humiliation, and loss of privacy when the truth is disclosed. Victim blaming by congregations is sometimes secondarily directed at other prominent women in the congregation, and wives of offending clergy are sometimes blamed for being inadequate spouses, unsupportive of their clergy husbands, or insufficiently involved in the life of the congregation.

Families of offending clergy also suffer direct economic consequences when offending clergy are disciplined. The clergyperson's salary may be terminated, and in cases of church-provided parsonages, housing may be abruptly terminated as well. Ann and Derek Legg[28] state that some con-

---

28. Ann and Derek Legg, "The Offender's Family," in Nancy Myer Hopkins and Mark Laaser, ed., *Restoring the Soul of a Church: Healing Congregations Wounded by*

gregations express anger over "sexual sin" through money, causing the offender's family to suffer financial punishment even though they themselves committed no wrongdoing.

Children of both victims and offenders may act out unhealed dynamics in the family after the disclosure of the abuse. Children of both families may blame the victim, lose respect for the clergyperson and by extension for the office of ministry and become mistrustful of all institutional religion. Children from both families may become scapegoated, especially if the abuse is given significant media coverage. "Good child/bad child" splits may begin to occur in both family systems, in which many interactions between children, or among children and adults, may begin to take on a parallel perpetrator-victim dynamic.

Spouses and family members frequently feel disregarded by institutional processes of adjudication that focus heavily on the victim and the offending clergy, but offer little in the way of emotional or material support to families. Counselors can help family members to identify and assert their own needs for support from their religious communities.

Whether the marital couple decides to stay together and work through the aftermath of the abuse together, or to divorce, both couples and their children need therapeutic help. Effective counseling can help both families to avoid the escalation of destructive projective processes and patterns of denial, and to engage fully in the emotional process of grieving, healing, and ultimately acceptance of new realities and integration of the truth of what occurred.

## Consulting to Congregations

There has been increasing recognition among clergy and judicatory executives that congregations are also traumatized by clergy sexual misconduct. It is now generally understood that when congregations are not offered an intentional, well-planned healing process, they continue to carry wounds that can affect future generations of future clergy and lay members, and are likely to pose significant if unspoken obstacles to effective ministry. Congregations are groups or systems which, just like individuals, have unconscious as well as unconscious dynamics. Traumatic events in the life of a congregation may be "forgotten," initially because of systemic taboos against telling the truth about what happened. Later, even if every person who was a member at the time the trauma has moved away or died, the post-traumatic dynamics persist. Old patterns of relating, of behavior,

---

*Clergy Sexual Misconduct* (Collegeville, MN: Alban Institute and Interfaith Sexual Trauma Institute, 1995) 140–54.

speech and silence, are taken up by new members without a conscious understanding of their origins. Like families with multi-generational patterns of incest, congregational dynamics can also be governed by a sexual abuse secret that is hidden from conscious awareness but can be recognized by the symptoms it produces.

Experts have identified a number of indicators of congregational symptoms in the aftermath of clergy sexual misconduct:[29]

1) anger that is displaced toward other authority figures such as congregation staff members, judicatory executives, interims and "after-pastors," and even toward lay leadership; 2) reactivity in the form of making unwise or hasty decisions; 3) a pattern of divisiveness within the congregation; 4) a sense of depression, malaise, and apathy among members toward routine tasks and programs; 5) excessive preoccupation with caring for the offending clergyperson (sometimes even after he has left the congregation) without similar apparent regard for other injured parties; 6) a loss of members and/or income which does not resolve in the usual "recovery period" of 6–12 months for these losses; 7) a climate of gossip and conjecture resulting from understandable attempts to find out "what happened?"; 8) conscious or unconscious embarrassment, leading to isolation from the surrounding community and from other congregations; 9) "sexualization" of the congregation, in which undue attention is given to matters of human sexuality; 10) "symbolic fights"—congregational conflicts that symbolize the pain (for example, conflicts about the priority of children's ministries, about job/role descriptions, about the external appearance of the congregation's building, about the newsletter and other means of communication, about "boundaries" such as keys to the building, office hours, outreach, etc.; 10) nostalgia for the "good old days" or idealization of previous clergy; suspicion or resistance to new ideas, programs, or forms of ministry; 11) despair about the future of the congregation, resulting in fear of making commitments or taking risks.

In order to heal from sexual misconduct, congregations need intentional, well-trained, and empathic intervention. First and foremost,

29. E.g., Chilton Knudsen, "Trauma Debriefing: A Congregational Model," *MCS Conciliation Quarterly* (Spring 1991); Nancy Myer Hopkins, "Symbolic Church Fights: The Hidden Agenda When Clerical Trust Has Been Betrayed," *Congregations: The Alban Journal* (May/June, 1993) 15–18; Nancy Myer Hopkins and Mark Laaser, ed., *Restoring the Soul of a Church: Healing Congregations Wounded by Clergy Sexual Misconduct* (Collegeville, MN: Alban Institute and Interfaith Sexual Trauma Institute, 1995); Nancy Myer Hopkins, *The Congregational Response to Clergy Betrayals of Trust* Collegeville, MN: Liturgical, 1998); Candace R. Benyei, *Understanding Clergy Misconduct in Religious Systems: Scapegoating, Family Secrets, and the Abuse of Power* (New York: Haworth, 1998).

congregations need information and education. Appropriate disclosure may be made by professionals who have authority in the religious institution with which the congregation is affiliated (judicatory executives), or consultants who are authorized officially to represent the institution by virtue of their particular training and expertise in working with congregations in the aftermath of sexual misconduct. Such initial disclosure gives permission for open discussion and processing of the traumatic events in the congregation's life. Appropriate disclosure serves two purposes: first, to reduce the congregation's anxiety about what happened and what has been kept from them; and second, to model permission for open discussion and truth-telling within the congregation itself. As with all trauma, truth-telling and open processing of feelings are at the heart of any congregational healing process. Information and education should at minimum include:

1. *Appropriate, ample disclosure of facts.* Congregations need fair and honest answers to the question "what happened?" Exceptions to full disclosure, such as withholding the identity of reporting victims to preserve their safety, or withholding of any information for specific, concrete legal reasons, should be explained. Secrecy is at the heart of the betrayal of the congregation's trust. The interruption of patterns of secrecy begins from the first disclosure to model a new way of congregational life based on honesty and sharing. Congregations that are "left in the dark" are more likely to engage in gossip, secrecy, victim-blaming, and covering up of the truth.

2. Access to the most recent *policies and procedures* pertaining to the case. They should be "walked through" the steps that will occur in their denomination's adjudication procedure, and be told what to expect at various stages in the process.

3. *Education about appropriate ministerial boundaries, the misuse of power inherent in clergy sexual misconduct, and a theological framework for sexual ethics.* Members should be helped to understand their institution's ethical mandates, and the rationale behind them. Educational efforts should give attention to issues of ministerial trust and responsibility for boundaries, power differentials inherent in the role of ministry, and theological understandings of abuse.

4. Education about the *stages in the congregational healing process*, which are not unlike the stages of grief experienced by a person in bereavement. The variety of commonly experienced feelings, reactions, and behavioral responses can be explained and normalized. A "Trauma De-Briefing Model," as developed by the Rev. Chilton Knudsen (1991),

is recommended for initial disclosure and early healing process. Her "Dimensions of Congregational Healing" wheel is helpful in explaining the range of reactions that may occur normally in a congregation in the aftermath of clergy misconduct. Reactions may include shock, denial, bargaining, anger (scapegoating), depression/sadness, anger (righteous rage), and (eventually), acceptance and integration.

A collaborative team approach is recommended, in which mental health/addictions professionals, denominational personnel, area clergy, attorneys, and (as appropriate) law enforcement professionals, may all potentially be of help to a congregation in the aftermath of sexual abuse. Lay leaders who have experienced misconduct in another congregation and have sufficiently moved through their own grief process can also be useful resources. Such a "response team" should be balanced to include both women and men, clergy and laity. The team should also include persons of varying ages and sociocultural perspectives, reflecting the nature and diversity of the congregation's own membership. A quiet room and a person designated simply to be a caring listener should be provided at any public meeting or event related to the misconduct. Local counseling resources should be posted so that members who wish to do so may seek further individual consultation and healing. Congregations can be helped in recognizing the need for a plan to respond to media in an appropriate and timely manner.

Finally, a consultant can help the congregation to realize that the healing process will take time. It is the disclosure of the information that initiates the crisis for the congregation, although the crisis was actually caused by the clergy misconduct. First disclosure opens a window for potential healing, but this window may shut down if ongoing support and education are not offered. Healing cannot be accomplished in a single congregational meeting. Follow-up meetings, both large and in small groups, should be planned at regular intervals. As with all grief processes, two years is a reasonable minimum length of time to expect that healing will occur, if the process is being regularly attended throughout that time. Knudsen has written, "No congregation that I know of has ever complained that 'too much was offered to us' for their healing process. Err on the side of offering more rather than less opportunity to discuss, process and accept/integrate the experience."[30]

After the initial crisis period, pastoral counselors who are well educated in these congregational dynamics may continue in an ongoing capacity to serve as consultants to interim clergy and "after-pastors." As consultants, pastoral counselors may help these clergy to stay differentiated from the

---

30. Chilton Knudsen, "Trauma Debriefing: A Congregational Model," *MCS Conciliation Quarterly* (Spring 1991) 12–13.

wounded congregational system into which they have been immersed. Consultants can help them to recognize post-traumatic "symptoms" as they occur in the congregational system. By integrating this knowledge, "after-pastors" may maintain a constructive, ongoing "non-anxious" pastoral presence[31] that helps move the congregation through healing to renewal of ministry and mission.

Pastoral counselors may also be a helpful resource to judicatory executives who need consultation in dealing directly with situations of sexual misconduct. Education in the dynamics of clergy sexual misconduct and guidance in appropriate methods of prevention and intervention can be invaluable to religious leaders. It is important to remember that judicatory executives are also secondary victims of clergy sexual misconduct. They may also experience a range of feelings including shock, anxiety, dread, disbelief, a wish to minimize, a pull to collude with the offender, or a desire to act impulsively from outrage or grief upon the discovery of clergy sexual misconduct in one of their congregations. Consultants can support judicatory executives in maintaining an educated, conscious nonanxious leadership presence, implementing (or creating) policies and procedures that enact at an institutional level both healing and justice.

## Conclusion

Pastoral counselors can make an important contribution to the prevention and healing of clergy sexual misconduct. This contribution can be made in a variety of ways—leading educational workshops for clergy and laity on the clergy sexual ethics and the prevention of sexual misconduct; counseling victims, offenders, and secondary victims; consulting to congregations, judicatory executives and "after-pastors," and engaging in active work for justice in our own denominations and institutions in which we serve. Finally, pastoral counselors must attend to our own ethical mandates, maintaining the highest standards of sexual professional ethics in our own practices, and refraining from colluding or "turning a blind eye" toward colleagues who cross sexual boundaries with clients, patients, congregation members, or others whom we serve. We must continue to strengthen our own policies and procedures, so that our own profession is a harbor of safety and justice for all who come to us for help.

---

31. Edwin H. Friedman, *Generation to Generation: Family Process in Church and Synagogue* (New York: Guilford, 1985).

# 8

## What Are We Teaching about Violence against Women?

2004[1]

THIS ARTICLE IS A summary of findings of a survey conducted in the Society for Pastoral Theology to investigate the current status of teaching about violence against women in SPT members' pastoral care/counseling and pastoral theology courses. The survey was emailed to all members of SPT during January-February, 2005. Members were informed that the survey is part of a larger project entitled "Intimate Violence against Women: Trajectories for Pastoral Care in a New Millennium."[2] The research was designed to gain information in three areas: the extent of the inclusion of gender violence issues in theological teaching by SPT members (who represent the largest organized body of teachers of pastoral theology/pastoral care and counseling in mainline theological education), the level of cooperation/collaboration in this teaching with domestic violence and rape crisis agencies beyond the walls of the educational institution, and teachers' perceptions of the level of awareness among entering M.Div. students about violence against women.

Although there was no formal Internal Review Board (IRB) process for this survey,[3] ethical care of research subjects was duly considered. The researcher's credentials were disclosed in the invitation letter. Surveys were designed to be anonymous—although they were to be returned via

---

1. Orig. publ. as "What Are We Teaching about Violence against Women?," *Journal of Pastoral Theology* 14/2 (2004) 48–69.

2. This longer project was originally written for Sheryl Kujawa-Holbrook and Karen Montagno, *Injustice and the Care of Souls: Taking Oppression Seriously in Pastoral Care* (Minneapolis: Fortress, 2009), but it outgrew that anthology and was subsequently published in *Pastoral Psychology* 60/6 (2011) 809–56—see Ch. 11, this volume.

3. My institution, the Lutheran Theological Seminary at Philadelphia (now United Lutheran Seminary), like most free-standing seminaries, did not have an IRB policy at that time; one was implemented a few years later.

email, participants were assured that completed questionnaires would be printed separately from the email or email header, and would remain anonymous in the compilation process. Risk of harm to participants was judged to be minimal, but participants were advised that if at any point during the survey they did not want to continue, they should feel free to stop at any time, and also feel free to leave out any questions they did not feel comfortable answering. In addition, if there was anything about the survey that they found disturbing in any way, or if they simply wanted to discuss any of the questions at more length, they were invited to contact the researcher. Counseling referrals were ready, if needed, but none were requested or deemed necessary.

The method used was primarily quantitative, with a few qualitative questions added to allow for subjects to explain or amplify on their responses.[4] The survey consisted of nine brief questions, which included 25 statistical data points—18 on the topic of teaching violence against women, and 7 demographic.

In addition to the survey, a follow-up workshop was offered at the Society's annual meeting in Atlanta, GA, June, 2005. Ten SPT members participated in the workshop and discussed the statistical findings.[5]

## Response Rate and Confidence Levels

Surveys returned netted a 33% response rate (N = 68),[6] with a margin of error for standard distribution (50%) of 9.82%+; margin of error for highly skewed distributions, of which there were many (80%+) = 7.8+ or better. The confidence level for standard distribution (50%) was calculated at 68%; confidence level for highly skewed distributions (80%+) = 79%; confidence level for 95%+ distribution = 98% (97.8%). Because the results were highly skewed toward positive responses, the outstanding question for this level of response was, of course, whether the respondents were truly representative. Did those members of the Society who did not return

---

4. Quantitative data was analyzed using the Statistical Package for Social Scientists (SPSS) 11.0 software. Qualitative data was compiled manually. Thanks to my work study student Research Assistant, Ann Colley, and my daughter Macrina Cooper-White, for their help with data entry and data checking.

5. Thanks to Brad Binau, Carrie Doehring, Jim Higginbotham, Markena Hill, Kristen Leslie, Sophie Park, Anne Sowell, Anne Ross Stewart, Gail Unterberger, and Elizabeth Zagatta for their participation and discussion of the survey results.

6. Surveys originally emailed = 269; - Emails "bounced" = 23; - Surveys sent back as "not applicable/do not teach" = 40; for a net population = 206. Number of valid surveys completed = 68; Invalid surveys = 0; Net response rate = 33%

surveys fail to do so because they do not teach pastoral courses at all (since many of our members are in clinical or other types of occupations), or because they do not include material on violence against women in their courses and were reluctant to reply?

The confidence level increases a good deal after surveying the complete list of then current SPT members. Roughly 52% *of those SPT members who teach*, as identified by their institutional affiliations on the 2003 membership list, did return surveys.[7] Of those who did not return surveys, only 29% were teaching in 2003 (including seminary, college, CPE settings, and as adjuncts), while 71% of non-respondents were in non-teaching occupations (publishing houses, clinical settings, independent scholars and other interested members) or were retired. A scan of the total 2003 SPT membership showed that about 40% of members were teaching, while 60% were in other occupations.

These adjusted response rates give us some confidence in the trends represented by the data among our Society members, although these cannot be considered definitive, since it is still not known whether respondents tended to have more positive responses than non-respondents. Trends reported on specific items for those who *do* include violence against women in their teaching may be considered to be highly reliable and representative.

## Who Responded?

Respondents to the survey appear demographically to reflect the overall profile of those members who teach in the Society. Respondents were almost evenly divided by gender: 51.5% female, and 48.5% male. Ethnicity generally seemed to reflect the overall membership of the Society at present. Respondents self-identified as: African American 10.4%; Asian American 7.5%; Caucasian/European American 74.6%; African (from Africa) 1.5%; Asian/Indian (from Asia) 1.5%; and identified as "Other"[8] 4.5%. (Note: no respondents identified as Hispanic, Latino, or Native American.) The following chart shows the ethnic breakdown of respondents graphically (shown in Figure 1 below).

---

7. It was not possible to survey the email list used for the actual survey, since the full 2003 membership list was needed to review institutional affiliations. The full membership list is actually larger than the 2003 email list.

8. "Other" included 1 "mixed" and 2 "Italian American/Italian descent"

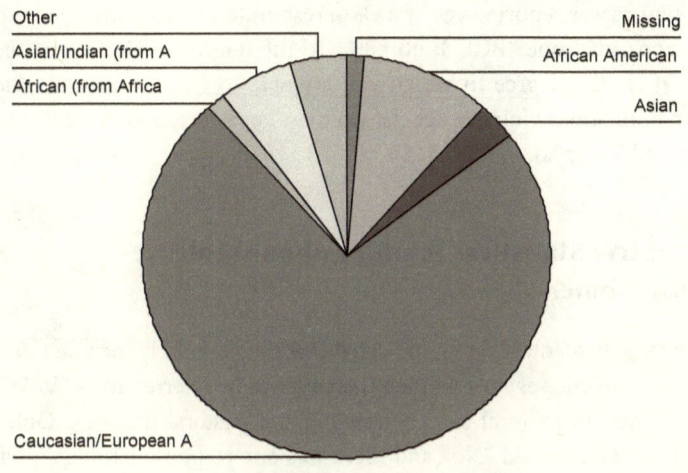

Figure 1

Ethnic Distribution of Survey Respondents
(Self-Identified Terminology, SPSS Output)

Other demographic questions addressed respondents' teaching positions and settings. Positions were fairly evenly distributed among tenure track positions: 26.2% Assistant Professor, 21.5% Associate Professor, and 29.2% Full Professor, with the remaining 4.6% Instructor, 3.1% Adjunct Professor, and 15.4% other title. 78% teach full-time; 3% half to 3/4 time, 17% as Adjuncts, and 3% identified as "other" time commitment. A large majority, 71.4% teach in seminaries, with 19% in divinity schools, and 9.5% in college/university settings.

Respondents were experienced teachers overall, with the median number of years teaching at their present institution = 6 years (mean = 8.4, mode = 8, range of 1–33); and median years teaching overall = 13 years (mean = 15, split mode = 6, 11 and 25, range of 1–40). Degrees varied among respondents, with 76% of all respondents listing an M.Div. degree; 12% with a master's degree in clinical counseling/pastoral counseling; 53% with a Ph.D.; 1.4% with a Psy.D., 10% with a D.Min. and 25% with another degree (these included Th.D., M.D., M.Th./Th.M./M.T.S./M.A. in Theology, M.Phil, M.S.W, C.A.S., and "licentiate in spiritual direction"). The *highest* degree earned by respondents was most often the Ph.D. (78%), with 1.4%

Psy.D., 6% D.Min., 2.9% M.Div. and MA/MS, respectively, and 7.3% "other" (Th.D., MD, M.T.S. and equivalent).

Tenure was reported yes by 42% of respondents (dates awarded ranged 1985–2001 plus one "BCE"); no 58%. To the question "Does your tenure status affect the degree to which you are able to teach courses including information about violence against women?" 93% responded "No," while 4 responded Yes (7%).

## Descriptive Statistics: Teaching about Violence against Women

A very large percentage, 97%, indicated that they regularly include information about violence against women (hereafter to be referred to as "VAW") in their courses on pastoral care, counseling and pastoral theology. Only one respondent (1.4%) said "No," and there was one response left blank. Of the courses listed on the questionnaire itself, 82% said they include VAW in their Introduction to Pastoral Care course (Yes 56, No 11); 40% in an Introduction to Pastoral Counseling course (Yes 27, no 37), 50% in a Marriage & Family course (Yes 34, no 29); 3% in a course on Death, dying and/or bereavement (Yes 7, no 55); 3% in a Group Counseling course (Yes 2, no 61); 21% in a course on Pastoral Care of Addictions (Yes 14, no 49) and 60% indicated that they include VAW in an "other" course (Yes 41, no 27).

"Other" courses listed represented a wide variety of topics, both in the pastoral field, but also including courses in church history, and systematic theology (see Figure 2).

Figure 2. Titles of Other Courses We Teach Including Violence against Women

American Church History
Bible and Pastoral Care
Crisis Counseling
Contemporary Issues in Pastoral Care
Early Church History
Human Sexuality and Pastoral Care/Sexuality
Medieval and Reformation History
Mental Health Skills for Pastors
Ministry Ethics
Multicultural Pastoral Care/Inter-cultural pastoral care and counseling
Pastor and Family Life
Pastoral Approach to Church Administration
Pastoral Care in Small Groups
Pastoral Care in a Violent World
Pastoral Care with Women
Practice of Ministry/Field Education
Professional Orientation and Ethics
Psychodynamics and Psychotherapy
Special Issues in Counseling: Spirituality
Systematic Theology III (Ecclesiology and Eschatology)
Theological Dimensions of Pastoral Care
Theology and Psychodyamic Theories of Personality/Personality Theory
Feminist, Womanist, Mujarista Ethics
Women and Men
Women and the Old Testament

In addition to these course titles, respondents indicated that they include information on VAW in clinical supervision, in the teaching of medical students, and one respondent stated that VAW is "included in all courses I teach."

Most members regularly assign readings on violence against women in their courses (87%), and of those who do, 44% assign 1–2 chapters, 44% assign all or most of a book, while 12% assign as many as 2 or more books. The texts and authors named in response to this question generated a large and varied bibliography, which is included here as Figure 3.

Figure 3
Bibliography of Authors Frequently Mentioned and
Titles if Mentioned [or may be safely assumed]:
\* = mentioned by more than one respondent

---

*Adams, Carol, *Woman-Battering*
*Adams, Carol and Marie Fortune, eds., *Violence against Women and Children: A Theological Sourcebook*
Benyei, Candace, *Understanding Clergy Misconduct in Religious Systems: Scapegoating, Family Secrets, and the Abuse of Power*
"Black Mountain Presbyterian Church's Response to Family Violence," in *Social Justice Actions of the 213th General Assembly* and *Family Ministry: Empowering through Faith* 17 (2003) 61–71.
Brock, Rita Nakashima and Rebecca Parker, *Proverbs of Ashes: Violence, Redemptive Suffering and the Search for What Saves Us*
Brown Douglas, Kelly, *Sexuality and the Black Church*
Carter, Betty, and Monica McGoldrick, [*The Expanded Family Life Cycle*, 3rd ed.]
*Chung, Hyun Kyung, *Struggle to Be the Sun Again*, and "Who is Jesus for Asian Women?" in *Asian Faces of Jesus*, ed. R.S. Sugirtharajah
*Cooper-White, Pamela, *The Cry of Tamar: Violence against Women and the Church's Response*;
Cooper-White, "Soul Stealing: Power Relations in Pastoral Sexual Abuse," *The Christian Century*, February 20, 1991, pp. 196–99;
Cooper-White, "Sexual Exploitation and Other Boundary Violations in Pastoral Ministries," Chapter 16 in *Clinical Handbook of Pastoral Counseling, Volume 3*; "Opening the Eyes: Understanding the Impact of Trauma on Development," Chapter 5 in *In Her Own Time: Women and Developmental Issues in Pastoral Care*, and other articles.
Crooks, Robert and [Karla] Baur, *Our Sexuality*, 8th ed.
Davis, Laura and Ellen Bass, [*The Courage to Heal*]
Doehring, Carrie, [*Taking Care: Monitoring Power Dynamics and Relational Boundaries in Pastoral Care and Counseling*; and *Internal Desecration*]
Dutton, Donald, *The Abusive Personality: Violence and Control in Intimate Relationships*
Eugene, Toinette and James Poling, eds., *Balm for Gilead: Pastoral Care for African American Families Experiencing Abuse*
*Fortune, Marie, *Is Nothing Sacred?: The Story of a Pastor, the Women He Sexually Abused, and the Congregation He Nearly Destroyed*
Fortune, [*Keeping the Faith: Guidance for Christian Women Facing Abuse*]
Fortune, *Love Does No Harm: Sexual Ethics for the Rest of Us* [and numerous articles]
Garma, JoAnn, "A Cry of Anguish: The Battered Woman," in Moessner and Glaz, eds. *Women in Travail and Transition*
Gebara, Ivone
Graham, Larry Kent
Gudorf, Christine
*Herman, Judith, *Trauma and Recovery*
Illinois Coalition against Domestic Violence, resource booklets
Isasi-Díaz, Ada-Maria, *Mujerista Theology*
*Isherwood, Lisa, Ed., *The Good News of the Body: Sexual Theology and Feminism*

*Journal of Religion and Abuse*
*Kornfeld, Margaret, *Cultivating Wholeness*
*Lebacqz, Karen, [*Ethics and Spiritual Care; PastorPower*]
Leslie, Kristin, *When Violence Is No Stranger*
*Livingston, *Healing Violent Men: A Model for Christian Communities*
Martin, Bernice
McClure, John, and Nancy Ramsay, eds., *Telling the Truth: Preaching about Sexual and Domestic Violence*
Meyeroff, Milton, *On Caring*
Miller-McLemore, Bonnie, and Brita Gil-Austern, eds., *Feminist and Womanist Pastoral Theology*
*Miles, Al, *Domestic Violence: What Every Pastor Should Know*
Miles, Al, and Marie Fortune, *Violence in Families: What Every Christian Needs to Know*
*Moessner, Jeanne Stevenson, ed. *Women in Travail and Transition*
Moessner, *Through the Eyes of Women*
Moore, Zoe, *Introducing Feminist Perspectives on Pastoral Theology*
Nobleman, Roberta, *Victim, Survivor, Celebrant: The Healing Journey from Childhood Sexual Abuse*
*Neuger, Christie, *Counseling Women*
*Neuger, Christie and James Poling, eds., *The Care of Men*
Odoyuye, Mercy, *Introducing African Women's Theology*
Patton, John, *Pastoral Care in Context*
*Poling, James, *The Abuse of Power; Deliver Us From Evil*
Poling, Understanding Male *Violence*
Poling, *Render Unto God: Economic Vulnerability, Family Violence and Pastoral Theology*
*Ramsay, Nancy
Rector, Lallene, "Are We Making Love Yet? Theological and Psychological Perspectives on the Role of Gender Identity in the Experience of Domination," in *The Good News of the Body: Sexual Theology and Feminism*, Lisa Isherwood, ed.
Rutter, Peter, *Sex in the Forbidden Zone*
Steinhauser, Karen
Stinson-Wesley, S. Amelia, articles: "Daughters of Tamar: Pastoral Care for Survivors of Rape," in *Through the Eyes of Women*
Stinson-Wesley, "Sexual Abuse in Christian Homes and Churches," *Daughters of Sarah* 20 (1994) 53.
Strozdas, Linda, "Moral Evil Close to Home: Domestic Violence," *New Theology Review* Winter/Spring 2004.
Suchocki, Marjorie, *Fall to Violence*
Thistlethwaite, Susan
*Weems, Renita, *Battered Love*
Werking Poling, Nancy, *Victim to Survivor: Women Recovering from Clergy Sexual Abuse*
West, Traci, *Wounds of the Spirit: Black Women, Violence, and Resistance Ethics*
Wicks, Robert, Richard Parsons, and Donald Capps, *Clinical Handbook of Pastoral Care and Counseling*, 3 vols.
Wink, Walter, series of titled on "the powers" re: evil, violence and the "domination system"

A few films were also mentioned in connection with teaching on VAW, including *In Love,* documentary, Rachel Zetland; Videos from the Faith Trust Institute (formerly the Center for the Prevention of Sexual and Domestic Violence/CPSDV), Seattle (*Broken Vows* on domestic violence and *Not In My Church* on clergy sexual abuse); and videos from U.S. Conference of Catholic Bishops (*When I Call for Help: A Pastoral Response to Domestic Violence against Women* and *When You Preach, Remember Me*).

Most respondents (79%) do not offer a single course dedicated entirely to some aspect of violence against women. However, 14% do offer such a course, and 8% report having done so in the past but not currently. Of those who do or have done so, 45% offer such a course yearly, and 54.5% offer it every 2–3 years.

## Collaboration with Community Agencies

The next set of questions addressed the level of involvement or collaboration with community agencies working to end violence against women. 34% of respondents indicated that in any of their assignments they do ask students to get involved in site visits or volunteer work at a local domestic violence or rape crisis agency. 54% invite a guest speaker from a local domestic violence or rape crisis agency to speak in your classes? Of those, 45% invite a guest expert every year, 32% every 2–3 years, and 23% less often. An impressive 27% of respondents indicated that they themselves had personally worked and/or volunteered at a battered women's or rape crisis agency. The number of years worked ranged from 1 year to 24 years, with a median of 4.5 years (mean 6, mode 2).

## Increasing Awareness?

The last topical question involved the level of awareness about violence against women among entering M.Div. students over the past 10 years. Of those who responded (10, or 15% did not respond), 70.7% felt that awareness is increasing; 8.6% felt it is decreasing, and 20.7% felt that it is about the same.

## Survey Results: Some Suggestive "Correlations"

In addition to the descriptive statistics described above, I ran tests for association among all the topical variables and the demographic variables.[9] While the caveat about confidence levels must be considered here, the following suggest interesting trends in the data received.

Teaching VAW in the introductory pastoral care course:

- The HIGHER the ACADEMIC RANK, the LESS likely to include VAW in the Intro course. ($p \leq .05$)
- Faculty employed HALF TO FULL-TIME are much more likely to include VAW in the Intro course than adjuncts or other instructors. ($p \leq .009$)
- Faculty employed in DIVINITY SCHOOLS are significantly more likely to include VAW in the Intro course than faculty in SEMINARIES; college/university faculty are about equally likely or not likely to include VAW in the Intro course. ($p. \leq .025$)
- Not surprisingly, those who believe that TENURE STATUS affects the degree to which they are able to teach courses including information about violence against women are significantly less likely to include VAW in the Intro course ($p \leq .027$).

Teaching VAW in other pastoral care courses:

- Only one type of course yielded further statistically significant results: Faculty teaching in SEMINARIES were much more likely to include VAW in their courses on MARRIAGE & FAMILY ($p \leq .02$) than those teaching in other types of institutions. *(Not known: is this because this type of course is offered more regularly in seminaries??)*

---

9. Since the data was nominal, not ratio level, true correlations could not be run. The test used was a standard Cross-Tab, or "Chi-Square" test ($X^2$).

### Regularly assigning readings on VAW in courses, and how much reading

- Faculty employed FULL-TIME are significantly much more likely to assign readings on VAW than adjuncts or other instructors, with half-3/4 time faculty somewhere in the middle. (p ≤ .014)
- Those who believe that TENURE STATUS affects the degree to which they are able to teach courses are statistically much more likely to assign MORE READING on VAW—2 or more books, while those who do not believe tenure status affects this generally assign 1-chapters or all or most of 1 book. (p ≤ .013)
- WOMEN are more likely to assign ALL OR MOST OF A BOOK, while men are more likely to assign 1–2 chapters, although the relatively fewer faculty who do assign 2 or MORE BOOKS on VAW tend to be MEN. (p ≤ .002).

### Have you ever offered a single dedicated course on some aspect of violence against women?

- Noting again that about 20% of faculty offer such a course, 80% do not, there is a *trend* showing that FULL-TIME faculty are perhaps somewhat MORE likely to offer a dedicated course on VAW than part-time or adjunct faculty (p ≤ .11).
- There were no statistically significant gender differences for this question overall (p ≤ .47), although a HIGHER % OF WOMEN (N = 9, or 26% of 34 women responding) than men (N = 5, or 16% of 32 men responding) have offered such a course. Those MEN who *do* offer such a course are statistically more likely than women to offer it EVERY YEAR as opposed to every 2–3 years (p ≤ .03).

### Faculty who have volunteered or worked at a battered women's or rape crisis agency:

- Perhaps not surprisingly, WOMEN have volunteered or worked in an agency devoted to VAW at over twice the rate of MEN. (39% of women vs. 16% of men; p ≤ .047) There were no statistically significant differences for the number of years volunteered/worked by women vs. men who did volunteer or work.

- A more surprising finding was that those who believe TENURE STATUS affects the degree to which they are able to teach courses including information about violence against women are much more likely (about 3.5 to 1) to have worked in a VAW agency ($p \leq .03$). (Does this suggest a more political outlook in general on the part of these respondents?)

*Do you feel that awareness about violence against women among entering M.Div. students in the last 10 years is increasing, decreasing, or about the same?*

GENDER was the significant difference on this question ($p \leq .04$):
- MEN were much more likely to believe that such awareness is INCREASING (86% of men vs. 55% of women).
- WOMEN were more likely to believe that it is about the SAME (31% of women vs. 10% of men) or even DECREASING (14% of women vs. 3% of men).
- SPT members WITH M.Div. degrees more often believed awareness was INCREASING, while those with other degrees but NOT M.Div.'s tended to believe awareness was DECREASING or REMAINING THE SAME ($p \leq .05$).
- Note: YEARS teaching at current institution, total years teaching, and tenure status (whether tenured or not) did *not* show statistically significant differences for this question.

## In the Respondents' Own Words: "The topic of violence against women should be a required component..."

In addition to statistical data, a number of respondents did add comments in their own words. All responses, from a variety of contexts, appeared to share the perspective that such teaching is a vital component of theological curricula, and their reflections showed a strong sense of commitment, sensitivity to students' own experiences with violence, and some frustration with colleagues or students showing lingering resistance to the subject. The overall attitude seemed to be one of continuing dedication to promoting awareness from a variety of disciplines, teaching methods, and cultural and gender perspectives.

A number of respondents wrote about their sense of commitment to the inclusion of violence against women in their courses, and elaborated on some of the methods they include in their teaching:

"I have moved from trying to introduce a variety of counseling theories to stressing many versions of narrative therapy as it deals with peer issues so well."

"I relate violence against women directly to lack of empathic capacity/ emotional disconnect in men."

"I've been teaching 'Domestic Violence and Pastoral Care' for 4 years and it was a course I proposed."

"In CPE: I include a module on crisis intervention that discusses violence. Also, it is part of the clinical experience of CPE residents . . . covers a spectrum: child abuse, peer to peer, women, etc."

"I regularly encourage students to continue reading and attending continuing education events on this topic after graduation, and stress the crucial importance of ongoing consultation with those specially trained in this work."

"As a male teacher I have read extensively, written a little bit and focused on the male formation process as an emphasis in dealing with violence toward women. I am pleased to have one of our male students see this as the focus for his future ministry."

"I assign students role-plays one per semester on some aspect of VAW; I assign each student an oral presentation on a subject of his/her choice and at least one per semester does report on some aspect of VAW; We talk about the ethics of reporting abuse/violence; We have a whole class devoted to clergy sexual misconduct; I have individual conversations with each student and some have told of their own experience with violence."

"There were 2 stories of violence toward women in prepared starter stories for role-playing exercises in the pastoral care class conducted in small groups. . . . [In] the course on women and men we dealt with the issue on at least 3 class periods. And in courses on the family, I had Mary Pellauer speak in the class 2 years and we dealt with the topic of a couple other occasions but not always. In the Intro to Pastoral Care the emphasis was on developing empathy skills—I did not deal with a whole range of specific life situations."

"The issue of violence is dealt with through case studies and often in the context of other issues such as ethnicity, culture, and administrative processes. Also in the last years especially, these courses are taught quite inductively. Hence violence and discrimination issues are studies in the context of cases and situations that others bring up. To me, the questionnaire implies a certain style of teaching and learning. In our work with field education, the matters of violence, discrimination and harassment are highlighted in cases brought by students. Resources such as your own book are then highlighted and discussed. There is not the structured approach in much of our work as the questions seem to imply."

"One assignment asks students to get involved in a site visit. Some choose on their own volition to visit an agency."

"Overall curricular demands affect what I teach much more than tenure status or probably any other factor."

"Also I challenge students to really understand the Canon Law re: church marriage . . . that because it is the couple who marries each other (the priest is simply witness), emotional, sexual, or physical violence renders a Catholic marriage invalid. I am always astonished at how few Catholics understand this. I charge them as responsible future parish leaders to construct a parish-wide pastoral plan for addressing domestic violence . . . they form groups that mimic a parish council. Each student group has to formulate a parish plan . . ."

[writing in the role of TA for an Intro to Pastoral Counseling course:] "The syllabus includes some readings about domestic violence. However, I do not find that the aim of class discussion has exclusively focused on violence against women. The class discussions have also included the distorted reality of children who are the victims of domestic violence."

A number of respondents pointed to other colleagues on their faculties who were teaching on the subject as well—or not:

"Each year our ethics professor whose expertise is in domestic violence offers a course on domestic violence."

"A female colleague and I have taught together a course on clergy abuse as an elective about four times over the year but that is no[w] being addressed in our Professional Ethics class, we hope."

"In my area, a number of faculty teach courses that focus on VAW ... They are all members of SPT."

"I alternate every 6–7 years teaching pastoral care and counseling core courses with my colleague whose approach to the topic is mostly theological. Hence, *those years I do not teach the core courses, students are less likely to be exposed to this topic.* One other female colleague addresses this topic in her theology courses and courses on sin/evil."

[same person as above:] "I am currently teaching a Pastoral Counseling course and have devoted a whole section to dealing with women and violence. I asked the class if they had done any readings on this topic or dealt with it in *any other class* during seminary. To my horror, this was the first time for most of the advanced students!!"

A few respondents offered some useful suggestions:

"This might be an interesting question to ask of a divinity school Dean—how/where in the entire curriculum is this issue addressed/explored? The question alone would raise consciousness that it deserves examination from several vantage points."

"Have abused seminarians on panels too."

"Do any of your pastoral care courses teach something about the history of violence against women before the 20th century?" [This respondent's courses did so.]

One respondent noted the presence of women on faculties was noted as an important factor in the inclusion of VAW in curricula. This perception was validated strongly by members of the follow-up discussion group:

> VAW began to be addressed when feminist women started teaching in theological schools. It is frequently taught in all fields where women are teaching, and some men are beginning to teach also. However, progress depends on the presence and power of feminist-oriented women on the faculty, in my opinion.

A few respondents also raised the issue of resistance they had experienced, or troubled feelings raised among students by the teaching of VAW:

"I still encounter great resistance from male students for discussing this. Many want to talk about violence against men; many say that concentrating on this is focusing on 'aberrant men.'"

> "When I did teach it . . . *Women in Travail* and *Through the Eyes of Women* were required and troubling reading for the men (and women) in the class, 40% of whom came from outside the U.S."

One respondent, whose sentiments were echoed by the discussion workshop, indicated how frequently students will disclose personal experiences of abuse as a result of the topic being raised in a class:

> Every time we finish a unit on DV in a class at CTU, there is at least one student who comes forward privately admitting having survived an abusive marriage.

The importance of cultural context and the setting for teaching were highlighted by some respondents:

> As an Emeritus . . . in a 'secular' setting MA-level [counseling program] . . . about 80% of my students are African American women. Domestic violence is an integral topic in most of these courses; and indeed many of these students have worked in, or are working in, domestic violence contexts and rape centers. Although only a very few students probably would see their counseling in a formal theological context, I am quite impressed with the fact that many of the topics in your survey are addressed and processed in our classes. Fact is that many of these first-generation to achieve higher education at the MA level have lived in—some still living in—communities where violence against women is an all too common factor. I only wish there were some way of linking these MA-level professional counselors to the theological community you are surveying.

> [from an international graduate student respondent:] My two teachers . . . did address the seriousness of domestic violence against women and children. I observed the impact of being informed among my fellow students. In addition, I took time to reflect upon whether there are some cultural myths and resistances among my American colleagues in dealing with violence against women and children. I temporarily drew a conclusion in thinking that people could try to avoid facing a distorted reality of violence because the lasting image of the U.S.A. and its citizenship is supposed to be based on egalitarianism and mutuality following the ideals of the fathers and mothers in the early American history. If the root of violence were embedded in the incomplete journey of the American people toward justice, the voice of the vulnerable population must be critically examined and evaluated to bring new insights in our understanding of

> psychosocial wellbeing. I now believe that embracing and addressing the American history could be a key to liberate many people across different backgrounds from false myths and resistance in the issue of violence against the most vulnerable population among us such as women and children.
>
> I teach in Sao Paulo, Brazil. There is not a great deal of awareness, or consciousness, regarding this topic, but it is growing. The topic of violence in general is very much in the forefront of discussions, but it is generally related to drugs and poverty. However, there is a growing awareness of how the question or problem of violence specifically affects women and children. Thank you for your research.

Finally, a number of respondents expressed a passionate concern about violence against women, advocating for inclusion of the topic in pastoral care courses, and for naming the problems of patriarchy and systems of domination more widely, in interfaith dialogue:

> The topic of violence against women should be a required component of Intro to Pastoral Care and Intro to Pastoral Counseling courses. At a minimum this would include domestic violence, incest and rape. Pastors and counselors should be able to recognize signs of abuse and be prepared to address the needs of those who have been abused either through counseling or appropriate referrals.
>
> I have not worked with abusers, but make sure that students are aware that they need to be identified while young. As Leonardo Boff noted . . . in *Liberating Grace*, culture can be both "graced and 'disgraced.'" In the case of domestic violence, we need to name patriarchal systems and power structures as vehicles of "disgrace" and wrestle them away from the endorsement of religious communities (whether Christian or non-Christian). We need to support our Muslim, Buddhist, Jewish, Hindi colleagues as they also work to separate the core of their religious beliefs from the "disgraced" violent aspects of cultural memory that impacts current violent behaviors. I believe that the whole community needs to be involved not just in providing care for victims, but in prevention at several levels.

## "Hawthorne Effect"!?;[10] Ways in Which This Survey Stimulated Further Activity:

A few additional comments suggested that the survey itself may have done some good, in stimulating members of the Society to think further about including information about violence against women in more of their courses, to include guest speakers, and to become more connected with community organizations working to end violence. Several such comments included:

"Made me realize what I have NOT done that I might!";

"My work on this matter is still minimal and primarily related to clergy sexual abuse. I am appreciative of your work and this further extension of it!"

"Using a guest lecturer is a very good idea and one I may pursue."

## Discussion of Results, Limitations, and Recommendations for Future Research

What do the results mean, in light of the findings here and the limitations of the present study, and what further research might be suggested? Although it is not known why SPT members who did not return the questionnaire decided not to respond, it is clear that among those who responded, there is a very high level of attention and seriousness given to the issue of violence against women in our teaching. Nearly all respondents teach about the issue in some course, and a very high 82 percent also include it in their introductory courses. A wide variety of readings are assigned to students in our classes. A number of course readings may be considered standard texts, including titles by Carol Adams, Pamela Cooper-White, Marie Fortune, Al Miles, Christie Neuger, James Poling, and Nancy Ramsay, as well as the three anthologies on pastoral care with women edited by Jeanne Stevenson Moessner, and Moessner and Maxine Glaz. But the variety of texts assigned beyond these "standards" represent a rich and varied bibliography, representing a greater multi-cultural diversity among authors beyond the texts used most often.

Single courses dedicated to the subject of violence against women are more rare than the incorporation of the topic into other courses, however

---

10. A term used to define positive results caused by the impact of being studied, rather than the actual variables being tested (named after the Hawthorne factory of Western Electric Company where it was first identified as a confounding factor in statistical research).

20% of SPT members do offer, or have offered such a course. This decision recognizes the importance not only of "mainstreaming" such issues as feminism and multi-culturalism into standard curriculum offerings—which sometimes, although not suggested in the present research, can have the feel of an add-on or a "nod" to the subject—but also taking the time in a curriculum to go into greater depth and detail into such subjects, which in prior generations were rarely mentioned at all. While it was not possible to compare the data in this survey to data from 20 years ago (no such study exists), participants in a follow-up workshop at the Society's annual meeting in Atlanta, George, June, 2005, agreed that few faculty were teaching about this issue at all 20 years ago. Given the fact that the first rape crisis and domestic violence agencies only began in the mid- to late-1970s, it is not surprising that the current level of attention given to these issues in pastoral care curricula has increased dramatically in the past two decades.

Involvement with outside agencies was higher than might be expected, with over 1/3 of respondents assignments requiring students to engage in site visits or volunteer work at a local agency, and slightly over half invited outside agency workers as guest speakers in classes (and almost half of those, yearly). In terms of respondents' own direct experience working in agencies, it was heartening to see that over ¼ of respondents indicated that they themselves had personally worked and/or volunteered. It was not surprising that more women (13, or 39%) had volunteered or worked at a rape crisis or domestic violence agency. This may be partly attributed to some agencies allowing only women to work in some or all of their programs for the sake of clients' sense of safety. Nevertheless, a fairly significant percentage of men (N =5, or 16%) had also done so. All these findings taken together are a strong indicator of the rise in awareness and commitment to these issues among our own membership.

The issue of student awareness was an interesting one as well. Although most a majority of respondents overall reported that they believe the awareness of entering level M.Div. students is increasing (over 70%), still nearly 21% feel that it is about the same, and almost 9% feel it is decreasing. This was the one question that showed marked gender differences. Not unlike a report we heard in Atlanta on the differences between white persons and persons of color regarding optimism about racism, in this study men were much more likely to believe that such awareness is increasing, while women (i.e., those most likely statistically to be affected personally by domestic violence, sexual assault, harassment, and other forms of gender violence) were more likely to believe that it is about the same (at a ratio of about 3:1) or even decreasing (14:3).

Rank, tenure, and years teaching had less effect than perhaps might have been expected. Both newer and more veteran faculty are taking up the issue of violence against women in their courses. The one main statistically significant finding about rank was that the higher the academic rank, the less likely the respondent was to include VAW in the Intro to Pastoral Care course. Participants in the follow-up workshop speculated that this might be generational, and that some senior faculty might have been less likely to include violence against women, or special topics more generally, in an introductory overview course than in other more topics courses (such as Marriage and Family, etc.) One respondent corroborated this—a senior faculty with many years of teaching indicated that the introductory course focused on listening skills and methods, and "I did not deal with a whole range of specific life situations." The finding that faculty employed half- to full-time are much more likely to include VAW in the Intro course than adjuncts or other instructors makes sense in terms of the freedom regular faculty have to offer the Introductory course, and/or to shape its contents.

The finding that faculty employed in divinity schools are significantly *more* likely to include VAW in the Intro course than faculty in seminaries was somewhat puzzling, since it would seem that seminaries may offer a wider variety of pastoral care courses and electives geared toward preparation for parish ministry. The follow-up workshop group considered however that some denominational schools self-identify as divinity schools, and some university-affiliated schools identify as seminaries, confusing the definitions. There may also be a slight tendency in divinity schools to offer more specialized course electives, and perhaps to offer more courses on challenging social topics that may be perceived as "too liberal" by some denominational seminary constituencies.

It was not surprising that those who believe that tenure status affects the degree to which they are able to teach courses including information about violence against women were significantly less likely to include VAW in the Intro course. Although the numbers here were small, others reported in the qualitative responses and in follow-up conversation that there is still some fear, particularly among junior faculty, about being perceived as too radical in their teaching and needing to "play it safe" until tenured. This finding must be balanced, however, with the overwhelming majority who reported that they believed tenure status did not affect their ability to teach about violence against women.

## Implications for the Future

Where do we go from here? It is clear that awareness and commitment are high among Society members. [For this current *Collected Essays* volume, a quick follow-up study in 2018 showed that this commitment has continued into the present decade, with younger scholars taking up the challenge alongside seasoned educators.[11]]

One follow-up group participant, who has significant teaching, clinical and agency experience on the issue of violence against women, commented that the Society itself is probably skewed toward members who are more "liberal" in social orientation, and given our research and programmatic emphases over the years, our membership tends to self-select toward faculty, researchers and clinicians who share common concerns for social justice as a core issue in pastoral care and pastoral theology. Both Roman Catholic and Evangelical Protestant theological schools are also under-represented in the Society, which is largely comprised of mainline Protestant seminary and divinity school faculties, as well as some independent researchers and interested pastoral counselors.

The consensus of the discussion group, as well as some survey respondents, was that others beyond the Society who teach pastoral care courses in seminaries—especially Roman Catholic and Evangelical schools—should be surveyed, and encouraged to consider increasing their teaching on these issues. It would also be valuable to survey faculties teaching in other fields such as social ethics, religious education, church history, and systematic theology. A separate survey of CPE supervisors would also be a worthwhile study. One workshop participant also suggested more formal research investigating outcomes assessment with students—i.e., developing instruments to investigate not only what we think we are teaching, but what students are actually learning!

---

11. The number of responses was very small (N=15), so it is assumed that those most committed to teaching on VAW issues were a self-selected response sample. All respondents regularly include information on VAW in their courses, and all but 1 incorporate relevant readings. Slightly less than ½ supervise outside agency placements, and slightly over ½ invite outside guest speakers. Two-thirds say they teach about VAW to the same degree as previously, 20% say they teach more and 13% (2 respondents) responded "no comparison—just began teaching." Almost half the respondents had worked or volunteered at a VAW agency. Academic rank was split fairly evenly among full professors 27%), tenured associates (20%), pre-tenure (20%), and part-time/adjunct (27%), plus one retired respondent. Two-thirds of respondents identified as female. Sixty percent were white (9), 20% African descent (3), and 7% (1 each) were international, Asian/Asian American, bi-racial, and prefer not to answer (non-mutually-exclusive categories). I did not run cross-tabs for any categories since the overall response rate was so low.

# WHAT ARE WE TEACHING ABOUT VIOLENCE AGAINST WOMEN?

Clearly, there is progress over the past 2-3 decades in the area of teaching on the subject of violence against women. This is enormously heartening for those of us who have worked to promote awareness and to build bridges to develop shared prevention, intervention, and political advocacy strategies across seminaries, counseling centers, agencies and congregations. There are yet so many miles to go, and much teaching and researching to be done, before violence against women is finally ended. Some of the areas specifically raised by workshop participants as needing even more attention in future teaching included . . .

- clergy sexual abuse
- sexual harassment (including harassment within institutions of theological education, and in related field education settings)
- war crimes against women and global issues of violence against women
- emotional and physical violence
- issues of shame, secrecy and under-reporting
- relating violence against women to developmental issues re: age, e.g., teen dating violence
- greater understanding of more communally based contexts of violence against women
- strategies to help men stop male violence: "We are pulling women out, but the men are still there in the community to hurt women!"
- revival of consciousness raising groups among younger women, and the importance of highly visible women telling their stories in the public arena
- issues of restorative justice
- especially in keeping with the theme of the Atlanta conference, to continue to make the conceptual linkages between violence against women and racism and other forms of oppression

Our dream is big! But the results of this research are heartening, and may serve to encourage all of us to "keep on keeping on," until all violence against women—and all violence—is ended. Let us hope for that day when we can finally teach about violence against women purely as a matter for the historians—as a memory of "the former things . . . the things of old" while God is indeed "doing a new thing!" (Isa 43:18).

# 9

# Feminism(s), Gender, and Power
*Reflections from a Feminist Pastoral Theologian*

2008[1]

WHAT IS FEMINISM? A general definition might be as follows: Feminism means taking seriously the call for social, economic and political parity, and equal rights and responsibilities, of women with men, and looking unflinchingly at the painful realities, and the negative impact on both men and women, of *patriarchalism* (literally, rule of the fathers), both historically (especially in Christian theology as it pertains to the history of the church[2]) and in contemporary societies.

Feminist *theologies*, then, point out the gaps and distortions both in the historical record and in the biblical witness itself—gaps and distortions *about* women—women's experiences, spirituality, and contributions, and the relative absence or discounting of women's voices in the theological tradition. In addition, feminist theologies take up issues that have historically been of *concern* to women, but often neglected in "traditional" theology, including such topics as the body, the role of subjective experience and relationships, and such socio-political issues as violence against women and children. Because oppression is both a catalyst and a theme for feminist theologies, the integrative linking of women's oppression with racial, class, sexual-orientation, and other forms of oppression is also always of central concern.

---

1. Earlier versions of this paper were presented at Princeton Theological Seminary, the annual Women in Church and Ministry Lecture, Feb. 28, 2008 (printed in *The Princeton Seminary Bulletin*, 2009, 38ff), and at the Society for Pastoral Theology annual study conference, June, 2008, published in the *Journal of Pastoral Theology* 18/2 (2008) 18–46.

2. This paper is written, necessarily, from my perspective as a Christian (Anglican) pastoral theologian, an ordained priest, and a white professional-class North American woman.

What are the implications of feminist movement for us, in our discipline of pastoral theology? As a feminist *pastoral* theologian, I will argue that all theology, but especially *pastoral* theology, which is concerned with care for suffering, must begin with embodied human experience. Pastoral theology begins with what Ada-María Isasi-Díaz calls *"lo cotidiano"*—the realities of daily life.³ In particular, it takes human suffering as its starting place⁴—in Jürgen Moltmann's words, "the open wound of life in this world."⁵ Moreover, as a *feminist* pastoral theologian, I must always work intentionally to resist the inertia that impedes awareness of oppression of women in our culture. This means being attentive to including and empowering women's voices in my research, and in my contexts of teaching and ministry; it means lifting up women's issues in my writing and preaching; and it means working on my own gender- and other culturally ingrained biases, and seeking collaborative partnerships across such socially constructed divides.

## Forms of Feminism

Feminism, however, is not a homogeneous movement. There are, of course, many feminisms. At the level of theoretical formulation, there have been increasingly over the past several decades a variety of forms of articulating justice for women, which in turn have had significant impact on theology in general, and pastoral theology in particular. To summarize, in somewhat chronological order, and using the language of the women who identify with each of these perspectives, these include radical, liberal, essentialist, and more recently Womanist, mujerista, global, two-thirds world, Lesbian, and postmodern and postcolonial feminisms.⁶

---

3. Ada Maria Isasi-Díaz, *Mujerista Theology: A Theology for the Twenty-first Century* (Louisville: Westminster John Knox, 1996).

4. This tradition runs deep in pastoral theology, including Anton Boisen's concept of "the living human document" (in *The Exploration of the Inner World*, New York: Harper, 1952); see also Bonnie J. Miller-McLemore, "The Living Human Web: Theology at the Turn of the Century," in Jeanne Stevenson-Moessner, ed., *Through the Eyes of Women: Insights for Pastoral Care* (Minneapolis: Fortress, 1996) 9–26. It is also part of a larger trend of "correlational theology," from Paul Tillich, *Systematic Theology*, Vols. 1 and 3 (Chicago: University of Chicago Press, 1973), esp. the introduction to Vol. 1; to David Tracy, *Blessed Rage for Order: The New Pluralism in Theology* (New York: Seabury, 1975); to Mark Kline Taylor, *Remembering Esperanza: A Cultural-political Theology for North America* (Maryknoll, NY: Orbis, 1989).

5. Jürgen Moltmann, *The Trinity and the Kingdom* (Minneapolis: Fortress, 1993) 49.

6. This portion of this paper is based on presentations for the Graduate Theological Union, Berkeley, CA, March, 2005, and Princeton Theological Seminary, Feb., 2008; see also Cooper-White, "The Early 1990s: Whose CWR? Whose Feminism?" In Rosemary

(1) The first form of feminism I have identified here is *"radical"* or *"progressive"* feminism (e.g., writings of bell hooks[7]). Grounded in Marxist-feminist ideals, this form of feminism involves critical analysis, public advocacy, and community organizing around concrete manifestations of oppression of women. The goal of this form of feminism is essentially revolutionary (even if the form it usually takes in an academic or church context is mainly via persuasion and education)—the overthrow of existing hierarchical structures, patterns, and institutions that perpetuate oppression, and the hope of a new, egalitarian social order.

This movement became manifest in Christian political activism beyond church walls, and in theological education through research and pedagogies that promote radical—that is to-the-root causes—analysis of economic injustice, violence against women, and a liberationist analysis of inter-related forms of oppression. Theologically, radical feminist method is guided by a politically informed hermeneutics of suspicion, critical analysis of power, and rejection of patriarchal images of God that reinforce women's subordination.

(2) The second form of feminism evident in the institutional church and theological education is what most North Americans would simply call "feminism," social analysts might call *"liberal feminism,"* and its detractors, as I once heard pejoratively spoken by some of the radical feminists, call "NOW-style bourgeois feminism." The goal of liberal feminism is not so much the overthrow of existing social structures, as the equal access of women to the privilege, decision-making, power and authority enjoyed by men within those structures. If Marxism is the underlying politics of radical feminism, then Enlightenment values of liberty, brother-and-sisterhood, and equality are the rallying cries of liberal feminism.[8] In the context of the church and theological education, this strand may be seen in the movement for the ordination of women; efforts to break through the "stained glass ceiling" of Assistant and Associate pastorates in those denominations that do ordain women; advocacy within seminaries for more women faculty and

---

Radford Ruether, ed., *Feminist Theologies: Legacy and Prospect* (Minneapolis: Fortress, 2007) 16–28.

7. E.g., bell hooks, *Feminist Theory: From Margin to Center* (Boston: South End, 1984).

8. This parallels Iris Marion Young's term "humanist" feminism: "Humanism, Gynocentrism and Feminist Politics," in Young, *Throwing Like a Girl and Other Essays in Feminist Philosophy*—Indianapolis: Indiana University Press, 1990) 73–91, cited in Bonnie J. Miller-McLemore, "Feminist Theory in Pastoral Theology," in Miller-McLemore and Brita Gill-Austern, eds., *Feminist and Womanist Pastoral Theology* (Nashville: Abingdon, 1999) 82.

the promotion of women faculty to tenured rank; and encouragement of women PhD students and faculty to publish feminist scholarship.

Theologically, at least one scholarly approach within the liberal feminist movement has been to appropriate the thought and/or methodology of major 19th and 20th century theologians such as Schleiermacher, Barth, or Niebuhr, or going back to ancient sources such as Augustine and Aquinas or even the Bible itself—recovering women's voices and leadership in antiquity—to show that women deserve an equal place of power in church and society (e.g., theologians Rosemary Radford Ruether,[9] Elisabeth Schüssler Fiorenza,[10] Clarissa Atkinson, Connie Buchanan and Margaret Miles,[11] and Letty Russell).[12] And of course, there has been the ongoing project of challenging sexist imagery in Christian tradition and patriarchal language in theology and liturgy (e.g., Ruether[13] and Russell[14].)

My own first pastoral theological book *The Cry of Tamar: Violence Against Women and the Church's Response*,[15] stands within both of these first two feminist movements: drawing from radical feminism in my critique of patriarchal structures that perpetuate the subjugation of women in our North American society, and calling on a more contextual understanding of power as accountable power-in-community,[16] while still drawing from liberal feminism in my continuing, dogged embrace of the church as a place of hope and redemption—in spite of its flawed, human history. As others have noted elsewhere, one of our own pioneers in pastoral theology and the teaching and ministry of pastoral care from a liberal/radical feminist per-

---

9. Rosemary Radford Ruether, *New Woman, New Earth: Sexist Ideologies and Human Liberation* (New York: Seabury, 1975); Rosemary Radford Ruether and Eleanor McLaughlin, *Women of Spirit: Female Leadership in the Jewish and Christian Traditions* (New York: Simon & Schuster, 1979)

10. Elisabeth Schüssler Fiorenza, *In Memory of Her: A Feminist Theological Reconstruction of Christian Origins* (New York: Crossroad, 1984).

11. Clarissa Atkinson, Constance Buchanan and Margaret Miles, *Immaculate and Powerful: The Female in Sacred Image and Social Reality.* (Boston: Beacon, 1985); Margaret Miles, *Augustine on the Body* (Missoula, MT: Scholars, 1979).

12. E.g., Letty M. Russell, ed., *Feminist Interpretation of the Bible* (Philadelphia: Westminster, 1985) and *Church in the Round: Feminist Interpretation of Church* (Louisville: Westminster John Knox, 1993).

13. Ruether, *Sexism and God-talk: Toward a Feminist Theology* (Boston: Beacon, 1983).

14. Russell, *The Liberating Word: A Guide to Nonsexist Interpretation of the Bible.* (Philadelphia: Westminster, 1976).

15. Pamela Cooper-White, *The Cry of Tamar: Violence Against Women and the Church's Response* (Minneapolis: Fortress, 1995; [2nd ed. 2012]).

16. Ibid., 30–40 [2nd ed. pp. 51–61].

spective is Peggy Way, whose numerous works since the 1960s challenged our own field to grapple with the social, political, and power realities of women in church and pastoral ministry.[17]

(3) Emerging especially in the 1980s, but drawing on much older threads of tradition regarding women's roles and definitions of the feminine, is a third form of feminism that might be termed *"essentialist feminism."* In the realm of women and religion, this form of feminism grew out of the women's spirituality movement, and has existed mainly in conversation and contrast to liberal feminism.[18] Whereas liberal feminists seek equality with men, essentialist feminists assert essential, even innate *differences* between women and men.[19] Like liberal feminists, they advocate for an equal valuation of women, but critique liberal feminists for "trying to be *like* men." In the social sciences, Carol Gilligan's 1982 work *In a Different Voice*,[20] and the work of Jean Baker Miller[21] and the Jean Baker Miller Training Institute (formerly known as the Stone Center[22]), would fall into this category of research.

17. E.g., Peggy Way, "What's Wrong with the Church: The Clergy," *Renewal*, 3/7 (1963) 8–9; and later, *Created by God: Pastoral Care for All God's People* (St. Louis: Chalice, 2005); See also Kathleen J. Greider, Gloria A. Johnson and Kristen J. Leslie, "Three Decades of Women Writing for Our Lives," and Bonnie Miller-McLemore, "Feminist Theory in Pastoral Theology," in Miller-McLemore and Brita Gill-Austern, ed., *Feminist and Womanist Pastoral Theology* (Nashville: Abingdon, 1999) 22, 88.

18. This is what Iris Marion Young terms "gynocentrism," in contrast with humanist feminist movements (op. cit.).

19. To varying degrees, this viewpoint is reflected in the works from the 1970s-early 80s, including Nancy Chodorow, *The Reproduction of Mothering: Psychoanalysis and the Sociology of Gender* (Berkeley: University of California Press, 1978); Dorothy Dinnerstein *The Mermaid and the Minotaur*, (New York: Harper & Row, 1976); Susan Griffin, *Women and Nature: The Roaring inside Her* (New York: Harper & Row, 1978); Carolyn Merchant, *The Death of Nature: Women, Ecology and the Scientific Revolution* (San Francisco: HarperSan Francisco, 1980). These authors recognize that both nature and nurture—including socialization and unconsciously internalized gender dynamics from infancy—are at play in gender inequality, but tend to emphasize women's distinctive differences.

20. Carol Gilligan, *In a Different Voice: Psychological Theory and Women's Development* (Cambridge: Harvard University Press, 1982).

21. E.g., Jean Baker Miller, op. cit.

22. Both schools of thought have roots in Sullivanian interpersonal theory, and both value reciprocity and mutuality in the therapeutic relationship. These authors challenge the developmental ideal of an autonomous self, replacing it with the paradigm of "self-in-relation." E.g., Jean Baker Miller, ibid. (2nd ed. 1986); Judith V. Jordan, Alexandra G. Kaplan, Jean Baker Miller, Irene P. Stiver, and Janet L. Surrey, ed., *Women's Growth in Connection: Writings from the Stone Center* (New York: Guilford, 1991); Judith Jordan, ed., *Women's Growth in Diversity: More Writings from the Stone Center* (New York: Guilford, 1997); Jean Baker Miller and Irene P. Stiver, *The Healing Connection: How Women*

This branch of feminism embraces a matriarchal or sororal ideal of women as nurturing, intuitive, creative, collaborative, and, like their radical feminist sisters, non-hierarchical. Their vision, however, at least at its extreme, is more utopian than revolutionary per se. Often somewhat separatist in their spiritual practices, many of these women have sought to recover or reconstruct ancient and pre-modern forms of goddess worship,[23] and "women's ways of knowing,"[24] which could be taught and practiced by both women and men alike.[25] The pastoral caregiver in me resonates with some of the healing that women have found in this movement, although I am too much of a psychoanalytic skeptic to fully embrace the over-idealization of women, and the denial of female aggression that I sometimes find there.[26] The goal of this form of feminism is to validate difference and to show that women should not be assessed by male norms and standards. But it begs the question of how uncritical acceptance of these differences as "natural" may also perpetuate stereotypes that in turn justify power inequities in the name of natural law. Maxine Glaz's influential article "Reconstructing the Pastoral Care of Women,"[27] and the four Fortress Press anthologies on pastoral care of women edited by Jeanne Stevenson-Moessner with Maxine Glaz and Teresa Snorton,[28] have taken the best of this women-centered approach to

*Form Relationships in Therapy and in Life* (Boston: Beacon, 1997). See also the Works in Progress Series, and many other papers available from the Stone Center, Wellesley College, Wellesley, MA [now online at https://www.wcwonline.org/JBMTI-Site/publications]. The Stone Center is now the Jean Baker Miller Training Institute, online at https://www.wcwonline.org/JBMTI-Site/introduction-to-jbmti. —PCW 2018]

23. E.g., Carol P. Christ, "Why Women Need the Goddess: Phenomenological, Psychological, and Political Reflections," in Judith Plaskow and Carol P. Christ, ed., *Womanspirit rising* (San Francisco: Harper & Row, 1979) 71–86; Charlene Spretnak, ed., *The Politics of Women's Spirituality: Essays by Founding Mothers of the Movement* (New York: Anchor, 1981).

24. Mary Field Belenky, Blythe McVicker Clinchy, Nancy Rule Goldberger and Jill Mattuck Tarule (1986). *Women's Ways of Knowing: The Development of Self, Voice, and Mind* (New York: Basic Books, 1986; 2nd ed., 2008).

25. Specifically in the context of ministry, see also Celia Hahn, *Sexual Paradox: Creative Tensions in our Lives and in Our Congregations* (New York: Pilgrim, 1991).

26. Cf., Kathleen Greider, *Reckoning with Aggression: Theology, Violence, and Vitality* (Louisville: Westminster John Knox, 1997).

27. Maxine Glaz, "Reconstructing the Pastoral Care of Women," *Second Opinion* 17/2 (1991) 94–107.

28. Maxine Glaz and Jeanne Stevenson-Moessner, eds., *Women in Travail and Transition: A New Pastoral Care* (Minneapolis: Fortress, 1991); Jeanne Stevenson-Moessner, ed., *Through the Eyes of Women: Insights for Pastoral Care* (Minneapolis: Fortress, 1996); Jeanne Stevenson-Moessner, ed., *In Her Own Time: Women and Developmental Issues in Pastoral Care* (Minneapolis: Fortress, 2000); Jeanne Stevenson-Moessner and Teresa Snorton, ed. *Women Out of Order: Risking Change and Creating Care in a Multi-cultural*

theology, theory and research, without abandoning the critical lens afforded by more radical social, psychological, and political analyses.

(4) A multiplicity of forms of feminism began emerging multi-culturally in the 1980s as *Womanist*,[29] *mujerista*,[30] *Asian*,[31] and *developing, "global," or "two-thirds world"* feminist voices,[32] as well as LGBTQ women's voices, began to be heard and published in both religious institutions and the academy.[33] Some important themes emerging from this dialogue included an emphasis on communal and context-oriented forms of care[34]; inductive rather than deductive methods of theologizing, especially naming women's experience as both source and norm[35]; valuing the power of narrative;[36] valuing friendship as a theological theme;[37] an emphasis on "God-praxis" rather than "God-talk," risking the traditional stigma of "syncretism" to

---

*World* (Minneapolis: Fortress, 2009).

29. E.g., classic Womanist texts include Emilie M. Townes, ed., *Embracing the Spirit: Womanist Perspectives on Hope, Salvation and Transformation* (Maryknoll: Orbis, 1997); Delores Williams, *Sisters in the Wilderness: The Challenge of God-Talk* (Maryknoll: Orbis, 2003); Jacqueline Grant, *White Women's Christ and Black Women's Jesus: Feminist Christology and Womanist Response* (Atlanta: Scholars Press/AAR, 1989); Renita Weems, *Just a Sister Away: A Womanist Vision of Women's Relationships in the Bible* (Philadelphia: Innisfree, 1988); Kelly Brown Douglas, *Sexuality and the Black Church: A Womanist Perspective* (Maryknoll: Orbis, 1999), among many others.

30. E.g., Isasi-Díaz, op. cit.; Ivone Gebara, *Longing for Running Water: Ecofeminism and Liberation* (Minneapolis; Fortress, 1999), among others.

31. E.g., Hyun Kyung Chung, *Struggle to Be the Sun Again: Introducing Asian Women's Theology* (Maryknoll: Orbis, 1991).

32. E.g., Mercy Amba Oduyoye, *Introducing African Women's Theology* (New York: Pilgrim, 2001); Kwok Pui Lan, *Postcolonial Imagination and Feminist Theology* (Louisville: Westminster John Knox, 2005); cf., Rosemary Radford Ruether, *Integrating Ecofeminism, Globalization and World Religions* (New York: Rowman & Littlefield, 2005) and Ruether, ed., *Feminist Theologies: Legacy and Prospect* (Minneapolis: Fortress, 2007).

33. E.g., Jane Adams Spahr, Kathryn Poethig, Selisse Berry, and Melinda V. McLain, ed., *Called Out: The Voices and Gifts of Lesbian, Gay, Bisexual, and Transgendered Presbyterians* (Gaithersburg, MD: Chi Rho Press, 1995); Letha Scanzoni and Virginia Ramey Mollenkott, *Is the Homosexual My Neighbor?: Another Christian View.* (San Francisco: Harper & Row, 1978); more recently, Virginia Ramey Mollenkott, *Omnigender: A Trans-religious Approach* (Cleveland: Pilgrim, 2001); and specifically in our field, Joretta Marshall, *Counseling Lesbian Partners* (Louisville: Westminster John Knox, 1997) and David J. Kuntz and Bernhard S. Schlager, *Ministry among God's Queer Folk: LGBT Pastoral Care* (Cleveland: Pilgrim, 2007).

34. E.g., Oduyoye, op. cit.

35. E.g., Isasi-Díaz, op. cit.; Emilie M. Townes, ed., *Embracing the Spirit: Womanist Perspectives on Hope, Salvation and Transformation* (Maryknoll: Orbis, 1997).

36. Isasi-Díaz, op. cit.

37. Mary E. Hunt, *Fierce tenderness: A Feminist Theology of Friendship* (New York: Crossroad 1989).

re-value local, particular cultural practices, religious traditions and "folk" religions, and claiming Christ as liberator, friend, and co-sufferer, "God-among-us" as well as "God-with-us."[38]

(5) Most recently, both *postmodern* and *postcolonial* feminisms have opened important new avenues in theology.[39] While postmodernism and postcolonialism[40] cannot be simply conflated, both approaches share a concern with deconstructing hegemonic or "dominant discourses" that perpetuate political and social inequalities. Both have, separately, offered conceptual frameworks and methods for analysis and dialogue, which are making important contributions to this very crucial question of how women—especially Black, Latina, Asian, African, third world, indigenous, and queer women, "can speak."[41] If language itself is the very medium of culture, and as infants we acquire language already infused with "the law of the father,"[42] then postmodern feminists such as Luce Irigaray ask the question in all seriousness: "Can women speak?"[43] And under colonial conquest, Gayatri Spivak further asks: Can the "subaltern"—that is, the subjugated one who has been made to be "other"—speak?[44]

What both postmodernism and postcolonialism represent in different ways—in a vastly over-simplistic generalization—is a critique of universal "truths" or truth claims, which have historically masked diversity of cultures, perspectives, and voices, particularly of those marginalized outside the so-called "mainstream" of white, western "dominant discourse." By now, growing numbers of us are engaging in serious dialogue with contemporary

---

38. E.g., Chung, op. cit.

39. Kwok Pui Lan, op. cit.; Musa W. Dube, *Postcolonial Feminist Interpretation of the Bible* (St. Louis: Chalice, 2000); Grace Jantzen, *Becoming Divine: Toward a Feminist Philosophy of Religion* (Indianapolis: Indiana University Press, 1999); Elaine Graham, *Making the Difference: Gender, Personhood, and Theology* (Minneapolis: Fortress, 1995); Ellen Armour, *Deconstruction, Feminist Theology, and the Problem of Difference: Subverting the Race/Gender Divide* (Chicago: University of Chicago Press, 1999); and Serene Jones, *Feminist Theory and Christian Theology: Cartographies of Grace* (Minneapolis: Fortress, 2000). [See also, e.g., Armour, *Signs and Wonders: Theology after Modernity* (New York: Columbia University Press, 2016). —PCW 2018]

40. A recent Society for Pastoral Theology study conference focused on these topics in the context of a meeting in San Juan, Puerto Rico, June, 2007, including a keynote by Luis Rivera-Pagán, "Doing Theology in a Postcolonial Context: Some Observations from the Caribbean," *Journal of Pastoral Theology* 17/2 (2007) 1–27.

41. Gayatri Chakravorty Spivak, "Can the Subaltern Speak?: Speculations on Widow Sacrifice," *Wedge* 7/8 (1985) 120–30.

42. Jacques Lacan, *Écrits: A Selection,* trans. A. Sheridan, (New York: Norton, 1977).

43. Luce Irigaray, *Speculum of the Other Woman,* trans. Gillian C. Gill (Ithaca, NY: Cornell University Press, 1985) 83, 89, 111.

44. Spivak, "Can the Subaltern Speak?" (1985).

European—especially French—expressions of feminist thought;[45] postmodern thinkers such as Jacques Derrida[46] and Michel Foucault[47]; postcolonial theorists across the globe like Homi Bhabha[48] and Gayatri Spivak[49]; and here in the U.S., gender theorists within cultural studies, queer theory, and contemporary psychoanalysis, such as Jane Flax[50] and Judith Butler.[51]

## Feminisms, Psychoanalysis, and Theology in Dialogue

Through my own forays, increasingly in the past fifteen years, into psychoanalytic theory at the intersection of feminism, I have been trying to forge a way for theology to become a third conversation partner in that dialogue.[52] In this work, the theme of multiplicity—of human beings, of God, and of modes of attention in pastoral practice—has become a central

45. E.g.,; Irigaray, *Speculum of the Other Woman*; and *This Sex Which Is Not One*, trans. Catherine Porter (Ithaca, NY: Cornell University Press, 1985); Julia Kristeva, *The Kristeva Reader*, ed. Toril Moi (New York: Columbia University Press, 1986); Julia Kristeva, *In the Beginning Was Love: Psychoanalysis and Faith*, trans. Arthur Goldhammer (New York : Columbia University Press, 1987); Hélène Cixous and Catherine Clément, *The Newly Born Woman*, trans. B. Wing (Minneapolis: University of Minnesota Press, 1986; orig. publ. 1975); Hélène Cixous, *The Hélène Cixous Reader*, ed. S. Sellers (London: Routledge, 1994). For a wonderful introduction to the implications of French postmodern feminism for feminist theology, also see C. W. Maggie Kim, Susan M. St. Ville, and Susan M. Simonaitis, S., ed., *Transfigurations: Theology and the French Feminists* (Minneapolis: Fortress, 1993).

46. Jacques Derrida, *Of Grammatology*, trans. Gayatri C. Spivak (Baltimore: Johns Hopkins University Press, 1976; orig. French ed. 1967); Jacques Derrida, *Writing and Difference*, trans. Alan Bass (Chicago: University of Chicago Press. 1978; orig. French ed., 1967).

47. E.g., Michel Foucault *Language, Counter-memory, and Practice: Selected Essays and Interviews by Michel Foucault*, ed. Donald F. Bouchard (Ithaca: Cornell University Press, 1977); Michel Foucault, *Power/Knowledge: Selected Interviews and Other Writings, 1972–1977*, ed. Colin Gordon (New York: Pantheon, 1980).

48. Homi Bhabha, *The Location of Culture* (New York: Routledge, 1994).

49. E.g., Gayatri Chakravorty Spivak, "Can the Subaltern Speak?: Speculations on Widow Sacrifice," *Wedge* 7/8 (1985) 120–30; *The Spivak Reader: Selected Works of Gayatri Chakravorty Spivak*, ed. Donna Landry and Gerald MacLean (New York: Routledge, 1996); and *A Critique of Postcolonial Reason: Toward a History of the Vanishing Present* (Cambridge: Harvard University Press, 1999).

50. Jane Flax, *Disputed Subjects: Essays on Psychoanalysis, Politics and Philosophy* (New York: Routledge, 1993).

51. Judith Butler (1990). *Gender Trouble: Feminism and the Subversion of Identity*. New York: Routledge; Judith Butler, *Undoing Gender* (New York: Routledge, 2004).

52. Cooper-White, *Shared Wisdom: Use of the Self in Pastoral Care and Counseling*, (Minneapolis: Fortress, 2004); *Many Voices: Pastoral Psychotherapy in Relational and Theological Perspective* (Minneapolis: Fortress, 2007).

organizing trope. Drawing both from postmodern understandings of the diversity of truths, and from the postcolonial notion of *hybridity*,[53] in which dialogue partners join together in new creative ways without losing their individual distinctiveness, I am interested in a pastoral theological anthropology that explores the multiplicity of persons (not only in terms of pluralism and diversity of human beings in our relations with one another, but multiplicity as internally constitutive of each individual mind/self/subject, at both conscious and unconscious levels.[54] An appreciation for this multiplicity informs a corresponding pastoral praxis, as a method of working with all the varied, contradictory and creative parts of each person—each parishioner or patient—in his or her many self-states. Imagine mind and self in terms of a three-dimensional multiplicity (or more)—neither vertical "depth" (as in Freud's topographical model of mind, or Jung's "depth psychology"), nor a purely horizontal "plane," but an infinitely dimensional, quantum space, with internal indeterminacy and some fluid external parameters. Imagine a subjectivity, a multiple self, identifiable simultaneously as both "I" *and* "Thou," subject *and* object, "self" *and* "other"—with a mobile consciousness that scans and networks various parts of the "self," in an illusory but functional sense of self-cohesion, self-regulation and self-continuity. Such a pastoral model of persons seeks to help us come to know, accept, and even appreciate all the distinctive parts—the many voices—that live within each one of us.

There is a political and ethical dimension to this reconceptualization as well. Being open to a variety of "others" within the web that constitutes oneself, it seems to me, should potentiate a greater openness to "others" beyond ourselves. The idea of a multiple self as emancipatory also relates to the flow of selves in our relations with other persons outside ourselves. Jane Flax describes multiplicity and fluidity of subjects as emancipatory:

> I believe a unitary self is unnecessary, impossible, and a dangerous illusion. Only multiple subjects can invent ways to struggle against domination that will not merely recreate it. In the process of therapy, in relations with others, and in political life we

---

53. Homi Bhabha, op. cit.; cf., Celia Brickman, *Aboriginal Populations in the Mind: Race and Primitivity in Psychoanalysis* (New York: Columbia University Press, 2003).

54. Pamela Cooper-White, "Higher Powers and Infernal Regions: Models of Mind in Freud's 'Interpretation of Dreams' and Contemporary Psychoanalysis, and Their Implications for Pastoral Care," *Pastoral Psychology* 5/5 (2002) 319–43. [Reprinted in Cooper-White, *Braided Selves: Collected Essays on Multiplicity, God, and Persons* (Eugene, OR: Cascade Books, 2011) 65–99.]; *Shared Wisdom* (2004); and Dissenting Dis-integration: Multiplicity as a Positive Metaphor in Therapy and Theology," *Pastoral Psychology* 57/1-2 (2008) 1–16. [Reprinted in Cooper-White, *Braided Selves: Collected Essays on Multiplicity, God, and Persons* (Eugene, OR: Cascade Books, 2011) 100–119.].

encounter many difficulties when subjectivity becomes subject to one normative standard, solidifies into rigid structures, or lacks the capacity to flow readily between different aspects of itself... No singular form can be sufficient as a regulative ideal or as a prescription for human maturity or the essential human capacity... [I]t is possible to imagine subjectivities whose desires for multiplicity can impel them toward emancipatory action. These subjectivities would be fluid rather than solid, contextual rather than universal, and [process-oriented] rather than topographical.[55]

Postmodern writers thus highlight the ethical implications of a nonunitary conception of self and mind, especially as they influence the social construction of self and others, and the resulting social construction of categories such as gender, race and class, and the distribution of power.[56] A corresponding pastoral approach would have as its goal an increasingly harmonious awareness and constructive dialogue among all the disparate parts, conscious and unconscious, of the person who comes for help, rather than an *integration* of conscious and unconscious into one homogenized whole.

As unsettling as we may find this more multiple, fluid, and spatially conceived model of mind—relational theory (the school of psychoanalytic thought that particularly embraces such a view of multiplicity[57]), philosophy, physics, and neurobiology are all converging to suggest that the postmodern view may be a more generous and apt description of the true complexity and multiplicity of mental life. In fact, given the demanding, pluralistic nature of our postmodern world, mental health may depend as much on the capacity for "identity complexity,"[58] as it does on a capacity for psychological "integration."

55. Jane Flax, *Disputed Subjects*, 93.

56. Ibid., 111-28.

57. The foundational text for this school of thought is Stephen A. Mitchell, *Relational Concepts in Psychoanalysis: An Integration* (Cambridge: Harvard University Press, 1988); see also Jay R. Greenberg, *Oedipus and Beyond: A Clinical Theory* (Cambridge: Harvard University Press, 1991; Lewis Aron, *A Meeting of Minds: Mutuality in Psychoanalysis* (Hillsdale, NJ: Analytic Press). The development of relational theory can be traced through the journal *Psychoanalytic Dialogues* (Vol. 1/1 in 1991), and in Stephen A. Mitchell and Lewis Aron, ed., *Relational Psychoanalysis: The Emergence of a Tradition*. (Hillsdale, NJ: Analytic Press, 1999). For more on the history of relational psychoanalysis, see Mitchell and Aron, Preface, and Greenberg and Mitchell, "Object Relations and Psychoanalytic Models," in Greenberg and Mitchell, eds., *Object Relations in Psychoanalytic Theory* (Cambridge: Harvard University Press, 1983) 9-20; Stephen A. Mitchell, *Relationality: From Attachment to Subjectivity* (Hillsdale, NJ: Analytic Press, 2004).

58. Carolyn Saari, "Identity Complexity as an Indicator of Mental Health," *Clinical*

Such an embracing of multiplicity has a particularly feminist ring, I think, because feminism/feminism(s)/Womanism/mujerisma, as I have already described, are multiple. Feminism is such a complex area of thought, it is not the case that we have proceeded in some linear fashion from Marxist and liberal feminism, to essentialism, to postmodernism and postcolonialism, to something more or better. Such a "progress model" would be both modernist and un-feminist! We bring it all along with us, in a big, roiling, complex mess of ideas, critiques, and practices. In the past three decades or so, we have, however, developed sharper and more discriminating tools to evaluate our work. With the influence of postmodern and postcolonial critiques, we are no longer able to embrace the sometimes simplistic and univocal (often white, middle-class) certainties of the 60s and 70s. It would nevertheless be a mistake to say that feminism in theology, including pastoral theology, is passé! Carrie Doehring has articulated one method for pastoral feminist theology in keeping with this more postmodern, postcolonial critique.[59] Her four criteria include being intentional about our methodologies, which are always cross-disciplinary; adopting feminist approaches that are poststructuralist, contextual, and pragmatic; being accountable for our work by explicitly naming our sources and norms; and having transformation as our central purpose.

## Gender and Power

One of the places where postmodern and postcolonial voices most converge with earlier feminisms is in the continuing call for increasingly sophisticated analyses of *power*, and an ongoing attentiveness to contexts of political, economic, and institutional subjugation of women's voices—together with, and in relation to, all other subjugated groups. A postmodern feminist pastoral theology begins with a consideration of the particularity of our subjectivities—our experiences, and our relative perspectives—and the ways in which these experiences and perspectives are gendered, as we are socialized into our identities and relative power positions as women and men.

As many of us in pastoral theology today would acknowledge, following 20th century "constructionist/constructivist" social scientists, reality is socially constructed.[60] As long as men and women do not have commensu-

---

*Social Work Journal* 21/1 (1993) 11–23.

59. Carrie Doehring, "A Method of Feminist Pastoral Theology," in Bonnie Miller-McLemore and Brita Gill-Austern, ed., *Feminist and Womanist Pastoral Theology*, (Nashville: Abingdon, 1999) 95–111.

60. This position is summarized in Cooper-White, *Shared Wisdom*, 35–56; Peter

rate options for political power, or even the same access to the *agora*—the marketplace of social dealings, we don't have equal access to the reality-*constructing* process. This essay focuses on gender, but similar dynamics pertain regarding, for example, race, class, sexual orientation, physical ability, and age. Certain groups have the authority to build and name reality for others. Although there is change, as evidenced by the presence of more women in formerly male-dominated professions—including ministry—it is still mostly the case that reality is built and named in our society by (mostly white) men and only a small percentage of (mostly white) women. Individual women are left with a terrible double bind: if reality is defined by men, then a woman must choose between convincing herself that the *other's* reality is the "real" one, or clinging perilously to her own perceptions and exposing herself to ridicule, ostracism, or worse. *Her* reality is *non*-reality. To choose her reality is therefore to choose being delusional.

To give a concrete example, some time ago, I treated myself to an expensive haircut. At the hairdressers', I was sitting looking like something out of an old "Jetsons" cartoon, with rods and pieces of tin foil sticking out of my head, with a drab, unisex robe draped around my shoulders, and suddenly I took a good look at the fashion poster that was proper up on display in front of the shampoo station. It was a black and white fashion photograph of a woman with her face unnaturally turned to one side, her hair blown across her face, and her shoulder visibly, obviously bruised. In this era of airbrushed perfection, the bruise could be no accident. I looked and blinked and really couldn't fathom what I was seeing—or why.

I walked out of my appointment a while later, and went to retrieve my car. While the parking attendant went with my key to get my car, I noticed a picture tacked up over his work station. Except for a small calendar with no pictures on it, this was the only decoration on his wall. It was a home-made xeroxed collage of nude female mannequins lying down at various angles, with arms and legs chopped off, and photographic faces of real women superimposed where the heads would have been.

My socially constructed reality said, "It's nothing. Forget it. So what?" My real, that is socially delusional, reality said "Today I have seen two photographs of violence against women, as style and as decoration. I'm a

---

L. Berger and Thomas Luckmann, *The Social Construction of Reality: A Treatise in the Sociology of Knowledge* (New York: Anchor, 1967); see also Egon Guba, "The Alternative Paradigm Dialog, in Guba, ed., *The Paradigm Dialog* (Newbury Park, CA: Sage, 1990) 17–27; Kenneth Gergen, "The Social Constructionist Movement in Modern Psychology," *American Psychologist* 40/3 (1985) 266–75; Kenneth Gergen, "Psychological Science in a Post-modern Context," *American Psychologist*, 56/10 (2001) 803–13; John Shotter and Kenneth Gergen, ed., *Texts of Identity* (Newbury Park, CA: Sage, 1989).

woman and this makes me feel very targeted and vulnerable." Well, what's a "girl" to do? I shook my newly permed hair, got in my car, and drove home. Whatever protest I might have felt was silenced by the utter, banal normality of both situations. To speak up would have been to be a trouble-maker, a fury, a crazy woman.

I did at a later time go back and lodge a complaint with the garage owner about the collage (which, thankfully, had already been removed)—but not until I had told this story in the context of teaching a seminary class, who by believing me provided me with a validation of the reality of my experience. It was this very important context of an alternative consensual reality that gave me the courage to go back and confront what I had seen.

## Power and Violence against Women

I've been asked why I have written and taught so much about violence against women specifically[61]—why not just talk about violence, period? In one sense, of course, all violence, whether against women, or men, or girls, or boys, is connected. Violence is never acceptable, and the pain and terror of a boy who is molested, or a man who is raped, mugged or murdered should not be minimized in any way. These are horrors which deserve to be spoken about and condemned.

The main reason why we need to talk about violence against women goes back to the gendered nature of *all* experiences, *including* violence, and the conjunction of gender and power that produces certain forms of violence that are targeted toward women. Violence specifically against women requires our focused analysis and attention in order to be competent, gender-sensitive pastoral caregivers, and advocates for prevention.

There are at least two aspects to the distinctiveness of violence against women. The first aspect is *proportionality*. Far more girls and women are disproportionately victims of certain types of violence, particularly sexual assault, sexual abuse, and intimate partner violence. The most recent very

---

61. [See chapters in this volume] and Cooper-White, "A Reply to Donald Capps: On Sex, Power and Scapegoating in the Parish," *Journal of Pastoral Care* 48/2 (1994) 193–95; *Women Healing and Empowering: A Small Group Resource for Abused Women* (Chicago, IL: Stop the Violence Project, Evangelical Lutheran Church in America/Minneapolis: Augsburg Fortress, 1996); "El Llamado de Reconciliación," in C. Roggeband (ed. and trans.), *Antología Módulo de Estudio: Teología desde las Mujeres* (Managua, Nicaragua: CIEETS—Centro InterEclesial de Estudios Teológicos y Sociales, 2000) 29–31; Bible study on 2 Samuel 13 in Taryn Montgomery et al., eds., *Tamar Campaign Bible Study Manual* (Nairobi: FECCLAHA—Fellowship of Christian Councils and Churches in the Great Lakes and Horn of Africa, 2008).

large-scale survey[62] estimates that 39% of women have experienced some form of abuse and/or sexual assault, and approximately 1/3 of American women are victims of domestic violence.[63] At least 1 in 6 women is sexually assaulted, compared to 1 in 33 men.[64] In its most recent comprehensive statistical report, the U.S. Department of Justice found that the number of reported violent crimes by intimate partners against women declined from 1.1 million in 1993, but still involved more than half a million (588,490) women, representing 85% of all nonfatal intimate partner victimization.[65] Intimate partner violence made up 20% of all nonfatal violent crime against women, compared to 3% against men and domestic violence was the cause of death in 33% of all female murder victims, compared to 4% of male victims, and this statistic has remained relatively stable for decades. Approximately 1 in 5 high school girls report physical or sexual abuse by a dating partner.[66] The most recent large-scale study, sponsored jointly by the National Institute of Justice and the Centers for Disease Control found that 25% of women have been raped or assaulted by an intimate partner, compared to 7.5% of men.[67] The authors of the study also stated:

---

62. The Commonwealth Fund commissioned a survey of 2,850 women and 1,500 men.

63. Karen Scott Collins, Cathy Schoen and Susan Joseph, S. et al., "Addressing Domestic Violence and its Consequences," in *Policy Report of the Commonwealth Fund Commission on Women's Health* (New York: Commonwealth Fund, 1998; Summary online at https://www.commonwealthfund.org/publications/publication/1999/may/violence-and-abuse.

64. Patricia Tjaden and Nancy Thoennes, *Extent, Nature, and Consequences of Intimate Partner Violence: Findings from the National Violence against Women Survey,* NIJ report #181867 (Washington, DC: National Institute of Justice and Centers for Disease Control and Prevention, 2000), online at https://www.ncjrs.gov/pdffiles1/nij/181867.pdf; National Institute for Justice (NIJ) (2007), *Victims and Perpetrators,* http://www.ojp.usdoj.gov/nij/topics/crime/rape-sexual-violence/victims-perpetrators.htm. [updated October, 2010—PCW 2018]

65. Dept. of Justice, Bureau of Justice Statistics (2003), *Intimate Partner Violence 1993-2001,* online at https://www.bjs.gov/index.cfm?ty=pbdetail&iid=1001. [In the most recent official report in 2016 by the U.S. Bureau of Justice Statistics, 5, there were over 300,000 incidents of rape/sexual assault, and 1,109,610 incidents of domestic violence/intimate partner violence. U.S. Department of Justice, Bureau of Justice Statistics, Criminal Victimization Summary, 2016, online at www.bjs.gov/content/pub/pdf/cv16.pdf—PCW 2018]

66. Lorelei A. Mucci, Jeanne A. Hathaway, Anita Raj, and Jay G. Silverman, "Dating Violence against Adolescent Girls and Associated Substance Abuse, Unhealthy Weight Control, Sexual Risk Behavior, Pregnancy, and Suicidality," *Journal of the American Medical Association* 286/5 (2001) 572-79.

67. Tjaden and Thoennes, *Extent, Nature, and Consequences* (2000).

Women experience more chronic and injurious physical assaults at the hands of intimate partners than do men. These findings suggest that research aimed at understanding and preventing intimate partner violence against women should be stressed.[68]

In 1993, the American Medical Association and the Surgeon General both named violent men as a major threat to women's health,[69] and in 2008, the American Psychological Association issued a Public Interest "Resolution on Male Violence against Women."[70]

The issue of international traffic in women and girls, enslaved by prostitution rings, is only now coming to light in the general media, in spite of a United Nations Convention for the Suppression of Traffic in Persons dating back almost 60 years (1949), and concern by feminist advocates for 150 years.[71] The UN estimates that trafficking is a five-to-seven billion dollar operation annually, mostly with women and children as its victims.[72]

Perhaps the most significant issue of proportionality, then, concerns who is committing violent crimes. Eighty-three to ninety-eight percent of perpetrators of all violent crimes are men.[73] In 2006, the most recent year's statistics published by the FBI, 90.9% of all murders (of both women and men) were committed by men.[74] So the issue becomes one of male violence,

68. Ibid., Executive Summary.

69. Nancy Gibbs, "'Til Death Do Us Part," *Time Magazine*, Jan. 18, 1993: http://www.time.com/time/magazine/article/0,9171,977464-3,00.html.

70. American Psychological Association, *Resolution on Male Violence against Women* (Washington, DC: APA, 2008): http://www.apa.org/about/policy/male-violence.aspx.

71. Peter Landesmann, "The Girls Next Door," *New York Times Sunday Magazine*, Jan. 25, 2004: http://www.nytimes.com/2004/01/25/magazine/25SEXTRAFFIC.html?ei=5007en=43dbe6ef76e45af8ex=1390366800; Rita Nakashima Brock, *Casting Stones: Prostitution and Liberation in Asia and the United States* (Minneapolis: Fortress, 1996); Rhonda Williams, "International slave traffic in women and children: A comparison of the institutional response versus the feminist response," unpubl. MA thesis, Carleton University, Canada, 1999: https://search.proquest.com/docview/303901686.

72. United Nations, *UN Resolution: Traffic in Women and Girls*, G.A. res. 51/66, 51 U.N. GAOR.

73. U.S. Department of Justice, Bureau of Justice Statistics, National Crime Survey: Statistics re: Offenders, 2005: http://www.ojp.usdoj.gov/bjs/pub/pdf/cvus/current/cv0538.pdf [website no longer available]; U.S. Sentencing Commission, *Statistics, 2007*, online at http://www.ussc.gov/ANNRPT/2001/table5.pdf [website no longer available].

74. U.S. Federal Bureau of Investigation (FBI), Expanded Homicide Data Table 3, (from statistics where gender was known), in *Crime in the United States*, 2006: http://www.fbi.gov/ucr/cius2006/offenses/expanded_information/data/shrtable_03.html [website no longer available—PCW 2018].

of which we are all to varying degrees, both women and men, socialized to protect ourselves against, to fear, and to avoid.

There is a second, perhaps even more compelling reason, however, why we must speak in the particular about violence against women. That is to *break silence*: to accurately name these various forms of violence. Violence against men is commonly understood in our culture *as* violence, a crime, a violation of a person's rights. Violence against women, however, in all its various forms, is all too often called something else: "just a little joke," "flirting," "making a mountain out of a molehill," "being in the wrong place at the wrong time," "asking for it," "poor communication skills," "poor impulse control" masochism, a "problem in the family system," "repetition neurosis."

Why is denial such a powerful force? In an important book entitled *Trauma and Recovery*, Dr. Judith Herman of Harvard Medical School has written:

> To study psychological trauma means bearing witness to horrible events. When the events are natural disasters or "acts of God," those who bear witness sympathize readily with the victim. But when the traumatic events are of human design, those who bear witness are caught in the conflict between victim and perpetrator. It is morally impossible to remain neutral in this conflict. The bystander is forced to take sides.
>
> It is very tempting to take the side of the perpetrator. All the perpetrator asks is that the bystander do nothing. He appeals to the universal desire to see, hear, and speak no evil. The victim, on the contrary, asks the bystander to share the burden of pain. The victim demands action, engagement, and remembering... After every atrocity, one can expect to hear the same predictable apologies: it never happened; the victim lies; the victim exaggerates; the victim brought it upon herself; and in any case it is tie to forget the past and move on. The more powerful the perpetrator, the greater in his prerogative to name and define reality, and the more completely his arguments prevail."[75]

In order for individual victims to be heard and to be met with justice and restitution, it takes a great deal of effort from the widest possible circle of bystanders, a social context of belief and action. Herman writes again:

> In the absence of strong political movements for human rights, the active process of bearing witness inevitably gives way to the

---

75. Judith Herman, *Trauma and Recovery* (New York: Basic Books, 1992) 8–9.

active process of forgetting. Repression, dissociation, and denial are phenomena of social as well as individual consciousness.[76]

Physical and sexual violence against women are the extreme (though not uncommon) example, as well as the reinforcing reality that maintain patriarchal power. But another less overtly violent nexus between the practice of ministry as a caring profession—or the practice of any profession for that matter—and the subject of gender, power, and violence against women, is the prevalence of sexual harassment and exploitation. Sexual harassment intersects with the practice of ministry in two ways—both how we conduct ourselves in relation to those who are in our care, and also how we respond to the stories of those who have been victimized and come to us for help and counsel. A thoughtful examination of sexual harassment can offer us another instructive example about the differing realities of women and men.

Because of the prevalence of violence against women, both in the images of women that surround us everywhere we go—more about that shortly—and in real life, no woman knows whether any form of supposedly mild, even joking sexual harassment will or will not escalate into more serious harassment, unwanted physical touching, stalking, or even rape. Men who actually have little more on their minds than relieving sexual tension with a little "dirty joke" are often baffled to be told that this behavior is inappropriate, partly because they do not recognize the more threatening context within which many women experience their behavior. But given the context of so many other forms of violence against women, a woman may always wonder, "who knows how far this man might go? Who knows if it's harmless or not?" This is precisely the reasoning behind the modern "reasonable woman" judicial standard for assessing the validity of sexual harassment claims in court:

In a landmark case in 1991, Ellison v. Brady,[77] (politically conservative) federal appellate court judges established the "reasonable woman" standard, with the following historic statement:

> We believe that in evaluating the severity and pervasiveness of sexual harassment, we should focus on the perspective of the victim. If we only examined whether a reasonable person would engage in allegedly harassing conduct, we would run the risk of reinforcing the prevailing level of discrimination. Harassers could continue to harass merely because a particular

76. Ibid., 9.

77. Kerry Ellison, Plaintiff-Appellant v. Nicholas F. Brady, Secretary of the Treasury, Defendant-Appelle, U.S. Court of Appeals, 9th Circuit, No. 89-15248, 1991; pp. 878ff.

discriminatory practice was common, and victims of harassment would have no remedy.

> We therefore prefer to analyze harassment from the victim's perspective . . . We realize that there is a broad range of viewpoints among women as a group, but we believe that many women share common concerns which men do not necessarily share.[78]

The authors continue with a quotation describing the prevailing societal context as one "where rape and sex-related violence have reached unprecedented levels, and a vast pornography industry creates continuous images of sexual coercion, objectification, and violence . . ."[79]

Even in situations where we, as women on the receiving end of harassment, are pretty sure that it won't escalate into violence, we experience the eroding of self-confidence, self-worth, and a feeling of adult well-being. Almost every clergywoman alive has experienced gender harassment by male colleagues. When I first moved to Chicago and was being introduced around my new diocese, I was called a "girl," a "little lady," and a "chickypoo"(!) by other clergy. A highly regarded bishop some time ago responded to a professional comment of mine—I was thanking him, ironically, for something he had said on behalf of women—by telling me how he loved the color of my hair, and that it was just like his daughters'. I had greeting him as a colleague, and he responded to me as a (sexualized) daughter. We might say that such remarks are no big deal in and of themselves, but the constant drip-drip-drip of hearing such remarks at almost every gathering of clergy—or analogously in other professional settings—begins to take on more seriousness. It says, "I don't see you as a colleague." "You don't belong here. Go back home where you *do* belong."

Power is expressed in many other ways besides sexual harassment, including in settings of ministry. In some ways, sexual harassment is just the tip of the iceberg. Social psychologists[80] have observed that power is expressed by who initiates touching—thereby presuming to enter the other's body and personal space; who stands closer to whom; who takes more personal space—for example, who sits in a more open posture, legs open or arms stretched out, and who sits more contained, taking up less space? Who controls time? Who is more likely to use familiarities of address first? Who

---

78. Ibid., 878.

79. Kathryn Abrams, "Gender Discrimination and the Transformation of Workplace Norms," *Vanderbilt Law Review*, 42 (1989) 1205.

80. E.g., Nancy Henley, *Body Politics: Power, Sex, and Nonverbal Communication* (New York: Prentice-Hall, 1977).

makes more jokes at the other's expense, who chooses topics of discussion, who interrupts more? Even such subtle behaviors as more relaxation, greater use of gesture, less tilting of the head, less smiling, and less eye aversion all subliminally communicate power, authority, and control.

These power behaviors happen to be stereotypical characteristics of masculine behavior. They are also common characteristics of behavior of white persons of either gender toward persons of color. The question of power is where the argument in favor of an "essentialist" view of masculine and feminine differences falls down. Yes, my husband would probably drive three miles out of his way to avoid asking directions while I'd jump out at the first available service station and strike up a "relationship . . ."[81] In such matters, masculine and feminine differences are almost cute. His self-sufficiency and independence; my resourcefulness and relationality. Much ink has been spilled in the last two decades about the characteristic—or so called essential—differences with which men and women relate, communicate, and make moral judgments. The thrust of such research is to validate difference and to show that women should not be assessed by male norms and standards. But it begs the question of how uncritical acceptance of these differences as "natural" may also perpetuate power, dominance, and striking inequality in the name of natural law and what is "normal."

It also begs the question concerning the poisonous, and often unrecognized effects these differences have on men. Stress-induced heart attacks and ulcers have long been associated with men more than women. A study by the Washington University Medical School reports that although twice as many women as men attempt suicide—at least 200,000 a year, which speaks volumes about women's depression—75% of the 30,000 completed suicides each year are committed by men.[82] Part of this is due to the more violent, immediately lethal methods of suicide chosen by men. But Dr. George Murphy, professor emeritus of psychiatry at Washington University, further attributes men's more deadly rate of suicide to their socialization not to reach out for help or to talk about feelings, to become emotionally isolated, and to dismiss the need for support with an over-reliance on logic, stoicism, and self-sufficiency.[83] Surely this has relevance for preventive pastoral care—inviting and creating an atmosphere of permission for men to share their inner thoughts, moods, and feelings, and creating better networks of friendship and support

---

81. A popular meme originally in Deborah Tannen, *You Just Don't Understand: Women and Men in Conversation* (New York: Harper, 2001) 40–44.

82. George E. Murphy, "Why Women are Less Likely than Men to Commit Suicide," *Comprehensive Psychiatry* 39 (1998) 165–75.

83. Ibid.

to counter some of the internal and external pressures to conform to stoic, life-denying expectations in the name of "being a man."[84]

Myths of "normality," and doctrines of "natural law" are constructed to explain the world, and more to the point, to try to control forces that are perceived as mysterious and threatening. It can be argued that at the deepest place in the collective psyche, the place that shapes the dominant masculine-constructed reality, Woman is such a force. Societal and cultural myths attempting to control Woman's power serve to lock unique, individual persons—both women and men—into stereotypes that are constricting, damaging, and ultimately death-dealing. In all cases where power is used to subjugate the other, there is a dynamic of objectification at work. The Other is not a "Thou" in such transactions—whether power is expressed consciously or unconsciously—but is treated instrumentally, as an "It."[85]

## Power and Objectification: An Analysis of Images of Women in the Media

This leads to an examination of the images of women that surround us in our culture. If pornography is defined not merely by erotic content, but by a standard of dehumanization and objectification of women,[86] then a preponderance of mainstream media images of women are, in fact, pornographic. Over many years, I have tracked images of women in a variety of mainstream news, fashion, and advertising publications, and the following themes emerge as just some of the forms of objectification that commonly appear:

- *Women as actual objects* (including objects for use, and trophies)

This postcard, distributed on the street for a now-closed diner in Berkeley, California, shows a woman as a utilitarian object on a table amid a variety of glassware.[87] Her scale, combined with proximity to an ashtray, suggests a cigar, which might be consumed and then snuffed. Her stereotypically pro-

---

84. E.g., Philip L. Culbertson, *Counseling Men*, Creative Pastoral Care and Counseling (Minneapolis: Fortress, 1994); Paul Kivel, *Men's Work: How to Stop the Violence that Tears Our Lives Apart* (New York: Ballantine, 1992); Christie Cozad Neuger and James Newton Poling, ed., *The Care of Men* (Nashville: Abingdon, 2011).

85. Buber, *I and Thou*.

86. Susan Griffin, *Pornography and Silence: Culture's Revenge against Nature* (New York: Harper & Row, 1981); Diana Russell, *Against Pornography: The Evidence of Harm* (Berkeley, CA: Russell, 1993).

87. A good faith effort was made to locate the original publisher and request permission to duplicate. The original entity "Iggy's" no longer exists.

vocative black lingerie, along with other obvious Freudian symbols such as the salt and pepper shakers, signify a fusion of sexualization and objectification. The possible ironic use of the vintage-style image does not negate its subliminal charge.

- *Women as faceless, anonymous bodies or body parts*

A prevalent genre of images of women in advertising shows nude or scantily clad women with their faces obscured by their hair, by hats and veils, by shadows, or cropped out altogether.[88] Considering this genre of images in light of philosopher Emmanuel Levinas' insistence that it is precisely the face of the other that illuminates his or her personhood and calls us to ethical responsibility,[89] this obscuring of the face in public images can only be understood as a deliberate objectification of women, and diminishing of the model's humanity.

- *Ideal women vs. bad women*, including . . .
  - *The bad woman as too powerful*—for example, during the 2008 primary campaign, the advertising of plastic "Hillary Nutcrakers" where the candidate's thighs were the actual nutcracker, packaged in a box with captions "Is America ready for this nutcracker?," "Stainless Steel Thighs!" and "Cracks Toughest Nuts!"[90]

---

88. E.g., *New York Times*, "Headless but Heady: An Image from Cedric Buchet's Cerebral Spring 2001 Advertising Campaign for Prada," *Fashion of the Times Section*, Feb. 22, 2004, 1; *New York Times*, "Mad about London Designers," *Sunday Styles*, Sept. 24, 2006, 1; BMW, 2002 print ad: http://www.coloribus.com/admirror/sex_with_a_cover_of_magazine/ [website no longer available—depicted a man having sex with a woman whose face was covered with a full-page ad for a BMW car—PCW 2018]

89. Emmanuel Levinas, *Totality and Infinity*, trans. Alphonso Lingis (Pittsburgh: Duquesne University Press, 1969).

90. Permission to copy stipulated on http://www.hillarynutcracker.com/HillaryN-webimages.html [website no longer available].

- *The bad woman as too old or too fat* . . . (sexism fused with ageism and body size discrimination)—for example, an ad for a Black&Decker power mower depicting a gray-haired couple with the husband pushing a mower with his wife riding on it, with the caption: "A solution for those who still think a powerful mower has to be heavy.")

- *The ideal woman as girl-woman*, inviting incestuous fantasies. This genre accelerated after a Calvin Klein advertising jeans campaign showing a then 14-year-old Brooke Shields with the caption "Nothing gets between me and my Calvins," and subsequent use of teenage (or teenage-appearing) models in nude or nearly nude poses in mainstream advertising, echoing images of bondage of girls in underground pornography,[91] e.g., nude images of an anorexic-appearing Kate Moss for *Obsession* men's cologne.

- *Women as animals or associated with animals: usually linked with racism.*

In an era when white women dominated the modeling profession, most images of women associated with animal skin or print clothing were African American women, often posed like wild animals (for example, a *Glamour* magazine "Do's and Don'ts" column with the title "Jungle Fever," featuring an African American model, and an *Elle* magazine full two-page centerfold showing a Black woman in a reptile skin suit, crouched in a hissing catlike pose with the title ". . . On the Wild Side.")

and finally,

---

91. Diana Russell, *Against Pornography* (1993).

# FEMINISM(S), GENDER, AND POWER 163

- *Overt violence against women as ...*

  - *Humor*: For example, a 1970s *New Yorker* cartoon showing a husband and wife sitting on opposite ends of a couch watching TV, with the caption "During the next commercial, I'm going to belt you one!" and ads for a movie "Faithful" showing the actress Cher tied to a chair with a red target on her chest, and the caption "After 20 years of marriage she thought she was the target of her husband's affection. She was half right."

  - *Eroticized bondage*: For example, a pair of 1980s ads for Boucheron women's and men's perfumes, showed a blue-tone photo of a woman's headless torso from behind, posed passively with her hands bound by a heavy jeweled bracelet, in contrast with a full-color photo of a man's hand, clad in expensive jacket, white shirt cuff and gold watch, posed actively tossing the men's cologne in the air. The caption of the men's cologne further suggested a fusion of wealth and violence or criminality: "Boucheron, parfum pour Homme, an accomplice..."

  - *Fashion*: This genre of violent imagery has become increasingly explicit in mainstream media over the past two decades. For example, in the 2007 season of the television show *America's Next Top Model*, the women were photographed in grisly blood-splattered poses as victims of a variety of forms of murder, and praised by the show's host as "very high fashion."[92]

## Conclusion: Implications for Pastoral Theology and Praxis

If we choose not to live in denial, and we dare to say that as pastoral caregivers we are called to be God's lovers and reconcilers (2 Cor 5:18-20), how can we face each other as women and men? How can we bridge our two separate realities? How can we ever talk to each other, talk about how much

92. America's Next Top Model, Season 8 (2007). *Murder Shoot*: http://tv.yahoo.com/americas-next-top-model/show/35130/photos/1#goto_1 [website no longer available], Thursday, Mar. 22, 2007, photos #318–327; [http://antm-archives.tumblr.com/post/123848127824/americas-next-top-model-cycle-8-season-8-photo accessed August, 2018; cf., "America's Next Top Controversy: ANTM Features "Murdered" Models," *Huffington Post*, Mar. 26, 2007/May 25, 2011, online at https://www.huffingtonpost.com/eat-the-press/2007/03/26/americas-next-top-contro_e_44291.html. Real violence impacted several ANTM models: several years later, a 2014 contestant, Mirjana Puhar, was murdered in real life - CNN, Feb. 26, 2015; Kimberly Rydzewski died, presumed suicide, Dec. 19, 2016; and Brandy Rusher, a 2005 contestant was wounded by her brother in a domestic violence shooting, Mar. 31, 2017—PCW 2018]

we care, talk about justice, talk about equality? How can we overcome our guilt, our shame, our rage and outrage? How can we talk to each other with tenderness and compassion?

"Deconstruction"[93] is not merely a semantic exercise, conducted by ivory tower academics hunched over printed texts like medieval monks with their parchments. In order to speak our truth(s) to power(s) in love, we must become adept at reading and interrogating the very culture(s) in which we live, in order not only to unmask the status quo that disguises power as natural law, but also to identify subversive truths that have been obscured and obfuscated, and most of all, to clear the way for previously silenced voices—for suppressed meanings, perspectives and experiences to come forth, and to resist. As we peel back layers of meaning, particularly meanings that reinforce hegemonic powers, we recognize and validate the claims of all those we have "othered," even including the "others" within ourselves. Acknowledging and having compassion for our own inner complexity and diversity, I believe, should have the ethical effect of making us more empathic and able to engage in true dialogue—both honest, open listening and honest, open speech. Such listening and speech are akin to Habermas' "ideal speech situation"[94]—they create the conditions for right relation.

As people of faith, and in our particular vocation as pastoral theologians, we are called toward the restoration of right relations, not just between individual men and women, and not in the sense of premature forgiveness or cheap grace, but in the context of the whole society. We are called to make connections between objectification, subjugation and violence against women and *all* forms of violence—racism, heterosexism, classism, able-bodyism, and *all* forms of oppression that serve to maintain structures of power and privilege at the expense of the majority of the planet's people and creatures.

Taking all this into consideration, then, our goal is not a gender-blind pastoral care, in which we simply try to treat women and men alike, nor is it our goal to be color-blind, or "neutral" toward all the various differences among individuals—but a gender- and culturally-sensitive pastoral care that recognizes all the unique particularities of each person's life, and celebrates them as precious in God's sight. My favorite quote from Martin Buber reads: "Inscrutably involved, we live in currents of universal reciprocity."[95] It is this "I-Thou" relationship that refuses to brand any person as an "It," and re-

---

93. Derrida, e.g., *Of Grammatology* and *Writing and Difference*.

94. Jürgen Habermas, *The Theory of Communicative Action*, trans. Thomas McCarthy (Boston: Beacon, 1984).

95. Martin Buber, *I and Thou*, trans. W. Kaufman (New York: Scribner, 1979) 67.

places aggression and domination with relationality, truth-telling, and care. Furthermore, an "It" is always monolithic. A "Thou" is vastly more complicated, because a "Thou" is real!

Objectification—regarding another living being as One Thing—I believe, is the root of all violence. The human person is not One Thing, and God, as I have argued elsewhere, expanding upon the idea of the Trinity, is not One Thing either.[96] Thanks be to this multiple, fluid, dynamic, relational and loving God, for at least the past decade-and-a-half we have begun talking to one another as theologians about these things—including taking these issues of gender and power into consideration in our own governance and formation of a new generation of scholars. It is a sign of hope to me that we *are* at many times, and in many places, breaking silence, and taking up our calling: to speak truth(s) to power(s) in love. In speaking these truths, we reverse patterns of privilege and discrimination, patterns of domination and objectification, and enter into possibilities for true relationship. This is the heart of all pastoral theology and pastoral care.

---

96. In Cooper-White, *Many Voices*, I have elaborated a theology of multiplicity, including a new formulation of pastoral Trinitarian language: "God as Creative Profusion, God as Incarnational Desire, and God as Living Inspiration," 67–94. See also Cooper-White, *Shared Wisdom*; "Interrogating Integration; and "Com|plicated Woman: Multiplicity and Relationality across Gender, Politics, and Culture," in Stevenson-Moessner and Snorton, *Women out of Order* (see above) 7–21, reprinted in Cooper-White, *Braided Selves: Collected Essays on Multiplicity, God, and Persons* (Eugene, OR: Cascade Books, 2011) 135–55; Catherine Keller, *Face of the Deep: A Theology of Becoming* (London: Routledge, 2003); Laurel C. Schneider, *Beyond Monotheism: A Theology of Multiplicity* (New York: Routledge, 2008).

# 10

## Forgiveness

*Grace, not Work*

2009[1]

ON THE POPULAR WEBSITE *WikiHow* (an online cousin of Wikipedia that publishes brief "how-to's" on virtually everything from washing a dog to running for political office), an article recently appeared entitled "How to Forgive."[2] It begins,

> One of the hardest, thorniest and most difficult things we humans are ever called upon to do is to respond to evil with kindness, and to forgive the unforgivable. We love to read stories about people who've responded to hatred with love, but when that very thing is demanded of us personally, our default seems to be anger, angst, depression, righteousness, hatred, etc. Yet study after study shows that one of the keys to longevity and good health is to develop a habit of gratitude and let go of past hurts. Want to live a long, happy life? Forgive the unforgivable. It really is the kindest thing you can do for yourself.

The tone of this essay is one of self-help, even self-improvement—like the Nike sneaker commercial: "Just do it!" (And you'll feel better when you do.)

And yet, there is good reason to believe that this popular emotional view of forgiveness is not only unhelpful—it is poor psychology and, from a Christian point of view, poor theology as well. This assertion may seem

---

1. Orig. publ. in *Journal for Preachers* (special issue on forgiveness), ed. T. Erskine Clarke and Walter Brueggemann, 32/2 (2009) 16–23. Further updated with discussion of racist violence in the 2015 Charleston church shooting, in Cooper-White, "Is Forgiveness Necessary?," International Association for Spiritual Care, Jerusalem, Israel, July 2017, online at https://www.youtube.com/watch?v=j2EeoqgLoNs.

2. http://www.wikihow.com/Forgive.

quite surprising, since forgiveness is a central theme in Christian scripture and tradition, and there is a strong strand of Christian thought that seems to advocate forgiveness as a hallmark of Christian piety. From the Lord's Prayer, which (in various English translations) includes "forgive us our debts/trespasses/sins as we forgive our debtors/those who trespass/sin against us," to the story of Jesus insisting that the disciple forgive "not seven times, but seventy times seven" (Matt 18:18–19), emotional forgiveness is often understood even as a command of Jesus himself.

The runaway Christian bestseller, *The Shack*,[3] offers a good example of how forgiveness is viewed as central to spiritual life, and even personal healing. The protagonist, Mack, is mysteriously summoned to a secluded shack where years before his youngest daughter Missy was murdered. The Trinity, in the form of a "large beaming African-American woman," a "Middle Eastern" man "dressed like a laborer," and a strangely translucent, "small, distinctively Asian woman" who collects tears in a crystal bottle, meet Mack at the site.[4] They spend time with him, giving him lessons and helping him to grieve. In a culminating lesson, Papa takes Mack to a clearing, and teaches him about forgiveness:[5]

> [Papa says,] "You already know what I want, don't you?"
> 
> "I'm afraid I do," Mack mumbled, feeling emotions rising as they seeped out of a locked room in his heart.
> 
> "Son, you need to speak it, to name it."
> 
> Now there was no holding back as hot tears poured down his face and between sobs Mack began to confess. "Papa," he cried, "how can I ever forgive that son of a bitch who killed my Missy. If he were here today, I don't know what I would do. I know it isn't right, but I want him to hurt like he hurt me . . . if I can't get justice, I still want revenge."
> 
> Papa simply let the torrent rush out of Mack, waiting for the wave to pass.
> 
> "Mack, for you to forgive this man is for you to release him to me and allow me to redeem him."
> 
> "Redeem him?" Again Mack felt the fire of anger and hurt, "I don't want you to redeem him! I want you to hurt him, to punish him, to put him in hell . . ." His voice trailed off.
> 
> Papa waited patiently for the emotions to ease.

---

3. William P. Young, *The Shack* (Newbury Park, CA: Windblown Media, 2007).

4. Ibid., 82–84. The romanticization of racial stereotypes in this image is also highly problematic.

5. Young, *The Shack*, 224.

> "I'm stuck, Papa. I just can't forget what he did, can I?" Mack implored.
> 
> "Forgiveness is not about forgetting, Mack. It is about letting go of another person's throat."

The dialogue continues, as Papa clarifies that Mack's forgiveness does not mean that "everything is okay," nor does he have to have a relationship with his daughter's killer, nor to forget what he did. Forgiveness does not excuse the man's crime. But Papa makes it clear that it is Mack's spiritual task, for his own well-being, to forgive the man:[6]

> "I don't think I can do this," Mack answered softly.
> 
> "I want you to. Forgiveness is first for you, the forgiver," answered Papa, "to release you from something that will eat you alive, that will destroy your joy and your ability to love fully and openly. Do you think this man cares about the pain and torment you have gone through? Don't you want to cut that off? And in doing so, you'll release him from a burden that he carries whether he knows it or not—acknowledges it or not. When you choose to forgive another, you love him well."
> 
> "I do not love him."
> 
> "Not today, you don't. But I do, Mack, not for what he's become, but for the broken child that has been twisted by his pain. I want to help you take on that nature that finds more power in love and forgiveness than hate." (225)

After further dialogue, Mack is finally convinced, and asks how to go about this task of forgiveness. Papa replies, "Just say it out loud. There is power in what my children declare." And Mack does so, at first in a whisper, and then "with increasing conviction." God tells him he is a joy, that he may have to declare this forgiveness "a hundred times the first day and the second day," but that eventually his forgiveness will be complete and God's love "will burn from [the murderer's] life every vestige of corruption." Mack groans, but "in his heart he knew that it was the truth."[7]

What is wrong with this picture, from a pastoral and theological perspective? Many faithful Christians, including many theologians, would say that it is both psychologically and theologically sound.[8] The theme of forgiveness as a cardinal virtue (however seemingly unattainable) is rampant in popular culture. Images of Amish girls, walking to the schoolhouse where their classmates were gunned down in Nickel Mines, Pennsylvania,

6. Ibid., 225.
7. Ibid.
8. E.g., Eugene Peterson's book endorsement, *The Shack*, front cover.

and accounts of their community's prayers for forgiveness of the gunman, held a strong fascination for weeks in the public media. People were riveted by media portrayals of the Amish as "Christ-like."[9] However, such portrayals even of the Amish, for whom forgiveness is a central spiritual discipline, neglected the more subtle and complex emotional nuances of Amish practice.[10]

## Forgiveness Is Not a Work

The portrayal of forgiveness in *The Shack* is less flat-footed than the "WikiHow" article cited above. Author William Young incorporates the understandings that forgiveness does not erase or excuse wrongdoing, and that forgiveness is a process, not a one-time action. The primary problem with all such emotional depictions of forgiveness, however, is that they define forgiveness as a human activity—in theological terms, as a *work*. Forgiveness becomes something we do, like exercise or healthy eating, in order to live a better life. In numerous popular accounts, forgiveness is increasingly being touted as a form of corrosion-prevention: "Unforgiveness is NOT normal or acceptable. It is a dysfunction, a sin. Like corrosive acid, it eats away at the soul and body of the possessor."[11]

In this way, the public interest in forgiveness in North America begins to be one more tool in the distinctively self-absorbed U.S. culture of self-actualization and the pursuit of happiness. Such depictions of forgiveness are perhaps not coincidental, coming at a time when self-improvement is a trademark of the good life, and advertisements for the good life have become all the more shrill in the aftermath of September 11, the war in Afghanistan and Iraq, and the current economic crisis. Notably, the primary motivation expressed in these calls for forgiveness is to release inner bitterness, pain, and anger, in order to heal from one's wounds and feel better. From another popular website, About.com's page on depression, we read:

> Forgiveness. It's such a hard thing to do, but it can be so liberating to the soul. What makes it difficult for most of us to do is the way we define it. We think of forgiveness as meaning that we should say all is forgotten and things will go back to what

---

9. E.g., "Amish Forgiveness Is Christ Like," MSNBC: http://www.youtube.com/watch?v=qjJt3wKXdRc.

10. E.g., Steven Holt, "Perspectives: Amish Forgiveness," Sept. 21, 2007: http://www.pbs.org/wnet/religionandethics/week1103/perspectives.html.

11. Junior DeSouza, "Forgiveness": http://www.openheaven.com/forums/forum_posts.asp?PN=1&TID=9616.

they were. This Biblical definition of forgiveness is very hard for most of us to swallow. How can you forget the unforgettable? How can you forgive the unforgivable? To enjoy the benefits of forgiveness, however, we needn't go that far. All that's really required is that we make the decision to move forward, to let go of the old hurts. We don't have to condone what's been done. What's wrong is still wrong. We don't have to invite the person back into our lives or even be friendly with them. What we do have to do is allow ourselves to release all the negative emotions associated with that person. As long as we hold onto the pain, we are choosing to allow that person's past actions to continue to hurt us. We can also choose to stop letting them hurt us. That's a definition of forgiveness that's more doable for those of us who are less than saintly.[12]

The article continues with "an exercise you can do right now to let go of pain and regain your life"—in other words, salvation.

How are such calls for forgiving one's way to healing and salvation likely to be heard by actual victims of violence, betrayal, and injustice? Any demand to forgive may be understood by the wounded individual as an impossible burden that adds insult—or guilt—to injury. Such advice all too often tends to heap new feelings of guilt and inadequacy on a person who makes an effort to forgive using such guidelines, and feels that he or she has failed. The most healing word we can offer a survivor of abuse or injury—*from* a Christian perspective—is this: that *forgiveness is not a human work*. The author of the About.com quotation has in fact misread and too quickly dismissed the Bible. A closer examination of biblical writings about forgiveness can help us to come to a better understanding of forgiveness—one that does not force forgiveness on the survivors of injury and violence.[13]

---

12. Nancy Schimelpfening, "The Healing Power of Forgiveness," July 25, 2008, formerly online: http://depression.about.com/od/copingskills/a/forgiveness.htm. [Archived at http://www.braintalkcommunities.org/~braintal/archives/06_11/showthread.php?t=5094. See also popular articles on forgiveness at https://www.verywellmind.com/celebrate-forgiveness-day-3144459 and https://www.verywellmind.com/the-benefits-of-forgiveness-3144954. —PCW 2018]

13. The following section summarizes a more detailed exegesis of forgiveness in the Bible in Pamela Cooper-White, "Conclusion: The Call to Reconciliation," *The Cry of Tamar: Violence against Women and the Church's Response* (Minneapolis: Fortress, 1995) 253–62. [Cf., *The Cry of Tamar*, 2nd ed. (2012) 251–61. —PCW 2018]

## What the Bible Really Says

The word most often used in the Gospel accounts of Jesus' teachings on forgiveness is the verb *aphiēmi*, which means "I send away," or "let off," in the sense of forgiving a loan. This is the word for forgiveness used, for example, in Matt 18:21–35 and in the Lord's Prayer (in both Matthew and Luke's Gospels). In Matt 6:12, the verse literally means "release us from our debts (*opheilēmata*) as we also have released those who are indebted to us (our debtors—*opheilētai*). We no longer hold them in obligation to us. This is also the sense of the most commandment-like passage about forgiveness in the Gospels, Mark 11:25 (literally): "Release whatever you may have down on someone, in order that your father in heaven may release your trespasses." There is nothing inherently emotional or psychological about this sense of the word. It is simply a cancelling of a balance due. Furthermore, in Mark 11:25, Jesus is more likely arguing against taking revenge than he is arguing for feeling forgiving. The Gospels and the Epistles both advocate turning away from active vengeance (e.g., Matt 5:38; Rom 12:17–21). However, refraining from personal retribution does not equate to feeling emotionally warm toward someone who has done us harm.

An examination of the parallel text of the Lord's Prayer in Luke further suggests that the emphasis in this passage is on the quality of *God's* forgiveness, and not on our effort to forgive. In Luke's version, the forgiveness of sins rather than debts is made explicit: "forgive us our sins" (*hamartia*)—literally, when we have missed the mark. But in Luke 11:4, God and human beings do not do exactly the same thing! The parallelism in the verse is not "as we forgive the *sins* of others," but again, as in Matthew, as we forgive our *debtors* (those who owe us—*opheilonti*). The Lucan version is not, in fact, a parallelism as in most English translations, but an *analogy*. In other words, we pray for God to release us from our wrongdoings *in the manner in which* we humans release our debtors. This is not the same thing as saying that we should forgive sinners as God forgives, and it is certainly not a legal contract by which God will only forgive us if we first forgive others. It is God in these texts who forgives sins, not human beings.

In this sense, *The Shack* almost gets it right—Papa tells Mack that Missy has already forgiven her murderer. Mack asks, "How could she?" Papa replies, "Because of my presence in her. That's the only way true forgiveness is ever possible."[14] The problem, of course, is that it is still framed as something the person him- or herself finally does, although s/he does it by God's help.

---

14. Young, *The Shack*, 226.

This sense of the Greek carries forward the understanding of forgiveness found in the Hebrew Bible. The word *kaphar*, to cover, is used by the ancient Hebrew writers to describe how God "blots out" sins. This word is never used in relation to human beings. It is only God who forgives in such a way. Note also that the English translation, "blots," implies an erasure, whereas a "covering" literally suggests a healing-over, but does not preclude a scar of remembrance.[15]

## Forgiveness as a Gift of Grace

The word for forgiveness found more often in the Epistles, *charizomai*, (e.g., 2 Cor 2:7, 10; 12:13; Eph 4:31–32; Col 2:13; 3:13) literally means to be gracious. Paul often exhorts the members of his churches to show forbearance, compassion, and kindness toward one another, and to "forgive each other as the Lord has forgiven you" (Col 3:13; also echoed in Eph 4:31–32). But this verb *charizomai* is too often misunderstood, again, as an effort on the part of the person. To be gracious is to be graced. It is a charisma, a gift of the Holy Spirit. It enables a person to let go of the person who wounded him/her, and perhaps, in time, to be less preoccupied with both the perpetrator and the wound. Moreover, as New Testament scholar Krister Stendahl pointed out, the modern church's emphasis on sin and forgiveness is not a correct interpretation of Paul.[16] From a post-Freudian perspective, we tend to psychologize biblical texts in ways that were unknown in the ancient world. Therefore, to assign a modern emotional understanding to the texts about forgiveness is anachronistic, and probably says more about our preoccupation with guilt and anxiety than the Bible actually says about God, Christ, or the early Christian community.

As I have written previously,[17] at certain times, for some people, when pain has been worked through and justice has in some sense been achieved, this gift simply descends. There may be a sense of anger, inner conflict, doubt,

---

15. contra Miroslav Volf, who has proposed an eschatological vision of a restoration of the world in which even the memory of evil is erased and forgotten, in *Exclusion and Embrace: A Theological Exploration of Identity, Otherness, and Reconciliation* (Nashville: Abingdon, 1996) 136; see also Volf, *The End of Memory: Remembering Rightly in a Violent World* (Grand Rapids: Eerdmans, 2006), and *Free of Charge: Giving and Forgiving in a Culture Stripped of Grace* (Grand Rapids: Zondervan, 2006). My view more resembles James Emerson, *The Dynamics of Forgiveness* (Philadelphia: Westminster, 1964).

16. Krister Stendahl, *Paul among Jews and Gentiles* (Philadelphia: Fortress, 1976) 85, 95; see also John Patton, *Is Human Forgiveness Possible? A Pastoral Care Perspective* (Nashville: Abingdon, 1985) 89, 127–30.

17. Cooper-White, *The Cry of Tamar*, 260–61; 2nd ed. (2012) 258–59.

fear, or hatred being lifted away. The experience of violation is not erased or forgotten, and anger and fear may still be present in very appropriate ways. But the experience no longer has power over the person in the same way as it did before. If *aphiēmi* is the word for release, then in this charism of forgiveness from God, it is we who are released—not by our own doing, but by God's action in us and for us. At times, this may come as a sense of realization or discovery after the fact.[18] There is a new lightness, a new ability to move on emotionally, a "peace that passes all understanding."

In another popular novel, *The Kite Runner*, the protagonist Amir discovers that without any conscious effort or intention on his part, he had finally experienced forgiveness toward his father Baba for secretly preferring his illegitimate half-brother:[19]

> Your father was a man torn between two halves, Rahim Khan had said in his letter. I had been the entitled half, the society-approved, legitimate half, the unwitting embodiment of Baba's guilt. I looked at Hassan, showing those two missing front teeth, sunlight slanting on his face. Baba's other half. The unentitled, unprivileged half. The half who had inherited what had been pure and noble in Baba. The half that, maybe in the most secret recesses of his heart, Baba had thought of as his true son.
> 
> I slipped the picture back where I found it. Then I realized something: That last thought had brought no sting with it. . . . I wondered if that was how forgiveness budded, not with the fanfare of epiphany, but with pain gathering its things, packing up, and slipping away unannounced in the middle of the night.

There is no English word that adequately expresses this sense of forgiveness as something we receive, rather than something we do. Rather than the transitive verb "to forgive him/her," which implies active effort, we need a word like "to be forgiven of him/her," which would convey the sense of *having been* released from pain and bitterness. This grace does not (and perhaps need not) come to everyone. It is not a matter of magic that we can invoke, or a prize we can earn. There are no "should's" in any of this, nor should we hold this in front of survivors of violence as a goal at the end of an emotional or therapeutic process. Perhaps the best pastoral counsel we can give to someone who may be feeling pressure (either internal or external) to forgive an offender is this: Sometimes people may have a feeling

---

18. Cf., Patton, "The Discovery of Human Forgiveness," in *Is Human Forgiveness Possible?*, 117–45; cf., Emerson's "realized forgiveness" in *Dynamics of Forgiveness*, 131–32.

19. Khaled Hosseini, *The Kite Runner* (New York: Riverhead, 2003) 359.

of having forgiven another person as a letting go and moving on, but do not blame yourself if you are not "there" in your own emotional life. Forgiveness is a gift of grace, and it may be given to you in God's own good time. In the meantime, don't worry, and don't be preoccupied with something that is God's job to do, not yours.

## Reconciliation as Communal

A related set of words in the New Testament, translated as "reconciliation" (*apokatallasso, katallasso,* and *diallattomai*) literally mean "thoroughgoing change" or "transformation." I have argued in my writings on the church's response to victims and survivors of violence, that this term represents a turn from insistence upon individual survivors forgiving their perpetrators, toward an emphasis on communal reconciliation. The root words for "reconciliation" are revealing—*katallasso* comes from *allasso*, to exchange, which in turn comes from the root word *allos*, meaning other.[20] Violence is, at its heart, always a result of an objectification, an "othering"—turning a "Thou" into an "It."[21] And such objectification can always be found operating not only at the level of individual relationships, but in the wider context of social injustice and unequal power, which serves in turn to undergird, goad, and/or reinforce individual acts of harm and violation.

Re-conciliation is therefore a corporate transformation—a turning toward those who have been "othered," a restoring of the *concilium*, the whole society.[22] Again, as in Paul's second letter to the Corinthians (2 Cor 5:18-19), reconciliation is *God's* work through Christ, and we are the ambassadors or messengers of that reconciliation. This reconciliation, or transformation, is not about individuals "making nice," or even about individuals' coming back into personal relationships at all. Rather, it is the promised unity and peace between whole groups of people, represented in Paul as Jews and Greeks, slaves and free, male and female (Gal 3:28; cf., the "reconciliation" between circumcised and uncircumcised peoples brought about in Christ, Eph 2:14-16), and between humanity and God (Rom 5:10; Col 1:19-23). Its sign would not be the oppressed forgiving their oppressors, but rather the hearts

20. John W. de Gruchy also uses this etymology in *Reconciliation: Restoring Justice* (Minneapolis: Fortress, 2002). While de Gruchy draws different conclusions, based on South Africa's Truth and Reconciliation Commission, he also emphasizes communal reconciliation.

21. Martin Buber, *I and Thou*, trans. W. Kaufmann (New York: Free Press, 1971).

22. Cooper-White, *The Cry of Tamar*, 262; cf., Emerson on community context, *Dynamics of Forgiveness*, 180. For further discussion of relationality and power, particularly power-in-community, see also *The Cry of Tamar*, 28-42.

of the oppressors recognizing the full dignity and humanity of those who had objectified, and entering into true repentance, true *metanoia*.

## Conclusion

All theology, but especially *pastoral* theology which is concerned with care for suffering, must begin with us, and in particular, the pain and brokenness of the human condition. Pastoral theology takes human suffering as its starting place—in Jürgen Moltmann's words, "the open wound of life in this world."[23] From the perspective of those who have been victimized, whether the injury has been emotional, physical, or sexual, classic and popular definitions of forgiveness as a spiritual work do not facilitate the healing that well-meaning Christians intend. Furthermore, when we urge someone else to forgive, we may be unconsciously wishing simply to avoid staying with them in their suffering and anger. As the Rev. Marie Fortune, longtime advocate for survivors of sexual and domestic violence, has put it: "We ask others to forgive and forget, and what we really mean is that we want them to forgive so we can forget."[24] When we shift our perspective in doing theology from one of power and privilege to the perspective of the "sinned-against,"[25] we are challenged to re-think simplistic notions of forgiveness as a work.

If forgiveness is God's job to do, and a gift of grace that we may receive but not forcefully achieve by our own effort, we no longer need to push forgiveness onto others—or ourselves! We may or may not ever feel as though we have forgiven those who have harmed us, but we can stop punishing ourselves and others for legitimate negative feelings of hurt, anger, humiliation, and grief. As we allow our feelings to flow through us, without self-recrimination or judgment, we may find that we have new freedom, because

---

23. Jürgen Moltmann, *The Trinity and the Kingdom*, trans. Margaret Kohl (Minneapolis: Fortress, 1993) 49.

24. Video "Broken Vows: Religious Perspectives on Domestic Violence," Seattle: Faith Trust Institute, https://store.faithtrustinstitute.org/collections/domestic-violence-resources/products/1-week-broken-vows-streaming-video.

25. Andrew Sung Park and Susan Nelson, eds., *The Other Side of Sin: Woundedness from the Perspective of the Sinned-Against* (Albany: SUNY Press, 2001); Park, *From Hurt to Healing: A Theology of the Wounded* (Nashville: Abingdon, 2004). [As I noted in my lecture in Jerusalem, 2017, sometimes a public declaration of forgiveness can also be an important assertion of one's dignity, as in the case of the survivors of the racially-motivated shootings at a Bible study at Emanuel African Methodist Episcopal Church in Charleston, SC, in 2015. Public declarations still do not prevent individual survivors from post-traumatic stress or from struggling with the emotional pressure to forgive on a personal level. —PCW 2018]

we are no longer using our energy to suppress emotions that we thought were un-Christian. In fact, the so-called "negative" emotions of hurt and anger can be channeled into acts of compassion for others who have been wounded, and collaborative actions with other Christians for constructive social change. Finally, as we re-shift our attention away from forgiveness as the central theme of our theology, we can be freed to engage in prophetic witness to the already-not yet reconciliation that God is calling forth from all creation, and an end to violence in all its forms.

# 11

## Intimate Violence against Women
*Trajectories for Pastoral Care in a New Millennium*

2011[1]

## Introduction

THIS ARTICLE REVIEWS PROGRESS made in the theory and practice of pastoral care and counseling with regard to the issue of intimate violence against women since the 1970s. It includes a comprehensive survey of sociological, psychological, and pastoral literature, and a summary of research on teaching about domestic violence in mainline Protestant seminaries. Social and theological themes, including gender, power, and social and political context, and the challenges of justice-making are traced historically. The article concludes with new recommendations for churches, pastoral caregivers, counselors, and theologians.

In an article for *Pastoral Psychology* published nearly fifteen years ago,[2] I outlined a program of recommendations regarding domestic violence[3] awareness, prevention and intervention strategies in pastoral care and counseling. These goals may be summarized as follows: 1) consistently, intentionally integrate the issue of domestic violence in seminary education; 2) develop models of pastoral counseling focused on empowerment

---

1. Orig. publ. in *Pastoral Psychology* 60/6 (2011) 809–56.

2. Pamela Cooper-White, "Opening the Eyes: Understanding the Impact of Trauma on Development," in *In Her Own Time: Women and Developmental Issues in Pastoral Care*, ed. Jeanne Stevenson-Moessner (Minneapolis: Fortress, 2000) 87–102.

3. *Intimate partner violence* is now the preferred term, recognizing that not all intimate violence occurs in the home (as implied by the term *domestic violence*) or in the context of heterosexual marriage (as implied in terms such as *spousal abuse* or *wife abuse*.) In this article, I will use intimate partner violence and domestic violence interchangeably, particularly with regard to the battered women's movement's historical usage of *domestic violence*.

of women, and maintaining vigilance against socially reinforced stereotypes that blame victims or minimize or excuse perpetrators of violence from direct responsibility; 3) develop collaborative partnerships with local battered women's shelters, domestic violence agencies, batterers' programs, and knowledgeable clinical and pastoral counselors in the wider community; 4) offer pastoral care for individual victims and survivors characterized by non-judgmental listening, interpretations of scripture that are healing and empowering, and faith-grounded advocacy in the wider community for justice; 5) work in congregations to foster communities of support for victims and survivors through education and other means; 6) identify responsible batterers' programs that recognize intimate violence as part of a larger pattern of socially sanctioned power and control over women, and uphold *safety* as the first priority.

Looking back on that article, now almost fifteen years ago, it is exciting to see a number of areas in which progress has been made. At the same time, violence against women, and domestic violence in particular, remains at epidemic proportions in North American society.

## The Continuing Prevalence of Intimate Partner Violence

A recent, large-scale survey sponsored by the Commonwealth Fund estimates that 39% of women have experienced some form of abuse and/or sexual assault, and approximately 1/3 of American women are victims of intimate partner violence.[4] In its most recent statistical compilation for the years 1993–2001, the U.S. Department of Justice[5] found that the number of *reported* violent crimes by intimate partners against women declined from 1.1 million in 1993, but still involved more than half a million (588,490) women, representing 85% of all nonfatal intimate partner victimization. In 2001, intimate partner violence made up 20% of all nonfatal violent crime against women, compared to 3% against men. Reported homicides by in-

---

4. Commonwealth Fund, *Addressing Domestic Violence and Its Consequences: Policy Report of the Commonwealth Fund Commission on Women's Health* (New York: The Commonwealth Fund, 1998), summary at https://www.commonwealthfund.org/publications/publication/1999/may/violence-and-abuse.

5. U.S. Dept. of Justice, Bureau of Justice Statistics," *Intimate Partner Violence 1993–2001*, 2003, https://www.bjs.gov/index.cfm?ty=pbdetailandiid=1001. For more recent statistics, see Shannan M. Catalano, Erica L. Smith, Howard N. Snyder and Michael R. Rand, "Female Victims of Violence" (Bureau of Justice Statistics, 2009), https://www.bjs.gov/index.cfm?ty=pbdetail&iid=2020. [Note that raw data is generally made available annually by the Dept. of Justice after one year, and digests and analysis of data occur within 2-3 years. —PCW 2018]

timate partners show some decline as well over the years 1976–2000, from 1,600 to 1,247 women, and from 1,357 to 440 men. But statistics continue to show domestic violence as the cause of death of 33% of all female murder victims, compared to 4% of male victims.

In the most comprehensive survey of the prevalence of intimate partner violence conducted to date, published in 2000 by the National Institute of Justice and the Centers for Disease Control and Prevention, researchers Patricia Tjaden and Nancy Thoennes found that "Intimate partner violence is pervasive in U.S. society."[6] Nearly 25 percent of 8,000 women surveyed women, as well as 7.5 percent of 8,000 surveyed men "said they were raped and/or physically assaulted by a current or former spouse, cohabiting partner, or date at some time in their lifetime; 1.5 percent of surveyed women and 0.9 percent of surveyed men said they were raped and/or physically assaulted by a partner in the previous 12 months," in contrast to the declines in officially reported victimization tracked by the Department of Justice, they write:

> According to these estimates, approximately 1.5 million women and 834,732 men are raped and/or physically assaulted by an intimate partner annually in the United States. Because many victims are victimized more than once, the number of intimate partner victimizations exceeds the number of intimate partner victims annually. Thus, approximately 4.9 million intimate partner rapes and physical assaults are perpetrated against U.S. women annually, and approximately 2.9 million intimate partner physical assaults are committed against U.S. men annually. These findings suggest that intimate partner violence is a serious criminal justice and public health concern.[7]

These researchers also found that stalking by intimates is more prevalent than previously thought: approximately 503,485 women and 185,496 men are stalked by an intimate partner annually in the United States, far exceeding earlier public "guesstimates."

This NIJ/CDC survey was also the first to address the full extent of intimate partner violence against both male and female victims, showing the seriousness of intimate violence against men as well as women. At the same time, the report solidly refuted the previously often-debated National

---

6. Patricia Tjaden and Nancy Thoennes, *Extent, Nature, and Consequences of Intimate Partner Violence: Findings from the National Violence against Women Survey* (Washington, DC: National Institute of Justice and Centers for Disease Control and Prevention, 2000), https://www.ncjrs.gov/pdffiles1/nij/181867.pdf.

7. Ibid, Executive Summary

Family Violence Survey, which asserted that male-female intimate violence was roughly equal or "mutual" in North American society.[8] Tjaden and Thoennes state:

> Women experience more intimate partner violence than do men ... These findings support data from the Bureau of Justice Statistics' National Crime Victimization Survey, which consistently show women are at significantly greater risk of intimate partner violence than are men. However, they contradict data from the National Family Violence Survey, which consistently show men and women are equally likely to be physically assaulted by an intimate partner.[9]

The authors confirmed long-held analyses by battered women's advocates that intimate violence is not primarily a matter of a batterer's poor impulse control, poor communication skills, or other interpersonal deficits,

---

8. Murray A. Straus and Richard J. Gelles, *Physical Violence in American Families: Risk Factors and Adaptation to Violence in 8,145 Families* (New Brunswick, NJ: Transaction, 1990). See also government-sponsored research by Michael S. Kimmel, "Gender Symmetry" in Domestic Violence: A Substantive and Methodological Research Review, *Violence against Women* 8/11 (2002) 1332–63; Callie Marie Rennison, *Crime Data Brief: Intimate Partner Violence, 1993–2001*, NCJ 197838 (Washington, DC: Bureau of Justice Statistics, Feb. 2003), https://www.bjs.gov/content/pub/pdf/ipv01.pdf; and Shannan Catalano, *Intimate Partner Violence in the United States* (Bureau of Justice Statistics, 2007), https://www.bjs.gov/content/pub/pdf/ipvus.pdf. The earlier disparity between the BJS statistics and those gathered by researchers at the University of New Hampshire through the 1985 National Family Violence Survey (the instrument used by Straus and Gelles in *Physical Violence in American Families*, see above) is best understood in terms of methodological problems with the UNH study's instrument, the Conflict Tactics Scale (CTS). For recent, comprehensive critiques of the CTS, see R. Emerson Dobash, Russell Dobash, Margo Wilson, and Martin Daly, "The Myth of Sexual Symmetry in Marital Violence, *Social Problems* 39/1 (1992) 71–91; Walter S. DeKeseredy and Martin D. Schwartz, *Measuring the Extent of Woman Abuse in Intimate Heterosexual Relationships: A Critique of the Conflict Tactics Scales* (Harrisburg, PA: VAWnet—a project of the National Resource Center on Domestic Violence/Pennsylvania Coalition against Domestic Violence, 1998), https://www.researchgate.net/publication/290448806_Measuring_the_Extent_of_Woman_Abuse_in_Intimate_Heterosexual_Relationships_A_Critique_of_the_Conflict_Tactics_Scale; Donileen R. Loseke and Demi Kurz, "Men's Violence toward Women is the Serious Social Problem," in *Current Controversies on Family Violence*, ed. Richard J. Gelles, Donileen R. Loseke and Mary M. Cavanaugh (Thousand Oaks, CA: Sage, 2005) 79–95. Tjaden and Thoennes go on to say in their Executive Summary, "Studies are needed to determine how different survey methodologies affect women's and men's responses to questions about intimate partner violence" (Tjaden and Thoennes, *Extent, Nature, and Consequences*, https://www.ncjrs.gov/pdffiles1/nij/181867.pdf).

9. Tjaden and Thoennes, *Extent, Nature, and Consequences*, Executive Summary at https://www.ncjrs.gov/pdffiles1/nij/181867.pdf.

but part of a larger dynamic of attempts to assert power and control over the victim. Their findings showed the following:

> Violence perpetrated against women by intimates is often accompanied by emotionally abusive and controlling behavior. The survey found that women whose partners were jealous, controlling, or verbally abusive were significantly more likely to report being raped, physically assaulted, and/or stalked by their partners, even when other sociodemographic and relationship characteristics were controlled," in*deed, having a verbally abusive partner was the variable most likely to predict that a woman would be victimized by an intimate partner. These findings support the theory that violence perpetrated against women by intimates is often part of a systematic pattern of dominance and control.*" (emphasis added)[10]

Finally, these researchers emphasized that not only quantity of assaults, but the repeated nature and level of injuriousness were unequal between women and men. They wrote:

> Women experience more chronic and injurious physical assaults at the hands of intimate partners than do men. The survey found that women who were physically assaulted by an intimate partner averaged 6.9 physical assaults by the same partner, but men averaged 4.4 assaults. The survey also found that 41.5 percent of the women who were physically assaulted by an intimate partner were injured during their most recent assault, compared with 19.9 percent of the men. These findings suggest that research aimed at understanding and preventing intimate partner violence against women should be stressed."[11]

Gender differentials in the extent of violence were further reinforced by a preliminary finding that women living with women experience less intimate partner violence (11%) than women living with men (21.7%), and men living with men experience considerably more such violence (23%) than men living with women (7.4%). The authors thereby conclude that "strategies for preventing intimate partner violence should focus on risks posed by men." This recommendation was echoed most recently on a national scale by the American Psychological Association in its "Resolution on Male Violence against Women."[12]

10. Ibid.
11. Ibid.
12. American Psychological Association, *Resolution on Male Violence against Women* (2008): http://www.apa.org/about/policy/male-violence.aspx.

Underreporting of intimate partner violence continues to be a problem, in spite of now three decades of increasingly public awareness and improved police and judicial training. These authors found the following:

> Most intimate partner victimizations are not reported to the police. Only approximately one- fifth of all rapes, one-quarter of all physical assaults, and one-half of all stalkings perpetrated against female respondents by intimates were reported to the police. Even fewer rapes, physical assaults, and stalkings perpetrated against male respondents by intimates were reported. The majority of victims who did not report their victimization to the police thought the police would not or could not do anything on their behalf. These findings suggest that most victims of intimate partner violence do not consider the justice system an appropriate vehicle for resolving conflicts with intimates.[13]

Combining this finding with other indications that battered women frequently seek help first from their clergy,[14] we must conclude that churches continue to play a crucial role in responding to victims. What more can religious institutions do to help stem this tide of violence?

In this article, I will consider what progress has been made in the theory and practice of pastoral care with regard to the issue of violence against women since the movement to name and end sexual assault and intimate partner violence began in the late 1970s. This will include a survey of pastoral literature, as well as church-related conferences and publications (e.g., denominationally sponsored brochures, websites, videos, etc.). I will also summarize a survey conducted during January 2004 of teaching members of the Society for Pastoral Theology, to determine the level of inclusion of these issues in theological teaching, as well as some informal research on the level of cooperation among domestic violence and rape crisis agencies and churches/denominations.[15] Major social and theological themes, including the rise in awareness of gender and power, the connection between personal, communal and political realities, the importance of social context, and the challenges of justice-making amid multiple forms of diversity in culture and society, will be traced through this historical development of a partnership to end violence against women. The article will conclude with observations about the distance we still have to go in ending violence against women,

---

13. Ibid.

14. Mildred Pagelow, *Woman-battering: Victims and Their Experience* (Beverly Hills, CA: Sage, 1981).

15. Pamela Cooper-White, "What Are We Teaching about Violence against Women?" *Journal of Pastoral Theology* 14/2 (2004) 48–69.

and recommendations re: the role of the church, pastoral caregivers and theologians in advocacy, activism and public witness toward achieving this long-desired goal.

## A Brief History of the Domestic Violence Awareness Movement

It is helpful first to survey the history of domestic violence awareness in the U.S., in order to understand the larger context for religious organizations' and congregations' efforts at prevention and intervention. The movement to end intimate partner violence grew out of the wider effort of "second wave feminism" in the late 1960s and early 70s[16] to identify the forms of violence against women that maintained and reinforced the subjugation of women in American society. The first battered women's shelter in North America, Haven House in Pasadena, was founded in 1964 by a local Al-Anon group.[17] Soon thereafter, arising from consciousness-raising groups and grass-roots movements to address violence, more battered women's shelters began to appear, sometimes simply as networks of underground emergency housing in volunteers' homes.[18] An early advocacy group for women struggling for free-

---

16. The term "second wave feminism" refers to the resurgence of movements for women's rights around the time of the civil rights movement in the U.S. The "first wave" refers to the feminist movement in the 19th and early 20th century, including the suffragists Elizabeth Cady Stanton and others, who drew on Enlightenment principles of equality and emancipation. "Second wave feminism" is also used, especially in literary theory, to refer to the shift to an emphasis on difference, and challenging of traditional cultural gender norms. A new "third wave feminism" is now being identified with postmodern efforts at deconstruction of binary categories, and an emphasis on social construction, gesture, performance, and fluidity of gender. For "a genealogy of gender from ancient times through three waves of feminist debate," see Claire Colebrook, *Gender* (New York: Palgrave Macmillan, 2004). For an accessible discussion of feminist literary theory, see Toril Moi, *Sexual/textual Politics: Feminist Literary Theory* (New York: Routledge, 1988).

17. Historians identify the underground movement of women sheltering abused women as beginning in the west at least many centuries earlier. The *Casa del Soccorso* in Bologna c. 1563 and the *Compagnia di Santa Maddalena sopra le Malmaritate* in 16th c. Florence are two examples (Sherrill Cohen, *The Evolution of Women's Asylums since 1500: From Refuges for Ex-prostitutes to Shelters for Battered Women* (New York: Oxford University Press, 1992); Lucia Ferrante, "Honour Regained: Women in the Casa del Soccorso di San Paolo in Sixteenth-century Bologna," trans. Margaret A. Gallucci, in *Sex and Gender in Historical Perspective*, ed. Edward Muir and Guido Ruggiero (Baltimore: Johns Hopkins University Press, 1990) 46–72. Thanks to Jennea Tallentire at the University of British Columbia for these references.

18. For a more detailed timeline, see SafeNetwork, "Herstory of Domestic Violence: A Timeline of the Battered Women's Movement" (California Department of Health

dom from domestic violence and/or substance abuse, Women in Transition, was started in 1971 in Philadelphia,[19] Chiswick Women's Aid was established in London by Erin Pizzey,[20] and Kvindehust was founded in Copenhagen by the Redstockings, a Danish women's liberation group.[21] A consciousness-raising group formed Women's Advocates, a legal aid and shelter program in Minneapolis/St. Paul on a collective model in 1972.[22] These were followed in North America by Rainbow Retreat in Phoenix, Arizona (in 1972), Interval House in Toronto (in 1972), Transition House in Vancouver (in 1974), Bradley-Angle House in Portland, Oregon (in 1975), Abused Women's Aid in Crisis in New York City (in 1975), and Transition House in Cambridge, Massachusetts (in 1975).[23] Other programs soon followed until many major cities had shelter programs by the late 1970s.

The first involvement of the religious community also began in this period. The Center for the Prevention of Sexual and Domestic Violence was founded in Seattle, Washington, in 1977 by the Rev. Marie Fortune (now the FaithTrust Institute).[24] A pioneering United Church of Christ minister dedicated to prevention and response to violence against women from within the religious community, Fortune has been honored for her tireless ecumenical and interfaith advocacy for victims of abuse, now for three decades. Programs began to expand beyond shelter in the mid 1970s. Haven House established the first program for children of battered women in 1974. Casa Myrna Vasquez, the first known bilingual battered women's program, was started in 1977 in Boston, MA by Latino, African American, Asian American and European American residents of the

---

Services and Interface Family Services, 1999): http://citeseerx.ist.psu.edu/viewdoc/download?doi=10.1.1.208.6955&rep=rep1&type=pdf. For more detailed historical accounts, see R. Emerson Dobash and Russell Dobash, *Women, Violence and Social Change* (New York: Routledge, 1992), and Sue Heinemann, *Timelines of American Women's History* (New York: Roundtable, 1996). For a legal history through 1995, see Nancy Lemon, *Domestic Violence Law: A Comprehensive Overview of Cases and Sources* (San Francisco: Austin & Winfield, 1996).

19. Website at http://www.helpwomen.org/.

20. Erin Pizzey, *Scream Quietly or the Neighbors Will Hear You* (London: Penguin, 1974). Pizzey was a controversial figure, whose subsequent co-authored book *Prone to Violence*, raised a storm of feminist protest against blaming—or pathologizing—the victim: Erin Pizzey and Jeff Shapiro, *Prone to Violence* (Feltham, UK: Hamlyn, 1982).

21. SafeNetwork, "Herstory of Domestic Violence: A Timeline of the Battered Women's Movement" (California Department of Health Services and Interface Family Services, 1999): http://citeseerx.ist.psu.edu/viewdoc/download?doi=10.1.1.208.6955&rep=rep1&type=pdf/.

22. Ibid.

23. Ibid.

24. http://www.faithtrustinstitute.org/.

South End (Casa Myrna Vasquez, 2009).[25] In 1977, the first program by men to end male violence against women, called Emerge, was also founded in Cambridge, Massachusetts.

State coalitions of advocates began forming around 1976-1978, often connected to the first statewide legislative initiatives, and now exist in every state in the U.S.[26] In January, 1978, over one hundred advocates for battered women gathered from across the country to attend the U.S. Commission on Civil Rights' first national hearing on domestic violence.[27] Hoping to gain strength from one another's individual efforts, these early leaders organized the National Coalition against Domestic Violence in Washington, DC.[28] The first Coalition volunteers and staff worked to identify battered women's programs and to help link them in a network that was philosophically bound by a common commitment to prevention, political analysis, and legislative advocacy, as well as victim services. A national toll-free crisis hotline was created to link victims with services nationwide. Currently, the national Coalition has its main offices in Colorado, and also maintains a public policy office in Washington, DC.

25. Some sources date this even earlier, in 1974, e.g., SafeNetwork, "Herstory of Domestic Violence (see web link above).

26. National Coalition against Domestic Violence (NCADV), links to state coalitions, 2009, https://ncadv.org/state-coalitions.

27. Two subsequent field hearings in Phoenix, AZ, and Harrisburg, PA, resulted in the report by the U.S. Commission on Civil Rights (USCCR), *The Federal Response to Domestic Violence: A Report of the United States Commission on Civil Rights*, also published as G. Gerebenics, *Under the Rule of thumb: Battered Women and the Administration of Justice* (Washington, DCP: U.S. Commission on Civil Rights, 1982), abstract online at https://www.ncjrs.gov/App/Publications/abstract.aspx?ID=82752. Subsequent state reports from Connecticut, New Hampshire and New Jersey have been submitted to the USCCR, and an article soon appeared in the *Civil Rights Journal*, Pamela Coukos (1998), "Outlawing Domestic Violence: What Works and What Doesn't," *Civil Rights Journal* 3/1(1998) 29-32. Coukos noted, "Four years after the passage of the Violence against Women Act (VAWA), and well over two decades after the founding of the nation's first battered women's shelters, domestic violence continues to plague women and children in the United States. The VAWA hearings provided a national wake-up call about a shockingly high rate of bartering in our society and a sadly inadequate response Congress documented that our police departments, prosecutors and courts, deeply infected with gender bias, often failed to respond to domestic violence as a crime or blamed the victim for the violence The VAWA began a major Federal commitment to improving the criminal justice system and services for battered women by providing Federal dollars and encouraging local partnerships among criminal justice systems and victim advocacy organizations. At this juncture we can report important progress, but tragic deficiencies remain" (29).

28. NCADV National Coalition against Domestic Violence, www.ncadv.org; https://ncadv.org.

Internationally, the United Nations held its first world conference on women in Mexico City in 1975, leading to the formation of UNIFEM (UN Development Fund for Women) and the declaration of a Decade for Women (1976–1985). Two more world conferences were held in Copenhagen (1980) and Nairobi (1985). Together, these conferences and organizational advances raised up violence against women for greater global visibility and activism, as well as numerous other platforms for economic, cultural and political action regarding women's rights and welfare.[29] The UN has remained committed to continuing conferences and review of the status of violence against women every five years. The fourth and largest global conference to date, involving over 50,000 participants, was held in 1995 in Beijing on the theme *"Equality, Development and Peace,"*[30] and this was followed five years later by a Special Session of the UN General Assembly entitled "Women 2000: Gender Equality, Development and Peace for the 21st Century, "Beijing+5," a "Beijing +10" conference at the UN Headquarters in New York in 2005, and a Beijing +15 conference in 2010.[31] The World Health Organization has initiated a program on Gender, Women, and Health, which published a groundbreaking study in 2005 of over 24,000 women in 10 countries, with recommendations for prevention and intervention of sexual violence as a pervasive and serious global health problem.[32] And finally, just

---

29. See United Nations, *UN Women Watch*: http://www.un.org/womenwatch/; for more on the history, see also United Nations, "About the UN Women": http://www.un.org/womenwatch/daw/daw/index.html.

30. For documents on the conference, and information on past and future developments, see United Nations, United Nations, "Gender Equality and Women's Empowerment Ten Years after Beijing—Where do we stand?" http://www.un.org/womenwatch/forums/review/; United Nations, *World Conference to Review and Appraise the Achievements of the United Nations Decade for Women,1985: Nairobi, Kenya* (Pleasantville, NY: UNIFO Publishers, 1986).

31. http://www.un.org/womenwatch/daw/beijing15/overview.html; see also UN Inter-Agency Network on Women and Gender Equality, Report of the Sixth Session, 10 April 2007 (for the most recent 2012 report: www.un.org/womenwatch/ianwge/annualmeetings/Report_of_IANWGE-2012.pdf). [*Update:* UN Women and the People's Republic of China co-hosted a "Global Leaders' Meeting on Gender Equality and Women's Empowerment: A Commitment to Action", in September 2015, in New York: http://beijing20.unwomen.org/en, and preparations are now underway for a 2020 "Beijing 25" conference: https://www.ngocsw.org/archive/ngo-csw-forum/preparing-for-2020. —PCW 2018]

32. Claudia García-Moreno, Henrica A.F.M. Jansen, Mary Ellsberg, Lori Heise, and Charlotte Watts, C., *WHO Multi-country Study on Women's Health and Domestic Violence against Women: Initial Results on Prevalence, Health Outcomes and Women's Responses* (Geneva, Switzerland: World Health Organization, 2005): http://www.who.int/gender/violence/en/.

in June, 2008, the International Criminal Tribunal in The Hague, Netherlands, defined rape as a war crime in its own right.[33]

In just slightly over three decades, the number of shelters and battered women's service programs has now grown to over 2,000 agencies. These agencies serve hundreds of women annually with emergency hotlines, shelter, legal assistance, police and courtroom advocacy, and other resources, while also serving their local communities through public education, legislative policy work, and training programs for the police, probation officers, and judges. More specialized programs grew in the 1980s to address the needs of Asian, Latina, and other ethnic groups and languages, programs for lesbians and gay men, and prevention programs targeting teen and dating violence. Programs to help women achieve greater economic stability including job training, economic literacy, and longer-term transitional residential programs, such as Second Step at Marin Abused Women's Services followed.[34] The mid-to-late 1980s also began to see the first cooperative training programs specifically designed for clergy sponsored by domestic violence agencies.[35]

Public awareness campaigns have grown, including the naming of October as Domestic Violence Awareness Month (first passed as state legislation in California in 1977) and a related purple ribbon campaign.[36] The "Stop Family Violence" postage stamp issued in October, 2003,[37] to help fund domestic violence programs through the U.S. Department of Health and Human Services, the children's art project "Hands Are Not for Hitting,"[38] the

33. Marlise Simmons, "For First Time, Court Defines Rape as War Crime," *New York Times*, June 28, 2008: http://www.nytimes.com/specials/bosnia/context/0628warcrimestribunal.html.

34. Marin Abused Women's Services (MAWS), 2009, www.centerfordomesticpeace.org/.

35. In addition to continuing work by the FaithTrust Institute in Seattle (see above), which had expanded to national programming and publication of resources, smaller cooperative groups of domestic violence workers and educated church leaders began to organize local prevention efforts. For example, the Family Violence Project (now called Futures without Violence in San Francisco (https://www.futureswithoutviolence.org/) began clergy trainings through the formation of a task force of battered women's advocates from local agencies and churches in 1987.

36. SafeNetwork, "Herstory of Domestic Violence (see above).

37. U.S. Postal Service, "Stop Family Violence" fundraising stamp, issued 2003: http://www.ncdsv.org/ncd_newsinterest_stamp.html, created through the "Stamp Out Domestic Violence Act," sponsored by U.S. Senator Nighthorse Campbell (R-CO) in 2001.

38. Slogan originated by the Minnesota Coalition for Battered Women and used in a variety of children's educational materials (Martine Aggasi, *Hands Are not for Hitting* (Minneapolis: Free Spirit, 2000).

Clothesline Project (begun at a Take Back the Night Rally in Hyannis, Massachusetts in 1990, the project involves traveling displays of hand painted T-shirts with art and statements against abuse - Clothesline Project, 2009), as well as newer programs with corporate sponsorship such as the Liz Claiborne "Love Is Not Abuse" campaign[39] developed in partnership with the Family Violence Prevention Fund,[40] a public policy advocacy organization founded in 1980 in San Francisco, Verizon's HopeLine program providing safe voice mail boxes for shelter residents and donating used cell phones for emergency use since 1995,[41] and Philip Morris' and its parent company Altria's "Doors of Hope" grant program developed in 1998 in partnership with the National Network to End Domestic Violence (a coalition of providers and state coalitions that first helped spearhead the Violence against Women Act in Congress).[42] Window Between Worlds, a project designed by an artist to use visual art as a tool for healing and public awareness was founded in 1991.[43] More recently the Family Violence Prevention Fund also initiated a "Coaching Boys into Men" media campaign and coaches' leadership program.[44] The Internet has also vastly changed the landscape of both service and advocacy work, and the broadened access to resources and exchange of ideas has accelerated in the past decade, as indeed in all political movements and helping professions. (Note how the references for this section of the article now include—for the first time in my research experience—more internet citations than print resources!)

Successful national legislative campaigns developed over many years have resulted in the passage in the 1990s of the federal Violence against Women Act, or "VAWA" first voted in 1994, renewed in 2000 and 2005, and currently due for reauthorization in 2010[45]; the Domestic Violence Offender

39. Liz Claiborne Corporation, Love Is not Abuse campaign (1991), http://www.loveisnotabuse.com/; [website no longer available; campaign archived with new resources at https://www.loveisrespect.org. —PCW 2018]

40. [Another earlier name for Futures without Violence (www.futureswithoutviolence.org) —PCW 2018]

41. Verizon Corporation HopeLine, 2009, described online: https://www.verizonwireless.com/dam/news/HopeLine_Press_Kit.pdf. Verizon also provided sponsorship for the Florida Clothesline Project: http://www.robertscommunications.com/verizon.htm.

42. National Network to End Domestic Violence (NNEDV): http://www.nnedv.org.

43. A Window between the Worlds: Art Transforming Trauma: http://www.awbw.org.

44. Futures without Violence: https://www.futureswithoutviolence.org/engaging-mencoaching-boys-into-men.

45. For full text see U.S. Congress, "Violence against Women and Department of Justice Reauthorization Act of 2005," https://www.congress.gov/bill/109th-congress/

Gun Ban (the "Lautenberg amendment") enacted in 1997; and the Victims of Trafficking and Violence Protection Act,[46] among others.[47] Many more bills are currently in Congress, including legislation to protect immigrant battered women, to provide health care, and to fund services for children exposed to domestic violence, including H.R. 739, the Security and Financial Empowerment "SAFE" Act of 2009–2010, originally introduced in 1996 as the Women's Health Equity Act, and reintroduced in Congress every year since).[48] Most programs also network closely with other victim services agencies, rape crisis organizations, child abuse prevention programs, police, district attorneys, and increasingly, coalitions of concerned clergy and lay leaders from the religious community.[49]

The NCADV and its member programs are distinguished from some social service agencies that may also serve battered women alongside other constituencies (for example, family service agencies, homeless women's shelters, and other social services), by an underlying philosophical commitment to understanding intimate partner violence and violence against women as part of a larger system of social injustice, encompassing not only sexism, but racism, heterosexism, and other forms of privilege and oppression. The Coalition's mission statement affirms a vision that goes beyond social services to social reform of the root causes of violence:

> The Mission of the National Coalition against Domestic Violence is to organize for collective power by advancing transformative work, thinking and leadership of communities and individuals working to end the violence in our lives.

NCADV believes violence against women and children results from the use of force or threat to achieve and maintain control over others in

---

house-bill/3402 . [*Update:* The VAWA was expanded in scope in 2013 amid considerable debate. It lapsed during the Dec. 2018 government shut-down, with some funding stopgaps. Conservative lawmakers have balked at expansion of services to LGBTQ persons and "red flag" gun laws, among other objections. (https://www.politico.com/story/2019/02/13/violence-against-women-act-budget-talks-1168924)—PCW 2019]

46. U.S. Congress, "Victims of Trafficking and Violence Protection Act of 2000," H.R. 3244: http://frwebgate.access.gpo.gov/cgi-bin/getdoc.cgi?dbname=106_cong_billsanddocid=f:h3244enr.txt.pdf [reauthorized in 2013; for a summary of current laws on trafficking, see https://www.state.gov/j/tip/laws/. —PCW 2018]

47. National Criminal Justice Reference Service, "Spotlight on Family Violence, Legislation," http://www.ncjrs.gov/spotlight/family_violence/Summary.html. See also the Dept. of Justice's Office on Violence against Women: https://www.justice.gov/ovw.

48. Lucille Roybal-Allard, "Security and Financial Empowerment Act (SAFE)," H.R. 739 (2009): http://www.govtrack.us/congress/bill.xpd?bill=h111-739.

49. National Criminal Justice Reference Service (NCJRS), *Special Feature: Family Violence,* 2009: https://www.ncjrs.gov/family-violence/.

intimate relationships, and from societal abuse of power and domination in the forms of sexism, racism, homophobia, classism, anti-semitism, able-bodyism, ageism and other oppressions. NCADV recognizes that the abuses of power in society foster battering by perpetuating conditions that condone violence against women and children. Therefore, it is the mission of NCADV to work for major societal changes necessary to eliminate both personal and societal violence against all women and children.[50]

The greatest challenge now within the battered women's movement is how to expand collaboration without sacrificing the political vision for justice and the original embedding of the movement in a larger effort to resist and dismantle structures of racism, heterosexism, classism, and other forms of oppression. One long-term veteran of the grassroots battered women's movement, Susan Schechter, has called publicly for greater openness to building alliances in order to advocate more effectively for public policy changes, especially on behalf of poor women.[51] Some partnerships, however, such as the Philip Morris campaign noted above, have given rise to ethical qualms within the battered women's movement, precisely because of the wider vision of that movement and its commitment to more than providing services, but addressing systemic exploitation in all its forms. Battered women's advocates schooled in radical politics and multi-national tobacco companies make strange bedfellows.[52] Domestic violence workers are divided in how far to compromise over-arching values, or, to put it differently, how stringent to be in their judgments of potential collaborators' politics, when pragmatic, even life-saving strategies and resources are on the table. This debate will not end any time soon, nor should it—keeping the wider ethical horizon in view is what has given the movement to end violence against women much of its passion and power.

---

50. "About Us," NCADV, 2009, www.ncadv.org. [Vision and mission statement shortened as of 2018, https://ncadv.org; similar language also found at https://ncadv.org/learn-more. —PCW 2018]

51. Susan Schechter, "New Challenges for the Battered Women's Movement: Building Collaborations and Improving Public Policy for Poor Women," in Schechter, *Building Comprehensive Solutions to Domestic Violence, Publication #1: A Vision Paper* (Pennsylvania Coalition against Domestic Violence/National Resource Center on Domestic Violence, January, 1999) [https://www.bcsdv.org/wp-content/uploads/2015/09/BCS-Pub1.pdf.

52. For a trenchant critique, see Marjorie Williams, "This Kills Women. Do Feminist Groups Even Care?" *Washington Post*, April 11, 2001, A27.

## Domestic Violence Literature in the Secular Press

Almost as soon as the first shelters were established, women began writing about the problem of intimate partner violence in an effort to expand the circle of awareness. The first popular volume was written by the children's novelist Erin Pizzey." In *Scream Quietly or the Neighbors Will Hear*, she chronicled her experience of helping a neighbor, which led to her founding of the first British women's shelter, described above.[53] The first social research books, also widely read, were written by lesbian and civil rights activist Del Martin,[54] psychologist Lenore Walker,[55] and the Duluth activist couple Rebecca and Russell Dobash.[56] Walker's book is the source for the often cited "Cycle of Violence," based on reports of women of an escalation phase, an acute battering incident, and a honeymoon or respite phase.[57] The Dobashes' book first published the "Power and Control Wheel," still commonly used to explicate the masculinist power dynamic underlying battering relationships. The first social scientific research book on domestic violence, *Battered Women: A Psychosociological Study*, was also published during the same time frame by AWAIC's founding director, Maria Roy.[58]

Journals dedicated entirely to issues of violence and victimization also began to be published as early as 1976, for example, *Victimology*[59] and *Response to the Victimization of Women and Children*,[60] and have continued to

---

53. Erin Pizzey, *Scream Quietly or the Neighbors Will Hear* (London: Penguin, 1974).

54. Del Martin, *Battered Wives* (1976; reprint, New York: Pocket Books, 1977, 1983). Del Martin and her partner Phyllis Lyon wrote the pioneering books *Lesbian/Woman* (San Francisco: Volcano, 1972) and were longtime advocates for the legalization of same-sex marriage. For a full bio, see William Grimes, "Del Martin, Lesbian Activist, Dies at 87," *New York Times*, Aug. 27, 1008, https://www.nytimes.com/2008/08/28/us/28martin.html.

55. Lenore E. Walker, *The Battered Woman* (New York: Harper Colophon, 1979).

56. R. Emerson Dobash and Russell Dobash, *Violence against Wives: A Case against the Patriarchy* (New York: Free Press, 1979).

57. Lenore E. Walker, *The Battered Woman* (New York: Harper Colophon, 1979).

58. Marla Roy, ed., *Battered Women: A Psychosociological Study of Domestic Violence* (New York: Van Nostrand Reinhold Company, 1977). Soon after, Roy also co-authored *Up from Battering* (with Marcia Wooding Caro, New York: Abused Women's Aid in Crisis, 1981) and also published *The Abusive Partner: An Analysis of Domestic Battering* (New York: Van Nostrand Reinhold, 1981). Roy went on to interview 146 children of battered women and published one of the earliest accounts of the damaging effects of domestic violence on children: *Children in the Crossfire: Violence in the Home—How Does it Affect Our Children?* (Deerfield Beach, FL: Health Communications, 1988).

59. *Victimology: An International Journal*, Vol. 1, Washington, DC: National Institute of Victimology/Visage Press, 1976)

60. *Response to the Victimization of Women and Children*, Vol. 1 (Washington, DC:

appear as recently as the 1990s, including the *Journal of Family Violence*,[61] the *Journal of Interpersonal Violence*,[62] *Violence and Victims*,[63] and *Violence against Women*.[64]

Two debates surfaced early among advocates for battered women, and were reflected in the expansion and divergence of perspectives represented in the literature. The first debate revolved around appropriate service approaches and who had legitimate authority to work most effectively with battered women, their children, and batterers. This debate could be termed the "peer vs. clinical counseling" debate.[65] The second debate was a larger philosophical one, addressing the necessity of including a political advocacy stance and a social power analysis alongside and undergirding any provision of services. This debate could be termed the "battered women's movement vs. social services" debate. The two debates also overlapped. It was battered women's workers, including early founders of the movement, growing numbers of formerly battered women who wanted to help others get free of violence, and many others who had been conscienticized about violence against women, who most often carried forward the necessity of understanding battering in a larger socio-political context. Those psychotherapists and social science researchers who had not been a part of the grassroots political movement tended to see victims' needs more in terms of clinical diagnosis and treatment models, or, as in the case of counselors who came to battered women's work from a substance-abuse treatment or 12-step background, tended to view battered women in terms of co-dependency or "relationship addiction."[66] Clinical authors, following gender-blind

---

Center for Women Policy Studies/Guilford, 1977); journal ended after 1992.

61. *Journal of Family Violence*, Vol. 1 (New York: Springer, 1986).

62. *Journal of Interpersonal Violence: Concerned with the Study and Treatment of Victims and Perpetrators of Physical and Sexual Violence*, Vol. 1 (University of Washington School of Social Work/Thousand Oaks, CA: Sage, 1986); https://us.sagepub.com/en-us/nam/journal/journal-interpersonal-violence.

63. *Violence and Victims*, Vol. 1 (University of New Hampshire Family Research Laboratory/New York: Springer, 1986): http://www.springerpub.com/violence-and-victims.html.

64. *Violence against Women*, Vol. 1 (Thousand Oaks, CA: Sage, 1994), http://journals.sagepub.com/home/vaw.

65. Cooper-White, "Peer vs. Clinical Counseling: Is There Room for Both in the Battered Women's Movement?" *Response to the Victimization of Women and Children*, 13/3 (1990) 2–6 [see Ch. 1, this volume.]

66. For critiques of this view, see Linda S. Brown, "What's Love Got to Do with It?: A Feminist Takes a Critical Look at the Women Who Love Too Much Movement," *Working Together* 7/2 (1986) (Seattle: Center for Prevention of Sexual and Domestic Violence [now the FaithTrust Institute]; Pamela Cooper-White, *The Cry of Tamar: Violence against Women and the Church's Response* (Minneapolis: Fortress, 1995) 253–62;

legal language, also tended to use the term "spousal abuse," obscuring the evidence that women were vastly more likely to be victims of intimate violence.[67] Two types of programs began to evolve over time: battered women's shelters and related services on the one hand, and services for battered women alongside other types of clients in family service agencies, homeless shelters, and various mental health programs.

At issue in both the "peer vs. clinical" and "movement vs. services" debates was a concern about blaming the victim.[68] Battered women's advocates (rightly) insisted that any analysis of battering needed to hold perpetrators accountable for the violence, rather than pathologizing the victim. They understood clinicians' and 12-step counselors' tendency to focus on victims' problems as part of a larger patriarchal societal pattern of minimization and denial, which diagnosed or blamed women for their victimization rather than holding batterers accountable for their violence. Lenore Walker's own later research occasioned one instance of this controversy, when her concept of the "battered women's syndrome"[69] based on her experience as an expert witness was critiqued by many in the battered women's movement as reductionistic, and open to being misused as another way to blame women psychologically for their own victimization.[70] The shift of attention from

---

[2nd ed. 2012, 251–61, esp. 111–12]; Rose Moore, "Co-dependency vs. Battered Woman Syndrome," *The Voice* (special edition), 1988, NCADV Reprints, P.O. Box 18749, Denver, CO 80218-0749.

67. As critiqued by Michele Bograd, "Introduction: Feminist Perspectives on Wife Abuse," in Kersti Yllö and Michele Bograd, eds., *Feminist Perspectives on Wife Abuse* (Newbury Park, CA: Sage, 1988).

68. A term first used in connection with the oppression of the poor, and an analysis of the politics around government welfare programs, by sociologist William Ryan in *Blaming the Victim* (New York: Vintage, 1976).

69. Lenore E. Walker, "The Battered Woman: Myths and Realities," in Kieran Scott and Michael Warren, eds., *Perspectives on Marriage: A Reader*, 2nd ed. (New York: Oxford University Press, 2000) 264–83; and a 3rd edition of Lenore E. Walker, *The Battered Woman Syndrome* (New York: Springer, 1984; 3rd ed., 2009; [4th ed. 2016]). Walker has continued to work in the field, e.g., Lenore E. Walker, *Terrifying Love: Why Battered Women Kill and How Society Responds* (New York: Harper & Row, 1989).

70. Mary Ann Dutton, *Critique of the Battered Women Syndrome Model* (Harrisburg, PA: National Resource Center on Domestic Violence, 2001), www.aaets.org/article138.htm; Donald A. Downs and James Fisher, "Battered Woman Syndrome: Tool of Justice or False Hope in Self-defense Cases?," in *Current Controversies on Family Violence*, 2nd ed., ed. Donileen R. Loseke, Richard J. Gelles, and Mary M. Cavanaugh (Thousand Oaks, CA: Sage, 2005) 241–56; Sue Osthoff and Holly Maguigan, "Explaining without Pathologizing: Testimony on Battering and Its Effects," in *Current Controversies on Family Violence*, 2nd ed., ed. Richard J. Gelles, Donileen Loseke and Mary M. Cavanaugh (Thousand Oaks, CA: Sage, 2005) 225–56. E.g., Dutton's work speaks to the inadequacy of battered woman syndrome for describing battered women's experiences,

perpetrator to victim was understood as subtly reinforcing batterers' socialized sense of entitlement to use force in order to maintain ownership and control of women and children.

One important way in which battered women's programs maintained their larger political vision was membership in the NCADV as well as state coalitions. Programs (including batterers' programs) were able to signal their ongoing commitment to the movement to end violence against women and children by their continued affiliation with other battered women's programs through the political advocacy done in coalition work. Advocates who joined together in this way also were able to hold one another accountable to a wider vision, including violence prevention and community education work in the short term, and legislative and educational advocacy to bring about long-term social change. NCADV also published resources, including an important guide for mental health professionals by Susan Schechter.[71]

Two strands of literature grew alongside the two types of programs. The battered women's movement generated a significant body of literature, mostly intended as guides for advocates and other helpers working with battered women, and/or as tools for wider education of the public, and empowerment and self-help for battered women themselves.[72] Two small presses took the lead in publishing resources for battered women and their advocates: Volcano Press in the San Francisco Bay Area, and Seal Press in Seattle.[73]

Volcano Press, which began as the publication arm of the Glide Foundation of Glide Memorial United Methodist Church in San Francisco,[74] published Del Martin's *Battered Wives* in 1976 before it was distributed by the mainstream press, and also in 1982 published the first book for battered men from the perspective of the men's movement to end violence against women.[75] Many other volumes followed, and Volcano continues to publish

---

whether for the purposes of expert testimony, counseling, or advocacy ... For example, 'There is no single profile of a battered woman"; the term "battered woman syndrome" is vague and creates an image of pathology; battered woman syndrome has often been defined as post-traumatic stress disorder yet "'post-traumatic stress disorder,' compared to other psychological reactions to battering, is not uniquely relevant for understanding legal (or other) domestic violence related issues." [n.p.]

71. Susan Schechter, *Guide for Mental Health Professionals* (Washington, DC: NCADV, 1987).

72. E.g., Linda Rouse, *You Are Not Alone: A Guide for Battered Women* (Holmes Beach, FL: Learning Publications, 1984).

73. [Seal Press is now part of the Hachette Book Group in New York. —PCW 2019]

74. For a history of Volcano Press, see http://www.volcanopress.com/ [website no longer active. —PCW 2018].

75. Daniel Jay Sonkin and Michael Durphy, *Learning to Live without Violence: A Handbook for Men* (Volcano, CA: Volcano, 1982).

books on intimate partner violence from a feminist perspective,[76] including an interfaith resource guide on family violence and religion.[77]

In 1980, Seal Press, a small press that had been publishing only poetry and fiction for just five years, took a leap of faith and began fundraising to publish NiCarthy's first book, *Getting Free: A Handbook for Women in Abusive Relationships*. In the words of their managing editor, Faith Conlon:

> Publishing it was a long labor of love. We had no resources, but there was no other book available to abused women. Nicarthy's book, though agented, had been turned down everywhere in New York publishing. Their overriding concern was that there wasn't a sufficient market. Because we were in the community more, we could see that there was, and you could reach that market in nontraditional ways . . . We all had other jobs, so we edited it in our free time and raised money for the actual production . . . At the time, we were a collective and not even paying ourselves . . . Our first run was a large one—5,000 copies. We raised the money for that with community fundraisers and an advance-publication mailing to women's shelters nationwide . . . We got a huge response, a literal flood . . . The story got picked up by the daily *New York Times*. They did a feature story and the phone just started ringing off the hook . . . It's remained a favorite of the shelters because it speaks directly to the women. It pushed Seal to think big and realize that we had a new mission—we could do more books about domestic violence.[78]

Seal Press went on to create the New Leaf series dedicated to books on domestic violence. This series subsequently published several more titles by Ginny NiCarthy alone and together with other advocates,[79] and *Getting Free* went into four editions.[80] It was also the first press to publish the voices of

---

76. E.g., Elaine Weiss, *Surviving Domestic Violence: Voices of Women Who Broke Free* (Volcano, CA: Volcano, 2000, 2004); Elaine Weiss, *Family and Friends' Guide to Domestic Violence: How to Listen, Talk, and Take Action When Someone You Love Is Being Abused* (Volcano, CA: Volcano, 2003).

77. Volcano Press Staff, *Family Violence and Religion: An Interfaith Resource Guide* (Volcano, CA: Volcano, 1995).

78. Ian Pitchford and Robert M. Young, "Interview with Faith Conlon," *The Human Nature Review* (Oct. 16, 1998): http://human-nature.com/interviews/seal.html/.

79. Ginny NiCarthy, *The Ones Who Got Away: Women Who Left Abusive Partners* (Seattle: Seal, 1987); Ginny NiCarthy and Sue Davidson, *You Can Be Free: An Easy-to-read Handbook for Abused Women* (Seattle: Seal, 1989); Ginny NiCarthy, Karen Merriam and Sandra Coffman, *Talking It Out: A Guide to Groups for Abused Women* (Seattle: Seal, 1984).

80. Ginny NiCarthy, *Getting Free: You Can End Abuse and Take Back Your Life*

women of color addressing the particular needs of battered women within various racial-ethnic communities—Evelyn C. White, Myrna Zambrano, and Jacqueline Agtuca among others—as well as a book by Kerry Lobel on the issue of lesbian battering,[81] and two books by Barrie Levy on teen dating violence.[82] The New Leaf series has kept these titles in print up to the present moment, while continuing to produce important titles grounded in the battered women's movement,[83] including a recent self-help book for friends and family members of battered women,[84] and a dramatic photographic essay of portraits of battered women.[85]

More specialized concerns of battered women were addressed by other authors beginning in the 1980s as well. Anti-rape activist Diana Russell,[86] and sexual assault researchers David Finkelhor and Kersti Yllö examined the issue of marital rape,[87] Ann Jones and Angela Browne researched the disproportionately harsh judicial treatment of women who commit homicide, including

---

(Emeryville, CA: Seal, 2004).

81. Evelyn C. White, *Chain, Chain, Change: For Black Women Dealing with Physical and Emotional Abuse* (Seattle: Seal, 1985; 2nd ed. 1995 with new subtitle: *For Black Women in Abusive Relationships*); Myrna M. Zambrano, *Mejor Sola que Mal Acompañada: Para la Mujer Golpeada/For the Latina in an Abusive Relationship.* (Bilingual Spanish/English) (Seattle: Seal, 1985); and Jacqueline R. Agtuca, *A Community Secret: For the Filipina in an Abusive Relationship* (Seattle: Seal, 1988; reissued 1994) among others—as well as a book by Kerry Lobel, *Naming the Violence: Speaking Out against Lesbian Battering* (Seattle: Seal, 1986) on the issue of lesbian battering. For later works on this subject, see also Claire M. Renzetti, *Violent Betrayal: Partner Abuse in Lesbian Relationships* (Newbury Park, CA: Sage, 1992), including an excellent section of resources as well as guidelines for shelters; Beth Leventhal and Sandra E. Lundy, eds., *Same-sex Domestic Violence Strategies for Change* (Newbury Park, CA: Sage, 1999); and Claire M. Renzetti and Charles H. Miley, *Violence in Gay and Lesbian Domestic Partnerships* (New York: Harrington Park, 1996), which addresses violence in both lesbian and gay partnered relationships.

82. Barrie Levy, *Dating Violence: Young Women in Danger* (Seattle: Seal, 1991; 2nd ed. 1998); Barrie Levy, *In Love and in Danger: A Teen's Guide to Breaking Free of Abusive Relationships* (Seattle: Seal, 1993). [More recently, see also Patti Occhiuzzo Giggins and Barrie Levy, *Dangerous: A Parent's Guide to Preventing Relationship Abuse* (Center City, MN: Hazelden, 2013) —PCW 2018]

83. For all current titles and a history of the press, see http://www.sealpress.com.

84. Susan Brewster (1997). *To be an Anchor in the Storm: A Guide for Family and Friends of Abused Women*, 2nd ed. (Seattle: Seal, 2000).

85. Vera Anderson, *A Woman like You: The Face of Domestic Violence* (photo-essay) (Seattle: Seal, 1997).

86. Diana E. Russell, *Rape in Marriage* (New York: Macmillan, 1982; expanded ed., Indianapolis: Indiana University Press, 1990).

87. David Finkelhor and Kersti Yllö, *License to Rape* (New York: Holt Reinhart & Winston, 1985). Later, see also Raquel Kennedy Bergen, *Wife Rape: Understanding the Response of Survivors and Service Providers* (Newbury Park, CA: Sage, 1996).

women who kill their batterers,[88] and Susan Schechter wrote one of the first over-arching analyses of multiple forms of violence against women, together with an analysis of the battered women's movement in its first decade.[89] Writings on interventions with batterers also began to emerge in the 1980s from the men's movement to end violence against women.[90]

The clinical/social services side of the debate was also represented in a growing body of social science research literature.[91] One strand of this

88. Ann Jones, *Women Who Kill* (1980; reprint, Boston: Beacon, 1996) and Angela Browne, *When Battered Women Kill* (New York: Free Press, 1987). Later on this subject, see also Charles Patrick Ewing, *Battered Women Who Kill: Psychological Self-defense as Legal Justification*. (Lexington, MA: Heath, 1987) and Lenore Walker, *Terrifying Love* (see above).

89. Susan Schechter, *Women and Male Violence: The Visions and Struggles of the Battered Women's Movement* (Boston: South End, 1982).

90. Daniel Jay Sonkin and Michael Durphy, *Learning to Live without Violence: A Handbook for Men* (Volcano, CA: Volcano, 1982); Edward Gondolf, *Men who Batter: An Integrated Approach for Stopping Wife Abuse* (Holmes Beach, FL: Learning Publications, 1985); Edward Gondolf, *Batterer Intervention Systems: Issues, Outcomes, and Recommendations* (Thousand Oaks, CA: Sage, 2002); Daniel Jay Sonkin, Del Martin and Lenore E. Walker, *The Male Batterer: A Treatment Approach* (New York: Springer, 1985); Paul Kivel, *Men's Work: How to Stop the Violence that Tears our Lives Apart* (New York: Ballantine, 1992); Lee H. Bowker, *Masculinities and Violence* (Newbury Park, CA: Sage, 1997); Donald G. Dutton and Susan Golant, *The Batterer: A Psychological Profile* (New York: Basic Books, 1997); R. Emerson Dobash, Russell Dobash, Kate Cavanagh, and Ruth Lewis, *Changing Violent Men* (Newbury Park, CA: Sage 1999); Donald G. Dutton, *The Abusive Personality: Violence and Control in Intimate Relationships* (New York: Guilford, 2002); Donald G. Dutton and Daniel Jay Sonkin, *Intimate Violence: Contemporary Treatment Innovations* (New York: Haworth Maltreatment and Trauma Press, 2003). For an excellent review of goals and methods of batterer intervention programs, written for courts and criminal justice agencies, see also Kerry Healey, Christine Smith, and Chris O'Sullivan. *Batterer Intervention: Program Approaches and Criminal Justice Strategies*, NCJ # 168638 (Washington, DC: National Institute of Justice, 1998.)

91. Lexington Press, Springer, and Sage Publications published the most domestic violence social-science research and clinical treatment manuals in the 1980s. Lexington's books include Lee H. Bowker, *Beating Wife-beating* (Lexington, MA: Lexington, 1983); Richard J. Gelles and Claire Pedrick Cornell, *International Perspectives on Family Violence* (Lexington, MA: Lexington, 1983); Anson Shupe, William A. Stacey and Lonnie R. Hazelwood, *Violent Men, Violent Couples: The Dynamics of Domestic Violence* (Lexington, MA: Lexington, 1987); Robert L. Hampton, *Black Family Violence* (Lexington, MA: Lexington, 1991; reissued 2001); Edward Gondolf and Ellen R. Fisher, *Battered Women as Survivors: An Alternative to Treating Learned Helplessness* (Lexington, MA: Lexington, 1998); and Tuyen Nguyen, ed. *Domestic Violence in Asian American communities: A Cultural Overview* (Lexington, MA: Lexington 2005). Springer's titles in family violence research are numerous, including Lenore E. Walker, *The Battered Woman Syndrome* (New York: Springer, 1984; 3rd ed., 2009, [4th ed. 2016]); Daniel Jay Sonkin, Del Martin and Lenore E. Walker, *The Male Batterer: A Treatment Approach* (New York: Springer, 1985); Daniel Jay Sonkin, ed., *Domestic Violence on Trial: Psychological and Legal Dimensions of Family Violence* (New York: Springer, 1987; Albert R. Roberts,

research in particular, the National Family Violence Survey conducted by researchers at the University of New Hampshire, caused great concern and protest among battered women's advocates. University of New Hampshire research psychologists Murray Straus, Suzanne Steinmetz, and Richard Gelles, using a structured interview survey, determined that battering was "mutual," and that violence was equally likely to be perpetrated by women and men.[92] Critiques from researchers within the battered women's movement revealed methodological flaws in the UNH study, including not considering whether violence was committed in self-defense, not measuring disparities in injury to men vs. women, repeatedness of assaults, or relative dangerousness of partners, and not considering safety issues for women in the interviewing process itself.[93] The Dobashes addressed this methodological problem in detail in their comprehensive book *Women, Violence, and Social Change*. From their perspective both as activists and researchers, they made the distinction between "family violence research," which adheres to a "value-free positivist stance," and "violence-against-women research," which takes safety and advocacy as its starting point.[94] These divergences are reflected, for example, in the titles of the specialized

---

*Battered Women and their Families: Intervention Strategies and Treatment Programs* (New York: Springer, 1998; 3rd ed. 2007); Robert T. Ammerman and Michel Hersen, ed. (1991). *Case Studies in Family Violence* (New York: Springer, 1991; 2nd ed., 2000); Pamela J. Jenkins and Barbara Palmer Davidson, *Stopping Domestic Violence: How a Community Can Prevent Spousal Abuse* (New York: Springer, 2001); Sana Loue, *Intimate Partner Violence: Societal, Medical, Legal and Individual Responses* (New York: Springer, 2001). Springer also published the *Journal of Family Violence* beginning in 1985.

92. Literature from this group includes Murray A. Straus, Suzanne Steinmetz, and Richard J. Gelles, *Behind Closed Doors: Violence in the Family (New York*: Anchor/Doubleday, 1980); David Finkelhor, Richard J. Gelles, Gerald T. Hotaling and Murray A. Straus, eds., *The Dark Side of Families: Current Family Violence Research* (Beverly Hills, CA: Sage, 1983); Richard J. Gelles and Claire Pedrick Cornell, *International Perspectives on Family Violence* (Lexington, MA: Lexington, 1983); Richard J. Gelles, *Family Violence*, Sage Library of Social Research 84 (Beverly Hills, CA: Sage, 1987); Richard J. Gelles and Murray A. Straus, *Intimate Violence* (New York: Simon & Schuster, 1988); Murray A. Straus and Richard J. Gelles, *Physical Violence in American Families* (see above).

93 Summarized in Cooper-White, "Peer vs. Clinical Counseling," 4 [see Ch. 1, this volume]; for more detailed arguments, see the journal debate between McNeely and Robinson-Simpson (Richard L. McNeely and Gloria Robinson-Simpson, "The Truth about Domestic Violence: A Falsely Framed Issue," *Social Work* 32/6 (1987) 485–90); and Daniel Saunders, "Other 'Truths' about Domestic Violence: A Reply to McNeely and Robinson-Simpson," *Social Work* 33/2 (1998) 179–83. See also R. Emerson Dobash, Russell Dobash, Margo Wilson, and Martin Daly, "The Myth of Sexual Symmetry in Marital Violence," *Social Problems* 39/1 (1992) 71–91.

94. R. Emerson Dobash and Russell Dobash, *Women, Violence and Social Change* (New York: Routledge, 1992), especially Ch. 8, "Knowledge and Social Change," 251–82.

journals listed above—emphasizing a victims' perspective, or a more clinical "family violence" perspective.

These methodological problems were also the catalyst for a meeting of the first Activist Research Task Force at the NCADV's annual conference in 1988. Principles for socially responsible research on domestic violence were presented at that meeting by Barbara J. Hart (1987), including a recognition of potential increased danger of violence due to participation in research and a presumption that any battered woman is a "subject at risk" rather than a standard "subject at minimal risk," voluntary, non-coercive and informed participation, confidentiality that recognizes the potential risk of violence if a participant's partner were contacted or even learned of her participation, communication with participants after the research is completed to provide any needed clarification, as well as pertinent resources. All research should "be undertaken with care to answer questions that will advance knowledge about ending violence against women and facilitating their access to community services and support," (p. 6) rather than focusing on etiology or demographics that do not help women to improve their lives. Ethical implications of the social and legal impact of any research should be considered in the research planning and design. Collaboration between academics and activists and agency workers was to be encouraged.

In the 1990s, a change may be felt in the research literature, toward a greater integration of the activist and clinical perspectives. Much of the newer research involves social-science methodologies that integrate the larger social and cultural dimensions of intimate partner violence with ethnographic and clinical treatment approaches to intervention. A turn toward a more inductive, qualitative research approach in the social sciences more generally gives strong support for research that recognizes the mutual impact of interaction between researcher and "subject" or research participant, does not pretend that researchers can be value-neutral, and builds theory from the "ground" of participants' reported experience rather than testing hypotheses generated by researchers in isolation from their subjects.[95] Combined qualitative and quantitative studies have also been used to illuminate

---

95. E.g., "Grounded Theory," in Juliet Corbin and Anselm Strauss, *Basics of Qualitative Research: Techniques and Procedures for Developing Grounded Theory*, 3rd ed. (Newbury Park, CA: Sage, 2008). For more on qualitative research methods, see John W. Creswell, *Qualitative Inquiry and Research Design: Choosing among Five Traditions* (Newbury Park, CA: Sage, 1997; 4th ed., with Cheryl N. Poh, 2017). For philosophical issues underlying qualitative vs. quantitative research, see Yvonna Lincoln and Egon Guba, *Naturalistic Inquiry* (Newbury Park, CA: Sage, 1985) and Egon Guba, ed., *The Paradigm Dialog* (Newbury Park, CA: Sage, 1990).

battered women's experiences.[96] Case studies were also used more often.[97] Some literature has also shown the integration of personal experience and professional advocacy, such as shelter director and survivor Karen Wilson's book *When Violence Begins at Home*.[98]

Research grounded in subjects' own experience further expanded the range of topics addressed from the 1990s to the present.[99] Greater attention was paid to the effects of domestic violence on children.[100] In 1996, a research press, Sage, inaugurated an extensive series of books on violence against women, building on an earlier body of work from the late 1980s[101] with an autobiographical account of a battered woman, Bethel Sipe.[102] A number of volumes followed,[103] addressing various specialized issues in intimate partner

96. E.g., Renzetti, *Violent Betrayal* (see above).

97. Ann Jones, *Next Time She'll Be Dead: Battering and How to Stop It* (Boston: Beacon, 1994).

98. K. J. Wilson, *When Violence Begins at Home: A Comprehensive Guide to Understanding and Ending Domestic Abuse* (Alameda, CA: Hunter, 1997).

99. E.g., Lee Bowker in *Ending the Violence: A Guidebook Based on the Experiences of 1,000 Battered Women* (Holmes Beach, FL: Learning Publications, 1986 [rev. ed. 1998]); Edward Gondolf and Ellen R. Fisher, *Battered Women as Survivors: An Alternative to Treating Learned Helplessness* (Lexington, MA: Lexington, 1988); Linda Gordon, *Heroes of Their Own Lives: The Politics and History of Family Violence* (1988; reprint, Urbana: University of Illinois Press, 2002); Lee Ann Hoff, *Battered Women as Survivors* (New York: Routledge, 1990). Bowker, a sociologist, was one of the first to undertake such ethnographic studies. Gondolf and Fisher analyzed 6,000 shelter intake and exit interviews to challenge the assumption that women are "unable to help themselves," but, rather, that "women's helpseeking efforts increase with the severity of battering" (27ff.).

100. Agnes Wohl and Bobbie Kaufman, *Silent Screams and Hidden Cries: A Compilation and Interpretation of Artwork by Children from Violent Homes* (New York: Brunner/Mazel, 1985); Peter G. Jaffe, David A. Wolfe, and Susan K. Wilson, *Children of Battered Women: Issues in Child Development and Intervention Planning*. (Thousand Oaks, CA: Sage, 1990); Einat Peled, Peter G. Jaffe, and Jeffrey L. Edleson, eds., *Ending the Cycle of Violence: Community Responses to Children of Battered Women* (Newbury Park, CA: Sage, 1994); George W. Holden, Robert Geffner, and Ernest N. Jouriles, eds., *Children Exposed to Marital Violence: Theory, Research, and Applied Issues* (Washington, DC: American Psychological Association, 1998); R. Lundy Bancroft and Jay G. Silverman, J., *The Batterer as Parent: Addressing the Impact of Domestic Violence on Family Dynamics* (Newbury Park, CA: Sage, 2002; 2nd ed., 2011).

101. Mildred Pagelow, *Woman-Battering: Victims and Their Experience* (Beverly Hills, CA: Sage, 1981); Kersti Yllö and Michele Bograd, eds., *Feminist Perspectives on Wife Abuse* (Newbury Park, CA: Sage, 1988); David Levinson, *Family Violence in Cross Cultural Perspectives* (Newbury Park, CA: Sage, 1989).

102. In Beth M. Sipe and Evelyn J. Hall, *I Am not Your Victim: Anatomy of Domestic Violence* (Newbury Park, CA: Sage, 1996; 2nd ed., 2013), Sipe gives an autobiographical account of her experiences of resistance and healing from domestic violence together with commentary from her therapist Evelyn Hall.

103. E.g., Peter G. Jaffe, David A. Wolfe, and Susan K. Wilson, *Children of Battered*

violence prevention and intervention, including marital rape,[104] health care for battered women and their children,[105] rural battered women and the justice system,[106] safety planning,[107] same-sex domestic violence,[108] a history of domestic violence research,[109] new treatment approaches for battered women and for batterers,[110] coordinating community responses,[111] an overview of domestic violence research,[112] a *Sourcebook on Violence against Women*,[113] and an *Encyclopedia of Interpersonal Violence*.[114] A dedicated journal, *Violence against Women*, has been published continuously since 1994.

---

*Women: Issues in Child Development and Intervention Planning* (Thousand Oaks, CA: Sage, 1990); Claire M. Renzetti, *Violent Betrayal: Partner Abuse in Lesbian Relationships* (Newbury Park, CA: Sage, 1991); Donileen R. Loseke, *The Battered Woman and Shelters: The Social Construction of Wife Abuse* (Albany: SUNY Press, 1992); Richard J. Gelles and Donileen R. Loseke, eds., *Current Controversies on Family Violence* (Thousand Oaks, CA: Sage, 1993); Richard J. Gelles, Donileen R. Loseke and Mary M. Cavanaugh, eds., *Current Controversies on Family Violence*, 2nd ed. (Thousand Oaks, CA: Sage, 2005).

104. Raquel Kennedy Bergen, *Wife Rape: Understanding the Response of Survivors and Service Providers* (Newbury Park, CA: Sage, 1996).

105. Jacquelyn C. Campbell, *Empowering Survivors of Abuse: Health Care for Battered Women* (Newbury Park: Sage, 1998).

106. Neil Websdale, *Rural Woman Battering and the Justice System: An Ethnography* (Newbury Park, CA: Sage, 1997).

107. Jill Davies, Eleanor J. Lyon and Diane Monti-Catania, *Safety Planning with Battered Women: Complex Lives/Difficult Choices* (Newbury Park, CA: Sage, 1998).

108. Beth Leventhal and Sandra E. Lundy, eds., *Same-sex Domestic Violence Strategies for Change* (Newbury Park, CA: Sage, 1999).

109. Jana L. Jasinski and Linda M. Williams, eds., *Partner Violence: A Comprehensive Review of 20 Years of Research* (Newbury Park, CA: Sage, 1998).

110. Zvi C. Eisikovits and Eli Buchbinder, *Locked in a Violent Embrace: Understanding and Intervening in Domestic Violence* (Newbury Park, CA: Sage, 2000); R. Emerson Dobash, Russell Dobash, Kate Cavanagh, and Ruth Lewis, *Changing Violent Men* (Newbury Park, CA: Sage, 1999)

111. Melanie F. Shepard and Ellen Pence, *Coordinating Community Responses to Domestic Violence: Lessons from Duluth and Beyond* (Newbury Park, CA: Sage, 1999).

112. Jana L. Jasinski and Linda M. Williams, eds., *Partner Violence: A Comprehensive Review of 20 Years of Research* (Newbury Park, CA: Sage, 1998).

113. Claire Renzetti, Jeffrey L. Edleson, and Raquel Kennedy Bergen, ed., *Sourcebook on Violence against Women* (Thousand Oaks, CA: Sage, 2000; 3rd ed., 2017).

114. Claire M. Renzetti and Jeffrey Edleson, eds., *Encyclopedia of Interpersonal Violence* (Thousand Oaks, CA: Sage, 2008).

Countless articles have now appeared in medical,[115] mental health,[116] and law journals,[117] among others. A few historical and legal studies have also appeared, from a variety of political perspectives and agendas.[118] Social constructionist and symbolic interactionist research has also been recently applied to the issue of intimate partner violence.[119] The impact of this form of research on battered women's advocacy is probably too limited to evaluate as yet. Another recent development is the effort to apply the method of Restorative Justice and "Intimate Abuse Circle teams" to intimate partner violence and other situations of intrafamilial abuse.[120] While potential lack of attention to safety for victims remains a lively concern in this literature, its effectiveness in some settings has been demonstrated by relying both on increased regard for the agency of victims, and on accountability of offenders and to those facilitating the process toward community, legal, and

115. National Institutes for Health (NIH), *Medline Database: Domestic Violence*: http://www.nlm.nih.gov/medlineplus/domesticviolence.html.

116. American Psychological Association (2009). PsycINFO Database: http://www.apa.org/psycinfo/. E.g., search "violence against women," "sexual violence," and "domestic violence."

117. Digested in Minnesota Center against Violence and Abuse, *MINCAVA Electronic Database*: http://www.mincava.umn.edu.

118. Sherrill Cohen, *The Evolution of Women's Asylums since 1500: From Refuges for Ex-prostitutes to Shelters for Battered Women* (New York: Oxford University Press, 1992); Elizabeth Pleck, *Domestic Tyranny: The Making of American Social Policy against Family Violence from Colonial Times to the Present* (New York: Oxford University Press, 1987); Daniel Jay Sonkin, ed., *Domestic Violence on Trial: Psychological and Legal Dimensions of Family Violence* (New York: Springer, 1987; Jean Bethke Elshtain, "Politics and the Battered Woman," in Elshtain, *Real Politics: At the Center of Everyday Life* (Baltimore: Johns Hopkins Press, 1997) 260–69. Elshtain, drawing in part on the work of Hannah Arendt, wrote a rebuttal of Schechter's *Women and Male Violence*: Susan Schechter, *Women and Male Violence: The Visions and Struggles of the Battered Women's Movement* (Boston: South End, 1982) as too universal in its blaming of patriarchy for violence, and too idealistic. Elshtain offers few alternatives, however, and ends by praising the battered women's movement on the grounds of "creation of political space, development of participatory capacities, and fundamental human decency" (269).

119. Donileen R. Loseke, *The Battered Woman and Shelters: The Social Construction of Wife Abuse* (Albany: SUNY Press, 1992); Sharon Lamb, *New Versions of Victims: Feminists Struggle with the Concept* (New York: NYU Press,1999).

120. E.g., Julie Stubbs, "Domestic Violence and Women's Safety: Feminist Challenges to Restorative Justice," in *Restorative Justice and Family Violence*, ed. Heather Strang and John Braithwaite (Cambridge: Cambridge University Press, 2002) 42–61; Donna Coker, "Transformative Justice: Anti-subordination Processes in Cases of Domestic Violence," in *Restorative Justice and Family Violence*, ed. Heather Strang and John Braithwaite (Cambridge: Cambridge University Press, 2002) 128–52; Linda G. Mills, *Insult to Injury: Rethinking our Responses to Intimate Abuse* (Princeton: Princeton University Press, 2003) esp. 103–48, also citing John Braithwaite, "Restorative Justice: Assessing Optimistic and Pessimistic Accounts," *Crime and Justice* 25 (1999) 26.

governmental authorities. The countertransference of helping professionals, and the unequal treatment of men of color in the criminal justice system have been examined as further complicating factors within current legal and service approaches.[121] More debate will no doubt be forthcoming on these new, complicating perspectives toward intimate partner violence.

The other important trend, beginning in the mid-1990s, coincident with the UN Decade for Women has been a widening of the scope of domestic violence literature to encompass global and multi-cultural issues in intimate partner violence. One of the earliest volumes in this area of study was by Gelles and Cornell.[122] David Levinson followed with the book *Family Violence in Cross Cultural Perspectives*.[123] Antonia Vann wrote a comprehensive guide on the Internet for culturally sensitive responses to African American battered women,[124] and there is a more recent book by Tuyen Nguyen on domestic violence in Asian American communities.[125] But beyond these two recent volumes and the earlier Seal Press titles, there still has been little written systematically on intimate partner violence in particular cultural and/or global communities. Battered women in many communities, for example, Native American women, are only minimally represented in the domestic violence literature.[126] Some resources, in the form of study

---

121. Mills, *Insult to Injury*, pp. 48–83, 119–142.

122. Richard J. Gelles and Claire Pedrick Cornell, *International Perspectives on Family Violence* (Lexington, MA: Lexington, 1983).

123. David Levinson, *Family Violence in Cross Cultural Perspectives* (Newbury Park, CA: Sage, 1989); see also Bowker, ed., *Masculinities and Violence* (see above).

124. Antonia A. Vann, *Developing Culturally-relevant Responses to Domestic Abuse* (Harrisburg, PA: National Resource Center on Domestic Violence, 2003), https://vawnet.org/material/developing-culturally-relevant-responses-domestic-abuse-asha-family-services-inc.

125. Tuyen Nguyen, ed. *Domestic Violence in Asian American communities: A Cultural Overview* (Lexington, MA: Lexington, 2005).

126. E.g., Paula Gunn Allen, "Violence and the American Indian woman," *Center for Prevention of Sexual and Domestic Violence Newsletter* 5/4 (1985) 5–7; Confronting Sexual Violence," (Enola, PA: National Sexual Violence Resource Center, 2000), on-line at https://www.nsvrc.org/publications/nsvrc-publications/sexual-assault-indian-country-confronting-sexual-violence. Gunn's *The Sacred Hoop* does include a chapter on women's anger (Paula Gunn, *The Sacred Hoop: Recovering the Feminine in American Indian Traditions* (Boston, MA: Beacon, 1986; reprinted 1992), and Mihesuah notes the rise of violence against Native American women (Devon Abbott Mihesuah, *"Indigenous American Women: Decolonization, Empowerment, Activism* (Lincoln: University of Nebraska Press/Bison Books, 2003). The Dept. of Justice has also very recently begun tracking domestic violence crimes specifically against Native American women (Dept. of Justice, Office on Violence against Women, https://www.justice.gov/ovw.)

papers, are beginning to appear online addressing these under-represented groups.[127] This is an area still needing further research.

## Domestic Violence in Pastoral and Christian Counseling Literature

From the 1980s onward, the pastoral and religious literature on intimate partner violence in Catholic, mainline Protestant, and more recently Jewish traditions, has followed the advances in the secular press, but progress was slow until the 1990s. Evangelical Christian literature has been slower to incorporate learnings from the domestic violence movement, although a few individual women advocates raised the issue in print within the Evangelical tradition from early on. Note that because pastoral care and counseling are not constituted in Islam as in western traditions,[128] there has not been a formal pastoral literature *per se*. Domestic violence remains a highly contested issue for women in Islam.[129] The internet has become an unexpected source of empowerment for battered women in the Muslim community, and a resource for new theological insights.[130]

---

127. *Violence against Women Online Resources* (Albuquerque: University of New Mexico, 2009 [2016]), website: https://women.unm.edu/resources/violence.html; National Sexual Violence Resource Center (NSVRC), continually updated resources: http://www.nsvrc.org/.

128. Margaret Kornfeld, presentation to Cooper-White, Advanced Pastoral Care Seminar, Lutheran Theological Seminary, Philadelphia, PA, Dec. 9, 2004, re: consultations with Muslim imams and community leaders in New York on pastoral care and counseling after 9/11.

129. A pioneer in this work was Sharifa Alkhateeb, who "created the Peaceful Families Project of FaithTrust Institute. She worked closely with Rev. Dr. Marie Fortune, Rev. Thelma Burgonio-Watson and Rabbi Cindy Enger to provide training for domestic violence advocates and religious leaders through our technical assistance grants from the Office on Violence against Women": http://www.faithtrustinstitute.org/. Resistance among Muslim women against domestic violence is beginning to appear on the Internet. For example, "What Does Islam Say of Domestic Violence?" Muslims against Domestic Violence [website no longer available]; F. Alam, *Domestic Violence: An Islamic Perspective*, 2009: http://www.geocities.com/Athens/Academy/7368/w_dv.htm. [website unavailable.] Cf. Salma Elkadi Abugideiri, "A Perspective on Domestic Violence in the Muslim Community" (Seattle: FaithTrust Institute, 2010), www.faithtrustinstitute.org/resources/articles/DV-in-Muslim-Community.pdf; Maha B. Alkhateeb and Salma Elkadi Abugideiri, *Change from Within: Diverse Perspectives on Domestic Violence in Muslim Communities* (Great Falls, VA: Peaceful Families Project, 2007); https://www.peacefulfamilies.org. See also Nazila Isgandarova, Muslim Women, Domestic Violence, and Psychotherapy: Theological and Clinical Issues (New York: Routledge, 2018). — PCW 2018]

130. Alexis Kort, "Dar al-cyber Islam: Women, Domestic Violence, and the Islamic

The earliest religious writings about domestic violence were incorporated in works addressing larger issues of abuse and sexual violence: Barbara Ann Stoltz's report for the U.S. Catholic Conference was one of the earliest pastoral studies,[131] followed by Peggy Halsey's *Abuse in the Family: Breaking the Church's Silence* for the United Methodist Church in 1982.[132] Marie Fortune's *Sexual Violence: The Unmentionable Sin*,[133] first published in 1983, remains a classic related work.[134] By the mid 1980s, there were a few more pastoral theological resources specific to battered women. Many of these were articles in anthologies: Janet Tanaka's contribution to a volume on women's issues in religious education,[135] articles by Mary D. Pellauer,[136] and Marie Fortune and Judith Hertz on theological and religious issues in violence against women,[137] Carole Bohn on domination and "a theology of ownership,"[138] Polly Young Eisendrath and Demaris Wehr on "The Fallacy of Individualism and Reasonable Violence against Women,"[139] and Susan Brooks Thistlethwaite's chapter on battered women in *Weaving the*

---

Reformation on the World Wide Web," *Journal of Muslim Minority Affairs* 25/3 (2005) 363–83.

131. Barbara Ann Stoltz, *Violence in the Family: A National Concern* (Washington, DC: Publications Office, U.S. Catholic Conference, Office of Domestic Social Development, 1979).

132. Peggy L. Halsey, *Abuse in the Family: Breaking the Church's Silence* (New York: Office of Ministries with Women, General Board of Ministry, United Methodist Church, 1982).

133. Marie M. Fortune, *Sexual Violence: The Unmentionable Sin* (New York: Pilgrim, 1983).

134. See also Marie M. Fortune, *Sexual Violence: The Sin Revisited* (Cleveland: Pilgrim, 2005).

135. Janet Tanaka, "The Role of Religious Education in Preventing Sexual and Domestic Violence," in *Women's Issues in Religious Education*, ed. Fern M. Giltner (Birmingham, AL: Religious Education Press, 1985) 81–114.

136. Mary D. Pellauer, "Violence against Women: The Theological Dimension," in *Sexual Assault and Abuse: A Handbook for Clergy and Religious Professionals*, ed. Pellauer, Barbara Chester, and Jane Boyajian (San Francisco: Harper, 1987) 51–61.

137. Marie M. Fortune and Judith Hertz, "A Commentary on Religious Issues and Family Violence," in *Sexual Assault and Abuse: A Handbook for Clergy and Religious Professionals*, ed. Mary D. Pellauer, Barbara Chester, and Jane Boyajian (San Francisco: Harper, 1987) 67–83.

138. Carole R. Bohn, "Dominion to Rule: The Roots and Consequences of a Theology of Ownership," in *Christianity, Patriarchy, and Abuse*, ed. Joanne Carlson Brown and Carole R. Bohn (New York: Pilgrim, 1989) 105–16.

139. Polly Young Eisendrath and Demaris Wehr, "The Fallacy of Individualism and Reasonable Violence against Women," in *Christianity, Patriarchy, and Abuse*, ed. Joanne Carlson Brown and Carole R. Bohn (New York: Pilgrim, 1989) 117–38.

*Visions*,[140] the sequel to the first groundbreaking anthology on feminist theology, *Womanspirit Rising*.[141] In this period, some of the distinctively pastoral, theological and ethical questions relating to intimate partner violence began to be addressed.

Earlier works in feminist theology from the 1970s and early 80s,[142] while not addressing battered women's issues *per se*, became important resources for feminist theological and ethical analysis that undergirded these efforts specifically to understand the spiritual and theological dimensions of intimate partner violence—in particular, the centrality of empowerment and the negative contributions of patriarchal religion. Feminist and womanist writers on violence more generally have also made contributions, for example Cheryl Kirk-Duggan's *Misbegotten Anguish: A Theology and Ethics of Violence*.[143] The *Journal of Feminist Studies in Religion*, begun in 1984, further expanded opportunities for women to write feminist theological research.

Longer monographs began to appear by the mid-1980s. The first sustained pastoral theological study on domestic violence was Joy Bussert's *Battered Women: From a Theology of Suffering to an Ethic of Empowerment*, published by the Lutheran Church in America.[144] Rita Lou Clarke's *Pastoral Care of Battered Women* and Marie Fortune's *Keeping the Faith: Questions and Answers for the Abused Women* directly addressed Christian battered women's questions about issues such as marriage vows, "turning the other cheek," and forgiveness.[145] In response to clergy concerns about divorce as a sin and the insolubility of Christian marriage, Mitzi Eilts first articulated the argument that in situations of domestic violence, it is the violence that has already broken the covenant of marriage, not the decision of the bat-

---

140. Susan B. Thistlethwaite, "Every Two Minutes: Battered Women and Feminist Interpretation," in *Weaving the Visions: New Patterns in Feminist Spirituality*, ed. Judith Plaskow and Carol Christ (San Francisco: Harper & Row, 1989) 302–13.

141. Carol Christ and Judith Plaskow, *Womanspirit Rising: A Feminist Reader in Religion* (San Francisco: Harper & Row, 1979; reissued 1992).

142. Ibid; Charlene Spretnak, *The Politics of Women's Spirituality: Essays on the Rise of Spiritual Power within the Feminist Movement* (Garden City, NY: Anchor, 1982).

143. Cheryl Kirk-Duggan, ed., *Misbegotten Anguish: A Theology and Ethics of Violence* (St. Louis: Chalice, 2001).

144. Joy Bussert, *Battered Women: From a Theology of Suffering to an Ethic of Empowerment* (Minneapolis: Division for Ministry in North America, Lutheran Church in America/Augsburg, 1986).

145. Rita-Lou Clarke, *Pastoral Care of Battered Women* (Philadelphia: Westminster, 1986); Marie M. Fortune, *Keeping the Faith: Questions and Answers for the Abused Woman* (San Francisco: Harper & Row, 1987; reissued in 1995 as *Keeping the Faith: Guidance for Christian Women Facing Abuse*) 33–39.

tered woman to leave the marriage.[146] Fortune has contributed some of the clearest, earliest thinking about forgiveness.[147] Using Luke 17 as a model, she emphasized that forgiveness is a process, which begins not with the victim making a decision to forgive, but with the abuser's genuine repentance—i.e., not just words of remorse, but evidence of lasting change of life. At minimum, the process of forgiveness requires justice.[148] Forgiveness (*aphíemi* in the biblical Greek)[149] literally means letting go, not forgetting.[150] The church has all too often pressured victims, as Marie Fortune succinctly put it: "We want you to forgive, so that we can forget."[151] Forgiveness may best be understood as a gift of grace, not a goal or task.[152] If and when conditions are right for a survivor, including an opportunity to process her pain and anger, and having been met with some form of justice, she *may* experience an internal sense of release from the perpetrator's former centrality, power and control over her emotional life. This is neither something she can decide, nor make happen. And it is not a "requirement" for her healing. I have also argued in *The Cry of Tamar* that forgiveness needs to be reframed ethically from an insistence on individual victims forgiving their abusers, toward an ethic of reconciliation (*katallagè*) that is a thoroughgoing transformation of the entire social fabric, a reorientation toward an "I-Thou-We" relationship, cre-

---

146. Mitzi Eilts, "Saving the Family: When is the Covenant Broken?" in *Abuse and Religion: When Praying Isn't Enough*, ed. Anne L. Horton and Judith A. Williamson (Lexington, MA: Lexington, 1988) 207–14.

147. Marie M. Fortune, *Keeping the Faith: Questions and Answers for the Abused Woman* (San Francisco: Harper & Row, 1987; reissued in 1995 as *Keeping the Faith: Guidance for Christian Women Facing Abuse*); Marie M. Fortune, "Forgiveness: The Last Step," in Carol Adams and Fortune, ed., *Violence against Women and Children: A Christian Theological Sourcebook* (New York: Continuum, 1995) 201–6.

148. Marie M. Fortune, *Keeping the Faith: Questions and Answers for the Abused Woman* (San Francisco: Harper & Row, 1987; reissued in 1995 as *Keeping the Faith: Guidance for Christian Women Facing Abuse*) 46–51.

149. For an exegetical examination of forgiveness and reconciliation in the biblical sources, see Pamela Cooper-White, *The Cry of Tamar: Violence against Women and the Church's Response* (Minneapolis: Fortress, 1995) 253–62; (2nd ed., 2012) 251–61, and "Forgiveness: Grace, not Work," *Journal for Preachers* 32/2 (2008) 16–23 [Ch. 10, this volume].

150. Rita-Lou Clarke, *Pastoral Care of Battered Women* (Philadelphia: Westminster, 1986); Pamela Cooper-White, *The Cry of Tamar*, 253–62 [2nd ed., 2012] 251–61; Carol Adams and Marie M. Fortune, ed., *Violence against Women and Children: A Christian Theological Sourcebook* (New York: Continuum, 1995); Al Miles, *Domestic Violence: What Every Pastor Needs to Know* (Minneapolis: Augsburg, 2000).

151. M. Garguilo, writer-director, *Broken Vows* [video recording] (Seattle: Center for the Prevention of Sexual and Domestic Violence [FaithTrust Institute], 1996).

152. Pamela Cooper-White, *The Cry of Tamar*, 260–61 [(2nd ed., 2012) 251–61; see also Ch. 10, this volume. —PCW 2018]

ating communities characterized by nonviolence and justice.[153] Awareness grew among clergy and pastoral care providers in the late 1980s. A clergy guide to laws against sexual and domestic violence first appeared in 1988.[154] Also in this time period, two evangelical women, Reta Halteman Finger and Kay Marshall Strom wrote for the journal *Daughters of Sarah*, and for Multnomah Press, respectively, on combating domestic violence from a Christian evangelical perspective.[155] James and Phyllis Alsdurf followed with a book for InterVarsity Press,[156] in which they confronted popular evangelical misconceptions that blamed women for their own victimization, such as James Dobson's statement on his "Focus on the Family" program:

> I've seen situations where the wife, I think, wanted most to be beaten up. There is a certain moral advantage that comes from having been hit by this man. Then you're in charge, you're self-righteous, you can leave, you have your exit. You want out, you can't find a moral way out because the Bible says marriage is forever, and if you can just push that guy until he turns around and blacks your eye, then boy the whole world, God included, can see that you were the one that's right and you were the one that was taken advantage of, and all of a sudden you're the martyr.[157]

As in the secular literature, as awareness grew, so did the divide between earlier, more advocacy-oriented approaches that adopted the feminist analysis of battering as an issue of power and control, and more clinically oriented approaches that described battering more in terms of family systems, communication issues, or other therapeutic paradigms.[158]

The 1990s saw a surge in pastoral literature on intimate partner violence from an advocacy perspective, including both practical workbooks and resources, and in-depth theological and ethical analyses. Building on the growth of requests for clergy training around the U.S., Marie Fortune

---

153. Ibid.

154. Mary S. Winters, *Laws against Sexual and Domestic Violence: A Concise Guide for Clergy and Laity* (New York: Pilgrim, 1988).

155. Reta Halteman Finger, "Too Close to Home: Domestic and Sexual Violence," *Daughters of Sarah* 13 (1987) 4–27; Kay Marshall Strom, *In the Name of Submission* (Sisters, OR: Multnomah, 1986).

156. James and Phyllis Alsdurf, *Battered into Submission: The Tragedy of Wife Abuse in the Christian Home* (Downers Grove, IL: InterVarsity, 1989; reissued 1998).

157. James Dobson, "Focus on the Family" (broadcast, 1984). Quote online at http://www.pollysplacenetwork.com/files/home/Church.pdf [website no longer available].

158. E.g., James Leehan, *Pastoral Care for Survivors of Family Abuse* (Louisville: Westminster John Knox, 1989); James Leehan, *Defiant Hope: Spirituality for Survivors of Family Abuse* (Louisville: Westminster John Knox, 1993)

published a workshop curriculum to train clergy on domestic violence prevention and intervention.[159] The National Conference of Catholic Bishops,[160] Forward Movement Publications,[161] the Episcopal Church's Committee on the Status of Women,[162] the Commission for Women of the Lutheran Church in America/Evangelical Lutheran Church in America,[163] among others,[164] began to offer short pamphlets, self-help tracts, and other congregational resources on domestic violence for both clergy and lay members of congregations. The FaithTrust Institute (then named the Center for the Prevention of Sexual and Domestic Violence) expanded their resources with award-winning training videos on domestic violence after the mid—1990s.[165] In 1995 a multi-division team of the Evangelical Lutheran Church in America commissioned and pilot tested a congregational small group resource for women seeking empowerment and new life after being in abusive relationships.[166]

159. Marie M. Fortune, *Violence in the Family: A Workshop Curriculum for Clergy and Other Helpers* (Cleveland: Pilgrim, 1991)

160. Bishops' Committee on Marriage and Family Life, Bishop's Committee on Women in Society and in the Church, and the National Conference of Catholic Bishops, *When I Call for Help: A Pastoral Response to Domestic Violence against Women* (Washington, DC: National Conference of Catholic Bishops, 1992).

161. Anne O. Weatherhold, *Are You Battered?* (Cincinnati: Forward Movement, 1991).

162. Nance A. Wabshaw, ed. *Now that the Silence is Broken* (New York: The Committee on the Status of Women and the Office of Women in Ministry and Mission, Episcopal Church Center, 2002).

163. Mary D. Pellauer, *If There Is Abuse in Your Home...* (Chicago: Commission for Women, Evangelical Lutheran Church in America, 1986; orig. publ. Family Resources, Division for Parish Services, Lutheran Church in America); Mary D. Pellauer, *Ministry to Abusive Families* (Chicago: Commission for Women, Evangelical Lutheran Church in America, 1986; orig. publ. Family Resources, Division for Parish Services, Lutheran Church in America); Mary D. Pellauer, "Violence against Women: The Theological Dimension," in *Sexual Assault and Abuse: A Handbook for Clergy and Religious Professionals*, ed. Mary D. Pellauer, Barbara Chester, and Jane Boyajian (San Francisco: Harper, 1987) 51–61; Mary D. Pellauer, *Lutheran Theology Facing Sexual and Domestic Violence* (Chicago: Commission for Women, Evangelical Lutheran Church in America, 1988).

164. See also tracts "About Wife Abuse," and "Family Violence" from Scriptographic Booklets (Deerfield, MA: Channing L. Bete, n.d.].

165. M. Garguilo, writer-director, *Broken Vows* [video recording] (Seattle: Center for the Prevention of Sexual and Domestic Violence [FaithTrust Institute], 1996); M. Garguilo, writer-director, *Wings like a Dove: Healing for the Abused Christian Woman* [video recording] (Seattle: Center for the Prevention of Sexual and Domestic Violence [FaithTrust Institute], 1997); M. Garguilo, writer-director, *To Save a Life: Ending Domestic Violence in Jewish Families* [video recording] (Seattle: Center for the Prevention of Sexual and Domestic Violence [FaithTrust Institute], 1997).

166. Pamela Cooper-White, *Women Healing and Empowering: A Small Group*

Community partnerships of clergy and domestic violence workers in various states and counties have also produced resource booklets for their own communities.[167] A major lay pastoral care training program, Stephen Ministries, does not include a training module on any form of abuse *per se*, regarding this exclusively as an area for professional referral, but Stephen Ministers are trained to be aware of signs of abuse, referral resources, and relevant reporting laws.[168] A recent *Sojourners* article lists actions taken by faith based community organizations,[169] and the Office on Violence against Women of the U.S. Department of Justice issued fact-sheets on "What Faith Leaders Can Do" and on faith-based community resources.[170]

In the pastoral theological literature, several significant contributions were added in the 1990s. James Poling's book *The Abuse of Power: A Theological Problem*[171] and *Deliver Us From Evil: Resisting Racial and Gender Oppression*,[172] and my own book *The Cry of Tamar: Violence against Women and the Church's Response*[173] were among the first single-author books to address the continuum of violence against women from an integrated social, ethical, and constructive theological perspectives. At the

---

*Resource for Abused Women* (Chicago: Stop the Violence Project, Evangelical Lutheran Church in America, 1996). This resource was intended for *formerly* battered women; for safety reasons, women currently in violent relationships were referred in the resource to local domestic violence agencies. The resource called for a confidential peer group format, and was not designed as a clinical/therapeutic group. A companion *Leader's Guide* emphasized safety, creating a safe climate for women in congregations, and practical information as well as biblical and theological resources for peer group leaders. The participants' guides offered spiritual, theological, and advocacy-based education and reflection exercises in an eight-week structured format.

167. E.g., Joan Chamberlain Engelsman, ed., *Helping Victims of Domestic Violence: A Guide for Religious Leaders* (Madison, NJ: Clergy Partnership on Domestic Violence, Inc., 2000).

168. J. Brescher, personal communication, Feb. 1, 2005 (Stephen Ministries, St. Louis; see also https://www.stephenministries.org.

169. Molly Marsh, "Out of Harm's Way: Faith-based Groups Fight Violence against Women," *Sojourners* 37/6 (2008) 9.

170. U.S. Dept. of Justice, Office on Violence against Women, Fact-sheet: What Faith Leaders Can Do (2000), http://www.ovw.usdoj.gov/docs/fs-whatfaithleaderscando.pdf. [website no longer available] and Fact-sheet: Faith-based and Community Organization Resources (2009), http://www.ovw.usdoj.gov/docs/fbco-resources051608.pdf. [website no longer available.]

171. James Newton Poling, *The Abuse of Power: A Theological Problem* (Nashville: Abingdon, 1991).

172. James Newton Poling, *Deliver Us from Evil: Resisting Racial and Gender Oppression* (Minneapolis: Fortress, 1996; reprinted 2006).

173. Pamela Cooper-White, *The Cry of Tamar: Violence against Women and the Church's Response* (Minneapolis: Fortress, 1995; 2nd ed. 2012).

same time, two pairs of editors—Elisabeth Schüssler Fiorenza and Shawn Copeland,[174] and Carol Adams and Marie Fortune[175]—contributed edited volumes of cutting edge theological and ethical analyses of violence against women and children, and the first anthology of voices of third world and western women on women resisting violence was also published by Mary John Mananzan, Mercy Oduyuye, Elsa Tamez and others,[176] including two chapters on domestic violence.[177] Books specifically on domestic violence also were added to the literature in the 1990s. Carol Adams wrote *Woman-Battering* for Fortress' Creative Pastoral Care and Counseling Series.[178] The first anthology on pastoral care with women also included a chapter on battered women.[179] Intimate partner violence was further addressed in articles in a few more journals and anthologies on women's spirituality, sexuality, and pastoral care during this time.[180]

Coinciding with the UN's increased attention to violence against women, noted above, churches began also to address intimate partner violence on a global scale. Spearheaded by Aruna Gnanadason of the World Council of Churches, several publications[181] and numerous conferences and

---

174. Elisabeth Schüssler Fiorenza and M. Shawn Copeland, eds., *Violence against Women*, Concilium 1994/1 (Maryknoll, NY: Orbis, 1994).

175. Carol Adams and Marie M. Fortune, ed., *Violence against Women and Children: A Christian Theological Sourcebook* (New York: Continuum, 1995).

176. Mary John Manzanan, Mercy Amba Oduyoye, Elsa Tamez, Shannon J. Clarkson, Mary C. Grey, and Letty M. Russell, eds., *Women Resisting Violence: Spirituality for Life* (1996; reprint, Eugene, OR: Wipf & Stock, 2004).

177. Elisabeth Schüssler Fiorenza, "Ties that Bind: Domestic Violence against Women," and Stella Baltazar, "Domestic Violence in Indian Perspective," in *Violence against Women*, Concilium 1994/1, ed. Elisabeth Schüssler Fiorenza and M. Shawn Copeland (Maryknoll, NY: Orbis,1994) 39–55, 56–65; reprinted in *Women Resisting Violence: Spirituality for Life*, ed. Mary John Mananzan, Mercy Amba Oduyoye, Elsa Tamez, Shannon J. Clarkson, Mary C. Grey, and Letty M. Russell (1996; reprint, Eugene, OR: Wipf & Stock, 2004).

178. Carol Adams, *Woman-Battering* (Minneapolis: Fortress, 1994).

179. JoAnn M. Garma, "A Cry of Anguish: The Battered Woman," in *Women in Travail and Transition: A New Pastoral Care*, ed. Maxine Glaz and Jeanne Stevenson-Moessner (Minneapolis: Fortress, 1991) 126–45.

180. E.g., Archie Smith, Jr., "The Transmission of Intergenerational Violence: Implications for the Pastoral Care of Families," *Memphis Theological Seminary Journal* 21/1 (1991) 13–29; Paula M. Cooey, "Remembering the Body: A Theological Resource for Resisting Domestic Violence," *Theology and Sexuality* 3 (1995) 27–47; and Marjorie Procter-Smith, "Reorganizing Victimization: The Intersection between Liturgy and Domestic Violence," in Elizabeth Stuart and Adrian Thatcher, ed., *Christian Perspectives on Sexuality and Gender* (Leominster, UK: Gracewing, 1996) 380–95.

181. Aruna Gnanadason, *No Longer a Secret: The Church and Violence against Women* (Geneva: World Council of Churches Publications, 1993); Aruna Gnanadason,

workshops were sponsored during the 1990s.[182] Thelma Burgonio-Watson soon addressed the relationship between globalization, global economics and domestic violence in an article for *Church and Society*.[183] A group of pan-African women theologians called The Circle of Concerned African Women Theologians, first organized by Mercy Amba Oduyoye, have addressed violence against women in an increasing number of published writings since the early 1990s.[184] Numerous books published by the Maryknoll Order (Orbis Books) since the 1980s have also given voice to third world women theologians, undergirding the work of churches worldwide against violence against women and other forms of sexism,[185] and very recently religion scholars from around the globe published an anthology addressing violence against women in contemporary world religions.[186]

The pastoral literature also began to expand in the 1990s to examine in more detail issues of intimate partner violence within particular religious communities. Increasing numbers of Jewish activists published resources,[187] and the film "To Save a Life: Ending Domestic Violence in Jewish Families"

---

Musimbi Kanyoro, and Lucia Ann McSpadden, *Women, Violence and Nonviolent Change* (Geneva: World Council of Churches Publications, 1996); Dept. for Mission and Development, Women in Church and Society, Lutheran World Federation, *Churches Say "No" to Violence against Women: Action Plan for the Churches* (Geneva: Lutheran World Federation, 2002).

182. Mercy Amba Oduyoye, *Who Will Roll the Stone Away: The Ecumenical Decade of the Churches in Solidarity with Women* (Geneva: World Council of Churches Publications, 1991).

183. Thelma Burgonio-Watson, "Globalization and Domestic Violence," *Church and Society* 92/1 (2001) 104–12.

184. E.g., Mercy Amba Oduyoye and Musimbi R. A. Kanyoro, *The Will to Arise: Women, Tradition, and the Church in Africa* (Maryknoll, NY: Orbis, 1992); Isabel Apawo Phiri and Sarojini Nadar, eds., *African Women, Religion, and Health: Essays in Honor of Mercy Amba Oduyoye* (Maryknoll, NY: Orbis, 2006).

185. For an overview of writers see Ursula King, ed., *Feminist Theology from the Third World: A Reader* (Maryknoll, NY: Orbis, 1994).

186. Daniel C. Maguire and Sa'Diyya Shaikh, eds., *Violence against Women in Contemporary World Religions: Roots and Cure* (Cleveland: Pilgrim, 2007).

187. E.g., Ian Russ, Sally Weber and Ellen Ledley, *Shalom Bayit: A Jewish Response to Child Abuse and Domestic Violence* (Panorama City, CA: Shalom Bayit Committee, 1993); Abraham Twerski, *The Shame Borne in Silence: Spouse Abuse in the Jewish Community* (Pittsburgh: Mirkov 1996); Gus Kaufman, Jr., Wendy Lipshutz, and Drorah Setel, "Responding to Domestic Violence," in *Jewish Pastoral Care: A Practical Handbook from Traditional and Contemporary Sources*, ed. Dayle Friedman (Woodstock, VT: Jewish Lights, 2001; 2nd ed. 2013) 237–63; for a comprehensive bibliography including a few earlier grassroots articles, see Marcia Cohn Spiegel, "Bibliography of Sources on Sexual and Domestic Violence in the Jewish Community," *Women in Judaism* 2/1 (1999); 2004 update online at http://wjudaism.library.utoronto.ca/index.php/wjudaism/article/view/180/201.

was released in 1997 by the Center for the Prevention of Sexual and Domestic Violence.[188] James Poling wrote on family violence in Nicaragua,[189] Toinette Eugene and Poling wrote *Balm for Gilead*, addressing pastoral care for abuse in African American families,[190] and most recently also Cheryl Kirk-Duggan.[191] Two chapters also appeared in 2000 in a volume on marriage and spirituality from a Roman Catholic perspective.[192]

The number of resources on domestic violence written from an evangelical and Christian/biblical counseling perspective also grew in the 1990s. Books by Patricia Gaddis,[193] Catherine Clark Kroeger and James Beck,[194] Nancy Nason-Clark,[195] Beaman and Nason-Clark,[196] and Aimee Cassaday-Shaw,[197] were published by church imprints as diverse as Judson Press, Baker Books, Westminster/John Knox, InterVarsity Press, and Haworth Pastoral Press. Three recent books by Al Miles, an African American hospital chaplain ordained in the Church of God, especially integrated advocacy, psychological research and biblical interpretation.[198] Miles,

188. M. Garguilo, writer-director, *To Save a Life: Ending Domestic Violence in Jewish Families* [video recording] (Seattle: Center for the Prevention of Sexual and Domestic Violence [FaithTrust Institute], 1997).

189. James Newton Poling, "Reflections on Family Violence in Central America," *Journal of Pastoral Care* 49/4 (1995) 417–22.

190. Toinette Eugene and James Newton Poling, *Balm for Gilead: Pastoral Care for African American Families Experiencing Abuse* (Nashville: Abingdon, 1998).

191. Cheryl Kirk-Duggan, ed., *Misbegotten Anguish: A Theology and Ethics of Violence* (St. Louis: Chalice, 2001); Cheryl Kirk-Duggan, *Violence and Theology* (Nashville: Abingdon 2006).

192. Gloria Durka, "Domestic Violence: The Long, Sad Silence," and Lenore E. Walker, "The Battered Woman: Myths and Realities," Chs. 23 and 24 in Kieran Scott and Michael Warren, ed., *Perspectives on Marriage: A Reader*, 2nd ed. (New York: Oxford University Press, 2000) 254–63, 264–84.

193. Patricia Riddle Gaddis, *Battered but not Broken: Help for Abused Wives and Their Church Families* (Valley Forge, PA: Judson, 1996).

194. Catherine Clark Kroeger and James R. Beck, eds., *Women, Abuse, and the Bible* (Grand Rapids: Baker, 1996).

195. Nancy Nason-Clark, *The Battered Wife: How Christians Confront Family Violence* (Louisville: Westminster John Knox, 1997).

196. Lori G. Beaman and Nancy Nason-Clark, "Evangelical Women as Activists: Their Response to Violence against Women," in *Shared Beliefs, different Lives: Women's Identities in Evangelical Context*, ed. Lori G. Beaman (St. Louis: Chalice, 1999) 111–32.

197. Aimee K. Cassaday-Shaw, *Family Abuse and the Bible: The Scriptural Perspective* (New York: Haworth Pastoral Press, 2002).

198. Al Miles, *Domestic Violence: What Every Pastor Needs to Know* (Minneapolis: Augsburg, 2000); Al Miles, *Violence in Families: What Every Christian Needs to Know* (Minneapolis: Augsburg, 2002); Al Miles, *Ending Violence in Teen Dating Relationships: A Resource Guide for Parents and Pastors* (Minneapolis: Augsburg, 2005).

who has worked with both victims and batterers since 1981,[199] confronted myths and stereotypes about abuse in the evangelical Christian community, including a critique of Promise Keepers' glorification of traditional masculinity, and advocated for a collaborative approach in which clergy challenge themselves to be more actively involved in preventing domestic violence. Most recently, Nason-Clark also advocated for greater recognition and inclusion of both victims' and batterers' religious perspectives as useful tools for intervention and accountability.[200]

A significant trend to be noted in the pastoral literature is a greater attention since the early 1990s to issues of men and male violence, largely due to the tireless work of James Poling and Christie Cozad Neuger. Poling first wrote an article on male violence against women and children for an anthology he co-edited with Neuger on pastoral care of men (the first of its kind),[201] followed by two monographs on men and prevention of male violence by Poling alone,[202] and by Poling and Neuger.[203] In the same time frame Neuger published an empowerment-based pastoral model entitled *Counseling Women: A Narrative, Pastoral Approach*, including a chapter "Coming to Voice in the Context of Intimate Violence."[204] Archie Smith

---

199. Miles serves as coordinator of the hospital ministry at The Queen's Medical Center in Hawaii. For a feature story on Miles' ministry, see http://starbulletin.com/2002/08/03/features/story1.html.

200. Nancy Nason-Clark, "When Terror Strikes at Home: The Interface between Religion and Domestic Violence," *Journal for the Scientific Study of Religion* 43/3 (2004) 303-10; see also Nancy Nason-Clark, "From the Heart of My Laptop: Personal Passion and Research on Violence against Women, in *Personal Knowledge and Beyond: Reshaping the Ethnography of Religion*, ed. James V. Spickard, J. Shawn Landres and Meredith B. McGuire (New York: NYU Press, 2002) 27-32.

201. James Newton Poling, Male Violence against Women and Children," in Poling and Christie Cozad Neuger, *The Care of Men* (Nashville: Abingdon, 1997) 138-62.

202. James Newton Poling, *Understanding Male Violence: Pastoral Care Issues* (St. Louis: Chalice, 2003).

203. Christie Cozad Neuger, "A Feminist Perspective on Pastoral Counseling with Women," in Robert J. Wicks, Richard D. Parsons and Donald Capps, eds., *Clinical Handbook of Counseling*, Vol. 3 (Mahwah, NJ: Paulist, 2003) 17-37.

204. Christie Cozad Neuger, *Counseling Women: A Narrative, Pastoral Approach* (Minneapolis: Fortress, 2001) 93-126; see also Christie Cozad Neuger, "A Feminist Perspective on Pastoral Counseling with Women," in Wicks et al., eds., *Clinical Handbook of Pastoral Counseling*, Vol. 3 (Mahwah, NJ: Paulist, 2003) 17-37; Christie Cozad Neuger, "Gender Narratives and the Epidemic of violence in contemporary families," in Herbert Anderson, Edward Foley, Bonnie Miller-McLemore, and Robert Schreiter, eds., *Mutuality Matters: Family, Faith, and Just Love* (Lanham, MD: Sheed & Ward, 2004) 83-92; Christie Cozad Neuger, "Power and Difference in Pastoral Theology," in Nancy J. Ramsay, ed., *Pastoral Care and Counseling: Redefining the Paradigms* (Nashville: Abingdon, 2004; reprinted in Appendix in Hunter and Ramsay, 2005) 74ff. See

drew on the biblical tradition of lamentation to address male violence,[205] and a general book on the issue of healing violent men was also published by David Livingston.[206]

Most recently, the pastoral literature on intimate partner violence has addressed more specialized subjects or issues. John McClure and Nancy J. Ramsay wrote a book specifically on preaching about sexual and domestic violence.[207] Marie Fortune and Joretta Marshall edited a volume entirely dedicated to evaluating issues of forgiveness and abuse from both Jewish and Christian perspectives.[208] In 2002, James Poling, Brenda Consuelo Ruiz and Linda Crockett co-authored a book *Render unto God: Economic Vulnerability, Family Violence, and Pastoral Theology*,[209] and the same year Kristen Leslie published a book on acquaintance rape, *When Violence Is No Stranger*.[210] The third in the series of Fortress anthologies on pastoral care with women included three articles on specific issues of violence against women/girls.[211] General examinations of the problem of violence against women have also appeared more recently, including Marie Fortune's *Sexual*

---

also Kevin T. Barry, "Domestic Violence: Perspectives on the Male Batterer," *Journal of Pastoral Counseling* 38 (2003) 58-68.

205. Archie Smith, Jr., "Look and See if There Is Any Sorrow Like My Sorrow?: Systemic Metaphors for Pastoral Theology and Care," *Word and World* 21/2 (2001) 5-15.

206. David J. Livingston, *Healing Violent Men: A Model for Christian Community*. (Minneapolis: Fortress, 2002).

207. John S. McClure and Nancy J. Ramsay, *Telling the Truth: Preaching about Sexual and Domestic Violence* (Cleveland: United Church Press, 1999).

208. Marie M. Fortune and Joretta Marshall, eds. *Forgiveness and Abuse: Jewish and Christian Reflections* (New York: Haworth Pastoral Press, 2004; orig. publ. as a special issue of the *Journal of Religion and Abuse*, 4, 2002).

209. James Newton Poling with Brenda Ruiz and Linda Crockett (2002). *Render unto God: Economic Vulnerability, Family Violence, and Pastoral Theology* (2002; reprinted, Eugene, OR: Wipf & Stock, 2012).

210. Kristen J. Leslie, *When Violence is No Stranger: Pastoral Counseling with Survivors of Acquaintance Rape* (Minneapolis: Fortress, 2002).

211. Pamela Cooper-White, "Sexual Exploitation and Other Boundary Violations in Pastoral Ministry," in Wicks, et al., eds., *Clinical Handbook of Pastoral Counseling*, Vol. 3 (Mahwah, NJ: Paulist, 2003) 342-65; Patricia H. Davis, "Horror and the Development of Girls' Spiritual Voices," in Jeanne Stevenson-Moessner, ed., *In Her Own Time: Women and Developmental Issues in Pastoral Care* (Minneapolis: Fortress, 2000) 103-14; Christie Cozad Neuger, "A Feminist Perspective on Pastoral Counseling with Women," in Wicks et al., eds., *Clinical Handbook of Pastoral Counseling* (Mahwah, NJ: Paulist, 2003) 17-37. See also Felicity Kelcourse, "Rape and Redemption," in Jane Ellen McAvoy, ed., *Kitchen Talk: Sharing our Stories of Faith* (St. Louis: Chalice, 2003) 60-71.

*Violence: The Sin Revisited*,[212] and Elizabeth Soto's *Family Violence: Reclaiming a Theology of Nonviolence*.[213]

Most recently in the field of pastoral theology, Jeanne Hoeft has incorporated a more postmodern, intersubjective approach, balancing the larger social and political construction of intimate partner violence with the particularity of individual women's experience—taking into consideration the ambiguities and contradictions of victimization, personal agency, and resistance.[214] Hoeft constructs a theological anthropology grounded in the particularity of battered women's "body and psyche, cultural construction and agency."[215] The complexity of this methodology carries certain potential dangers, such as being used again to point to the complicity to victims, or to reify theories of mutual violence. Hoeft acknowledges these risks, but stresses the importance of women's agency in order to resist violence and join with others for social and political change.[216]

In addition to books, numerous articles have appeared, sporadically at first, and more consistently from the mid-1990s, in religious professional journals. The first articles to appear were "Battered Woman," published in the United Methodist Church's journal *Engage/Social Action*[217] and an article by E. Joan Edwards Lepley entitled "Pastoral Counseling: Battered Women," for the *American Protestant Hospital Association Bulletin*.[218] Jour-

---

212. Marie M. Fortune, *Sexual Violence: The Sin Revisited* (Cleveland: Pilgrim, 2005).

213. Eleanor Soto, *Family Violence: Reclaiming a Theology of Nonviolence* (Maryknoll, NY: Orbis, 2008). [More recently, see also Stephanie Crumpton, *A Womanist Pastoral Theology against Intimate and Cultural Violence* (New York: Palgrave Macmillan, 2014); Rachel Starr, *Reimagining Theologies of Marriage in Contexts of Domestic Violence: When Salvation Is Survival* (Abingdon, UK: Routledge, 2018). —PCW 2018]

214. Jeanne M. Hoeft, *Agency, Culture, and Human Personhood: Pastoral Theology and Intimate Partner Violence* (Eugene, OR: Pickwick, 2009).

215. Ibid, p. x.

216. Important sources for this argument include Sharon Lamb, *New Versions of Victims: Feminists Struggle with the Concept* (New York: NYU Press, 1999), and from the Restorative Justice perspective, Julie Stubbs, "Domestic Violence and Women's Safety: Feminist Challenges to Restorative Justice," in *Restorative Justice and Family Violence*, ed. Heather Strang and John Braithwaite (Cambridge: Cambridge University Press, 2002) 42–61; and Mills, *Insult to Injury* (see above).

217. [n.a.] (1978). Battered women. *Engage/Social Action* (Board of Church and Society, United Methodist Church), 6, 32–34.

218. E. Joan Edwards Lepley, "Pastoral Counseling: Battered Women," *American Protestant Hospital Association Bulletin* 42/2 (1978) 32–35. Other early articles included Lib McGregor Simmons, "Domestic Violence," *Journal for Preachers* 5/1 (1981) 31–32 and Lee H. Bowker, "Battered Women and the Clergy: An Evaluation," *Journal of Pastoral Care* 36 (1982) 226–34.

nals including articles on intimate partner violence since then have ranged from progressive publications, including an article by the late Senator Paul Wellstone in *Tikkun*,[219] to evangelical, such as *Christian Ministry*[220] to progressive-evangelical—*Sojourners*[221]—and many in between, such as *The Christian Century*,[222] and *Currents in Theology and Mission*.[223] Articles have appeared in religious periodicals focused on women's issues including both the *Feminist Studies in Religion*,[224] and the more evangelical *Daughters of Sarah*.[225] The trend toward greater specialization of topics within intimate partner violence is also seen in the periodical literature, including an article by a biblical scholar on intimate partner violence in Ezekiel 16[226] and a sociological study of religious affiliation and domestic violence,[227] and in 2001 a theological review article drawing on liberation theology to equip

---

219. Paul Wellstone, "Domestic Violence as a Health-Care Issue," *Tikkun* 9 (1994) 19-20, 106.

220. Sherry Lundberg, "Ministering to Victims of Domestic Violence," *Christian Ministry* (Mar. 18, 1987) 25-27; James Leehan, "Domestic Violence: A Spiritual Epidemic," *Christian Ministry* (May 23, 1982) 15-18; Al Miles, "Helping Victims of Domestic Violence," *Christian Ministry* (Mar. 28, 1997) 33-34.

221. E.g., Judy Webb, "Binding Up the Wounds: A Grassroots Movement is Giving Haven to Battered Women," *Sojourners*, 13 (1984) 25-27.

222. Carol Adams, Help for the battered: Stopping violence against women. *Christian Century* (June 29-July 6, 1994) 628-29.

223. Carol J. Schlueter, "Creating a New Reality: No More Domestic Violence," *Currents in Theology and Mission* 23/4 (1996) 254-64. Three other Lutheran journals also published articles on domestic violence in the 1990s, including Anne Castleton, "Speaking Out on Domestic Violence," *Dialog* 23 (1990) 90-100; Carol J. Schlueter, "Valiant Women: Survivors of Domestic Violence," *Consensus* 20/2 (1994) 91-106; and Robert A. Erickson, "Supervised Self-help Group Counseling of Male Perpetrators of Domestic Violence, Using a Church Based Delivery System," *Lutheran Theological Journal* 28/2 (1994) 80-86.

224. Marie M. Fortune and Frances Wood, "The Center for the Prevention of Sexual and Domestic Violence: A Study in Applied Feminist Theology and Ethics," *Journal of Feminist Studies in Religion*, 4 (1988) 115-22; Beverly Mayne Kienzle, and Nancy Nienhuis, "Battered Women and the Construction of Sanctity," *Journal of Feminist Studies in Religion* 17/1 (2001) 33-61.

225. Reta Halteman Finger, "Too Close to Home: Domestic and Sexual Violence," *Daughters of Sarah* 13 (1987) 4-27; Linda Midgett, "Silent Screams: Do Evangelicals Hear the Cries of Battered Women?" *Daughters of Sarah* 20 (1994) 43-45; Carol Shimmin Nordstrom, "Domestic Violence and Hagar," *Daughters of Sarah* 20 (1994) 34-35.

226. Linda Day, "Rhetoric and Domestic Violence in Ezekiel 16," *Biblical Interpretation* 8/3 (2000) 205-30.

227. Christopher G. Ellison and Kristin L. Anderson, K., "Religious Involvement and Domestic Violence among U.S. Couples," *Journal for the Scientific Study of Religion* 40/2 (2001) 269-86.

religious professionals to "engage effectively with domestic violence."[228] In 1998, Marie Fortune and Carol Adams also started the *Journal of Religion and Abuse*, the first journal entirely dedicated to the intersection of religion and violence in the family.

Among the pastoral theology journals, the *Journal of Pastoral Care*, edited by Orlo Strunk, was the first to publish an article on domestic violence by the sociologist Lee Bowker, "Battered Women and the Clergy: An Evaluation,"[229] followed by two articles in *Pastoral Psychology* in 1987 and 1988.[230] By 1993, *Pastoral Psychology* followed with an entire issue dedicated to a symposium on domestic violence including authors Marie Fortune, Larry Kent Graham, Gail Ryan, and Karen Steinhauer.[231] Since that time, Lew Rambo, the editor of *Pastoral Psychology*, is credited with publishing five more articles on the subject between 1994 and 2004, the most of any pastoral theology journal to date.[232] The *Journal of Pastoral Care/Pastoral Care and Counseling* published two articles, a decade apart, between 1995 and 2005,[233] and *The Journal of Pastoral Theology* published three from 1999 to 2004, including a literature review,[234] the first article on pastoral theologians' teach-

---

228. Colin A. Phillips, "Equipping Religious Professionals to Engage Effectively with Domestic Violence," *Journal of Religious and Theological Information* 4/1 (2001) 47-70. See also Marie M. Fortune, "Picking up the Broken Pieces: Responding to Domestic Violence," *Church and Society* 85 (1995) 36-47.

229. Lee H. Bowker, "Battered Women and the Clergy: An Evaluation," *Journal of Pastoral Care* 36 (1982) 226-34.

230. Edward V. Stein, "Violence Begins at Home," *Pastoral Psychology* 35/4 (1987) 288-96; Michael J. Garazani, "Troubled Homes: Pastoral Responses to Violent and Abusive Families," *Pastoral Psychology* 36/4 (1988) 218-29.

231. Larry Kent Graham, ed., Symposium on Sexual Abuse and Domestic Violence (with articles by M. Fortune, L. K. Graham, G. Ryan and K. Steinhauer), *Pastoral Psychology* 41/2 (1993) 273-345.

232. Alberta D. Wood and Maureen C. McHugh, "Woman Battering: The Response of the Clergy," *Pastoral Psychology* 42/3 (1994) 185-96; Gerald W. Gross, and Sandra M. Stith, "Building Shelters for Battered Women and Religious Organizations: Advice from Victim Advocates," *Pastoral Psychology* 45/2 (1996) 107-17; Pamela Cooper-White, "An Emperor without Clothes: The Church's Views about Treatment of Domestic Violence," *Pastoral Psychology* 45/1 (1996) 3-20. [Ch. 3, this volume.]; Myra N. Burnett, "Suffering and Sanctification: The Religious Context of Battered Women's Syndrome," *Pastoral Psychology* 45(1997) 107-17; and Robert J. Rotunda, Gail Williamson and Michelle Penfold, "Clergy Response to Domestic Violence: A Preliminary Survey of Clergy Members, Victims, and Batterers," *Pastoral Psychology* 52/4 (2004) 353-65.

233. James Newton Poling, "Reflections on Family Violence in Central America," *Journal of Pastoral Care* 49/4 (1995) 417-22; Nancy E. Nienhuis, "Theological Reflections on Violence and Abuse," *Journal of Pastoral Care and Counseling* 59/1-2 (2005) 109-23.

234. Christie Cozad Neuger, "Intimate Violence and Pastoral Theology: A Review

ing on domestic violence in the *Journal of Pastoral Theology*,[235] and an article on Korean victims of domestic violence.[236] Iona College's Journal of Pastoral Counseling recently published an excellent article on perspectives re: the male batterer,[237] and the relatively new *American Journal of Pastoral Counseling* has published one article focused on pastoral counseling with abused women.[238] One very brief article on spirituality and domestic violence has also appeared in *Chaplaincy Today*.[239]

Since 2000, following a virtual silence previously, there has been a significant increase in attention to the issue of violence against women in academic theological journals.[240] There has been a particular rise in articles on issues of violence against women in specific ethnic and cultural

---

of Recent Literature," *Journal of Pastoral Theology* 9 (1999) 113-20.

235. Pamela Cooper-White, "What Are We Teaching about Violence against Women?" *Journal of Pastoral Theology* 14/2 (2004) 48-69.

236. Hee Sun Kwon and Carrie Doehring, "Spiritual Resources Used by Korean Victims of Domestic Violence," *Journal of Pastoral Theology* 14/2 (2004) 70-86.

237. Kevin T. Barry, "Domestic violence: Perspectives on the Male Batterer," *Journal of Pastoral Counseling* 38 (2003) 58-68.

238. Richard T. Frazier, "Objects of Care: The Use of Transitional Objects in Pastoral Counseling with Abused Women," *American Journal of Pastoral Counseling* 2/2 (1999) 21-65; see also on a related subject Leah Coulter, "A Pastoral Theology for the Sinned against: Adult Christian Women Sexually Abused as Children. *American Journal of Pastoral Counseling* 3/3-4 (2000) 187-205.

239. Richard B. Gilbert, "The spiritual Dimension of Domestic Violence: Challenges for Spiritual Caregivers," *Chaplaincy Today* 16/2 (2000) 31-34.

240. E.g., Anne Marie Dalton, "The Challenge of Violence: Toward a Theology of Women's Bodies," *Toronto Journal of Theology* 16/2 (2000) 235-50; Susan E. Hylen, "Forgiveness and Life in Community," *Interpretation* 54/2 (2000) 146-57; Yvette Noble-Bloomfield, "Partnership and Empowerment: Overcoming Violence against Women," *Reformed World* 53/3 (2002) 130-35; Marylou Fusco, "Breaking the Chains," *The Other Side: A Magazine of Christian Discipleship* 39/3 (2003) 22-26; Lisa Isherwood, "Marriage: Heaven or Hell? Twin Souls and Broken Bones," *Feminist Theology* 11/2 (2003) 203-15; Debra L. Duke, "The Blood of the Martyrs Can Be the Seed of Life: Violence, Abuse, and the Prophetic Dimension of Theology," *Koinonia* 16 (2004) 42-50; Kerry L. Fast, "Religion, Pain, and the Body: Agency in the Life of an Old Colony Mennonite Woman," *Journal of Mennonite Studies* 22 (2003) 103-29; Barbara W. Schaffer, "Domestic Abuse in Christ's Kingdom," *Reformation and Revival* 13/2 (2004) 87-100; Carol Winkelmann, "'In the Bible, It Can Be So Harsh!' Battered Women, Suffering, and the Problem of Evil," in *Christian Faith and the Problem of Evil*, ed. Peter van Inwagen (Grand Rapids: Eerdmans, 2004) 148-84.

contexts.[241] Entire issues of the *Journal of Theology for Southern Africa*,[242] the *Pacific Journal of Theology*,[243] and the World Council of Church's journal *Ministerial Formation*[244] were devoted to the subject of violence against women, and a subsequent issue of *Ministerial Formation* on issues of resistance to violence included three articles specifically on violence against women in various global contexts.[245] Given the burgeoning of attention to

241. E.g., Fanny Gerymonat-Pantelis, "Domestic Violence against Women in the Andean-Bolivian Context," *Voices from the Third World* 23/1 (2000) 36-50; Denise Ackermann, "Ein neuer Blick auf einen alten Text: Die Geschichte von Tamar," *Zeitschrift für Mission* 29/3 (2003) 237-42; NirmalaVasanthakumar, "International Day for the Elimination of Violence against Women," *Reformed World* 53/1 (2003) 54-57; Norah Almosaed, "Violence against Women: A Cross-cultural Perspective," *Journal of Muslim Minority Affairs* 24/1 (2004) 67-88; Hee Sun Kwon and Carrie Doehring, "Spiritual Resources Used by Korean Victims of Domestic Violence," *Journal of Pastoral Theology* 14/2 (2004) 70-86; Carol Winkelmann, "'In the Bible, It Can Be So Harsh!' Battered Women, Suffering, and the Problem of Evil," in *Christian Faith and the Problem of Evil*, ed. Peter van Inwagen (Grand Rapids: Eerdmans, 2004) 148-84; Stephanie Crumpton, "No Safe Space: The Impact of Sexist Hermeneutics on Black Women Survivors of Intimate Abuse: A Womanist Pastoral Care Perspective," *Journal of the Interdenominational Theological Center* 32/1 (2005) 99-121. [See also Crumpton, *A Womanist Pastoral Theology against Intimate and Cultural Violence* (New York: Palgrave Macmillan, 2014)]; Jacqueline Grant, "Freeing the Captives: The Imperative of Womanist Theology," in *Blow the Trumpet in Zion!: Global Vision and Action for the 21st-century Black Church*, ed. Iva E. Carruthers, Frederick D. Haynes III, Jeremiah A. Wright, Jr. (Minneapolis: Fortress, 2005) 86-90; Alexis Kort, "Dar al-cyber Islam: Women, Domestic Violence, and the Islamic Reformation on the World Wide Web," *Journal of Muslim Minority Affairs* 25/3 (2005) 363-83; Brenda Consuelo Ruiz, "Domestic Violence and the Church in Nicaragua: Hearing the Silenced Voices," *Ministerial Formation* 104 (2005) 13-23; Julienne Wangahemuka Kavira, "De la violence contre les femmes et les enfants à l'Est du République Démocratique du Congo: Vers une culture de la paix/ Violence against Women and Children in Eastern Democratic Republic of Congo: Moving toward a Culture of Peace," *Ministerial Formation* 104 (2005) 24-44; Aruna Gnanadason, "'We Have Spoken So Long O God: When Will We Be Heard?': Theological Reflections on Overcoming Violence against Women," *Theology and Sexuality* 13/1 (2006) 9-21, http://tse.sagepub.com/cgi/content/abstract/13/1/9.

242. Tinyiko Sam Maluleke, and Sarojini Nadar, eds., Special Issue: Overcoming Violence against Women and Children, *Journal of Theology for Southern Africa* 114 3-106.

243. Virginia Fonasa and Bryce Tilisi, eds., "Violence against Women and Children: A Theological Problem for the Church," special issue of *Pacific Journal of Theology* 30 (2003) 1-65.

244. Nyambura J. Njoroge, ed., special issue, "Tamar Campaign: Breaking the Chains of Silence," *Ministerial Formation* 103 (2004) 1-51.

245. Liza B. Lamis, "Passion for Peace: From Victims of Violence to a Healing Community," *Ministerial Formation* 104 (2005) 4-12; Brenda Consuelo Ruiz, "Domestic Violence and the Church in Nicaragua: Hearing the Silenced Voices," *Ministerial Formation* 104 (2005) 13-23; Julienne Wangahemuka Kavira, "De la violence contre les femmes et les enfants à l'Est du République Démocratique du Congo: Vers une culture

violence against women and the increase in general of women's publications internationally,[246] this global literature will no doubt increase dramatically over the next decade.

This survey of the pastoral literature, therefore, shows considerable attention to the issue of intimate partner violence, and to violence against women more generally, as well as growing consideration, especially from the mid-1990s, in professional religious journals. More general pastoral literature on closely related subjects such as marriage[247] and divorce[248] shows a lack up to the present day of integration of the issues into the mainstream of pastoral care. A survey of resources on premarital counseling, for example, shows at best a brief mention of the possibility of domestic violence.[249] One of the most extensive premarital preparation and

---

de la paix/ Violence against Women and Children in Eastern Democratic Republic of Congo: Moving toward a Culture of Peace," *Ministerial Formation* 104 (2005) 24-44.

246. Helen Hood, "World Council of Churches' Project on Overcoming Violence against Women: A Progress Report," *Feminist Theology* 12/3 (2004) 373-77.

247. In Herbert Anderson and Cotton Fite, *Becoming Married* (Louisville: Westminster John Knox, 1993), Anderson and Fite helpfully discuss power sharing, mutual recognition and empathy (127-33), but there is no explicit mention of violence in marriage. Anderson, Hogue and McCarthy focus on mature marriage and "empty-nesters" (Herbert Anderson, David Hogue, and Marie McCarthy, *Promising Again* (Louisville: Westminster John Knox, 1995). A variety of crises are addressed in some detail, including infidelity, but not violence. Abuse is mentioned only once in passing (94) in the context of the need for ritualizing the ending of a marriage when such ending is necessary. Butler helpfully links the evils of sexism and racism, and the rage of invisibility and post-traumatic effects of a history of enslavement, but does not address domestic violence directly; Lee H. Butler, *A Loving Home: Caring for African American Marriages and Families* (Cleveland: Pilgrim, 2000); cf. Toinette Eugene and James Newton Poling, *Balm for Gilead: Pastoral Care for African American Families Experiencing Abuse* (Nashville: Abingdon, 1998).

248. J. Randall Nichols, *Ending Marriage, Keeping Faith: A New Guide through the Spiritual Journey of Divorce* (New York: Crossroad, 1991) is one of the best and most sensitive books on divorce, from a liberal theological perspective, written in part from his own divorce experience. However, perhaps because his own experience as a divorced man, he mentions "abuse of tolerance" (134), but nowhere explicitly addresses the possibility of overt violence. In his chapter "Facing the Lost Cause," he affirms the importance for marital partners of setting boundaries, and states that forgiveness does not mean one has to keep putting up with emotional pain. However, he continues to frame this pain in terms of mutual emotional harm: "sometimes divorce can itself be a form of reconciliation: when the destructiveness ends because people have recognized a lost cause and refuse to go back for more *mutual hurting*" (emphasis added, 140).

249. The best is a recent workbook, Norma Schweitzer Wood and Lisa M. Leber, *Now Bring Your Joy to This Wedding: Couples in Premarital Preparation* (Lima, OH: CSS Publishing, 2002). While brief, the authors state, "Of course when anger leads to physical violence this is never acceptable. Violence not only destroys conditions that allow for trust and intimacy to flourish, but it seriously endangers personal safety." This

marital enrichment programs, the *Prepare/Enrich* counselor's manual[250] does include four queries to couples about abuse in its "Background Inventory,"[251] but only makes brief mention of these items in the *Counselor's Manual*, simply recommending that the counselor discuss the items individually in more detail, and being prepared to report and make referrals, as appropriate.[252] There is no guidance given regarding the safety of including such items in the inventory, or its possible subsequent dangers for a battering victim. The couple inventory also has an assessment scale for "partner dominance,"[253] which includes items that would be included in many abuse inventories, but the issue of violence is not addressed directly, although it includes extensive materials on conflict styles and communication. Related research at the University of Minnesota by the author of *Prepare/Enrich*, David H. Olson and Shuji Asai,[254] frame abuse from an "ecological systems" approach as *"couple abuse,"* with a typology including "husband-abusing couples," "wife-abusing couples," and "volatile couples," and a "non-abusing couple" in which abuse could nevertheless be scored by either partner as either "never" or "seldom." Much of this echoes both the methodological and ethical problems of the UNH study, its clinical family systems orientation, and the limitations and dangers of relying on self-reports in cases where violence is present in the relationship.

---

statement is well placed in the section on "Understanding Power and Anger." Donald Luther, in his otherwise comprehensive premarital workbook (Donald J. Luther, *Preparing for Marriage* (Minneapolis: Augsburg, 1992), includes a sidebar cautioning against physical violence. He frames it appropriately as a "means of control" (52), however this is misplaced in the section on alcohol and drugs, and not alluded to anywhere in the sections on conflict styles and "Our Worst Behavior."

250. David H. Olson, *Prepare/Enrich Counselors' Manual, Version 2000, including Question Booklets* (Minneapolis: Life Innovations, Inc., 2000). See also http://www.prepare-enrich.com. [An updated 2009 "Customized Version," https://webcache.googleusercontent.com/search?q=cache:DWqez1OPE5kJ:https://www.prepare-enrich.com/pe/pdf/research/2011/pe_customized_version_overview.pdf+&cd=8&hl=en&ct=clnk&gl=us, adds items including cultural/ethnic issues, interfaith/interchurch, several parenting scales, and notably, forgiveness. The overall philosophy of the program appears to remain as described above. —PCW 2018]

251. David H. Olson, *Prepare/Enrich Counselors' Manual, Version 2000, including Question Booklets* (Minneapolis: Life Innovations, Inc., 2000), Items 26–29.

252. Ibid, 59.

253. Ibid, Appendix A, 17.

254. Shuji G. Asai and David H. Olson, "Spouse Abuse and Marital System: Based on ENRICH" (2000), https://www.prepare-enrich.com/webapp/pecv/about/template/DisplaySecureContent.vm;pc=1533842112946?id=pecv*about*research.htmlandxlat=Yandemb_org_id=0andemb_sch_id=0andemb_lng_code=ENGLISH.

This mirrors the secular literature on marriage, including two resources often used in pastoral care curricula: Harville Hendrix,[255] whose "imago relationship therapy" approach frames all marital conflict within a paradigm of unconscious mutual projection of childhood wounds in order to seek healing, and John Gottman, who names "criticism, contempt, stonewalling, and defensiveness" as the "four horsemen of the apocalypse" for destroying marital relationships. These otherwise very useful books never explicitly address violence, in spite of decades of observation by the authors of conflict in couples in both clinical and research settings. However, although the Imago website still does not address intimate partner violence,[256] Gottman's lab has begun to address the issue in its research.[257]

The most helpful exceptions in the pastoral marriage and family literature are Edward Wimberly's excellent chapter on abuse and pastoral counseling in *Counseling African American Marriages and Families*,[258] and an anthology edited by Herbert Anderson, Edward Foley, Miller-McLemore, and Robert Schreiter, *Mutuality Matters: Family, Faith, and Just Love*.[259] Wimberly meets the issues of sexism head on, and advocates for a "love ethic" in which all family members equally support one another in living out their eschatological vocation as members of God's Realm.[260] *Mutuality Matters* incorporates Christie Neuger's "Gender Narratives and the Epidemic of Violence in Contemporary Families,"[261] together with essays

255. Harville Hendrix, *Getting the Love You Want* (New York: Harper & Row/Perennial, 1988).

256. http://www.imagorelationships.org/.

257. E.g., James Coan, John M. Gottman, Julia Babcock, and Neil Jacobsen, "Battering and the Male Rejection of Influence from Women," *Aggressive Behavior* 23/5 (1997) 375–88. [When this article was first written, the National Domestic Violence Hotline was listed under resources on the lab's website: http://www.gottman.com/about/resources but cannot be found there now. Level 2 therapist training at the Gottman Institute now includes a segment on "situational" vs. "characterological" domestic violence, and "when it is appropriate and inappropriate to use Gottman Method Couples Therapy with a couple dealing with domestic violence" https://www.gottman.com/product/gottman-method-couples-therapy-level-2/—a controversial matter, as noted above. —PCW 2018]

258. Edward P. Wimberly, *Counseling African American Marriages and Families* (Louisville: Westminster John Knox, 1997) 113–27.

259. Herbert Anderson, Edward Foley, Bonnie Miller-McLemore, and Robert Schreiter, eds., *Mutuality Matters: Family, Faith, and Just Love* (Lanham, MD: Sheed & Ward, 2004).

260. Ibid, chapters 1–2.

261. Christie Cozad Neuger, "Gender Narratives and the Epidemic of Violence in Contemporary Families," in *Mutuality Matters: Family, Faith, and Just Love*, ed. Herbert Anderson, Edward Foley, Bonnie Miller-McLemore, and Robert Schreiter (Lanham,

on justice, power and equality in marriage by Kleingeld, Herbert Anderson, Joel Anderson, and Osiek.[262] The entire volume affirms an ethic of mutuality and power sharing as a foundation for just love in family life.

In the secular marriage and family literature, a textbook by Betty Carter and Monica McGoldrick, *The Expanded Family Life Cycle*, which is often used in pastoral care courses on relationships, marriage and family), consistently integrates perspectives on sexism, racism, and other forms of oppression as enduring stressors on individuals and family systems, and includes chapters specifically on abuse.[263]

While anthologies on the pastoral care of women do include chapters on violence and abuse, as noted above, the pastoral literature on men, which has emerged more recently, often neglects the issue of male violence.[264] An exception to this is the impressively comprehensive anthology, *The Care of Men*, edited by Christie Neuger and James Poling, including a lengthy article by Poling on male violence against women and children.[265]

The most problematic approaches to pastoral care for marriage and divorce are found in the evangelical Christian/biblical counseling literature.

---

MD: Sheed & Ward, 2004) 83–92.

262. Pauline Kleingeld, "Just Love: Marriage and the Question of Justice," 23–42, Herbert Anderson, "Between Rhetoric and Reality: Women and Men as Equal Partners in Home, Church, and the Marketplace," 67–82, Joel Anderson, "Is Equality Tearing Families Apart?," 93–106, and Carolyn Osiek, RSCJ, "Who Submits to Whom? Submission and Mutuality in the Family," in Herbert Anderson, Edward Foley, Bonnie Miller-McLemore, and Robert Schreiter, ed., *Mutuality Matters: Family, Faith, and Just Love* (Lanham, MD: Sheed & Ward, 2004) 57–66.

263. Betty Carter and Monica McGoldrick, eds., *The Expanded Family Life Cycle: Individual, Family, and Social Perspectives*, 3rd ed. (Boston: Allyn & Bacon, 2005; 5th ed., with co-editor Nydia A. Garcia, 2015).

264. E.g., Phillip Culbertson, *Counseling Men* (Minneapolis: Fortress, 1994) briefly addresses violence as "self-destructive urges misdirected externally", but neglects the primary issue of power and control (65–66). In Culbertson's edited volume (Phillip Culbertson, ed., *The Spirituality of Men: Sixteen Christians Write about Their Faith*. (Minneapolis: Fortress, 2002), violence against women is not addressed specifically in any single chapter. The anthology does include two thoughtful essays by Poling on "Masculinity, Competitive Violence and Christian Theology": James Newton Poling, "Masculinity, Competitive Violence and Christian Theology," in *The Spirituality of Men: Sixteen Christians Write about Their Faith*, ed. Phillip Culbertson (Minneapolis: Fortress, 2002) 122–24, and Ellison on same sex domestic violence: Marvin Ellison, "Setting the Captives Free: Same-sex Domestic Violence and the Justice-loving Church," in *The Spirituality of Men: Sixteen Christians Write about Their Faith*, ed. Phillip Culbertson (Minneapolis: Fortress, 2002) 145–62.

265. James Newton Poling, "Masculinity, Competitive Violence and Christian Theology," in *The Spirituality of Men: Sixteen Christians Write about Their Faith*, ed. Phillip Culbertson (Minneapolis: Fortress, 2002) 122–24.

At least two different strands of biblical counseling can be articulated:[266] a fundamentalist biblical or "nouthetic" counseling approach, developed by Jay Adams,[267] in which the Bible is considered literally to provide guidance for all pastoral situations; and a "Christian counseling" approach, represented by Gary Collins,[268] in which a foundation of knowledge in clinical psychology is integrated with an evangelical biblical counseling method.

For Adams, and his followers, abuse was simply not addressed as an issue for many years.[269] In his foundational textbook, *Competent to Counsel*, Adams makes no explicit mention of violence."[270] in a section called "Anger and Resentment," he states the "undisciplined anger is totally wrong," however, he later asserts without qualification that "love is a forgetting kind of forgiveness."[271] Most disturbing is Adam's insistence, common among fundamentalist Christians, that "only adultery and desertion can break a marriage. Apart from these exceptions, marriage is for life."[272] In Adams' companion volume, *Christian Counseling Manual*, marital conflict is framed in terms of an ethic of reconciliation and maintaining the marriage at all costs.[273] The wife's role as reconciler is stereotypically used as the single example of marital conflict: If a wife's attempts at reconciliation are rebuffed by her husband, she must take it officially to the church. If he refuses to be reconciled, he can be excommunicated.[274] Neither book includes any mention, or biblical remedy recognized for a wife fleeing domestic violence. Although these books were published in the early 1970s, there is little evidence of improvement among nouthetic counselors to this day.[275] [Since 2016,

266. Thanks to Charles Scalise of Fuller Theological Seminary for this distinction.

267. Jay Adams, *Competent to Counsel* (Grand Rapids: Zondervan, 1970; reprint, 1985); see the Association of Certified Biblical Counselors (formerly the National Association of Nouthetic Counselors), https://biblicalcounseling.com/.

268. Gary R. Collins, *Christian Counseling: A Comprehensive Guide*, 3rd ed. (Irving, TX: Word, 2007).

269. A search of the NANC website http://www.nanc.org as of July, 2007, for "abuse" and "violence" yielded no articles. [Website no longer available.] A previous search in January, 2005, yielded one article on counseling adult survivors of child sexual abuse (no longer on the site), and none on violence.

270. Jay Adams, *Competent to Counsel* (Grand Rapids: Zondervan, 1970; reprint, 1985); Association of Certified Biblical Counselors (see above).

271. Adams, *Competent to Counsel*, 221, 228.

272. Ibid, 248. Citing an exegesis of 1 Corinthians 7, John Murray, *Divorce* (Philadelphia: Presbyterian & Reformed, 1961.)

273. Jay Adams, *Christian Counseling Manual* (Grand Rapids: Baker, 1973).

274. Ibid, 61.

275. Tom Whiteman retains the evangelical perspective that divorce is only for cases of adultery or desertion, although he acknowledges that Christians sometimes

there have been some efforts to address the problem more appropriately, still with some serious caveats.[276]]

---

do divorce because of abuse ("substance, physical, and emotional"), in *Surviving Divorce and Living Again* (Forest, VA: American Association of Christian Counselors/Life Source, 2005), a course offered online at http://old.aacc.net/courses/biblical-counseling/marriage-works/, http://jmm.aaa.net.au/articles/4903.htm: "The good news is we are staying together longer and taking marriage seriously, but the bad news is we're putting up with a lot more pain and ending up getting divorced anyway."

276. [*Update:* A conference lecture by Heath Lambert, "Biblical Counseling and Domestic Violence," presented at the ACBC Counseling and Discipleship Training in Jacksonville, FL, 2016, https://biblicalcounseling.com/store/all-products/biblical-counseling-domestic-violence-heath-lambert/. He specifies "opposite sex" partners, and asserts that roughly 1/3 of women experience domestic violence, which is his focus, although he makes the point that in his own counseling practice most abuse victims were husbands. He states that the statistics are under-reported, and domestic violence is in every congregation, and asserts that it is "never under any circumstances appropriate for a husband to use physical force against his wife for the purpose of compelling her submission to his authority . . . Any use of physical force by a husband against his wife is abuse, *ab-use*, a wrong use of force. You're not allowed to do it." He then poses the question "What's wrong with it?" He asserts three authorities ordained by God with the means to enforce them: the state ("the sword"), the church ("the keys"), and the home ("the rod"—"spank your kids if they disobey.") He notes the relationship of husband and wife as a notable absence—the person given authority is not given the means to enforce. "The Bible teaches that husbands have real authority in the home . . . are called to lead in their home; wives are called to submit. There is real authority that exists in the office of the husband . . . A husband can never enforce it. He is never given the means . . ." So that means that God has called husbands to exhibit a kind of authority that is never enforced. The only mechanism men have of enforcing their authority with their wives is their kind, loving godliness. That's the mechanism of authority . . . Husbands are called to lead with passive enforcement. But there's never any justification in the Bible for husbands to enforce their authority. So this truth will rule out on theological and biblical grounds any forceful acts by a husband against his wife." He is arguing against books and websites that argue that husbands can discipline wives as well as children, which he says has no biblical justification. (In a long excursus he advocates for the use of "controlled" force, tempered by love, in discipline of children, particularly by fathers, on biblical grounds.) In another section, he argues that abusers can change because Jesus' power overcomes all sins (drawing a parallel with the assumed definite potential for gay persons to be converted to straight.) The biblical response: first, listen—to the abused and the abuser (our goal is "restoration, not stigmatization.") "Consider whether and how to involve law enforcement." Here he confuses "adult protective services" (which normally refers to elder abuse services), and laws re: abuse reporting (normally only referring to child abuse), and does not engage the issue of taking the decision out of the victim's hands "even if she begs me not to." Then, shockingly, "You may or may not involve the authorities, but you always involve the church . . . give them a place to stay." There is no reference to community battered women's shelters. In the conclusion, he outlines a process for repentance and reconciliation, including intensive (even daily) Christian couples' counseling focused on the man's frustrated desires and the need for genuine repentance and forgiveness. "God can turn evil in to good." The same lecture is also digested as a weekly resource "Biblical Counseling

Collins' approach is only somewhat better. In the 2nd and 3rd editions of his major textbook, *Christian Counseling*, Collins does include a

---

and Domestic Violence" by Lambert, https://biblicalcounseling.com/2017/02/weekly-resource-biblical-counseling-domestic-violence/. From April 5, 2017, Lambert offers a podcast "Truth in Love: Restoration after Abuse," in which "Dr. Lambert addresses two extremes that are prevalent in the church. First, people in the church assume that an abuser can never change. Second, people in the church err on the side of sending an abused woman back to their husband. Dr. Lambert addresses these two extremes and helps listeners think through these issues biblically. He also gives practical advice for how to minister to a family in this situation." https://biblicalcounseling.com/2017/04/til-045-restoration-abuse/ . A transcript is also available at https://biblicalcounseling.com/2016/12/restoration-abuse-transcript/, in which Lambert makes it clear that a woman should call police "because we're told in Romans 13:4 that God has established the state to enforce law and order. It's biblical to look for help from the governing authorities. When a man abuses his wife he not only sins against God and sins against her, also he commits a crime against the state." He then advocates for pastors calling the police (controversial in the battered women's movement) and further states, "She says, 'I don't feel scared. He says he's never gonna do it again. We're getting help,' then you probably don't need to pick up the phone and call the police in that situation. But if she says over the phone through tears, 'My husband just hit me. I have a black eye. I'm scared. I don't know what's gonna happen next,' then you have to call the police." Neither response shows awareness of current best practices re: safety of the victim. He urges reconciliation, within limits: "Christians always should be interested in pursuing restoration and reconciliation in having our relationships be restored. But the other side of that is we should never send a woman or anybody into a situation that we know to be or suspect is unsafe." But the plan most highlighted is separation to re-establish trust, and then a gradual re-joining as a household. A conference is planned for October, 2018: https://biblicalcounseling.com/conference/abuse/, featuring 5 men and 1 woman as plenary speakers. Overall, there is a real effort here to educate an often resistant community with facts and a reasonable clinical approach, but the absence of consultation with domestic violence advocacy organizations and experts in batterers' rehabilitation is troubling. It's an earnest effort (decades after the work with battered women began in other Christian contexts on very different theological grounds), but irreparably limited by the insistence on husbands' authority over their wives and children, and, worse, in some instances it is dangerously unaccountable to best practices established for safety by battered women's advocates over three decades and accountable batterers' treatment programs. This raises the thorny question whether, if some communities would have no help without a flawed resource, how can the battered women's movement help improve these resources—and would we ever be invited to do so? Marie Fortune's *Keeping the Faith* was written for just such communities: Marie M. Fortune, *Keeping the Faith: Questions and Answers for the Abused Woman* (San Francisco: Harper & Row, 1987; reissued in 1995 as *Keeping the Faith: Guidance for Christian Women Facing Abuse*). Sadly, her work is not referenced in any of these materials, nor has the evangelical Christian author Nancy Nason-Clark, whose well-researched writings also frame traditional views on wifely submission in terms of a framework of mutuality and the right to safety, e.g., in Catherine Clark Kroeger and Nancy Nason-Clark, *No Place for Abuse: Biblical Practical Resources to Counteract Domestic Violence*, rev. ed. (Downers Grove, IL: InterVarsity, 2010). —PCW 2018]

discussion of abuse.[277] The latest version of the chapter, entitled "Abuse and Neglect," encompasses and conflates child abuse, "mate abuse," elder abuse, sexual abuse, emotional abuse, neglect, spiritual abuse, harassment, together with examples of sexual assault (not separately identified as such).[278] In this edition he adds paragraphs on the prevalence of abuse, and is more sympathetic to battered women's suffering and need for safety and support. However, this sympathetic stance is diminished by a consistent failure to recognize either the historical role of Christian theology and ecclesiology in perpetuating violence against women, or any analysis of gender and power dynamics, in spite of his effort to incorporate some secular research in his counseling approach.[279]

Collins seems unaware of important distinctions among the various forms of violence and related approaches to intervention, as are all framed together as expressions of human sinfulness. For example, regarding domestic violence, he erroneously states that "whenever you suspect abuse, you must report it,"[280] failing to recognize the needs of adult victims to manage their own safety and self-determination.[281] Collins rightly corrects the impression that violence does not occur in Christian homes.[282] He counters the view that rape victims "really want to be raped" as "cruel and inaccurate."[283] He qualifies this, however, with the dangerous statement that "on rare occasions, victims may subtly invite the attacker's assaults" although he goes on

---

277. Gary R. Collins, *Christian Counseling: A Comprehensive Guide*, 2nd ed. (Dallas: Word, 1988); and Collins, *Christian Counseling*, 3rd ed. (see above).

278. Collins, *Christian Counseling*, 3rd ed.

279. The clinical literature Collins cites is a strangely uncritical admixture, including legitimate experts on child abuse, but systematically ignoring literature on domestic violence other than the mutual violence research. There is no systematic review of established literature on any of the topics he addresses in this chapter. A bibliography for further reading in the 2nd edition, including Mary D. Pellauer, "Violence against Women: The Theological Dimension," (51–61), is removed in the 3rd ed. His primary source in the 3rd ed. for intimate partner violence is Grant L. Martin, *Counseling for Family Violence* (Waco: Word, 1987), with one footnote citation (909n) to Michelle Harway and Marsali Hansen, *Spouse Abuse: Assessing and Treating Battered Women, Batterers, and Their Children*, 2nd ed. (Sarasota, FL: Professional Resource Press, 2004).

280. Collins, *Christian Counseling*, 3rd ed., 413.

281. The battered women's movement successfully advocated against mandatory reporting of adult-to-adult intimate violence on the grounds of self-determination and safety of adult victims. Well-meaning counselors can cause more harm than good by reporting against a victim's wishes, due to the potential for retaliation by the abuser. Reporting only of child abuse and the abuse of elderly or legally incompetent adults is legally mandated in all 50 U.S. states.

282. Collins, *Christian Counseling*, 3rd ed., 401.

283. Ibid, 403.

to say "this is unusual and certainly not the norm."[284] He assigns the causes of domestic abuse only to "environmental stress" (including Walker's cycle of violence, without attribution), "learned abuse," and "personality influences" such as insecurity, low self-concept, or "feeling jealous, possessive or intimidated by their wives,"[285] not recognizing that jealousy and possessiveness are classic expressions of dominance and control. In 2007 he also added "cultural issues" to the list of causes, including tolerance for violence in the media, and the pervasiveness of violence in society "modeled by our governments in their aggressive actions against other nations." He cites another author, Grant Martin, who also names "the reluctance of our police to intervene in cases of domestic violence, clergy who encourage the abused woman to be submissive to the husband, and mental-health workers who blame women for violence."[286] These two paragraphs, which do condemn the demeaning of women and children, are drawn directly from Martin, and although they point in a very helpful direction, they stand alone in the chapter in a cut-and-paste fashion. This framework does not appear to be fully understood or integrated throughout the chapter or the book.

In the 2007 edition, Collins replaces the exhortation in the 2nd edition that "people in time can learn to love their persecutors."[287] with a better statement that Christian forgiveness and turning the other cheek does not "prevent victims and their families and counselors from taking action to bring justice within the legal system, to prevent further abuse, to protect victims from additional harm . . ."[288] Even this statement, however, is confusing as he adds "and ultimately to bring about the non-abusive ideals that the Scriptures clearly teach," assigning this responsibility to victims and their families and advocates, without specifying accountability and responsibility on the part of the abuser. Counseling of abusers is solely focused on communication, problem-solving, conflict-resolution, and stress and anger management, without an examination of issues of power and control, although Collins does acknowledge the evidence in support of group

---

284. Ibid., 403.
285. Ibid., 404.
286. Grant L. Martin, *Counseling for Family Violence* (Waco: Word, 1987).
287. Collins, *Christian Counseling*, 2nd ed., 296.
288. Collins, *Christian Counseling*, 3rd ed. 402. [Note: 2007 is the last published edition of Collins' *Christian Counseling*, and there is no clear successor as a textbook. A more recent text, Everett L. Worthington, Eric L. Johnson, Joshua N. Hook, and Jamie D. Alten, *Evidence-Based Practices for Christian Counseling and Psychotherapy—Christian Association for Psychological Studies* (Downers Grove, IL: Intervarsity Press/IVP Academic, 2013), does not pro-actively address intimate partner violence or sexual assault, but rather offers a forgiveness-based approach to couples' counseling. —PCW 2018]

treatment educating men in "violence-free living."[289] In 2007 he advocates changing abusers' erroneous beliefs that victims enjoy abuse or "that violence is the macho way to assert authority and demonstrate masculinity,"[290] but does not contest the fundamental belief in male authority itself as problematic. Heterosexuality is assumed throughout the chapter.[291]

In a section specifically on helping victims of "mate abuse" (an idiosyncratic term used virtually only by Collins), he bends over backwards to

---

289. Gary R. Collins, *Christian Counseling*, 3rd ed., 414–415.

290. Ibid, 414.

291. Violence within same-sex relationships is never considered, except in a separate chapter on homosexuality, in which clinical research cited is dubious and one-sided, and the goal of all counseling of homosexuals, while urged to be compassionate, is "change from homosexual tendencies and behaviors" (ibid, 389) and "prevention of homosexuality" (ibid, 394–96). The AACC Code of Ethics absolutely requires Christian Counselors to subscribe to this point of view, and advocates "reparative therapy" to convert clients to heterosexuality (American Association of Christian Counselors, AAAC Law and Ethics Committee, *AACC code of ethics: The Y2004 Final Code*, 2004, http://www.aacc.net/about-us/code-of-ethics/ [website no longer available]. Section I-126 (7) reads: "Christian counselors refuse to condone or advocate for the pursuit of or active involvement in homosexual, transgendered, and cross-dressing behavior, and in the adoption gay and lesbian and transgendered lifestyles by clients. We may agree to and support the wish to work out issues of homosexual and transgendered identity and attractions, but will refuse to describe or reduce human identity and nature to sexual reference or orientation, and will encourage sexual celibacy or biblically prescribed sexual behavior while such issues are being addressed. Christian counselors differ, on biblical, ethical, and legal grounds, with groups who abhor and condemn reparative therapy, willingly offering it to those who come into counseling with a genuine desire to be set free of homosexual attractions and leave homosexual behavior and lifestyles behind. Either goal of heterosexual relations and marriage or lifelong sexual celibacy is legitimate and a function of client choice in reparative therapy. It is acknowledged that some persons engaged in same-sex change or reparative therapy will be able to change and become free of all homo-erotic behavior and attraction, some will change but will still struggle with homosexual attraction from time to time, and some will not change away from homosexual practices." [*Update*: As of 2014, the most recent AACC Code of Ethics (https://www.aacc.net/code-of-ethics-2/ ), Section 1-120f, has deleted the discussion of reparative therapy, but still takes a strong stance against all non-heterosexual sexuality: "Christian counselors do not condone or advocate for the pursuit of or active involvement in homosexual, bisexual or transgendered behaviors and lifestyles. Counselors may agree to and support the desire to work through issues of homosexual and transgendered identity and attractions, but will not describe or reduce human identity and nature to sexual orientation or reference, and will encourage sexual celibacy or biblically-prescribed sexual behavior while such issues are being addressed. Counselors acknowledge the client's fundamental right to self-determination and further understand that deeply held religious values and beliefs may conflict with same-sex attraction and/or behavior, resulting in anxiety, depression, stress, and inner turmoil." There is no mention of domestic violence, rape, or sexual assault in the code of ethics; the general duty to warn of immediate harm to self or others (the "Tarasoff" duty) is mentioned. —PCW 2018]

exclude gender differences, citing only the research described earlier in this article on mutual violence, and even making the unsupported statement that "husband abuse does occur and is increasing."[292] Because of their greater strength, men are better able to inflict injury on their wives, but women often do more physical harm because they attend to attack with something other than their hands."[293] These statements are not only erroneous but dangerous, as they are being used by generations of Christian counseling students to form their approaches to those in their future care.

Later in the book, in a chapter on divorce and remarriage, divorce is framed almost entirely as a negative.[294] Like Adams, Collins sees divorce as biblically permissible only on two grounds: "when one's mate is guilty of sexual immorality," or "when one of the mates is an unbeliever who willfully and permanently deserts the believing partner."[295] Abuse is not included in a list of causes of divorce.[296] He acknowledges that

> All of this appears to overlook those marriages where there is no infidelity or desertion, but where homes are filled with violence, physical and mental abuse, deviant forms of sexual behavior (including forced incest), foul language, failure to provide for a family's physical needs, alcoholism, a refusal to let other family members worship, or a variety of other destructive influences ... Here the Scriptures appear to be silent. Some might encourage the victims of abuse to stay in their difficult circumstances and to suffer in silence, hoping that this behavior might lead to the mate's conversion or change. However, submitting meekly to physical and mental attack *seems to be* neither wise nor healthy. The abuser is psychologically and spiritually unhealthy."[297]

---

292. Collins, *Christian Counseling*, 3rd ed., 412-17.

293. Collins, *Christian Counseling*, 2nd ed. only, 304, cites Richard L. McNeely and Gloria Robinson-Simpson, "The Truth about Domestic Violence: A Falsely Framed Issue," *Social Work* 32/6 (1987) 485-90; and Karen Diegmueller,"The Battered Husband's Case Shakes up Social Notions," [*Insight*, Mar. 7, 1988]. The same statement is made in the 3rd ed., 412, but drops the citation. For a careful refutation of McNeely and Robinson-Simpson (Richard L. McNeely and Gloria Robinson-Simpson, "The Truth about Domestic Violence: A Falsely Framed Issue," *Social Work* 32/6 (1987) 485-90) published in the next issue of the same journal (not cited by Collins), see Daniel Saunders, "Other 'Truths' about Domestic Violence: A Reply to McNeely and Robinson-Simpson," *Social Work* 33/2 (1998) 179-83; also Jack C. Straton, "The Myth of the 'Battered Husband Syndrome'" (2008): http://nomas.org/the-myth-of-the-battered-husband-syndrome.

294. Collins, *Christian Counseling*, 3rd ed., 412-17, 607-8.

295. Ibid, 610, citing Matthew 19:9 and 1 Corinthians 7:15.

296. Ibid, 611-14.

297. Ibid, 611-12, emphasis added.

However, regarding the abuser, Collins goes on to say "In addition, he or she is sinning. While such behavior *must be forgiven*, it cannot be condoned by a mate who *passively stands by*, says nothing, and lets various family members, including children, get hurt. Legally, the mate who allows this to continue could be in violation of the law and seen as an accomplice to child abuse, even though he or she resists it and tries to stop it,"[298] thus placing the blame on victims and other family members for their supposed "passivity." In the 2007 edition of the book, he adds that "Common sense, love for one's family members, and regard for one's personal safety would all indicate that such victims need to get out. The church and the Christian counselor surely have no alternative but to support such a decision and to assist victims in finding a place of safety."[299] However, he still grapples with biblical injunctions against divorce. He concludes (more definitively in 2007) that "in itself, abuse does not appear to be a stated biblical justification for divorce, even though many divorces occur because of this."[300] He wanly suggests that "at least a temporary separation may be necessary for the physical, psychological, and spiritual well-being of the abused mate and family members."[301] He adds, 'Sometimes as a result of separation" (and not, notably, any specified intervention), "the recalcitrant, hard-hearted person comes to a place of repentance and determination to reconcile."[302] No distinction is made between transient remorse and genuine amendment of life, and his ambiguous conclusion is hardly empowering of battered women to resist abuse in any definitive way: "This is one of those many cases where problems arise that are not addressed specifically in Scripture but where Christians seek to act in accordance with our God-given wisdom, Christian compassion, and general biblical guidelines."[303] While apparently more nuanced and sympathetic than hard-line biblically-based injunctions against divorce, Collins' approach, common among many Christian and biblical counselors, continues to reinforce misinformation and re-victimizes battered women by conveying mixed messages about responsibility, compassion, and forgiveness, and framing divorce even when violence is present as both sin and a failure.

At the root of the problem across the spectrum of Christian and biblical counseling is the fundamentalist biblical belief that wives must be under

---

298. Ibid., 612, emphasis added.
299. Ibid.
300. Ibid.
301. Ibid.
302. Ibid.
303. Ibid.

submission to their husbands, taking the statement in Ephesians 5:22 "Wives, be subject to your husbands" out of its context in verse 21: "Be subject to *one another* out of reverence for Christ."[304] Domestic violence has finally been included just in the past few years in the American Association of Christian Counselors' biblical counseling courses, as one segment of a distance-learning curriculum "Marriage Works," where violence is attributed to "distorted views of male headship"[305] and in a more empowerment-oriented segment of a curriculum entitled "Extraordinary Women," both available through the organization's website.[306] Searchable postings of links to articles and reviews of books on the topic "domestic violence" began to appear in 2006, mostly from the AACC-related website www.ecounseling.com,[307] many with citations from reliable domestic violence experts). A few further resources were added in the past decade.[308] Although some evangelical writers have con-

304. Emphasis added. See Marie M. Fortune, *Keeping the Faith: Questions and Answers for the Abused Woman* (San Francisco: Harper & Row, 1987; reissued in 1995 as *Keeping the Faith: Guidance for Christian Women Facing Abuse*). See also Philippians 2:4. Fortune has made the classic exegetical argument against taking v. 22 in isolation (15–17); see also Rita-Lou Clarke, *Pastoral Care of Battered Women* (Philadelphia: Westminster, 1986) 61–74. The Alsdurfs attempt to retain an evangelical framework, while restating the idea of submission and the husband's headship in terms of "equality in being, but inequality in function," and the man's power as sacrificial agape-love: James and Phyllis Alsdurf, *Battered into Submission: The Tragedy of Wife Abuse in the Christian Home* (Downers Grove, IL: InterVarsity, 1989; reissued 1998). They challenge the idea of family as a "chain of command" structure, and clearly define violence as misuse of power (82–95) They do not, however, in my view, go far enough in confronting an essentialist division of roles between the sexes that perpetuates hierarchy and inequality of power.

305. Leslie Vernick, L. *Domestic Violence: Confronting Physical and Sexual Abuse*, course offered online, 2009, at http://old.aacc.net/courses/biblical-counseling/marriage-works/. [See also "Domestic Abuse Counselor Training," https://leslievernick.com/training/courses/domestic-abuse/. —PCW 2018]

306. J. Hunt, "No more! Standing against and healing spousal abuse," course description, 2009, http://www.aacc.net/courses/biblical-counseling/extraordinary-women/curriculum-ew/ (website no longer available).

307. E.g., D. Bain, "Relationship Cancer: Understanding the Psychological Dynamics of Domestic Violence," 2008, http://www.ecounseling.com/articles/921 [website no longer available. There are no articles on domestic violence currently listed under Resources at ecounseling.com. —PCW 2018]

308. [*Update:* One Christian Counseling DVD training packet is offered on the AACC website, entitled "Domestic and Community Crisis Response https://www.lightuniversity.com/product/domestic-and-community-crisis-response-no-videos-provided/. Two course segments (10 and 11) address domestic violence and sexual assault, respectively. Segment 3, however, could undermine women's determination to seek safety: "The family is also part of the caregiving equation, and counselors need to understand their important role. In this lesson, Dennis Rainey will discuss God's plan and tools for marriage, and will provide encouragement to people who have difficult

tributed important arguments toward the empowerment of battered women in the specialized literature on domestic violence since the late 1990s,[309] violence in intimate relationships, and violence against women more generally, will continue to be overlooked and minimized until they are fully and appropriately addressed by Christian and biblical counselors, and safety is valued over the "sanctity of marriage."

Turning to mainline Protestant and Catholic pastoral theologians' general resources on pastoral care and pastoral theology are more likely to include considerations of intimate partner violence in the last decade or so. A survey of articles in the first edition of the *Dictionary of Pastoral Care and Counseling*,[310] shows attention to the issue in articles mostly among women authors, including both a specialized article "Family Violence,"[311] and articles on pastoral care of women,[312] and on feminist therapy.[313] An article on feminist theology and pastoral care,[314] however, inexplicably does not mention violence. Articles by men uniformly ignore the issue of male violence and intimate partner violence, except for J. C. Wynn's excellent article on marriage,[315] although there is some consideration of gender inequality—

---

situations within their family settings. He will also discuss how families can be victorious and overcome traumatic scenarios by the grace and power of God." More promising, in 2012 AACC trained 1,000 caregivers in domestic violence response (https://www.aacc.net/2012/06/14/aacc-trains-1000-caregivers-in-domestic-violence-response/) and declared a zero-tolerance policy toward domestic violence on the related web page. More recently, solid information with a link to NCADV was provided at https://www.aacc.net/2015/10/30/domestic-violence-awareness-month-three-steps-to-break-the-cycle/. Much would be up to the individual Christian counselor, and a commitment to value safety over and above "sanctity of marriage." —PCW 2018]

309. E.g., Lori G. Beaman, ed., *Shared Beliefs, Different Lives: Women's Identities in Evangelical Context* (St. Louis: Chalice, 1999) 111–32.

310. Constance Doran, "Family Violence," in *Dictionary of Pastoral Care and Counseling*, ed. Rodney J. Hunter (Nashville: Abingdon, 1994) 426–29.

311. Constance Doran, "Family Violence," in *Dictionary of Pastoral Care and Counseling*, ed. Rodney J. Hunter (Nashville: Abingdon, 1994) 426–29.

312. Peggy Garrison and Emma Justes, "Women, Pastoral Care of," in *Dictionary of Pastoral Care and Counseling*, ed. Rodney J. Hunter (Nashville: Abingdon, 1994) 1329–31

313. Charlotte Ellen, "Feminist Therapy," in *Dictionary of Pastoral Care and Counseling*, ed. Rodney J. Hunter (Nashville: Abingdon, 1994) 436.

314. Patricia Zulkosky, "Feminist Theology and Pastoral Care," in *Dictionary of Pastoral Care and Counseling*, ed. Rodney J. Hunter (Nashville: Abingdon, 1994) 433–35.

315. J. C. Wynn, "Marriage," in *Dictionary of Pastoral Care and Counseling*, ed. Rodney J. Hunter (Nashville: Abingdon, 1994) 678. In contrast, Giblin's article on the Marriage Encounter/Marriage Enrichment, does not acknowledge the critique of these programs' failure to attend to domestic violence: Paul R. Giblin, "Marriage Encounter/Marriage Enrichment," in *Dictionary of Pastoral Care and Counseling*, ed. Rodney J.

including articles on pastoral care of men,[316] and psychology of men.[317] In one article entitled "Violence," gender violence is mentioned in passing, but intimate partner violence is not mentioned at all, nor is racial violence.[318] The first two volumes of the *Clinical Handbook of Pastoral Counseling* did not include issues of violence against women.[319]

Since 2000, both of these important resources have issued updated volumes that have rectified these omissions.[320] Intimate partner violence is surveyed in several chapters in Nancy J. Ramsay's edited supplement to the *Dictionary*.[321] The third volume of the *Clinical Handbook* includes articles by both Neuger and myself addressing violence against women, and boundary violations, respectively, as well as a comprehensive article on trauma by David Foy and colleagues.[322]

---

Hunter (Nashville: Abingdon, 1994) 688-89.

316. Wimberly, *Counseling African American Couples and Families* (2004), frames issues of men as "slaves to the cult of masculinity" but no mention of violence—only "aggressiveness" (705).

317. Goldberg mentions "control vs. submission and "self destructive effects" but not violence: Herb Goldberg, "Men, Psychology of," in *Dictionary of Pastoral Care and Counseling*, ed. Rodney J. Hunter (Nashville: Abingdon, 1994) 705. Curiously, he names many psychological elements on the spectrum of aggression, but not violence itself.

318. Donald E. Miller, "Violence," in *Dictionary of Pastoral Care and Counseling*, ed. Rodney J. Hunter (Nashville: Abingdon, 1994) 1303-5.

319. Robert J. Wicks, Richard D. Parsons and Donald Capps, eds., *Clinical Handbook of Pastoral Counseling*, vol. 1 (Mahwah, NJ: Paulist, 1985); Robert J. Wicks, Richard D. Parsons and Donald Capps, eds., *Clinical Handbook of Pastoral Counseling*, vol. 2 (Mahwah, NJ: Paulist, 1993).

320. The website of the American Association of Pastoral Counselors (http://www.aapc.org) does not contain a systematic listing of publications and resources, so no specific resources on domestic violence are officially offered or endorsed there. Individual members may post their own publications. To date, there is one video recording listed on domestic violence (Angie Panos, *Survival from Domestic Violence: Stories of Hope and Healing* [video recording], 2005, available at http://www.giftfromwithin.org/html/video8.html#8). AAPC's linked online journal *Sacred Spaces* has not yet addressed the topic specifically—online at https://www.aapc.org/page/sacredspaces.

321. Nancy J. Ramsay, *Pastoral Care and Counseling: Redefining the Paradigms* (Nashville: Abingdon, 2004; reprinted as Appendix in Hunter and Ramsay, eds., 2005); Herbert Anderson, Edward Foley, Bonnie Miller-McLemore, and Robert Schreiter, eds., *Mutuality Matters: Family, Faith, and Just Love* (Lanham, MD: Sheed & Ward, 2004); Christie Cozad Neuger, "Gender narratives and the epidemic of violence in contemporary families," in Anderson et al., eds., *Mutuality Matters: Family, Faith, and Just Love*, (Lanham, MD: Sheed & Ward, 2004) 83-92.

322. Christie Cozad Neuger, "A Feminist Perspective on Pastoral Counseling with Women," in Robert J. Wicks, Richard D. Parsons and Donald Capps, eds., *Clinical Handbook of Pastoral Counseling*, Vol. 3, (Mahwah, NJ: Paulist, 2003) 17-37; Pamela Cooper-White, "Sexual Exploitation and Other Boundary Violations in Pastoral Ministry," in

Another avenue to understand how awareness of intimate partner violence has grown over the past three decades is to examine how domestic violence is included in the pastoral care curricula of theological schools. In order to probe this, I conducted a survey to all members of Society for Pastoral Theology during January-February, 2004. The survey was designed to gain information about the extent of the inclusion of gender violence issues in theological teaching by SPT members (who represent the largest organized body of teachers of pastoral theology/pastoral care and counseling in mainline theological education), the level of cooperation/collaboration in this teaching with domestic violence and rape crisis agencies beyond the walls of the educational institution, and teachers' perceptions of the level of awareness among entering M.Div. students about violence against women. Detailed results of this research were published in the *Journal of Pastoral Theology*[323]—See Chapter 8, this volume. Among those who responded, the survey demonstrates that there is currently a very high level of attention and seriousness given to the issue of violence against women in our teaching. (For this current Collected Essays volume, a quick follow-up study showed that this commitment has continued into the present decade, with younger scholars taking up the challenge alongside seasoned educators.[324])

## Where Are We Now?

In reviewing the goals articulated in 1996 and summarized at the beginning of this article, we can observe some important advances: 1) There has been considerable effort in the past decade or more to consistently, intentionally

---

Wicks et al., eds., *Clinical Handbook of Pastoral Counseling*, Vol. 3 (Mahwah, NJ: Paulist, 2003) 342–65; David W. Foy, Kent D. Drescher, Allan G. Fitz, and Kecin R. Kenney, "Post-traumatic Stress Disorder," in Wicks et al., eds., *Clinical Handbook of Pastoral Counseling*, Vol. 3 (Mahwah, NJ: Paulist, 2003) 274–88.

323. Pamela Cooper-White, "What Are We Teaching about Violence against Women?" *Journal of Pastoral Theology* 14/2 (2004) 48–69 [Ch. 8, this volume.]

324. The number of responses was very small (N=14), so it is assumed that those most committed to teaching on VAW issues were a self-selected response sample. All respondents regularly include information on VAW in their courses, and all but 1 incorporate relevant readings. About ½ supervise outside agency placements, and ¾ invite outside guest speakers. 64% say they teach about VAW to the same degree as previously, 21% say they teach more and 14% (2 respondents) responded "no comparison—just began teaching." Half the respondents had worked or volunteered at a VAW agency. Academic rank was split evenly among full professors, tenured associates, pre-tenure, and part-time/adjunct. 71% of respondents identified as female. About 2/3 were white (8), 20% African descent (3), and 10% (1 each) were international, Asian/Asian American, bi-racial, and prefer not to answer (non-mutually-exclusive categories). I did not run cross-tabs for any categories since the overall response rate was so low.

integrate the issue of intimate partner violence in seminary education, as shown in the research reported above. Evangelical schools (with the notable exception of Fuller Seminary's forward-looking curriculum in pastoral psychology) lag behind, hampered by a literalist theological approach to the Bible and a prescriptive counseling model that has taken little account of battered women's experiences—although this is just now beginning to change—but mainline Protestant schools have made important gains in this area. (Little is still known empirically about Roman Catholic seminaries).

2) As the review of the pastoral literature has shown, models of pastoral counseling have been developed, in which the focus is on empowerment of women, and maintaining vigilance against socially reinforced stereotypes that blame victims or minimize or excuse perpetrators of violence from direct responsibility. This is mostly evident in specialized books on the subject of intimate partner violence. Much important work is still needed in order to integrate such approaches to the general literature on relationships, marriage, and family.

3) What about collaboration in the community with local battered women's shelters, domestic violence agencies, batterers' programs, and knowledgeable clinical and pastoral counselors in the wider community? Teaching members of the Society for Pastoral Theology showed a considerable amount of collaboration in their classroom teaching and assignments in the community, as well as personal involvement with local shelters and agencies. There has also been considerable growth of clergy training programs, both nationally through the FaithTrust Institute, and at the local level through coalition-building efforts by community activists and church members.

4) What are clergy actually doing? We do not have an empirical window into the offices of pastoral caregivers nationwide, so it is difficult to assess the degree to which pastoral care for individual victims and survivors is characterized by non-judgmental listening, interpretations of scripture that are healing and empowering, and faith-grounded advocacy in the wider community for justice. The lack of attention to intimate partner violence in training programs such as Stephen Ministries shows some distance yet to go in this area. However, the vast majority of teachers of pastoral care in mainline churches, as well as the pastoral care literature, advocate a non-directive, empathic approach to care. Again, evangelical approaches, which direct church members and counseling clients through biblical prescriptions and homework, need to be challenged in light of battered women's felt experiences of oppression, blame, and invisibility.[325] Often in the evangeli-

---

325. In their survey of 238 evangelical clergy, Beaman and Nason-Clark learned

cal context, the most effective pastoral care for battered women is provided by other church women.[326]

5) Many mainline denominations have produced a variety of resources to promote and undergird work in congregations to support victims and survivors through education and other means. Posters, tracts, pamphlets, small group resources, and materials for clergy are now available through many national church offices. More ecumenical sharing and "cross-pollenization" of creative resources and programming would significantly help advance this resourcing of congregations, particularly those in smaller denominations or in church bodies where domestic violence has not yet been addressed as thoroughly.

6) Works by Poling and Neuger have begun to promote understandings of male violence and appropriate care of men that would help pastoral caregivers to identify responsible batterers' programs that recognize intimate violence as part of a larger pattern of socially sanctioned power and control over women and uphold *safety* as the first priority. This work is still just beginning, and a broader dissemination of information and theological reflection on accountable care of men is still needed.

## Where Do We Go from Here?

The foregoing survey suggests at least four trajectories for continued advancement of pastoral caregivers and theologians in advocacy, activism and public witness to end violence against women, and intimate partner violence in particular: teaching, research, pastoral care and counseling, and public advocacy.

### Teaching

In the follow-up workshop with SPT members described above, workshop participants raised several specific areas that could use even more attention in future teaching. Topics mentioned were wide ranging, and included

- clergy sexual abuse

---

that most pastors feel inadequately prepared, and tend to frame abuse in terms of poor communication skills rather than power and control, although they do not condone violence and do not turn women away: Lori G. Beaman and Nancy Nason-Clark, "Evangelical Women as Activists: Their Response to Violence against Women," in *Shared Beliefs, different Lives: Women's Identities in Evangelical Context*, ed. Lori G. Beaman (St. Louis: Chalice, 1999) 126.

326. Ibid.

- sexual harassment (including harassment within institutions of theological education, and in related field education settings)
- war crimes against women and global issues of violence against women, including traffic in women and girls
- emotional and physical violence
- issues of shame, secrecy and under-reporting
- relating violence against women to developmental issues re: age, e.g., teen dating violence
- greater understanding of more communally based contexts of violence against women
- more teaching about effective strategies to help men stop male violence: "We are pulling women out, but the men are still there in the community to hurt women!"
- revival of consciousness raising groups among younger women, and providing forums for "highly visible women to tell their stories in the public arena," to make the point that violence is neither rare nor targeted only toward poor or disadvantaged women
- issues of restorative justice
- consistently and *per*sistently making the conceptual linkages between violence against women and racism and other forms of oppression.

## Research

Further research on the extent of teaching about intimate partner violence would be valuable in assessing both the quantity and quality of preparation of seminarians to provide appropriate pastoral care in their ministries. One limitation of the study of members of the Society for Pastoral Theology just conducted is that SPT has a "skew" in favor of professors of pastoral care who are more liberal, even progressive, in social orientation. Given their research priorities, and SPT's meeting themes over the years, SPT members tend to self-select toward those who share a concern for social justice as a core issue in pastoral care and pastoral theology. Roman Catholic, Orthodox, Evangelical Protestant, and Jewish theological schools are under-represented in the Society, which is largely comprised of mainline Protestant seminary and divinity school faculties, as well as some independent researchers and interested pastoral counselors.

It would be valuable in the future to survey professors who are not members of SPT, but who teach pastoral care courses in Roman Catholic, Evangelical, and other theological schools, as well as CPE supervisors.[327] It would also be valuable to survey faculties teaching in other fields such as social ethics, religious education, church history, and systematic theology. More formal research investigating outcomes assessment with students would also be useful—to investigate not only what we think we are teaching, but what students are actually learning! Surveys of clergy in communities, including surveys of general knowledge about intimate partner violence, before-and-after studies to test the effectiveness of community clergy training programs, and other research into clergy awareness and effectiveness would be another useful area of investigation.

Beyond what is being taught in seminaries, and what seminarians and clergy know, it would be even more important to explore battered women's own experiences of pastoral care, and the responsiveness of their religious communities. While research among battered women should only be undertaken with the utmost sensitivity, confidentiality, and above all care for safety (see above), respectful surveys of battered women's experiences and perceptions of how clergy and congregations have helped and/or harmed them would add an empirical base of knowledge to the currently large anecdotal pool of evidence available.

## Pastoral Care and Counseling

As noted above, there has been much writing about sensitive and empowerment-based pastoral care, especially in the last decade. Perhaps one of the greatest challenges in the new millennium is to avoid the temptation of clergy and seminary faculties alike to say "Oh, we've covered that now," and through complacency, to allow awareness of intimate partner violence and violence against women to begin to fade from consciousness. Violence against women and children is still pandemic. There has been a significant growth in high-quality, specialized literature on intimate partner violence. However, the topic is still mostly lacking in the general pastoral care literature. Pastoral counselors certified through the American Association of Pastoral Counselors,[328] and professional chaplains[329] need regular continuing education and in-service training to remain up to date on re-

---

327. Association for Clinical Pastoral Education (ACPE), http://www.acpe.edu.

328. American Association of Pastoral Counselors (AAPC), http://www.aapc.org.

329. Association of Professional Chaplains (APC), http://www.professionalchaplains.org; Association for Clinical Pastoral Education (ACPE), http://www.acpe.edu.

search, community resources, and intervention strategies, while Christian Counselors[330] need more rigorous clinical training and certification generally, including on issues of intimate partner violence. Domestic violence awareness, prevention and intervention needs to be "mainstreamed" much more effectively, especially in pastoral literature on premarital counseling, marriage and family, and divorce, and in evangelical Christian resources. In addition, new technologies including the media, video games, digital photography and camera phones, and the Internet are continually developing new forms of victimization and objectification of women, requiring new knowledge and strategies for helping victims and survivors.

Moreover, given that we continue to live in a "rape culture,"[331] we must maintain vigilance, in order to keep the truths about violence against women and girls from fading into chronic cultural patterns of minimization and denial," in the words of Judith Herman of Harvard Medical School:

> To hold traumatic reality in consciousness requires a social context that affirms and protects the victim and that joins victim and witness in a common alliance. For the individual victim, this social context is created by relationships with friends, lovers, and family. For the larger society, the social context is created by political movements that give voice to the disempowered . . . The study of trauma in sexual and domestic life becomes legitimate only in a context that challenges the subordination of women and children," in the absence of strong political movements for human rights, the active process of bearing witness inevitably gives way to the active process of forgetting. Repression, dissociation, and denial are phenomena of social as well as individual consciousness.[332]

This is not only a political or social vigilance—it is a spiritual discipline, a *habitus*, or habit of mindfulness, in which we remember the cries of those who live in terror, upheld by a faith in God's own "preferential option" for the orphan and the widow, the sojourner and the stranger, the poor, the least, and the lost.

---

330. American Association of Christian Counselors (AACC), https://www.aacc.net.

331. Emilie Buchwald, Pamela R. Fletcher, and Martha Roth, ed., *Transforming a Rape Culture* (Minneapolis: Milkweed Editions, 1983; 2nd ed. 2005).

332. Judith Herman, *Trauma and Recovery* (New York: Basic Books, 1992) 8.

## Public Advocacy

Such an approach to pastoral care also means that pastoral care of abuse victims and survivors can never occur in a vacuum, simply as an exercise of individual compassion, even empowerment, but must be part of a larger commitment to working to end violence against women," in this sense, pastoral care can never be separated from the prophetic witness for social change. Even as we do education, preach, provide resources, offer a ministry of presence with victims and their family members, and speak the truth to batterers in love, we must take part in community efforts to speak truth to power, raising awareness in the public arena, and confronting institutional and systemic injustices with strategies for transformation.

Perhaps the most important thing we can do is to make coalition with others in our communities, our nation, and the world, to end violence against women, and intimate partner violence in particular. We should be read, and be proactive, to join in the call for greater collaboration that is emerging from battered women's advocates themselves—and prepare ourselves to be good partners in the struggle.

Longtime battered women's advocate Susan Schechter wrote:

> Right now we [in the battered women's movement] offer women shelter, support, and protection orders to stop the violence, and they are telling us that this often doesn't meet their needs as human beings. This isn't because we do our work poorly; it is because we are looking only at the violence and making that primary. But women don't necessarily experience their lives and needs that way. Domestic violence organizations have often offered women a menu that is service driven—i.e., these are the services that will help you because these are the services we have. We need now to think about the women's lives and needs more broadly and ask how we can assist them [citing Davies et al., 1998]. We will never do this without collaborating with the poverty organizations, teachers, day care centers, and *clergy in our communities*.[333]

We are invited! Sincere religious leaders in the past may have found activists difficult to work with. As Schechter acknowledges, "Our collaborative

---

333. Susan Schechter, "New Challenges for the Battered Women's Movement: Building Collaborations and Improving Public Policy for Poor Women," 14, in Schechter, *Building Comprehensive Solutions to Domestic Violence, Publication #1: A Vision Paper* (Pennsylvania Coalition against Domestic Violence/National Resource Center on Domestic Violence, January, 1999) [online (cached) at https://www.bcsdv.org/wp-content/uploads/2015/09/BCS-Pub1.pdf, 2018], emphasis added.

partners—those who consider themselves our allies—find some of us discouraging to work with. This is an unpleasant truth to hear . . . Professional allies are annoyed that domestic violence organizations won't let them do more."[334] But this should not deter us from reaching out, repeatedly if necessary, to join in coalition with those who are most passionate and most knowledgeable about ending domestic violence—those whose pioneering vision created the battered women's movement three decades ago, and those who have since been formed in the front lines of shelter, hotline, and agency work, and community advocacy.

Schechter enumerates criteria for good collaborators, based on feedback she solicited through research.[335] To paraphrase, her recommendations are to see both sides of an issue, to develop empathy for the other field's perspective; to understand the other field's parameters and limits—what other people can and cannot do; to articulate positive possibilities; to target energy on what can realistically be done; to articulate needs clearly; to be patient in explaining issues—no screaming or yelling!; to realize that partners in collaboration sometimes needs to be protected, too; to never be "too tired to talk and explain;" to know how to listen, how to say one's piece, how to see other points of view, and how to communicate."[336] These recommendations are not very different from what we teach and practice in our pastoral care classrooms and congregations as good empathic listening and responding. They apply equally well to us as to battered women's activists.

## Conclusion: Pastoral *and* Prophetic— Our Call to Stand for Justice

In this invitation toward greater collaboration, we have something, I believe, that we can uniquely bring to the table: a steadfast, theologically grounded vision for *justice*. At a time when, as described above, the battered women's movement has often found itself "mainstreamed," and its vision even occasionally compromised through corporate sponsorships and governmental partnerships, there is an ever-present danger of sliding exclusively into a service-provider mentality, and compromising or softening the vision for justice for women that powered the movement in its earliest years. Schechter calls in particular for a more integrated vision that recognizes the multiple problems battered women face, and particularly the pressures of poverty

---

334. Ibid, 10.
335. Ibid.
336. Ibid.

and economic injustice.[337] I would further include racism and heterosexism on this list of priorities.

As pastoral theologians, caregivers and counselors, *we have a vocabulary, and a passion, that weds care for the vulnerable with an eschatological vision of hope.* As the field of pastoral care in the last decade and a half has embraced a widening beyond "relational humanness" to also encompassing "relational justice,"[338] we are invited by our colleagues in community—but further, we are called by the same God who called the ancient Israelites out of slavery through the wilderness to freedom—to join with our activist partners in community, to shore up the vision for social transformation, to encourage those who are working in the trenches, and together to keep working and living toward a world that as a people of faith we name God's Realm of Peace and Justice:

> The wolf shall live with the lamb, the leopard shall lie down with the kid, the calf and the lion and the fatling together, and a little child shall lead them . . . They will not hurt or destroy on all my holy mountain; for the earth will be full of the knowledge of the Lord as the waters cover the sea. (Isaiah 11:6, 9)

---

337. Ibid, 6–7, 14.

338. Larry Kent Graham, "From Relational Humanness to Relational Justice: Reconceiving Pastoral Care and Counseling," in *Pastoral Care and Social Conflict*, ed. Pamela D. Couture and Rodney J. Hunter (Nashville: Abingdon, 1995) 220–34.

# 12

## Denial, Victims, and Survivors

*Post-traumatic Identity Formation and Monuments in Heaven*

2012[1]

### Remembering Trauma in Psychotherapy

IN THE 1980S AND 90S, much of the clinical therapeutic literature (including books and articles in pastoral care and counseling) advocated that persons with a history of abuse or other personal trauma be helped to move from a defensive denial of abuse ("Nothing bad ever happened to me" or "I'm done with it") to the more vulnerable and at times regressive identity of "victim," in order finally to arrive at an identity of empowered survivor. As most clinicians will agree, without digging for memories of abuse or suggesting abuse to the patient (which would be frankly harmful[2]), creating a safe space in which traumatic memories can gradually emerge—in an organic process led by the patient's own unconscious dreams, fantasies and gestures—from dissociation into consciousness is an important, even central, aspect to the healing of trauma. Because traumatic memory differs—structurally, in the brain—from ordinary, even unpleasant memories which retain a narrative

---

1. Orig. publ. in the *Journal of Pastoral Theology* 22/1 (2012) 2.1–2.16.

2. This is the correction to over-zealous therapists in the 1980s and 90s toward whom Elizabeth Loftus' research was most constructively directed. E.g., Elizabeth Loftus and Katherine Ketcham, *Witness for the Defense: The Accused, the Eyewitness and the Expert Who Puts Memory on Trial* (New York: St. Martin's, 1992). However, a thorough examination of the so-called "False Memory Syndrome" shows a mixture political motivations as well as clinical research. Methodologically, a straight-line analogy cannot be made between the planted memories, e.g., Loftus' experiments involving implanted memories of being lost in a shopping mall (in the context of otherwise normal childhood experience) and the different neurological mechanism of memories of actual traumatic experience. The debates on this issue are discussed in Cooper-White, *The Cry of Tamar: Violence against Women and the Church's Response*, 2nd ed. (Minneapolis: Fortress, 2012) 2nd ed., 181–183, 317.

shape—the process is not akin to opening a locked file cabinet and retrieving a folder with readable documents. Trauma, because it is by definition an experience of threatened bodily and/or psychic annihilation, floods all the normal coping mechanisms, and is "recorded" in the brain in fragments, traces and bruises that change the neural pathways in the brain and are experienced (if at all) as separate domains of affective reactivity, cognitive perception (or distortion), bodily sensation, and behavioral repetition.[3]

Thus, the retrieval of traumatic memories is not a linear process in which "bad" memories are fished for, hooked, and brought up for a cathartic cure of neurotic symptoms (as Freud and Breuer had initially hoped, prior to 1895). The "talking cure" involves a gradual, often two-steps-forward-one-step-back process of allowing (not forcing) glimpses of traumatic memory to emerge from bodily and behavioral traces, to symbolization, and finally verbalization,[4] in a therapeutic relationship in which both therapist and patient are deeply immersed in an intersubjective state of knowing/not-knowing, and the meaning that is made of past violations is continually shaped and re-shaped, with the patient having the final say—contingent and in process though that "final say" must be. Thus "memories" of abuse are more like shapes viewed through a cloud than a sharp-focused story book.[5] The capacity to suspend certainty and to grapple with multiple layers and dimensions of "truth" is a significant developmental achievement. In the open-endedness of such working-through, memory and its sequelae begin to take on recognizable shapes, but traumatic memory cannot be pinned down like a specimen under a glass. The movement is one away from de-

---

3. These four elements are adapted from Bennet Braun's "The BASK Model of Dissociation: Clinical Applications," *Dissociation* 1/2 (1988) 116–23. Some key texts for understanding the mechanism of trauma include Judith Lewis Herman, *Trauma and Recovery* (New York: Basic Books, 1992); Bessel Van der Kolk, "The Body Keeps the Score: Memory and the Evolving Psychobiology of Posttraumatic Stress," *Harvard Review of Psychiatry* 1/5 (1994) 253–65; Van der Kolk and and Rita Fisler, "Dissociation and the Fragmentary Nature of Traumatic Memories: Overview and Exploratory Study," *Journal of Traumatic Stress* 8 (1995) 505–26; Van der Kolk, Alexander C. McFarlane, and Lars Weisaeth. *Traumatic Stress: The Effects of Overwhelming Experience on Mind, Body, and Society* (New York: Guilford, 1996); and Lenore Terr, *Too Scared to Cry: Psychic Trauma in Childhood* (New York: Basic Books, 1992) and *Unchained Memories: True Stories of Traumatic Memories Lost and Found* (New York: Basic Books, 1995).

4. Jody Messler Davies and Mary Gail Frawley, *Treating the Adult Survivor of Childhood Sexual Abuse: A Psychoanalytic Perspective* (New York: Basic Books, 1994).

5. For further discussion of this quality of the therapeutic process, see Philip Bromberg, "'Speak! That I May See You': Some Reflections on Dissociation, Reality, and Psychoanalytic Listening," *Psychoanalytic Dialogues* 4/4 (1994) 517–47; see also *Standing in the Spaces: Essays on Clinical Process, Trauma, and Dissociation* (Hillsdale, NJ: Analytic Press, 1998).

fensive amnesia/amnesty toward a wider and wider acknowledgement, acceptance of past experiences, working through the pain and grieving the attendant losses (past and present), creating multi-layered understandings of what those experiences meant and mean now. In this arduous process, less and less is lost to consciousness, as both memory and meaning are continually co-constructed in the container of the therapeutic relationship, in order that growth and empowerment may increase.

The goal of such therapy is for the patient gradually to move from an identity of "victim" to "survivor," as the process of grief and anger gives way to a sense of empowerment and ability to move forward in life "strong at the broken places." This literature has been important in countering denial of abuse, both historically and in current times, both in terms of psychiatric formulations (e.g., Freud's re-orientation of his theory away from the trauma-based "seduction theory"), and socio-political forces that reinforced oppression by "blaming the victim."

In fact, the renewal of awareness and interest in abuse was part of a larger cultural movement in North America, Europe, and arguably all over the globe, toward the liberation of oppressed groups and the overthrow of tyrannical regimes. We can trace the liberation movements of the 1960s, 70s, and 80s in North America to influence of Marxism in the 19th and 20th centuries, and even earlier to Enlightenment revolutionary movements that swept Europe in the 18th century and laid the philosophical foundations of both the American and French Revolutions, and the anti-slavery movements of the 19th century. "Second wave feminism" in the 1960s and 70s in particular was the most immediate catalyst for the rediscovery of the extent and severity of domestic violence, sexual assault and rape, elder abuse, and child abuse in all its forms. Holocaust survivors decried the denial of genocide under the Nazi regime even as evidence of mass torture and murder was available during World War II, and the vow, "Never forget!" became a crucial call to conscience—best exemplified in the writings of Elie Wiesel,[6] and expanded to include numerous other victims of genocide and violence across the globe in the 2nd half of the 20th century. The increase of public memorials—including the contested World Trade Center site in New York—represent the growth of public movements, often led by the survivors of mass atrocities, to remember. The needs of returning Vietnam veterans concurrently raised awareness and legitimated the clinical study and treatment of post-traumatic stress. It was therefore not only individuals and families who had closed their eyes (or had their eyes closed) to abuse, but society as a whole, which had mostly entered (or re-entered after the late

---

6. E.g., Wiesel, *Night* (New York: Bantam, 1960), and numerous other writings.

19th century psychologists' brief revelations) a long sleep of denial throughout most of the 20th century. Judith Herman addressed such societal denial head on in her important book *Trauma and Recovery*:

> The knowledge of horrible events periodically intrudes into public awareness but is rarely retained for long. Denial, repression, and dissociation operate on a social as well as an individual level. The study of psychological trauma has an 'underground' history. Like traumatized people, we have been cut off from the knowledge of our past. Like traumatized people, we need to understand the past in order to reclaim the present and the future. Therefore, an understanding of psychological trauma begins with rediscovering history.[7]

Furthermore, as history bears out, denial and dissociation are never complete, and memory—however suppressed and fragmented—seems inherently to demand release. Again, quoting Herman:

The ordinary response to atrocities is to banish them from consciousness. Certain violations of the social compact are too terrible to utter aloud: this is the meaning of the word unspeakable. Atrocities, however, refuse to be buried. Equally as powerful as the desire to deny atrocities is the conviction that denial does not work. Folk wisdom is filled with ghosts who refuse to rest in their graves until their stories are told. Murder will out. Remembering and telling the truth about terrible events are prerequisites for the restoration of the social order and for the healing of individual victims.[8]

However, as Herman also cautions, it is in perpetrators' interests to enlist the denial of bystanders, and to marginalize the voices of victims as part of a larger pattern of power and privilege at the expense of the oppressed. Thus movements for raising awareness of abuses of all sorts have repetitively fallen into "rational" arguments for minimizing and denying their full reality. In Herman's words:

> Advances in the field [of trauma in sexual and domestic life] occur only when they are supported by a political movement powerful enough to legitimate an alliance between investigators and patients and to counteract the ordinary social processes of silencing and denial. In the absence of strong political movements for human rights, the active process of bearing witness inevitably gives way to the active process of forgetting.

---

7. Herman, *Trauma and Recovery*, 2. See also Susan J. Brison, "The Politics of Forgetting," in Brison, *Aftermath: Violence and the Remaking of a Self* (Princeton: Princeton University Press, 2002) 85–99.

8. Ibid., p. 1.

Repression, dissociation, and denial are phenomena of social as well as individual consciousness.[9]

## Memory in Philosophy and Theology

It is perhaps no surprise, then, that memory and forgetting have constituted a significant—and contested—theme in recent decades in both philosophy and theology. I will turn now to address some recent philosophical and theological literature exploring themes associated with trauma and victimization, including trauma, memory, and forgiveness. In philosophy, probably the most important contribution (and certainly the longest, weighing in at 642 pages!) is Paul Ricoeur's 2004 *Memory, History, Forgetting*.[10] In theology, there are several important contributions including Anglican theologian Flora Keshgegian's *Redeeming Memories*(2000)[11] and Reformed theologian Miroslav Volf's *The End of Memory: Remembering Rightly in a Violent World*.[12] I will briefly examine Keshgegian's and Volf's perspectives, with Ricoeur's insights as a backdrop. Keshgegian and Volf both claim the credibility not only of rigorous scholarly training and research, but of personal traumatic memory—Keshgegian as the daughter of survivors of the Armenian Holocaust during World War I, immersed in "their feelings of emptiness and deprivation, . . . tutored . . . in narratives of deportation and brutality, of loss and abandonment, of displacement and poverty,"[13] and Volf as a survivor of a series of psychologically traumatic interrogations during which the threat of torture and death was never absent (though never carried out directly), by totalitarian Communist security forces in Yugoslavia in 1984.[14] These theologians, however, represent quite different points of view about the meaning and ultimate disposition of memory (and they do not appear to be aware of each other's contributions). Keshgegian

> draws our attention once again to those who have suffered childhood sexual abuse, those in the Armenian genocide and the Jewish Holocaust, and those historically disinherited

---

9. Ibid., 9.

10. Paul Ricoeur, *Memory, History, Forgetting*. Trans. Kathleen Blamey and David Pellauer (Chicago: University of Chicago Press, 2004).

11. Flora Keshgegian, *Redeeming Memories: A Theology of Healing and Transformation* (Nashville: Abingdon, 2000).

12. Volf, *The End of Memory: Remembering Rightly in a Violent World* (Grand Rapids: Eerdmans, 2006).

13. Kesgegian, *eeming Memories*, 12.

14. Volf, *The End of Memory*, 3–8.

peoples and groups, especially women and African Americans. With such human memories of suffering in mind, she insists that redeeming memories is the purpose and mission of the church. The church's structure and practices are measured by how well they enable and enhance the work of remembering as a multiform and ongoing process. She challenges us to understand that the redemptive potential of the memory of Jesus Christ will be made known and realized by the capacity of that memory to hold and carry not only the story of Jesus, but of all those who suffer, struggle, live, and die. She invites [her readers, with a double-entendre] to understand Christianity as *saving memory*.[15] (emphasis added)

Well versed in trauma literature, Keshgegian argues for a process of "re-membering," in which the remembrance of suffering paves the way for transformation and redemption—in the form of both personal healing and wider socio-political change. She likens the recollection of truths about past abuse and violence to the anamnesis of the Eucharist, in which the dangerous memory of Jesus Christ can empower a resurrection faith in the form of "remembering resistance, resilience, and agency"—"resurrecting hope." Her focus is not on a future-oriented eschatology, or redemption in "the by and by," but redemption as

> the going on, the continuing to embrace living with commitment and faith ... For those who have been victimized, the partnership is realized through their struggle for life, their witness of remembering and *re-membering*. For others of us, it is manifest in faithful and effective witness that begins in listening and ends in transformation of ourselves and the world. Witnessing is a shared and universal task that does not end in time or space. There is no resolution, no realized redemption. In the place of resolution, this theology offers remembrance and witness. Indeed, remembering replaces resolution in the story of redemption. Remembering bears witness to life, ever-threatened, ever-renewed.[16] (emphasis added)

Volf's focus, on the other hand, is *both* on the here-and-now, advocating for "right remembering" as a practice of humility, recalling that each of us, victim and perpetrator, is also a sinner, *and* on the eschatological future, as Volf envisions an ultimate fulfillment, initiated by God, in which all suffering

---

15. Keshgegian, *Redeeming Memories*, back cover.
16. Ibid., 235–36.

would be forgotten, and all injury reconciled by grace—a future heaven without recall of offenses or monuments to the past and its losses.[17]

As a pastoral theologian with a commitment to bringing feminist, postmodern, psychoanalytic, and (like Keshgegian) Anglican perspectives into constructive dialogue in my work, I must "come clean" that I do not remain neutral with regard to these diverging theological approaches to memory and forgetting. I will take a side. I also believe there are some problems with the popular clinical idea that there is any sort of linear (even if circuitous) movement from "denial" to "victim" to "survivor" as clearcut stances or identities. In this final section of the paper, I argue for both a psychology and a theology that I believe do justice to memory, and enlist memory to do justice—both for individual victims of trauma, and for the larger social and political domain to which all theology, but especially pastoral and practical theology, as public theology,[18] must address itself.

## On Memory and Individual Healing

First, to take up the question of individual healing through the process of retrieving and grieving memories of past abuse. Keshgegian's discussion of remembering as "re-membering" rings true to clinical experience, and presents a more organic process of recovery from trauma, I believe, than Volf's model of "right remembering"—which, however ethically and theologically well motivated, could still become a kind of cognitive strait-jacket that, by naming forgetting and individual reconciliation as the end-goal, could be experienced as a form of re-victimization by traumatized individuals. (Volf himself acknowledges this possibility, and acknowledges his own struggle to comply, but claims that "loving those who do me harm was precisely the hard path on which Jesus called me to follow him . . . Not to

---

17. Volf does not invent this conclusion from whole cloth. He draws on Augustine of Hippo for this formulation of the Heavenly City, citing Augustine's *City of God* (XXII.30; cited in *The End of Memory*, 22–23), as well as John Calvin's *Institutes* and Karl Barth's *Church Doagmatics* (cited in *The End of Memory*, 133–34). Volf actually draws a different conclusion in his earlier book *Exclusion and Embrace: Theological Reflections of Identity, Otherness, and Reconciliation* (Nashville: Abingdon, 1996). As he notes in The End of Memory (191n23), he originally proposed that "the cross will be eternally remembered. I have come to believe that the proposal offered here is more plausible." (191n23).

18. My method here obviously draws on David Tracy, especially *The Analogical Imagination* and also Mark Kline Taylor, *Remembering Esperanza*; as well as other works (e.g., Browning, *A Fundamental Practical Theology*) that have been influential in pastoral theology as a discipline addressed not only toward individual suffering but also advocacy and social change.

follow on that path would be to betray the One who is the source of our life and miss the proper goal of all our desires. It would also be a reckless squandering of my own soul."[19])

Philosophically, Ricoeur points out a flaw in presupposing a symmetry between forgetting and memory. Ricoeur bases this on his distinction between memories (the content of what we remember—*souvenirs*) and memory itself (*memoir*—the process of remembering, which may include an effortful attempt to remember, which he calls *anamnesis*), and between what is remembered and the awareness that something is forgotten—i.e., what he calls "memories *in reserve*" (analogous to memories that have either faded or been repressed). For Ricoeur, forgetting itself is a monument to having remembered, and therefore there can never be total erasure of memory. Traces always remain. To the question "Should we confess *in fine* something like a wish for a happy forgetting?"[20] Ricoeur therefore gives a more complex and ambiguous answer: there is no "carefree memory," only "Carefree memory *on the horizon of concerned memory*, the soul common to *memory that forgets and does not forget*."[21]

Clinically, I believe the exhortation to "forgive and forget"—even if only envisioned in a future End-time—may, in fact, set up an impossible agenda that reinforces some form of psychological splitting to accomplish—a victim/survivor would have to split off fear, anger, hate, and more, in order to fully "forget" his or her abuse.[22] Volf here seems to be conflating the emotion of love (as in *eros* or *philia*) with the commandment of non-retaliation represented by the Greek word *agape*. I do believe that Christ's call to "turn the other cheek" was a call to non-violence, as in non-retaliation and refraining from vengeance. At the same time, I do not believe it is a call to passivity or trying to "like" one's abuser. (On the contrary, the relevant biblical passage has been thoughtfully interpreted to mean non-violent resistance against one's persecutors.[23])

Volf and Ricoeur both reflect in depth on the issue of forgiveness in relation to memory and forgetting, and a detailed examination of their differing arguments exceed the scope of this paper. To address this only very

19. Volf, *The End of Memory*, 17.
20. Ricoeur, *Memory, History, Forgetting*, 500.
21. Ibid.; emphasis added.
22. For more views on forgiveness from a clinical perspective, see also Sharon Lamb and Jeffrie G. Murphy, eds., *Before Forgiving: Cautionary Views of Forgiveness in Psychotherapy* (Oxford: Oxford University Press, 2002).
23. Walter Wink, "Neither Passivity nor Violence: Jesus' Third Way (Matt. 5:38-42)," in W. M. Swartley, ed., *The Love of Enemy and Nonretaliation in the New Testament* (Louisville: Westminster John Knox, 1992) 102-25.

briefly, I have argued since my earlier work on violence against women in the 1980s and 90s that forgiveness is a gift of grace, not a work on the part of the victim.[24] Further, "reconciliation" should be reframed as a communal rather than individual process:

> It is, finally, in community that we are all called to account. Power-in-community, whether it is a nurturing, caretaking power-for, an interpersonal power-with, or a charismatic power-within, is power authorized by the whole people. Violence against women is not only an abuse of individual person, but a violation of trust and a rupturing of right relation with the entire community.
>
> When viewed in this light, insisting upon the forgiveness of an individual perpetrator by an individual victim misses the point. Even if such forgiveness were accomplished, if it takes place in private, or relatively so, the wound to the community is not healed. Deep change must put down roots and when those roots go deep into the earth, the whole earth is rearranged by their movement. This is the thorough change, not of individual forgiveness, but of reconciliation [the word for the biblical Greek *apokatallásso*, which means thorough-going transformation.][25]

To the extent that reconciliation is human work, even if empowered by God, it is *communal* work—the working together of communities to forge peace and right relationship, without forgetting the past or erasing differences, akin to the postcolonial notion of "hybridity" in which the oppressed and oppressors meet around negotiated terms for justice and mutual influence. This differs significantly, I believe, from individuals striving for interpersonal forgiveness (which in any case, I believe theologically and with good biblical foundations to be God's work, not our own, and the subjective experience of having forgiven to be a gift of grace, not works' righteousness.)

From a relational-psychoanalytic perspective, I would also argue against a straight line progression of healing from denial, to acknowledgement of victimization, to empowered survivor identity. Rather, I would like to propose that there is no single, univocal identity to be achieved as an arrival point, or one normative psychological "position" that characterizes recovery from trauma. On the contrary, I believe the effort to remain in a singular identity or regulative position is problematic for mental and

---

24. Cooper-White, *The Cry of Tamar*, 2nd ed., esp. "Conclusion: On Forgiveness and Reconciliation," esp. 258–259. See also Cooper-White, "Forgiveness: Grace, not Work," *Journal for Preachers* special issue on forgiveness, ed. T. Erskine Clarke and Walter Brueggemann, 32/2 (2009) 16–23. [Ch. 10, this volume.]

25. Ibid., 259–260.

emotional health and healing. To insist upon a normative arrival point for healing may well be to split off aspects of one's self/selves, in a Kleinian paranoid-schizoid mode.[26]

Instead, drawing on the idea of normative multiplicity as a model for mental, interpersonal, and social/political health, I have come increasingly to believe that all three self-states—denial, victim, and survivor—as well as many *more*(!)—remain a part of a survivor's complex identity. And none of these three, moreover, is a monolithic state.

Denial lessens as traumatic memories emerge and are processed, but denial remains an important ongoing coping mechanism. Who could hold everything in mind all the time without going mad? Dissociation and even repression are necessary defenses and a regulative aspect of everyday living, negotiated in an ongoing pattern and flux of consciousness and unconsciousness.

The identity of "victim" may initially emerge out of denial in the form of total vulnerability and dependence, and for a time, may claim a stance of purity and innocence. This, too, is untenable long-term. As psychologist Sharon Lamb has pointed out:

> The problem with wanting to see victims as absolutely pure and perpetrators as absolutely evil is that few in either group actually live up (or down) to these expectations. In order for our prescribed story line to work, they would need to transform themselves into our view of them. And if they cannot change themselves to fit into our molds of purity and monstrosity then we tend to blame the victims more, the perpetrators less, and sometimes even reverse blame by holding the victim (who may be more privileged, intelligent, and sane) ultimately responsible and seeing the perpetrator (who may come from a disadvantaged background, be less intelligent, and less sane) as ultimately a victim. Our expectations of victims force them to paint a public picture of themselves as more innocent and less self-blaming than they actually are.[27]

---

26. E.g., Melanie Klein, "Notes on Some Schizoid Mechanisms" (1946), in *Melanie Klein: Envy and Gratitude and Other Works, 1946–1963*, ed. Robert Money-Kyrle (New York: Free Press, 1975) 1–24. See also Thomas H. Ogden, *The Primitive Edge of Experience* (Northvale, NJ: Aronson, 1989).

27. Sharon Lamb, *The Trouble with Blame: Victims, Perpetrators, and Responsibility* (Cambridge: Harvard University Press, 1996) 88–89. Lamb also makes the point that "The current overemphasis on victimization and the concomitant overpurification of victims have actually been helpful to perpetrators looking to escape responsibility. Through all-embracing victim's rights movement, where victims can be rendered into passive, incapacitated shells of people whose acts are seen not as emanating from any

In the words of feminist pastoral theologian Jeanne Hoeft,

> Another area for consideration in pastoral relationships is the way in which ministers of pastoral care and victims themselves construct the category 'victim.' With the heightened awareness of the widespread problem of abuse and its effects on victims, 'victim' has, in many ways, become an identity category lacking in ambiguity ... To be a 'victim' has come to mean that one has no responsibility for the situation that has victimized them, that one cannot also be a 'perpetrator,' that one must always be helped but not confronted or held accountable ... [W]hile it was once important for the purpose of heightening public awareness to stress the harm done to individual women by abuse it is now used to pathologize (post trauma) victims and to test for the validity of their victimhood ... "Here, the image of the victim is one who is pure, innocent, blameless, and free of problems (before the abuse)."[28]

Hoeft advocates for "[a] pastoral care of resistance" that "must attend to the exclusions made in attempts to categorize and identify victims."[29] Victims, even in the midst of their traumatization, have some agency and often do find ways to resist—although such resistance will be circumscribed by the culture in which their experience is embedded, and the socio-political systems that perpetuate injustice and the inequality of power. Especially in situations of extreme helplessness and threat, dissociation itself may be the only form of resistance available—as resistance is not only a conscious, but also, often, an unconscious process.

In the process of healing from trauma, the sense of oneself as "victim" may gradually shift away from the center of identity as healing and transformation take place in the container of the therapeutic relationship and

---

self within, but as mere reactions to the abuse and victimization suffered, perpetrators who were once victims themselves can now escape blame" (8). See also Lamb, ed., *New Versions of Victims: Feminists Struggle with the Concept* (New York: New York University Press, 1999), and Lamb and Murphy, eds., *Before Forgiving*. Feminist theologian Christine E. Gudorf similarly cautioned against romanticizing victims of oppression, in *Victimization: Examining Christian Complicity* (Philadelphia: Trinity, 1992). See also Keshgegian, *Time for Hope: Practices for Living in Today's World* (New York: Continuum, 2008) 110.

28. Jeanne Hoeft, *Agency, Culture, and Human Personhood: Pastoral Theology and Intimate Partner Violence* (Eugene, OR: Pickwick, 2009) 162–63, also citing Lamb, "Constructing the Victim: Popular Images and Lasting Labels," in Lamb, ed., *New Versions of Victims: Feminists Struggle with the Concept* (New York: New York University Press, 1999) 108.

29. Hoeft, *Agency, Culture, and Human Personhood*, 163.

in other contexts of safety and new life, toward a more empowered sense of self—the shift in identities from "victim" to "survivor." But the reality of past victimization does not magically evaporate. It will always be a part of a survivor's personal history, and as such, a part of who he or she continues to be. It may also become a *positive* source of wisdom for living, and empathy toward others who have been injured, and as such, a catalyst for action in the wider sphere of advocacy and work for justice.

The identity of "survivor," however, like that of "victim," is still problematic if it becomes frozen as a monolithic sense of one-self. If a survivor continues over time to foreground the experience of trauma to the exclusion of other foci of awareness, this is not helpful or salutary either to the survivor or to others with whom s/he relates. If my primary identity is "survivor," is trauma still at the center of my personal history in such a way that I am unable to define myself creatively in a myriad of other ways? I want a position *beyond* survivor that both retains the history of trauma and resistance, and the empowerment that the term "survivor" implies, but that also makes room for entirely new possibilities that neither deny nor focus exclusively upon past injuries in the formation of who I am today.

Both Kesgegian and Volf are intuiting such a further identity formation where transcendence is possible, albeit in very different ways.[30] Volf does so by attempting to cut off negative feelings toward the oppressor, while Keshgegian points to a more holistic moving-through in which nothing is lost, but more becomes possible. In her own words, she describes "an on-going multiple memorative practice that consists of remembering victimization, remembering survival, and remembering one's larger life narrative . . . three strands being woven and held together." She also claims "memory work as communal and socio-political."[31] Keshgegian's views are compatible with a relational-psychoanalytic perspective of multiplicity of the self as a network of subjectivities, as I have argued previously.[32]

A more linear model of healing (neither Keshgegian's nor my own) that progresses from denial to victim to survivor tends to reiterate and reinforce

---

30. See also Marilyn Nissim-Sabat, *Neither Victim nor Survivor: Thinking toward a New Humanity* (Lanham, MD: Lexington, 2009). Nissim-Sabat examines the category of "victim" as a construct of capitalism and Marxist anti-capitalist theory, and argues, drawing from both philosophy and contemporary psychoanalysis, for a "radical socialist-humanist" understanding that moves beyond simplistic, ideological notions of victimization to ones that can account for greater complexity and new collaborations for social change.

31. Keshgegian, personal communication, Nov. 29, 2010.

32. E.g., Cooper-White, *Many Voices: Pastoral Psychotherapy in Relational and Theological Perspective* (Minneapolis: Fortress, 2007), and *Braided Selves: Collected Essays on Multiplicity of God and Persons* (Eugene, OR: Cascade Books, 2011).

monolithic positions of identity, whereas in a conception of multiplicity of the self/selves, all these positions can co-exist in varying proportions, moving from background to foreground in relation to contextual pressures and seductions. They also can co-exist alongside many other creative possibilities for self-identification—from a narrative point of view, we are all, within ourselves, multiple authors of multiple stories about what we intuit about our pasts, what we "re-member." The flux from one self-state, one identity, to another is, moreover, always in|fluenced by other persons with whom we relate, both past and present, and the larger social and cultural context in which we live. I am therefore advocating for a model of healing understood as expansion of the self without leaving anything behind. Such a model of expansion of the self/selves makes more space for new directions in living, greater openness to others, and a widened capacity for empathy—without losing sight of the necessity for compassion for one's own inner, wounded, fearful, and angry self-states, and the concomitant need for self-care as an inherent part of engaging in justice-making in the wider world.

Serene Jones, in her recent book *Trauma and Grace*, identifies this movement in theological terms, as the expansive arrival of grace:

> Fully, we are undone and yet also held together in the strong grip of divine compassion. Then comes the third surprising moment. At the same instant that you are undone and held, you are thrown wide open. With each breath and needle prick, the world around you and within you becomes more spacious and boundlessly present to you ... Theologically cast, the moment enacts the embodied grace feeling of accepting your life as a gift and a promise, and living in the expansive sense of time and space that this gift provides. In full abundance, this grace strengthens the capacity to act at the very same time it invites you to fuller love of neighbor and ever-deepening love of the God who both frees and holds.[33]

It is also critical to remember that identities, wounded, healing, and beyond, are not formed in the isolation of intrapsychic development, or even just in the matrix of individual relationships—however therapeutic and transformative these may be. As Hoeft has pointed out, identities are formed in and through the larger culture in which they are embedded:

> [T]he boundaries between internal and external are called into question since psyche/body/culture are identified as made of and by each other. Agency arises in that construction, not as

---

33. Serene Jones, *Trauma and Grace: Theology in a Ruptured World* (Louisville: Westminster John Knox, 2009) 160–61.

the self-determined action of an autonomous subject but as the ambiguous working of the dynamic of power of interrelatedness that both constrains and enables the activity of the subject.[34]

The personal *is* political—in perhaps more interpenetrating ways than the originators of this slogan in the 1970s could have envisioned. To quote Hoeft again:

> There are victims and there are perpetrators; both act but the extent to which each can act in resistance varies according to the political regulations for what it means to be a subject, male/female, wife/husband, married/partnered, dependent/independent, making love/making war. The extent to which one 'has' agency is linked to the extent to which an act of the subject is recognized. The terms of 'choice' to act or not act in particular ways are set by political structures and ideologies that determine what choices are allowed, how they will be received, the costs and benefits at stake, and even which choices are conceivable.[35]

## On Memory as a Function of Public Theology

Finally, what are the implications of this revised pastoral-clinical perspective for theology? Just as Judith Herman (rightly, I believe) has insisted that individual healing cannot take place without a larger social and political context of awareness and advocacy for justice, theology—including pastoral and practical theology—is challenged to consider how our theological constructions actively contribute to the remembering and righting of injustice—or, as theology is always a product of culture itself, do our theologies simply aid and abet the "active process of forgetting" against which Herman cautions? In this regard, I don't think Volf and I are so much at odds in terms of the practical and ethical application of our theological positions in this life, here and now. However, I find myself challenging Volf's ideas of the "logic of grace," as it leads to an eschatological reconciliation in which there is no more memory of suffering.

To come full circle, back to denial, can the theological desire for purity—even an envisioned future or eschatological purity, or even if conceived in *kairos* rather than linear *chronos* time—ever be fully distinguished from the ubiquitous human desire for denial of pain (including collective, social pain, going back to Herman)? Theology, as well as individual psychology,

34. Hoeft, *Agency, Culture, and Human Personhood*, 151.
35. Ibid., 165.

must give up the purity of Klein's paranoid-schizoid position, to enter the tragic dimensionality of the depressive position in which all experiences can be known and held in creative tension. Such a view of the complexity of the moral life incorporates what feminist theologian Wendy Farley has identified as the classical tragic components to human suffering: finitude, conflict, and fragility.[36] This is not to abandon ethical responsibility or to collapse into a claim of perfect purity and innocence (a real peril of the victim identity, as Volf points out). Ethics governs how one behaves toward the other (and this certainly could encompass even one's own persecutors, choosing, for example, not to seek revenge or retribution), but it also stands firm on the truth/truths of one's own experience, as one continually forms and reforms understandings of it—without collapsing back into denial or attempting to "forgive and forget." Ethics *also* includes a demand for compassion toward oneself—with all one's personal history of both joy *and suffering*. The first, and perhaps most difficult *reconciliation* is among warring parts of one's own psyche. Tragic theology and relational psychoanalysis together suggest an ethical capacity to hold together the realities of both good and evil—to quote another feminist theologian, Kristine Rankka:

> What a tragic view of reality and suffering might do, for example, is move one from self-blame or from the projection of responsibility to change things outside oneself to a more mature realization of one's own appropriate responsibility within a context of limitation and finitude.[37]

The depressive position relinquishes, albeit with sadness, the possibility of perfection, and acknowledges the seeming inextricability of evil from the very fabric of the good, and the ever-present reality of suffering, at least from this side of the Eschaton. The grief work involved in such healing flows together with the grief work involved in adopting the tragic in our theologies.[38] Our theological work, through the depressive position, turns away from abstract argumentation about the nature of good and evil and visions of a perfect Heaven in some other realm. Tragic theology does not attempt

---

36. Wendy Farley, *Tragic Vision and Divine Compassion: A Contemporary Theodicy* (Louisville: Westminster John Knox, 1990) 27–31; see also Kristine Rankka, *Women and the Value of Suffering: An Aw(e)ful Rowing Toward God* (Collegeville, MN: Liturgical, 1998), esp. 174–81; Edward Farley, *Good and Evil: Interpreting a Human Condition* (Minneapolis: Fortress, 1990); Flora Keshgegian, *Time for Hope*, 96–127.

37. Kristine Rankka, *Women and the Value of Suffering: An Aw(e)ful Rowing Toward God* (Collegeville, MN: Liturgical, 1998) 196.

38. Ricoeur affirms the close relationship between mourning and memory, including an in-depth discussion of Freud's *Mourning and Melancholia* in dialogue with other sources, ancient and modern (*Memory, History, Forgetting*, 69–80).

to split off the most brutal and horrific aspects of our own experiences, but, rather, focuses our work on compassionate solidarity with the suffering and concrete acts of healing. As Jürgen Moltmann wrote in *The Trinity and the Kingdom*, "the question of theodicy is *not a speculative question*; it is a critical one . . . [the question] is the open wound of life in his world."[39] (emphasis added) Jones sees recovery and transcendence in the creative tension between two "habits of spirit": "mourning and wonder."[40] At the very end of her book, she asserts:

> This is a profoundly *presentist* vision of life, *landing us hard in the here and now*: to be saved is *not to be taken elsewhere*. It is to be awakened—to mourn and to wonder. And to stand courageously on the promise that grace is sturdy enough to hold it all—you, me, and every broken, trauma-ridden soul that wanders through our history. To us all, love comes. (emphasis added)[41]

Whatever "Heaven" or the final redemption of time may be or not be, eschatological symbols have a profound impact on the way people believe and behave *in the present*.[42] As we "remember the future,"[43] we shape the present in ways that can be either healing or collusive with present systems of abuse and injustice. I should confess here, probably, that I don't believe in a concrete future Heaven (or Hell). But I do believe that we are held by God's unfathomable love, both "now and in the hour of our death."[44] As God holds *all* the parts of who we are now—complicated, aching, wounded, healing, hopeful, angry, fearful, loving, hating, zealous and at peace—nothing that has composed who we are in this life is lost in God's *oikos*, God's economy.[45]

39. Moltmann, *The Trinity and the Kingdom*, trans. Margaret Kohl (Minneapolis: Fortress, 1993) 49.

40. Jones, *Trauma and Grace*, 161.

41. Ibid., 165.

42. Volf acknowledges that his "thought experiment" has such implications: "Theology is different [from the hard sciences]. It does not simply explain. It proposes a way of life—and one that sometimes crosses our expectations" (142n34).

43. Borrowing this term from David Hogue, *Remembering the Future, Imagining the Past: Story, Ritual, and the Human Brain* (Cleveland: Pilgrim, 2003), and Letty Russell's term "memory of the future," in *Human Liberation in a Feminist Perspective: A Theology* (Philadelphia: Westminster, 1979) 72ff, 133ff. Volf also refers briefly to "remembering the future" (100), citing Reinhard Koselleck, *Futures Past: On the Semantics of Historical Time*, trans. Keith Tribe (Cambridge: MIT Press, 2004) 287–88. I also am reminded of Letty Russell's argument for the eschatological "authority of the future" in which justice is at the center of God's "household," in *Household of Freedom: Authority in Feminist Theology* (Louisville: Westminster John Knox, 1987).

44. Quote from the prayer *Ave Maria*.

45. It is interesting to note that Volf himself describes an inner multiplicity when he

Every hair on our heads is counted, and every memory cherished and redeemed as a part of who we are. (When Jesus appeared to the disciples after his resurrection, he still bore the marks of his wounds on his hands, feet, and side!—John 20:20, 27[46])

Rather than envisioning a future Heaven in which all the bad things that have happened to us are erased, I choose a Heaven in which those bad things are healed, and no longer have power over us or those who have harmed us. Whatever may await us in the fulfillment of time, I believe it will leave *nothing* behind. An eschatological vision of ultimate reconciliation will be large enough to encompass it all. "Right remembering"/"re-membering" is ultimately God's work, not ours—but the hope we envision for such re-membering matters greatly for the way we try to cooperate with God's present work of the mending of creation (*tikkun 'olam*) in the here and now. We need both a psychology and a theology that do justice to memory, and enlist memory to do justice. Both psychologically and theologically, there must be monuments in our Heaven(s)!

---

writes: "[E]very time I wrote about 'loving' Captain G., a small-scale rebellion erupted in my soul. 'I love my parents and relatives, I love my wife and children, I love pets and wild geese. I might even love nosy neighbors and difficult colleagues, but I *don't love abusers*—I just don't and never will,' screamed the leader of my internal insurrection. And at times as I wrote it would not have taken much to make me switch sides . . . except that loving those who do me harm was precisely the hard path on which Jesus called me to follow him—a path that reflects more than any other the nature of his God and mine. Not to follow on that path would be to betray the One who is the source of our life and miss the proper goal of all our desires. It would also be a reckless squandering of my own soul" (*The End of Memory*, 17). The latter half of the paragraph, in light of multiplicity of the self, reads almost like an exorcism. From the perspective of relational psychoanalysis, and tragic theology, however, there would be no need to try to eliminate the "internal insurrection," but rather to try to understand with empathy its own piece of truth. Such self-compassion often leads to a modulation of affect, and new options for how to proceed with ethical living.

46. Thanks to both Martha Moore Keish and Michael Cooper-White for making this connection.

# 13

## Sexual Violence and Justice
*Toward an Ethic and Theology of Sexual Justice*

2013[1]

### Introduction

IN TAHRIR SQUARE, CAIRO, Egypt, a group of young boys chase women through crowds of political protestors, taunting them with sexual epithets. The *PBS News Hour* recently reported, "While trying to participate in recent protests and the shaping of their country's future, nearly 100 Egyptian women have been sexually assaulted in Tahrir Square by attackers who may be systematically planning their crimes."[2]

> Such sweet boys full of energy and fun. They have just been chasing a young woman up the street. The interviewer asks them why. "If a lady is respectable, no one will harass her," says a kid in red. The others pile in. "Why do they wear short skirts or tight trousers?" "Some young women, when we flirt with them, they smile." That's how it starts. This is how it ends. A mob attacks a young woman on the corner of Tahrir Square . . . This is one of more than a hundred assaults in Tahrir Square during last week's demonstrations. This is the very place. Women still come to the square, but it's dangerous. This corner of Tahrir Square has become notorious for attacks on women. . . .
> And the most horrific thing I have heard is that these attacks are planned, and, sometimes, women think that the men

---

1. Orig. publ. as "Violence and Justice" in *The Oxford Handbook of Theology, Sexuality and Gender*, ed. Adrian Thatcher (Oxord: Oxford University Press, 2015) 487–504.

2. Lindsey Hilsum, "In Tahrir Square, Recent Protests Have Been Scene of Rampant Sexual Assault," *PBS News Hour*, July 11, 2013, https://www.pbs.org/newshour/show/recent-protests-have-been-scene-of-rampant-sexual-assault#transcript.

coming for them are trying to save them from being assaulted, but in fact they take them away and attack them again.[3]

In seemingly peaceful fields across the United States, migrant women workers are repeatedly sexually assaulted and harassed by employers exploiting their poverty, sometimes illegal status, and fears of deportation, loss of work, or further violence to themselves and their families:

> In Molalla, Ore., a worker at a tree farm accused her supervisor of repeatedly raping her over the course of several months in 2006 and 2007, often holding gardening shears to her throat. If she complained to anyone, he allegedly told her, he would fire her and kill her entire family."[4]

In a news investigation based on thousands of documents and interviews from California to Florida to the Pacific Northwest, University of California journalists documented that

> Hundreds of female agricultural workers have complained to the federal government about being raped and assaulted, verbally and physically harassed on the job, while law enforcement has done almost nothing to prosecute potential crimes. In virtually all of the cases reviewed, the alleged perpetrators held positions of power over the women. Despite the accusations, these supervisors have remained on the job for years without fear of arrest.[5]

Thousands more individuals, mostly women, experience sexual violence every day, including rape, assault, stalking and sexual harassment. The World Health Organization, extrapolating from research in thirty-five countries, estimates that between 10% and 30% of women worldwide are sexually assaulted, and from 10% to 52% of women are victims of intimate partner violence.[6] Literally millions of women and young girls are kidnapped and held captive as sex slaves in a vast underground network of sex trafficking.[7] In the U.S. alone, not just in dark alleys and in parks at night

3. Ibid.
4. Bernice Yeung and Grace Rubenstein, "Female Workers Face Rape, Harassment in U.S. Agriculture Industry," June 25, 2013, Center for Investigative Reporting, University of California at Berkeley. http://www.pbs.org/wgbh/pages/frontline/social-issues/rape-in-the-fields/female-workers-face-rape-harassment-in-u-s-agriculture-industry/.
5. Ibid.
6. World Health Organization (2005). *WHO Multi-Country Study on Women's Health and Domestic Violence against Women: Summary Report.* Geneva: WHO, 1, online at http://www.who.int/gender/violence/who_multicountry_study/summary_report/summary_report_English2.pdf.
7. United Nations Population Fund, "Ending Violence against Women and Girls,"

but on dates, at work, and in the sanctity of their own homes and bedrooms, close to 1 in every 5 women experience attempted or completed rape in their lifetimes, as well as 3 in every 100 men.[8] In spite of recent improvements in U.S. law enforcement resulting in significant decreases in reported rapes, approximately 350,000 rapes and sexual assaults are still reported to police annually (U.S. FBI 2009a, 2009b) with many more left unreported,[9] and over 200,000 women are raped each year by a husband or intimate partner.[10] Sexual assaults, especially by acquaintances, is still estimated by rape crisis experts to be under-reported by as much as 90%, for reasons ranging from fear of revictimization by the judicial process, fear of reprisal by the offender, or shame and humiliation compounded by a culture that still too often blames victims and makes excuses for the perpetrators. In U.S. society, experts estimate that only 1/4 of rape suspects are arrested, only slightly over half are convicted,[11] and when factoring in under-reporting, "only 3% of rapists will ever serve a day in prison."[12] In spite of slowly improving arrest rates, there are still more deterrents to victims' reporting sexual assaults than to offenders' committing them.

Sexuality is a domain of experience that has been variously described as embodied, deeply personal, intimate, ecstatic, and even sacred. Yet precisely because of some of these qualities and the emotions associated with them, it is also a domain that entails not only pleasure but also the possibility of intrusion, coercion, harassment, violation, assault, pain, and even terror.

---

Ch. 3 in *State of the World Population 2000* (New York: United Nations, 2000), Ch. 3, online at http://www.unfpa.org/swp/2000/english/ch03.html.

8. Patricia Tjaden and Nancy Thoennes, *Extent, Nature, and Consequences of Violence against Women: Findings from the National Violence against Women Survey*, NCJ 181867, National Institute of Justice and Centers for Disease Control and Prevention, November, 2000, pp. iii, 13, online at https://www.ncjrs.gov/pdffiles1/nij/181867.pdf. For more statistics and information on prevalence studies, see also Cooper-White, *The Cry of Tamar: Violence against Women and the Church's Response*, 2nd ed. (Minneapolis: Fortress, 2012) 2, 107.

9. Cooper-White, *The Cry of Tamar*, 265n9.

10. Tjaden and Thoennes, *Extent, Nature, and Consequences of Violence against Women*, 9–10.

11. National Center for Policy Analysis (1999). *Crime and Punishment in America, 1999*. Washington, DC: NCPA; U.S. Department of Justice, Bureau of Justice Statistics (1998). "Crime and Justice in the United States and in England and Wales, 1981–1996," https://bjs.gov/content/pub/pdf/cjusew96.pdf.

12. Harriet Jameson, "Reporting Rates." Washington, DC: Rape, Abuse & Incest National Network (RAINN), May 2, 2013. http://www.rainn.org/print/288. [Website no longer avaiable. For more recent account of under-reporting see U.S. Bureau of Justice Statistics, Police Response to Domestic Violence, p. 5, online at https://www.bjs.gov/index.cfm?ty=dcdetail&iid=245. —PCW 2018]

It is a ground on which wars are fought (including intrapsychic, familial, social, political, and even military) over issues of desire and fulfillment, personal morality and boundaries, social mores and taboos, groundrules for procreation and child-rearing, commodification and exploitation, politics of privacy, and civil and criminal safeguards. Because social constructions of "sex" and "gender" are so closely identified, sexuality is also intertwined with definitions of gender—including psychological identifications, performativity, social norms and transgressions, and access to privilege and power. By extension, these categories further implicate race, age, ability/disability, and virtually all arenas of embodied experience. Therefore, sexuality, and in particular sexual violence, constitute a domain that calls for ethical reflection regarding multi-dimensional and multi-textured issues of sexual justice, and in particular, the use and abuse of power.

## Sex and Power

In the anti-rape movement in the 1970s, a pithy slogan signaled the gist of the feminist political analysis of sexual assault: "Rape is about power, not sex." This saying contradicted the (still common) myth that men cannot control their sexual impulses once aroused. It rightly shifted the definition of rape from uncontrollable lust to inexcusable violence, in which sexual body parts are used to dominate and subjugate victims, but the primary motivation is physical force, not sexual desire. As an object lesson, we taught that any body part could be used or targeted for tenderness or violence: a hand can gently caress or bring healing, or it can be made into a fist to pummel another person; a penis can be an instrument of mutual desire and love, or a weapon. Sexual assault is an extreme form of violence precisely *because* erogenous zones of the body are experienced as the most intimate and vulnerable; however, the primary *purpose* of sexual assault is not to discharge sexual tension, but to conquer, humiliate, and violate. The victim of sexual assault is not an "object of desire," but a literal object of domination and dehumanization.

At the same time, the statement that "rape is about power, *not* sex," perhaps deserves further clarification and examination. As a slogan, it conveys an important message sharply and memorably. However, there are complexities involving both power and sex that invite further analysis. More nuanced substitutes might lose the pithy utility of a slogan, but might be helpful in understanding the ways in which sex, power, aggression, and violence can overlap and intertwine. Simple slogans, further, tend toward simplistic solutions. The saying "rape is about power, not sex," helpfully combats myths about sexual assault, but the solution it implies simply to work to stop perpetrators from abusing power. While this is, indeed, a core insight of prevention and education programs, perpetrators rarely stop abusing power simply because they are taught or told to do so. Neither re-education/therapy nor containment—mainly through incarceration (where further sexual violence often occurs)—have a strong track record in ending sexual assault.

What, then, would a more nuanced statement be? The following are three possible alternatives that are not meant to undo the important insights of the anti-rape movement, nor to offer an all-encompassing substitutions, but to bring greater complexity to bear on the causes and dynamics of sexual injustice: "Rape is about power, *and* sex"; "Rape is about power, *using* sex"; and "Rape is about power, gender, and race."

Rape is about power, and sex.

The main objection to the original slogan is that one cannot escape the fact that sexual assault involves sexual acts. "Of course rape is sexual," some argue, "after all, it's *sexual* assault." If rape is about power, *not* sex, how do we account for the sexual arousal of the offender?

Physiologically, there is a link between sex and aggression—intuited by Freud as the two primary instincts or "drives" of human nature.[13] Freud viewed sex (libido) and aggression as having their origins, respectively, in the instincts for procreation and for self-defense or self-preservation. Viewed more broadly, if sex is the drive for pleasure, which (at least some of the time) is connected with the potential to propagate the species, aggression is the drive to have an impact, to make a difference in one's environment, to move forward and to live for oneself. Pastoral theologian Kathleen Greider has pointed out that especially in Christian theology aggression has been branded as negative and sinful, a sign of human brokenness. However, she argues:

> The brokenness in our aggression is perhaps most easily identified in its two extremes: violence and passivity, or lack of vitality. At one extreme, aggression explodes into incalculable incidents of hatred and violence. When violent, we are not adequately in charge of our aggression and overuse it, which results in injury and sometimes death . . . At the other extreme, aggression

---

13. Sigmund Freud, *Beyond the Pleasure Principle,* in James Strachey, ed. and trans., *The Standard Edition of the Complete Psychological Works of Sigmund Freud* (London: Hogarth, 1955), Vol. 18, 1–64 (orig. publ. 1923).

implodes, a major source of our passion and power drains away, and we are left with too little vitality and vulnerable to passivity. When passive, we are not adequately in charge of our aggression, and underuse it, resulting in ineffectualness.[14]

Sexual activity requires a certain degree of aggression—well modulated between the extremes of violence and passivity—in order for anything to happen. Initiative is required to move sexual relating from the realm of fantasy to mutual activity. Healthy sexual activity requires energy and agency—that is, healthy aggression. Libido, as life force or energy for life, therefore encompasses both sex and aggression, and is necessary to all forms of creativity.

There is an important difference, of course, between healthy aggression and violence. Without aggression, we would have no motivation to get up and do anything at all. Violence, on the other hand, as the word implies, involves violation. Rape and sexual assault are by definition violent, not merely aggressive, because the offender forces unwanted sexual touching or penetration on the other—who becomes a victim. Here physiological explanations for sexual violence become troubling with regard to human nature, and perhaps especially masculinity. There is some emerging scientific research that identifies sex and aggression as involving the same neuronal networks in the brain.[15] This view converges with earlier psychoanalytic theories suggesting that sexual fantasies and behaviors labeled as "perversions" exist on a spectrum with "normal" sexuality, rather than belonging to entirely separate domains of pathology vs. health. Robert Stoller, in particular, whose writings focused on gender identity and the dynamics of erotic life, even proposed that aggression in the form of *hostility* (i.e., aggression directed toward another person) was a necessary ingredient in healthy sexual excitement—albeit in minute proportions, comingled with love and intimacy:

> as one proceeds along the continuum toward less use of hostile mechanisms, one is proceeding from the bizarre (psychotic) through the character disorders we diagnose as perversions and on into the range of the normative, where the mechanisms propelling the excitement are energized by hostility but where affection and capacity for closeness also thrive. At the far end of the spectrum is a small group of contented people who enjoy

---

14. Greider, Kathleen, *Reckoning with Aggression: Theology, Violence, and Vitality* (Louisville: Westminster John Knox, 1997) 13–14.

15. Ewen Calloway, "Sex and Violence Linked in the Brain," *Nature: International Weekly Journal of Science*, Feb. 9, 2011, online at http://www.nature.com/news/2011/110209/full/news.2011.82.html.

(even in fantasy) loving, unhostile relationships with others and who are not so frightened by intimacy that they must fetishize the other person. For them the other is a person; they do not have to dehumanize. If hostility is present in their excitement, it is microscopic... Is it, nonetheless, essential? ... Perhaps this dynamic [of tension and climax] holds for all excitements, rites of passage, myths, and miracles. What we call "sublimation" may be a state that has been non-hostilely depleted of hostility.[16]

Stoller is quick to observe, however, that the amount of hostility present in fantasy and modulated in healthy sexuality is not equivalent to violence: "we should not equate the small amount of hostility that powers a daydream with the much greater degree of hostility needed for hostile acts in the real world."[17]

If healthy sexuality, then, contains at least a minute component of aggression, does the converse also hold, that violence contains an element of sexual arousal? The answer from both social and biological sciences would seem to be a qualified "Yes." This is in no way to undermine the essential insight of the anti-rape movement that rape is primarily about power—since rape and sexual assault, and other forms of sexual abuse and exploitation are defined by the use of coercion, unequal power and authority, and/or physical force. Yet the phenomenon of physiological arousal to violence exists, and if there is a tincture of hostility in loving sex, there is more than a tincture of sexual excitement in violence—perhaps especially male violence. While neither a single biological explanation (e.g., it's all about testosterone) nor a simplistic social analysis that *all* men are socialized to use violence[18] are sufficient to explain the connection between sex and violence, history attests to a long record of sexual excitement in violent settings that are not primarily intended as erotic, particularly in war. Numerous ancient frescoes and vases depict scenes of men with full erections competing in athletic races (e.g., Panathenaic Amphora, c. 530 BCE),[19] chasing after women, and raping or murdering women in enemy tribes (e.g., the "Tydeus and Ismene" Amphora, c. 560 BCE).[20] In ancient Rome, gladiators were imbued with sexual magne-

---

16. Robert Stoller, *Sexual Excitement: Dynamics of Erotic Life* (1979; reprint, London: Karnac, 2012) 31–32.

17. Ibid., 31.

18. For a more nuanced multi-variate model, see Michele Harway and James M. O'Neill, *What Causes Male Violence against Women?* (Thousand Oaks, CA: Sage, 1999).

19. Metropolitan Museum of Art (2013). Panathenaic Amphora, c. 530 BCE. New York. http://www.metmuseum.org/toah/works-of-art/14.130.12.

20. Musée du Louvre (2013). "Tydeus and Ismene" Amphora, c. 560 BCE. Paris. http://www.hellenicaworld.com/Greece/Mythology/en/TydeusIsmeneLouvreE640.html.

tism even after death—new brides sought to have their hair parted by a spear, preferably dipped in the blood of a slain gladiator—and the word for sword, *gladius*, was common slang for penis.[21] Rape, military conquest, and colonization were intertwined in both rhetoric and image in the ancient world, and rape was a tool of domination by both men and gods.[22]

Women were regularly regarded worldwide as part of the "property" belonging to the enemy, and therefore were part of the "spoils of war" that went to the victor in the form of rape and sexual slavery. Only in the eighteenth century were efforts to respect the sanctity of the family and the rights of civilians, or non-combatants, commonly written into legal codes for the conduct of war in the west, although some attempts were made in the middle ages in Europe as well.[23] Only as recently as 2008 the United Nations classified rape as a "war tactic."[24] However, rape as a form of terrorizing the enemy and a crude and brutal form of reward for conquest reach back to the dawn of human history and persist in wars throughout the world today.[25] This long history of rape in war has fed a military culture of hyper-masculinity that, in turn, is all too prone in spite of a rhetoric of honor to turn a blind eye to sexual assault within the ranks of the military (an estimated 26,000 victims, both women and men, in 2012 alone[26]) and leads to sadistic acts of torture and sexualized degradation against enemies objectified as the "other," as in the prison at Abu Ghraib.[27]

21. Keith Hopkins, *Death and Renewal: Sociological Studies in Roman History*, Vol. 2 (Cambridge: Cambridge University Press, 1983) 12. The word *vagina*, which means "sheath" or "scabbard" in Latin was not used in the anatomical sense in ancient times, but the sword-and-covering etymology pertains to its first use in English, late seventeenth century—Douglas Harper "Vagina." *Online Etymology Dictionary*, 2013, online at http://dictionary.reference.com/browse/vagina/.

22. Carol Dougherty, *The Poetics of Colonization: From City to Text in Ancient Greece* (Oxford: Oxford University Press, 1993); Lin Foxhall and John Salmon, eds. *When Men Were Men: Masculinity, Power, and Identity in Classical Antiquity* (London: Routledge, 1999).

23. Kelly Dawn Askin, *War Crimes against Women: Prosecution in International War Crimes Tribunals* (The Hague: Nijhoff, 1997).

24. United Nations Security Council (2008). Resolution 1820, online at http://www.un.org/News/Press/docs/2008/sc9364.doc.htm/.

25. Askin, *War Crimes against Women*.

26. Jennifer Steinhauer, "Sexual Assaults in Military Raise Alarm in Washington," *New York Times*, May 7, 2013, online at http://www.nytimes.com/2013/05/08/us/politics/pentagon-study-sees-sharp-rise-in-sexual-assaults.html?pagewanted=all/.

27. *New York Times*, digest of articles on Abu Ghraib, 2013, online at http://topics.nytimes.com/top/news/international/countriesandterritories/iraq/abu_ghraib/index.html.

Sexual arousal to violence is more common than is often supposed or admitted.[28] It should be noted, in this regard, that male erections occur not only as arousal to pleasure, but to fear and more mundane urges such as the need to urinate.[29] At the same time, sexual excitement can be produced in direct connection with exposure to violence. That the connection between penises and swords, sex and war, is not relegated only to ancient times is attested by the very existence of the contemporary slang term "war boner" defined in the *Urban Dictionary* as "the process of an erection due to being aroused by machine gun fire, explosions, jet engines and large amounts of blood and gore"—as in "As I was massacring my opponents in COD I earned a chopper gunner and the sound of the chain and the propeller meshing together fueled my raging war boner ... Dude I noticed in the middle of *Apocalypse Now* you had a total war boner!"[30] To complicate the categories of sex, aggression, power, and violence, then, it must be acknowledged that there is often an element of sexual arousal in violence, as well as a well sublimated and modulated element of aggression, if not hostility, in healthy sexuality.

All too often, moreover, there is a dangerous fusion of sex and violence, not only in a hypermasculinized psychology of war, but also in pornography, and in mainstream cultural media.[31] This is where biology may entail a link between sexuality and aggression, but socialization can strongly enhance or incite a more dangerous merger of the two. Pornography is not obscene because it is too sexual, per se, but because it is dehumanizing. If *Eros* is love that includes physical passion but also includes the whole person, body and soul together, then the *erotic* is that life force that reaches out toward the other for intimacy, mutual creativity, and exchange. The erotic is, in the words of Audre Lorde, "a measure between the beginnings of our sense of self, and the chaos of our strongest feelings."[32] In contrast,

28. Neil Malamuth, Seymour Feshbach, and Yoram Jaffe, "Sexual Arousal and Aggression: Recent Experiments and Theoretical Issues," *Journal of Social Issues* 33/2 (1977) 110–33; http://www.sscnet.ucla.edu/comm/malamuth/pdf/77jsi33.pdf.

29. Sexual Medicine Society of North America, Inc. (SMSNA) "Male Erection Frequency," SexHealth Matters, 2013; http://www.sexhealthmatters.org/did-you-know/male-erection-frequency/.

30. Valley's Own (pseudonym) "War Boner," *Urban Dictionary*, April 5, 2011; https://www.urbandictionary.com/define.php?term=Warboner.

31. For further analysis, see Cooper-White, *The Cry of Tamar*, 64–82. This paragraph draws especially from 80–81.

32. Audre Lorde, "Uses of the Erotic: The Erotic as Power," in *Take Back the Night*, ed. Laura Lederer (New York: Harper Perennial, 1980) 296; Susan Griffin, *Pornography and Silence: Culture's Revenge against Nature* (New York: Harper & Row, 1981); Carter Heyward, *Touching Our Strength* (San Francisco: HarperSan Francisco, 1989);

pornography "is a direct denial of the power of the erotic, for it represents the suppression of true feeling. Pornography emphasizes sensation without feeling."[33] The erotic is relational, empathic, whole, spirited and imaginative; pornography is episodic, performance-oriented, fragmented, standardized, and addictive.[34] The root word *porne* has nothing to do with love—in classic Greek *porne* or *porneia* were sexual slaves held captive in low-cost brothels.[35] Pornography is obscene precisely because its aim is to deny and even murder the soul of those portrayed in it—by *de*eroticizing them, robbing them of their deepest life-giving and life-seeking energy.[36] These observations lead to the second alternative statement about rape, power and sex: that rape is about power *using* sex.

## Rape Is about Power, Using Sex

In an often cited typology of sex offenders developed in the late 1970s,[37] the "angry-hostile offender" was understood to be the type of rapist who used sexual assault to act out his anger and hostility toward women, while the power rapist used rape primarily to enforce dominance. The aim of the third type, the sadistic rapist, was explicitly to inflict pain and torture. However, all these typologies implicate power, and all forms of rape, sexual assault and abuse, stalking and harassment, are abuses of power using sexual language and/or contact as their medium—whether that power is physical force (including the use of weapons), psychological coercion, professional authority, or the use of other means such as alcohol, drugs, or threats to overcome a victim's resistance. Sexual violence is sexual*ized* violence—dominating power exercised through sexual words and deeds. Sexualized violence exists on a spectrum from seemingly "milder" forms of sexual harassment and exploitation (as in professionals crossing sexual boundaries with those over whom they have authority, for example, to hire and fire, teach, preach, or

---

Rita Nakashima Brock, *Journey by Heart: A Christology of Erotic Power* (New York: Crossroad, 1988).

33. Lorde, "Uses of the Erotic," 296.

34. Anthony Giddens, *The Transformation of Intimacy: Sexuality, Love and Eroticism in Modern Societies* (Stanford, CA: Stanford University Press, 1992) 119–20; Mary Eberstadt and Mary Anne Layden, eds., *The Social Costs of Pornography* (Princeton: Witherspoon Institute, 2010).

35. Maggie Hays, "Pornography: A Definition," https://www.againstpornography.org/definition.html. [Website no longer available.]

36. Griffin, op. cit.

37. Nicholas Groth, *Men Who Rape: The Psychology of the Offender* (New York: Perseus, 1979).

counsel), to stalking and threats, to sexual abuse and molestation, sexual assault, trafficking and sexual enslavement, and rape. The psychological impact of these behaviors, however, is not a simple series of gradations. All can cause trauma. The younger or more vulnerable the victim, and/or the more overpowering, overwhelming, and/or painful the act, the greater the victim's terrorization and often, as well, the greater her subsequent second-guessing, guilt, and self-blame. It does not really help to compare victimizations, since experiences of dehumanization, humiliation, confusion, terror, and pain—emotional, mental, and physical—all fall within a place in the psyche that survives at times by multiple self-numbing mechanisms of rationalization, fragmentation, rage, depression, and self-destructiveness. All such acts of violence are violations of the fundamental personhood of the victim, and are at their core an abuse of power in relation to another human being—which is a theological problem.[38]

No single etiology/ theory of causation for sexual violence fully accounts for its prevalence, or for its dehumanizing acts. "Single factor theories" that focused narrowly on particular biological, behavioral, or social causes have been found wanting by social scientists and law enforcement professionals.[39] Sexual violence is caused by a confluence of factors that lead a perpetrator to violating another person's humanity. These can include biological, developmental, environmental, cultural, and situational factors in combination with an offender's personal character formation, impairments, and vulnerabilities.[40] Abnormally high testosterone, relational deficits in early parenting (including but not limited to sexual abuse), violence and aggression learned from parents and/or others in the childhood environment, and a culture saturated in film and media images of sexualized violence may all contribute to damaging a child's developing sense of identity, self-esteem, self-control, capacity for empathy, and relationally directed sexual intimacy—although it should be cautioned that many adults experience some or all of these factors and do not become violent. Both internal and external factors are also considered important in the acting out of sexual domination: there must be an internal motivation involving fantasies of violation, but these must be further fa-

---

38. James Newton Poling, *The Abuse of Power: A Theological Problem* (Nashville: Abingdon, 1991).

39. Rachel West, "The Etiology of Sexual Offending Behavior and Sex Offender Typology: An Overview," Center for Sex Offender Management (CSOM), U.S. Dept. of Justice, 2013; www.csom.org/train/etiology.

40. William L. Marshall and Howard E. Barbaree, "An Integrated Theory of the Etiology of Sexual Offending," in Marshall, D. Richard Laws, and Barbaree, eds., *Handbook of Sexual Assault* (New York: Plenum, 1990) 257-75.

cilitated by opportunity (either discovered or premeditated). Often some disinhibition precedes the offender's final step of taking action—either by rationalizing the violence through objectification of the victim, and/or by using drugs, alcohol, pornography, or other means to desensitize himself from the meaning and impact of his desired violent behavior.[41]

Further, individuals who engage in sexual assault, rape, exploitation and harassment share a common trait of narcism which, either situationally or permanently, impairs their ability to feel empathy for their victims, or to fully comprehend the meaning and impact of their actions.[42] The sociopathic individual, defined by a complete lack of a social sense and conscience, is only the extreme version of the more garden variety narcissist who exploits and uses other persons because his own needs and wishes are the only ones he can see and feel. As the early British psychoanalyst and pediatrician D.W. Winnicott observed, the "antisocial" or sociopathic personality type is one who inwardly feels "the world owes me," often because of a very early childhood sense of some perceived goodness that was withheld or taken away.[43] While this does not fully explain individuals who for some hormonal or other physiological reason cannot control their sexual and aggressive impulses (e.g., due to traumatic head injury[44]), Winnicott's observation implicates not only individual parents and families, but entire communities and the wider society in our failure to provide the reasonable supports necessary to help households become places of safety and nurture, and, moreover, to become "crucibles of justice,"[45] fostering in children a sense of openness and generosity toward others in the wider world.

---

41. Neil Malamuth, Christopher Heavey, and Daniel Linz "Predicting Men's Antisocial Behavior against Women: The Interaction Model of Sexual Aggression," in Gordon C. Nagayama Hall, Richard Hirschman, John R. Graham, and Maira S. Zarazoga, eds., *Sexual Aggression: Issues in Etiology, Assessment, and Treatment* (Washington, DC: Taylor & Francis, 1993) 63–97.

42. Cooper-White, *Shared Wisdom: Use of the Self in Pastoral Care and Counseling* (Minneapolis: Fortress, 2004) 110–16, 172–80.

43. D. W. Winnicott, "The Antisocial Tendency," in Winnicott, *Through Paediatrics to Psycho-Analysis: Collected Papers* (New York: Basic Books, 1975) 306–15.

44. Theresa A. Gannon and Tony Ward, "Rape: Psychopathology and Theory," in D. Richard Laws and William T. O'Donohue, *Sexual Deviance: Theory, Assessment, and Treatment*, 2nd ed. (New York: Guilford, 2008) 356–83.

45. Herbert Anderson and Susan Johnson, *Regarding Children: A New Respect for Childhood and Families* (Louisville: Westminster John Knox, 1994).

## Rape Is about Power, Gender, and Race

The injustice of sexual abuse and assault is, therefore, also connected to the wider realm of injustice, including social and institutional structures of domination along the lines of gender, race, sexual orientation, class, and other systemic inequalities. Although a generous humanistic analysis would want us to equalize such demographic factors, and say that women are as prone to violence as men—"they just express it differently"—or that violence is color-blind, statistical research and studies of the specific dynamics of sexual violence (as well as all violent crime) consistently show that sexual and intimate partner violence are overwhelmingly perpetrated by men against women. And contrary to the myth of the Black rapist, statistics show that white men are three times more likely to be the perpetrators of sexual assaults (extrapolating from U.S. Bureau of Justice Statistics in 2008[46]).

Sexual violence, then, is unavoidably an issue not only of sexual words and acts, but of gender—in the vast majority, a crime of men against women. Reinforced and exacerbated by patriarchal myths about women as property, possessions, and conquests, sexual violence actually fits the definition of a hate crime, although in the U.S. it is not prosecuted as such. The distinguishing feature of a hate crime is that it is motivated by bias against an entire category of persons.[47] The U.S. Congress, however, still declines to include "women" in its list of protected categories: "race, religion, disability, ethnic origin and sexual orientation."[48] Nevertheless, given the vast preponderance of sexual violence directed by men against women, it is difficult to see how rape, sexual assault, and other forms of sexual violence do not constitute a gender-based hate crime. Gender is considered a protected characteristic in the legal codes of a number of European and other countries, including,

---

46. U.S. Department of Justice, Bureau of Justice Statistics (2011) "Personal Crimes of Violence, 2008"; https://www.bjs.gov/content/pub/pdf/cvus0802.pdf; U.S. Federal Bureau of Investigation (2009a). "2008 Crime in the United States," Table 1, http://www2.fbi.gov/ucr/cius2008/data/table_01.html; U.S. Federal Bureau of Investigation (2009b). "2008 Crime in the United States," Table 1a, http://www2.fbi.gov/ucr/cius2008/data/table_01a.html. [For updated crime statistics, see U.S. Department of Justice, Bureau of Justice Statistics (2016). Criminal Victimization Summary, online at www.bjs.gov/content/pub/pdf/cv16.pdf. —PCW 2018]

47. Office for Democratic Institutions and Human Rights, *Hate Crime Laws: A Practical Guide* (Warsaw, Poland: ODIHR, 2009) 16; http://www.osce.org/odihr/36426?download=true.

48. U.S. Federal Bureau of Investigation (2013) "Hate Crime—Overview"; http://www.fbi.gov/about-us/investigate/civilrights/hate_crimes/overview. Hate crime based on sexual orientation was added in 2009 (the Matthew Shepard and James Byrd, Jr., Hate Crimes Prevention Act).

for example, Canada and France.[49] Sexual violence, then, is fundamentally a violation of human rights, and needs to be addressed not only in relation to individual victims, but as a systemic and societal injustice.

## Toward an Ethic and Theology of Sexual Justice

No one of the alternative sayings described above entirely captures the motivation of perpetrators, nor the suffering of victims. Nor do the three alternative statements exhaust the possible understandings of sexual violation. What the alternatives do, perhaps, is point toward the need for a both an ethic of sexual behavior *and* an ethics of power. Further, as theologians, we need a theology that emphasizes the relationality of both God and humanity—to provide an adequate and appropriate foundation for an ethic of sexual justice.

### Sexual Ethics

Too often, sexual ethics have been reduced to traditional moral teaching about specific *acts* that are considered inherently taboo. These are presented in numerous cultures and religions, including the Judaeo-Christian biblical tradition, as deontological—"natural" laws and purity codes deriving from the very essence of life and goodness, even commanded by God. Yet in other ancient cultures, such as Rome, both homosexual and bisexual relationships were permitted as equal to heterosexual relationships for both gods and men, in part because they were thought to reinforce virtues of brotherly love, and to provide the social glue of a civil society.[50] Ancient "natural laws" prohibiting homosexuality and bisexuality often disguised a teleological intent, however—to maximize procreation for the purposes of increasing a tribe, a religion, and a people. Certain other sexual acts, such as masturbation, were not necessarily considered harmful in and of themselves, but were described as sinful in certain contexts because they did not lead to the increase of the tribe, as when Judah's Onan "spilled his semen on the ground whenever he went in to his brother's wife, so that he would not give offspring to his brother" (Gen. 38:10). The mystification of the teleological foundation—procreation—has resulted in the unmooring of sexual laws and taboos from their original purpose, thereby holding the (false) status of

---

49. ODIHR, 16.

50. John Boswell, *Christianity, Social Tolerance, and Homosexuality: Gay People in Western Europe from the Beginning of the Christian Era to the Fourteenth Century* (Chicago: University of Chicago Press, 1980).

unquestionable divine law. While the idea of sin is a constant in Christian moral teaching, much of what is considered to be sinful behavior is socially constructed, and changes according to cultural norms[51]—often using biblical interpretation to support contextual morés.

Whenever sexual morality has been justified deontologically on the grounds of acceptable vs. unacceptable acts, rather than a transparent teleological foundation, many issues of gender injustice, the treatment of certain persons as property—notably women, children, and servants—and larger issues of sexual ethics based on justice, equality and freedom have been obscured in moral discourse. For example, Christian moral teachings have traditionally defined marriage as a sacred sexual preserve of one man and one woman largely for the purpose of procreation, and have prohibited sexual activity outside an officially sanctioned marital bond. But this narrow definition of appropriate sexuality has had unintended consequences of turning a blind eye toward rape in marriage (reframing it as the husband's right to sexual congress), sexual abuse of children, and historically the rape of one's slaves or servants (as *droigt du seigneur*—a man's right to treat his property as he wishes). It has demanded celibacy and chastity of loving and committed gay and lesbian persons, and viewed sexual harassment and exploitation in both church and workplace only as moral lapses or "affairs" rather than abuses of professional power and authority.[52] The emphasis on procreation has further narrowed the definition of what constitutes sexual activity to sexual intercourse per se, rendering invisible or unimportant those forms of sexual assault and harassment that do not involve penetration.

What is needed in sexual ethics is not a new set of deontological rules—simple "do's and don't's"—but a transparent teleological foundation that is informed by modern scientifric and psychological understandings of sexuality, as well as by modern problems facing humanity and the planet. Many myths and superstitions about sexual behavior have long been scientifically unfounded—such as notions that certain acts would lead to insanity, blindness, or hairy palms(!). The ancient drive toward propagation of the human species no longer makes good sense in a world plagued by overpopulation, pollution, and endangered food supplies. For modern Jews and Christians, the Bible still offers sacred truths as a foundation for ethics, but not by proof-texting individual verses anachronistically and out of context. Rather, the Bible offers an over-arching ethical norm of love and justice, expressed by the ten commandments, the prophetic witness of care for the poor and the

---

51. John Portman, *A History of Sin: How Evil Changes, but Never Goes Away* (New York: Rowman & Littlefield, 2007).

52. See Ch. 2, this volume.

vulnerable, the injunction to "do justice, love kindness, and walk humbly with your God" (Micah 6:8), and the centrality in both the Hebrew Bible and the New Testament of loving one's neighbor as oneself (Lev 19:18; Mark 12:31, Rom 13:9, etc.)—even loving one's enemies (Matt 5:43).

With this biblical foundation, individual sexual activities are re-evaluated in light of their ultimate aim and consequences. Actions are ethical when they promote love and justice, protect the vulnerable, and hold the other in mutual regard and respect. They preserve life in its abundance (John 10:10). Some acts, under this teleological view, will remain forever taboo because by their very nature they violate another person: physical violence, sexual assault or rape, and sexual abuse of children or other persons who are unable to give authentic consent by their relative lack of power, authority or physical or mental capacity. Other sexual behaviors, however, can be evaluated situationally, taking into consideration such issues as context, intent, and the personal and social meaning of the act in a given place and time. A whole array of formerly taboo activities may or may not be ethical depending upon complex—and at times, competing—factors.

To use the example already given above, masturbation may be healthy or unhealthy depending on its purpose. If a person masturbates compulsively to the detriment of forming loving intimate relationships and even as a form of addiction that diminishes his or her overall thriving, then we might well view this activity as a problem (although, along the lines of other addictions, it might not be considered sinful per se unless it causes harm to others (as in frotteurism and exhibitionism). Researchers have also documented harm associated with "offence-specific fantasies," or masturbating to pornographic material that fuses sex with violence.[53] On the other hand, masturbating in order to explore what is pleasurable, to learn about one's own body, to ease loneliness, or to enhance a loving and mutual sexual relationship, can be both healthy and ethical.

The line between what is morally sinful vs. what is scientifically pathological or "deviant" is complex, since scientific norms are socially constructed, and shift across continents and centuries regarding what is considered deviant.[54] Some "deviant" behaviors may be considered harmless unless they are distressing to the person or others in his environment,

---

53. Dion Gee, Grant Devilly, and Tony Ward, "The Content of Sexual Fantasies for Sexual Offenders," *Sexual Abuse: A Journal of Research and Treatment* 16/4 (2004) 315–31.

54. Philip Cushman, *Constructing the Self, Constructing America: A Cultural History of Psychotherapy* (New York: Perseus, 1995); Michel Foucault, *The History of Sexuality*, Vol. 1: *An Introduction*, and Vol. 2: *The Use of Pleasure*, trans. Robert Hurley (New York: Random House/Pantheon, 1978 and 1985).

while sexualized violence nearly always requires both clinical treatment and incarceration or inpatient containment for the sake of safety.

Following this reasoning, a number of formerly taboo behaviors can be re-examined in light of modern understandings of sexuality. Sexual fidelity in marriage and committed partnerships remains an ethical norm, not any more to protect a man's assurance that his children are "really his," but because deception, secrecy, and the violation of solemn vows inherently cause pain and suffering. At the same time, the impulse to cheat on a partner can be an important signal of deeper trouble within the relationship, and require honest mutual dialogue in order to address what needs to change—including, in some cases, the need to separate. New biomedical issues present further ethical dilemmas regarding extramarital sex—for example, should a spouse with dementia be prohibited from extramarital sexual activity when there is no longer comprehension of the marital vows? Should a non-impaired spouse likewise be prohibited from all extramarital intimacy when this is no longer possible with his or her legal spouse?[55]

Even the issue of informed consent, which is key to most ethical decision-making, is fraught with complexity. In an "open marriage," where partners have agreed to have other sexual relationships outside their own relationship, do both partners truly consent to sexual relationships outside their primary bond, or is unequal consent or subtle coercion present? In the practice of sadomasochism, does one person ever truly consent to acts of sexual violence in a relationship, or are other psychological dynamics of power and control subtly or not-so-subtly involved? How do unconscious dynamics come into play in sexual relationships where there is a potential for physical or emotional harm, or in relationships where there has been overt violence? When is consent freely given, and when is engaging in certain activities a reenactment of previous experiences of abuse? Some theorists would further question the entire social construction of gender as binary, with its stereotypical norms of masculinity and femininity, as both a reflection of culture and a reinforcer of male, heterosexist domination. They advocate for a queering, or interrogation, of gender dichotemy through the performance of multiple, alternative, and expanded gender identities.[56]

These questions, and more, complicate any attempt to lay down universal rules for behavior in the gray areas beyond outright sexual violence and abuse.[57] Often, when intentions are hard to determine, and outcomes

55. John Portman, *The Ethics of Sex and Alzheimer's* (New York: Routledge, 2013).

56. Judith Butler, *Undoing Gender* (New York: Routledge, 2004).

57. For thoughtful essays dealing further with these questions, see, e.g., James Nelson, ed., *Sexuality and the Sacred: Sources for Theological Reflection* (Louisville: Westminster John Knox, 1994); Marvin Ellison and Kelly Brown Douglas, *Sexuality*

difficult to predict, the grounds for discerning ethical vs. unethical behavior do circle back to the statement "rape is about power," because sexual ethics often depend finally upon an examination of the dynamics of power in relationships.

An Ethic of Power

Power finally is inseparable from an over-arching ethic of love and justice. The concept of justice itself depends upon a framework of the rights of individuals and groups to exercise power with responsibility, mutual accountability, and care. This is not to argue for an absolute leveling of all power, which, given the multiplicity of forms of power, and the interconnectedness of all living beings, is unlikely within the web of competing human interests and desires—at least this side of the Eschaton. Nevertheless, every form of power has both strengths and limitations, and beyond every well-intended act of power lies the potential for unintended consequences. Furthermore, power cannot be self-regulated as if it were only a phenomenon of conscious intent. The unconscious of each individual has multiple wishes, anxieties, aims and powers of its own. Families, groups, and nations are, then, an almost impossibly rich amalgam of such contending and contesting motivations.

An ethic of power, therefore, in my view, requires a corresponding ethic of *community*. Hannah Arendt located power finally not in any one individual or group, but in the *polis*, the collective.[58] Tyranny succeeds, in Arendt's view, more effectively through the isolation of people from one another than through brute force. Relationship is required for the peaceful negotiation of power, and solidarity through knowledge of the other is made possible. In truth, every theory of power implies a corresponding theory of community. An ethic of constructive, communally shared and mutually authorized power—what I have termed *"power-in-community,"*[59] is a vision not unlike Isaiah's vision of the peaceable kingdom (Isaiah 11:6, 9): "The wolf shall live with the lamb, the leopard shall lie down with the kid, the calf and the lion and the fatling together, and a little child shall lead them...They will not hurt or destroy on all my holy mountain; for the earth will be full

---

*and the Sacred: Sources for Theological Reflection*, 2nd ed. (Louisville: Westminster John Knox, 2010); and Adrian Thatcher, *God, Sex, and Gender: An Introduction* (Oxford: Wiley-Blackwell, 2011).

58. Hannah Arendt, *The Human Condition* (Chicago: University of Chicago Press, 1958) 201.

59. Cooper-White, *The Cry of Tamar*, 52–63.

of the knowledge of the LORD as the waters cover the sea." This last phrase further suggests that as humans we do not achieve this on our own, but we require a theology, a "knowledge of the Lord," to support and inspire such cooperation and justice.

## A Trinitarian Theology of Relationality

Within Christianity, we have the deep symbol of the Trinity to support an ethic of power-in-community. Following Catholic theologian Elizabeth Johnson:

> At its most basic the symbol of the Trinity evokes a livingness in God, a dynamic coming and going with the world that points to an inner divine, circling around in unimaginable relation . . . God's relatedness to the world in creating, redeeming, and renewing activity suggests . . . that God's own being is somehow similarly differentiated. Not an isolated, static, ruling monarch—but a relational, dynamic, tripersonal mystery of love. Who would not opt for the latter?[60]

The Trinity is itself an image of power-in-community, the dynamic power (*dunamis*) of mutually empowering and empowered love and care. While it would be unwise to ascribe human character traits to the "persons" of the Trinity, the image of *perichoresis* with its inherent relationality reveals the ultimate floundering emptiness of narcissism and unempathic self-preservation. The Trinity is a symbol of life that is eternally mutual in its sustenance—enlivened by relationship, the love of the Divine spills over into the creation, and animates us as creatures to reach out similarly in trust and love.

This is by no means a naive exhortation to victims to suppress their righteous outrage and to offer instant forgiveness to individual perpetrators.[61] This line of thinking tends to revictimize survivors, and to aid bystanders in retreating from the reality of violence into a mist of sentimental pseudo-Christian niceness. Jesus stood for justice, and for a love that is deeper and stronger than mere sentimentality. In keeping with the communal ethic of power advocated above, the relationality of the Trinity calls us to a relational form of restoration of justice—not to be carried out on the backs of individuals victims—who are revictimized by communities' insistence that they forgive—but to be carried out on the shoulders of all of us together, in community, as we see, hear, and tell the truth of the horrors of violence, and

---

60. Elizabeth Johnson, *She Who Is: The Mystery of God in Feminist Theological Discourse* (New York: Crossroad, 1994) 192.

61. Cooper-White, *The Cry of Tamar*, 51–61.

hold up an alternative Trinitarian vision of life lived most fully in mutual communion and kenotic, self-giving joy.

Is this possible, given the human condition? I honestly do not know. As Freud famously said, "Man is wolf to man"[62]—and to woman. It is inherent in human nature to project human nature onto God and in our depictions and doctrines—even our sacred texts—and make God over in our own image.[63] So our theologies from ancient times and multiple cultures all too often reflect a God-imago of patriarchal lordship that serves to reinforce structures of domination and violence. Yet a central symbol of Christian theology is the Incarnation. Iin spite of many Christian doctrines that perpetuate images of divine domination, the God revealed in Christ is not a dominating lord and master, but a refugee baby in a borrowed feedstall, a poor itinerant prophet, and a broken body dangling lynched on an instrument of imperial torture. The Jesus of the Gospels and the doctrine of his Resurrection anticipated the coming of God's Realm of peace and justice on earth, and an apocalyptic overturning of the world's structures of oppressive power. We are not yet given a present time that is so full of the knowledge of God that we and the earth are healed of all violence. But through scripture, tradition, and our own reason and experience, we have a vision of the peaceable Realm of God—an erotics of justice that points, however haltingly, toward to God's gift of abundant life.

62. Sigmund Freud, *Civilization and Its Discontents*, in James Strachey, ed., *The Standard Edition of the Complete Psychological Works of Sigmund Freud* (London: Hogarth, 1961), Vol. 21, 58 (orig publ., 1931).

63. Ana-María Rizzuto, *The Birth of the Living God: A Psychoanalytic Study* (Chicago: University of Chicago Press, 1979); see also Cooper-White, *Many Voices: Pastoral Psychotherapy in Relational and Theological Perspective* (Minneapolis: Fortress, 2007) 36–38.